A Century of the ENGLISH NOVEL

Being a *Consideration* of the place in *English Literature* of the *Long Story;* together with an estimate of its *Writers* from the heyday of Scott to the death of Conrad.

By CORNELIUS WEYGANDT

Professor of *English Literature* in the *University* of *Pennsylvania.* Author of "Irish Plays and Playwrights"

"The truth of humanity goes on forever, unchangeable and inexhaustible in the variety of its disclosures."—CONRAD

Published by THE CENTURY CO. in *New York City*   *1925*

Printed in U. S. A.

FLIC005

5xx '77

18 febr.

DATE DUE

DEMCO, INC. 38-2931

A Century of the
ENGLISH NOVEL

To
S. M. W.

PREFACE

A book such as this, which is the outcome of the reading and talk of a lifetime, owes more than its maker can acknowledge to other people. As I read the proof of it I heard many voices, most often, perhaps, the voice of my father. He began to gather together a library in 1848, and he talked of its books to me, off and on, from about 1880 until his death in 1907. Under my own roof we have talked of the novelists again and again, sometimes all of us at once. There have been stout and pleasant quarrels with friends, too, of which I find echoes here. There are echoes also from the classroom, of the give and take of teacher and those who have suffered him, some with agreement with what he had to say, and some with dissent from it. I hope that others can hear these voices. I should like to believe that the book is a summing up of talk with many people.

I know very few of the many contemporary writers considered here, but I am under obligation to a number of them for their answers to inquiries about their work. Three, at least, I must mention. Maurice Hewlett wrote me in detail about his theories of art, and Mr. Eden Phillpotts casually, but to the point, about his "modest comedy of Dartmoor," in letters in praise of shrubs. Mr. James Stephens made me read Powys. My colleague, Professor C. G. Child, has been patient under daily questioning by me. He has read the proof, too. Another colleague, Mr. T. E. M. Boll, read the book in manuscript. His familiarity with the English novel, and with the bibliography of the English novel, has been of help in many ways.

CORNELIUS WEYGANDT.

North Sandwich,
New Hampshire.

CONTENTS

A CENTURY OF THE ENGLISH NOVEL

A CENTURY
OF THE ENGLISH NOVEL

CHAPTER I

THE DOMINANCE OF THE NOVEL

FOR about a century the novel has been dominant, save for short periods, over every other form of English literature. Poetry, essay, short-story and drama have had their vogues, but these vogues have been only momentary, and, persistently, year in and year out, from the heyday of Scott to today, the novel has held first place in the interest and affections of readers. That some form of story should occupy this place is in the nature of things, but that it should be the novel does not follow inevitably. The long story in prose does not have a more fundamental appeal in it than other narrative forms.

It would, indeed, seem probable that in the hurried world of today a shorter story than the novel would prevail. But popular as is the short-story and popular as is that longer form, the condensed novel, or "novelette," the novel is still more popular. Can it be that a very material reason accounts largely for this dominance of the novel? Is its very length a source of its popularity? A book of the proportions of a novel keeps the reader in a bright world of the imagination, and away from the dull world of his daily round for a longer time, than any other form. The shortest novel lasts out the longest evening; the novel of average length three evenings; the novel in the old English or the modern Russian manner six evenings and all spare time of a Sunday, too.

There is another reason for the dominance of the novel in its very absorption into itself of nearly all literary forms. Poetry, essay, short-story, drama—you will find them all in the novels of the great. Poetry, lyric feeling, lyric passages are so constant to the greater stories and so uniformly absent from the lesser ones that you are driven to say that a novel can hardly be great if it has not poetry in it.

Think of the many names among the great in the English novel who are poets first of all. Scott and Meredith and Hardy are masters of verse as surely as Byron and Browning and Masefield, but there are those who will say there is as much poetry in certain passages of their prose, in the exultations of Eddie Ochiltree, in the tranced meeting by the weir of Richard Feverel and Lucy, in the lament of Marty South over Winterbourne, as in "Marmion," or "Love in a Valley," or "Julie-Jane."

And who will deny that Charlotte Brontë, whose verse is negligible, has in passage on passage in *Jane Eyre* (1847) and *Villette* (1853), that lift of the heart, that quickening of life, that thrilling revelation of the wonder of the world which turn lyric the words that express such moments, which must so turn lyric the words or the moments will not be expressed?

Conrad is as surely lyric. He is so aware of the beauty of a moonlit landfall or a landless sunset heavy with clouds, of a jungle hour or an island as lonely in the sea as the first star of evening in the sky, that his expression of such beauty is often too poignant, too disturbing, for those who would have their reading bring only quiet joys. And his conception of character and his revelation of it in its environment, have intensities that rival those of a Turgenieff or an Ibsen. Heyst gives a kind of significance to *Victory* (1915) such as Gemma gives to *Spring Floods* (1871) or Solness to *The Master Builder* (1892).

That poetry is necessary to writing of first power was maintained by Charlotte Brontë. In a letter to G. H. Lewes she queries, "Can there be a great artist without poetry?" She thought not, and so she wrote down Jane Austen as a novelist of second power. She was wrong in that. Miss Austen thought abandon bad form; she was dedicated to "sense" rather than "sensibility." She might, conceivably, be remembered for "miniatures etched on ivory" in verse had she practiced the art of Prior. She had the temperament for "society verse." Few of her admirers could imagine her an emotional poet, however, and few of them would hold that she plumbed the depths of life in her novels. And yet, because she was almost perfect of accomplishment within her chosen range, these admirers will maintain Miss Brontë was wrong in denying Miss Austen greatness. Miss Austen had the gift of character creation. She added portraits to the great gallery of portraits from English poetry and drama and novel, an Elizabeth Bennett and a Mr. Woodhouse and a score others, that have their place there as surely as the portraits from Chaucer or Shakespeare or Hardy.

Fielding himself allied the novel with poetry by calling *Joseph Andrews* (1742) "a comic epic poem in prose." There is, however, nowhere in his writing that exaltation without which there cannot be poetry. Yet nobody dare argue that Fielding is not a great novelist. The truth is, of course, that the gift of storytelling and power of characterization and insight and a prose style of distinction can make a novelist with little or no poetry in him a novelist of first power. There is, for instance, less poetry in Thackeray than in most great writers and what there is, is oftenest of the repressed or gallant eighteenth century sort. Yet no man who knows the novel, in English and elsewhere, doubts that Thackeray is a great novelist. More clearly still Fielding and Jane Austen point the truth that a novel can be great without poetry, because each is great and neither has lyric passages or poetical conception of character. No, poetry is not necessary to a great novel, but there are only a few novelists without poetry in them who are great.

The essay is almost as constantly present as poetry in the novel. Fielding introduces the various "books" of his novels with a chapter of familiar criticism or moralizing more or less related to the stories the chapters of the "book" are to unfold. In the chapters themselves are often to be found passages of like nature, sometimes in the first person and sometimes as dialogue, between, for instance, a poet and a player. Thackeray and George Eliot moralize in like pleasant spirit on topics suggested by the action of their characters, owning allegiance to Fielding in this as in many other matters. And that habit persists down even into our own time. One wonders if James E. Agate is not more interested in the thirty pages of familiar essay of the "introduction" to his *Responsibility* (1918) than in the rest of the book. If he is not, it is because in that rest of the book he has recorded enough of the musing of his youth to content him. What professes to be the story of one Edward Marston is principally what a young man talked and felt and— incidentally—idly did in the Manchester of the eighteen nineties.

The essay that appraises painting and music is almost an integral part of the novels of George Moore. Half-chapters of Phillpotts might have been put with as much propriety into a collection of sketches of out-of-doors as into *The River* (1902) or *Widecombe Fair* (1913). In *Marius the Epicurean* (1885) of Pater the novel assimilates even the weightiest kind of sententious essay, as well as matter of scholarship alien to the passions and adventures of men with which novels have usually to do.

A tale of separate entity, a short recital having no real connection with the main plot, is so often interpolated between the many incidents of that plot in the novel of the eighteenth century as to be a feature of it. Fielding and Sterne love such digressions, and Scott, in later days, was prone to them. Such tales are not always, in the present interpretation of the term, short-stories, but in Scott, at any rate, they sometimes are. "Wandering Willie's Tale" in *Redgauntlet* (1824), is for instance, as exactly a short-story as "The Murders in the Rue Morgue" of Poe. Today such short-stories as are to be found embedded in novels are justified by being made episodes in the plot. So Stevenson justifies "The Tale of Tod Lapraik" in *David Balfour* (1892), although it is not really necessary to the progress of the story.

A variant of this method is followed by Wells in *The Secret*

Places of the Heart (1922). Here Chapters VI, VII, and VIII read like a readjustment and expansion of a short-story to illustrate the character of Sir Richmond Hardy. Such an explanation is that of an indulgent critic. One unsympathetic might say that *The Secret Places of the Heart* is but a clumsy splicing together of a "writeup" of neurosis with a Glynian short-story.

Leonard Merrick believes so stoutly that the form of the novel possesses an efficacy beyond the form of the short-story that he prints *While Paris Laughed* (1918) as a novel when it is but a series of short-stories loosely connected through the Tricotrin who is hero of them all.

In his "Life of Henry Fielding" (1821) Scott pointed out, in an analysis of admirable clarity, how different are the powers of novelist and playwright. And yet the connection between the novel and the drama has always been very close. From its beginnings in Richardson and Fielding the younger form has borrowed from the older. The eighteenth century novel drew in large part its characterization and its dialogue from the drama that preceded it. An almost equal debt the novel of the earlier nineteenth century owes to that old drama. Scott confessed his obligations to Miss Edgeworth for his delineation of peasant characters, but who that knows his hags and beggars, his herds and plowmen, his fishermen and fantastics, will deny his greater obligation to Shakespeare? Dickens has frankly owned his discipleship to Ben Jonson, whose "humours" reappear in his caricatures, his eccentrics, his grotesques.

So many elements are, in the nature of the forms, common to drama and novel, that it is difficult to determine just which are borrowed by the one from the other. Yet it is safe to say that for the fifty years from 1840 to 1890 much of the energy the natural expression of which would have been through the drama was forced into the novel to gain a hearing. Charles Reade is the outstanding example. His bent was for the stage, but the conditions of the time were against him and he was driven to novels for his livelihood. He was an early practitioner of that dubious art of turning a play into a novel. *Masks and Faces*

(1852), which Tom Taylor helped him to put into form for the boards, he rewrote as *Peg Woffington* within a year of its successful production.

As earlier the novel borrowed from the drama so later the drama borrowed from the novel. Tom Robertson thought that his attempts at realism in *Society* (1865) and *Caste* (1867) were putting characters from the world of Thackeray upon the stage. Sir Arthur W. Pinero has been the follower of Robertson in this practice as in many others. His Duke of St. Olpherts in *The Notorious Mrs. Ebbsmith* (1895) is but Lord Steyne reincarnated. And Hoggard and Prabble in *Saints and Sinners* (1884) of Henry Arthur Jones! Do they inherit directly from *The Alchemist* (1610) or by way of *Hard Times* (1854)?

The novel has lent those voluminous prefaces and stage directions and addenda of all sorts to the versions of his plays Shaw prints for us to read. These devices enable Shaw to inform us, almost as freely as can the novelist, how to interpret the actions of his characters and how to visualize the characters themselves. Not Thackeray himself choruses more over his dramatis personæ, is more explicit in telling us how to take them.

We might point to novels printed in dialogue, like *The Story of the Gadsbys* (1888) of Kipling or *Dolly Dialogues* (1894) of Anthony Hope, as borrowings of form from the play by the novel. All dialogue in the novel is really in ultimate origin such a borrowing, a borrowing that the novel can ill do without. That is a dull book, more than nine times out of ten, the novel with but little dialogue.

Taking the place of the play as it did in so many households for so many years, the novel necessarily took over some of the functions of the play. An important one of these was the visualization of the scene of action, a function performed in the theatre, of course, by scenery and lighting. Scott found very little background in the novels of his predecessors. Fielding was interested in his story and his style and human nature. Landscape, political questions, social and industrial conditions, meant little to him. Smollett, in *Humphrey Clinker* (1771), mellows a little in memories of his Vale of Leven and paints in a scene or two of a beauty unusual to him. Mrs. Radcliffe delighted in landscape but trusted more often to intuition than memory in describing it. It remained for Scott to set a standard for the description of landscape and a standard for explanations of political conditions that bring about crises in the affairs of characters.

Galt pictured the changes that factories brought to his corner of Scotland in his *Annals of the Parish* (1821), and Dickens and Reade made certain of their stories outgrowths of social and industrial conditions which they almost painfully elaborated in the progress of those stories.

This emphasis of background has increased and increased until not a few late Victorian and contemporaneous novels are dramatizations of places and forces of nature and social conditions rather than narratives of the adventures of men and women and records of their changing fortunes and emotions. Gissing in *The Whirlpool* (1897) shows London as a force that draws in and overwhelms even determined and self-seeking characters, but the Rolfes and Carnabys are relatively important in themselves. So it is in *The River* (1902), for all the prominence given the Dart itself. "John Trevena," using the same Dartmoor as background, makes it an even more sinister and oppressive agency than does Phillpotts in crushing the people who trusted it for their livelihood and happiness. Even in *Furze the Cruel* (1907), though, the characters are not wholly dwarfed by their environment.

In *The Nigger of the Narcissus* (1897), however, the background is all important. James Wait and Donkin and Singleton count hardly at all in comparison with the sea, which Conrad makes the real protagonist. In the later books of Wells, despite his passionate devotion to heroes and heroines that herald his new day, it is the principles of that day that chiefly concern him and in their exploitation the people are minimized. So it is in *The New Machiavelli* (1910). Isabel and Remington are forgotten in all the welter of the New Liberalism or the New

Toryism. So, too, it is in *The Passionate Friends* (1913).
Jealousy, the villain of the story, obscures Lady Mary and
Stephen Strafford.

From the time of Richardson the novel has been used as a
tract. Richardson himself so regarded his *Pamela* (1740), begun, as we have so often heard, as a model letter-writer of moral
purpose for servant girls. Godwin, as optimistic as Wells once
was as to the perfectibility of human nature, so used it in *Caleb
Williams* (1795) and Charles Kingsley in *Alton Locke* (1850).
So, too, did Grant Allen in *The Woman Who Did* (1895) and
Samuel Butler the Lesser in *The Way of All Flesh* (1903). So,
too, do the earnest young men who follow Wells. W. L. George
preaches, if he does not always practice, such use of it. The advancement of the race should be, he holds, the chief use of the
novel. "A hand grenade flung at the bourgeoisie" is the kind
of novel he admires most. "Ashamed as we are of the novel
with a purpose," he says, "we can no longer write novels without
a purpose." He is proud that "aspiration toward truth" has
broken up "the old form," and he is equally proud to admit that
"you cannot tell a story in a straightforward manner when you
do but glimpse it through the veil of the future."

Whatever the moral value of such preaching as this of George
it does not affect in any way the old standards of judgment of
the novel or of any other kind of literature. If we will only
keep steadily before us all the time the truth that poetry is the
highest expression of literature in English, and make a practice
of putting the other forms of literature over against poetry to
see how they measure up to poetry, we are little likely to be
led astray by the vagaries of these other forms. If the qualities
of the tract are put into poetry we see at a glance they are out
of place there. If we demand that the novel shall be, in accordance with the requirements of its form, a something beautiful made out of a man's experience or dream of life, as we demand that poetry shall be, in accordance with the requirements
of its form, we will realize clearly how negligible as art are a
Way of All Flesh of Butler and a *Marriage* (1912) of Wells.

Why should the novelist insist on putting his hobbies, or his prejudices, or his politics, or his schemes for the regeneration of mankind, into his stories any more than the poet into his verses, or the essayist into his essays? And this out of season as well as in season. Such topics he should draw upon only as the story demands, only as he draws upon all other experience he has had. But a certain kind of novelist very prevalent today thrusts such pre-occupations of his into every book, and defends himself by the plea that a man must stand by his convictions. It is an obsession in a writer to think that he is always on the stand giving testimony.

Ralph Hodgson is the expert on bull terriers in England today, but does he devote poem on poem to a consideration of whether one should snip off or bite off the puppies' tails, or passionately protest against the shortening of their tails at all?

W. H. Hudson left his little all to help toward the preservation of birds in England, but, much as there is about them in his best writing, it is in definite tracts issued by the Humanitarian League or the Royal Society for the Protection of Birds that you find almost all of his propagandist writing. Such as is included in his collected essays is in what he frankly calls his "bread and cheese" books, the "stuff" he did for the market and not for himself.

Rupert Brooke was a convinced Fabian but there is no plea for Socialism in his poems.

Frank Bolles thought the importance of mankind in the scheme of nature absurdly overestimated by man but he did not harp upon this conviction.

And the better novelists, of course, have not the habit of propaganda, or only now and then, when the tune of the time momentarily masters them, or they "get religion." Conrad is a staunch supporter of authority, as you would expect a sea-captain to be, but he does not turn his books into tracts for the continuance of the old order of things.

A realistic novel that is not first of all loyal to life, to truth, to things as they are; that warps character or incident to prove a thesis held by the author; that is chiefly concerned, in short, with anything but the revelation, in terms of beauty, of human nature as it is, need not be taken seriously in any discussion of the art of fiction. Beauty, in the novel, springs from material, the selection from life of certain people and certain incidents and certain environments; from form, the architectonics of the story; and from style, that is to say, the way the writer has of expressing himself, the very quality of himself as it colors his telling of the story.

Justification of the novel with a purpose is frequently accompanied by a plea for a changed form of novel, for a departure from the narrative novel of Scott or Hardy. The novel with a purpose or the novel that is a cross-section of modern civilization at some political or industrial or commercial center is necessary, we are told, as new forms or old forms in a new guise are always necessary, to express a changed world. As a matter of fact almost every novelist of power changes to some degree the form of the novel he inherits from the writer he calls master. A writer nine times out of ten begins in the manner of some elder he admires. Change of form in the story will come about in such cases just as soon as the writer begins to be himself. He finds the form of story suited to him just as he finds his style.

This change of form of each succeeding new writer of power is just as great and just as small as the change in the world of which he writes. One must platitudinize so that one may not be misunderstood, and say that the world changes in essentials hardly at all. Human nature is, the better and worse of it, what it has been for ages. Our progress, if progress it is, has been in material comforts; and in a distribution of wealth a little more in accordance with the earning of it; and in the lessening of intolerance. These changes though are little enough in all. The increase of comforts, through sanitation and preventive medicine, telephones, new systems of power and heating and lighting, new methods of transportation, seems to make our day very different from that even of our parents or grandparents. And yet the differences these material agencies have brought about are hardly more than differences of manners. Character is what character has long been. The old truths are the old truths yet. The old lies the old lies. We are a little more hurried than our ancestors, a little less proud of our trades, a little more avid of pleasure. The basic instincts, for self-preservation, for the continuation of the race; love; self-esteem; ambition; and the rest; remain unchanged.

The use of the novel as a tract, as a medium for propaganda, is but another proof of its dominance today. The novel has not only to a large degree absorbed the literary forms of poetry, short-story, and essay, but the bulk of propagandist writing. The novel has, too, absorbed no small part of such quasi-literary writing as history, philosophy, and criticism. Hewlett avowed that he had read all the state papers and historical articles on Mary Queen of Scots for his *Queen's Quair* (1904); Wells plays prophet in *The World Set Free* (1914), and philosopher in *The Research Magnificent* (1915); George Moore, as I have said, is critic of many arts in his long list of books from *A Modern Lover* (1883) to *Héloïse and Abélard* (1921).

The novel that draws into itself matters extraneous to literature often falls outside of literature, but if its author have the genius he can, as I have said, compel his story to assimilate such matters. If it does it may be the work of art he intended it to be, despite its lapses from the accredited standards. Such a novel is *Jude the Obscure* (1895). The power of Hardy enables him to subdue even pathological data to the purposes of art. Yet experiment of this kind is always dangerous, and in the hands of a lesser man, as so often with Wells, results in failure. Even Hardy cannot achieve his best when burdened with progaganda. *Jude the Obscure* is not a *Return of the Native* (1878), a *Mayor of Casterbridge* (1886), or a *Woodlanders* (1887), not even a *Tess* (1891).

CHAPTER II

THE INCLUSIVENESS OF THE NOVEL

ANOTHER phase of the dominance of the novel is discovered if you examine critically the long roll of the novelists from Richardson to Conrad. You will find that a good many of them, especially among those of the second century of the novel, are not basically novelists, and that many of them had a very strong penchant for other literary forms than the novel, but had to be novelists most of the time because of the "laws of demand," and not by choice alone. Richardson was basically a novelist, although he stumbled into the novel by chance, and spent a great deal of time in what we today would call psychological detail for its own sake rather than for the sake of the story.

Fielding began as a dramatist. He was driven to the novel after the Licensing Act of 1737 deprived him of his living from the stage. In later years he said that he left off playwriting when he ought to have begun, a judgment of himself that is well taken, for his plays are thin compared to his novels. The genius of Smollett, too, is for the novel; he is a story-teller before he is anything else.

Sterne is a familiar essayist with a gift for dialogue, a man whose two so-called novels are novels largely by courtesy. Incident succeeds incident in *A Sentimental Journey* (1768) more logically than in *Tristram Shandy* (1767), among whose chapters a story wanders in and out but casually. Miss Austen is novelist by nature. It is not until we come to the nineteenth century that we find novelist after novelist much else than novelist or fundamentally something else.

Scott was a fellowly human being, the friend of all Scotland, even before he was Scott of Abbotsford, country laird of ducal

importance. He was Scott of Abbotsford before he was collector of folklore, and collector of folklore before he was poet.
He was all these before he was novelist, to his advantage without doubt as novelist.

Galt would have been a diarist if he had not had to make his
living by his pen. He had tried biography, drama and travels
before he published any fiction, and it was in the chronicling of
the small beer of country places that he won his sure if modest
place.

Bulwer-Lytton was playwright as well as novelist to his own
age. The theatricality that is of the very fibre of him has stood
the years as well in *Richelieu* (1838) as in *The Last Days of
Pompeii* (1834).

Dickens has told us that he was a writer from the cradle, an
actor always. His readings bore him out in this self-criticism.
As Tom Moore gave to his songs by his singing of them something he could not put into the printed words of them, so
Dickens gave to his reading from his stories a something he
could not put into them by their writing alone. Dickens could
give more of himself to the written word than Moore could and
a good deal of that was of real dramatic quality. In an age
more congenial to drama than the Victorian he might well have
been a playwright, but his attempts at drama are none of them
comparable to his stories.

Thackeray was much slower coming to the novel than was
Dickens. He tried journalism and illustrating before he tried
literature, and in literature he tried nearly every form before he
girded up his loins for *Vanity Fair* (1848). That Thackeray is
story-teller first of all is so obviously true it needs hardly to
be stated, but it did not appear so to everybody in 1850. Charlotte Brontë found it to be true and was disappointed. She
wished him to be the scourger of all the wickedness of the time.
But how much else Thackeray is than novelist! Leave out his
black and white work, and list but his writings. Burlesque;
satire; society verse; travels; essays familiar, sententious, critical; short-stories and long, tales and sketches; everything but

drama this consummate craftsman turned his hand to successfully.

Borrow is not so surely a novelist as he is a writer of travels.
A book of travels, *The Bible in Spain* (1843), brought him to the
attention of the public and a book of travels, *Wild Wales* (1862),
was the last book of his that mattered. Between these two
came *Lavengro* (1851) and *The Romany Rye* (1857), novels
maybe, but more like the picaresque story than most novels of
their generation.

Reade is, as I have said, instinctively a dramatist, and Charles
Kingsley is as much honored today as a poet for "Airly Beacon"
as he is as a novelist for the best of his novels, say *Hypatia*
(1853).

The first try of the Brontës was in *Poems* by "Currer,
Ellis and Acton Bell," in 1846. The volume was passed by with
little attention then, but a critical position long held by many
is that Emily is to be valued more for her verses than for
Wuthering Heights (1847). No one questions, however, that
Charlotte is novelist rather than poet, though poet she is, too,
in her prose if not in her verse. Both *Jane Eyre* (1847) and
Villette (1853) have in them much of the intimacy that belongs to the kind of journal that is almost a "confession" but
they were novels in intention and as novels they were received.
There were those who gossiped and those who scandalized about
Jane Eyre, delighted to consider it more of a personal record than
it was, but time has had its way with them and *Jane Eyre* owes
the place it has so long held to its own merits.

There were many forces working to make George Eliot something else than a novelist,—to make her a translator and scholar,—
but her bias toward the novel and the careful pilotage of Lewes
brought her through triumphantly. Despite the overburdening
of her later books with issues of the hour she stuck constantly to
her trade. She was not known for her fund of stories or her
humor or for beauty of writing as a young woman down in
Warwickshire, but even if she was not instinctively the novelist
almost all that she is remembered for is her novels. Her short-

stories are really condensed novels and almost the only value her narrative poems have is the story in them.

Meredith was philosopher and poet from his first writing. His first verse, *Poems* (1851), antedates by eight years, and his first prose, the extravagant and questioning *Shaving of Shagpat* (1856), by three years, his first novel, *The Ordeal of Richard Feverel* (1859). And philosopher and poet, in prose and verse, he remained through his long life, sometimes fusing their qualities with those of the novelist and sometimes failing to so fuse them.

The *Wessex Poems* of Hardy was a great surprise on its publication in 1898. A few sets of verses of his had been published, but so inconspicuously and with so little acclaim that no one thought of him as a poet in verse. Howells had the perspicacity to write him down "a great poet as well as a great humorist" in 1894, but he based that judgment on the lyric moments in the novels. No one had suspected that during the years his novels had been welcomed by a steadily widening public Hardy had been all the time writing verses, indeed, from 1860 on, even before he had written novels at all. Hardy is a man of stories, in his verse as well as in his prose, but he has been always just as surely poet as story-teller.

Robert Buchanan belongs to literature only by "The Ballad of Judas Iscariot" and a few other poems, yet for a decade he was a rival of William Black as a purveyor of novels of romantic life. He was, too, a writer of melodrama that filled the theaters.

Stevenson had all the cardinal virtues of an essayist in as large measure as Lamb himself. He began with the essay, he returned to it time and again, and there is little doubt that had not the story been that for which people would pay he would have devoted his greatest energy to the essay. At the end, in 1894, he was engaged on *Weir of Hermiston* (1896), his first attempt at a story of the caliber of a novel, and there is no doubt it promised largely. The pity is that as we have it it is but a fragment. Gallant as his earlier stories are they are not so good in their kind as his essays and his verses in their kinds.

Essayist, poet, romancer—it is in this order I would rate his accomplishment as writer. His letters, of course, are familiar essays in little and their brightness and charm seem to me to make sure the rating of him as essayist first. His short-stories rank with his long ones. His plays have qualities like his novels, but whether because of his shortcomings as dramatist or those of his collaborator Henley, they are lesser things.

There was never a writer less of a novelist by nature than Gissing. By temperament he was a commentator and what impulse toward creative writing he had was in journalizing and the essay. But never until nearly the end of his career was he able to follow his bent. Then he had leisure and enough of income and reputation to indulge himself in *By the Ionian Sea* (1901) and *The Private Papers of Henry Ryecroft* (1903). For the first time now he wrote with gusto and for the first time with the full power he had. For twenty years he had made his way by writing novels, almost all of which were earnest, creditable work, but none the less work done against the grain. No writer in the whole range of English fiction is so completely the product of the tyranny of the novel as George Gissing. For the man who refused to do newspaper work or hackwork the novel was the only kind of writing that offered a living in Gissing's period.

George Moore took to the novel after he had been balked as painter and writer of verse. There is no question at all of his mastery of it in *Esther Waters* (1894) and *The Lake* (1905), but he is natively critic of art and writer of confessions rather than novelist. *Modern Painting* (1893) is creative criticism and *Hail and Farewell* (1911-1914) about the best book of its kind in English. Moore has tried his hand, too, at drama and short-story, without distinguished accomplishment in either form. His polemical writing, effective as it is, is not more than journalism. He has yet to achieve an *Areopagitica*.

Sir James M. Barrie has endeared himself to a very wide public through his stories, a wider public perhaps than he has reached through his plays. For years he refused to publish these plays, but now that he has published them, and we can consider them in the library as well as see them on the stage, we know they are what he has done of highest value. They get to the inwardness of things with a downrightness the novels are wanting in.

There is almost no literary form that Maurice Hewlett did not experiment with. None of these experiments had so great a popularity as his first romance, *The Forest Lovers* (1898), a warm-hearted harking-back to Malory. Yet the best work of Hewlett is to be found in the tale of the order of "Madonna of the Peach Trees" that is not novel or romance or short-story but just as surely a distinctive sort of narrative. Novels and romances of all kinds he wrote and short-stories and essays of many kinds, and a play, and verse galore of every description. His chief concern was with verse but readers would not have it and would have his stories; so he became story-teller willy-nilly.

Phillpotts was stage-struck in his youth and he has never wholly recovered. He dallies with drama off and on and carries situations in his novels very close to dramatic form in their presentment. We find in him that love of "scenes" that is so characteristic of Dickens. Plays of Phillpotts have run the gauntlet of the stage, two being produced within a fortnight in October, 1913. *The Shadow* was put on at the Gaiety in Manchester and *The Mother* at the Repertory Theatre in Liverpool. Yet neither these nor their fellows, except *The Farmer's Wife* (1924), have succeeded in their kind at all.commensurately with the novels in theirs. Nor are his verses, fresh as is their material, more than 'prentice work. Nor do his sketches of out-of-doors have a life of their own; they seem like rejected passages from the descriptive background of the stories. Despite his desire Phillpotts cannot escape being novelist before he is anything else.

All that we have from Conrad, except for articles on seamanship and the sea, a couple of attempts at plays, and a few critical papers on novelists and the novel, is autobiography or stories. There are points of view from which these two forms almost coincide. It is not a matter-of-fact chronological account of his life that Conrad gives us in *A Personal Record* (1912) but a selection from the events of his life marshalled together by mood and not set down as they occurred year on year. Are such stories as *The Nigger of the Narcissus* (1897) or *Youth* (1903) or *Typhoon* (1902) very different in kind from *A Personal Record,* or for that matter from *The Mirror of the Sea* (1906)? In two of the three stories first mentioned, in *The Nigger of the Narcissus* and *Typhoon,* Conrad chooses another protagonist than himself but the experiences recorded must be those he underwent or very intimately observed. In *Youth* there is no assumption of any other person between author and story. It is of himself that he writes, but of himself not only personally but as the symbol of youth. All three are what might be called dramatized biography, biography projected somehow so as to be a reflection of the man writing and not that man himself. *The Mirror of the Sea* is partly chapters from the biography of Conrad, and partly the gathering together of facts from his experience and partly comment on that experience. Papers of this last sort approximate to the essay, as indeed do some of the passages of autobiography. One chapter, "The Tremolino," is almost a short-story.

There is evidence in the writing of Conrad that he has read English poetry and evidence of his poetic temperament. Yet so far as I know he has written no verse. It was not to be expected he would. A man who did not write English until he was past thirty would hardly attempt so difficult a technique as that of our verse. His prose style as we know it could never be forced into the straightjacket of that verse, however much it might have simplified that style had he made the attempt so to do. But, as I have said, his conception of character is poetic and his ecstasy in intense life and in the beauty of the world lifts his writing often to lyric bursts. His short-stories are, many of them, condensed novels, and his novels sometimes are only short-stories whose significance to him compels him to explain them at the length of novels. And others of these short-stories, like the longer ones of them I have already alluded to, are very like heightened logs of voyages, sublimated chapters of auto-biography.

Galsworthy is another of the novelists who like Barrie bulks big as a dramatist too. It is true that his *Man of Property* (1906) is finer as a novel than any of his plays, a *Pigeon* (1912) say, or a *Skin Game* (1920), as a play. The contemporaneous English drama is, however, relatively to the contemporaneous English novel, so scant of accomplishment, that his plays take on, in comparison with the characteristic plays of their day, a greater importance than his novels among their kind. He has done a good many short-stories too, good, bad and indifferent. There is not much poetry in Galsworthy, but what there is is to be found in his stories rather than in his plays or his verse. There is just a flash of poetry in *A Bit O' Love* (1915) and dimmer flashes here and there in *Moods, Songs and Doggerels* (1911). Galsworthy has written criticism of a good deal of value, as his sayings that Conrad and W. H. Hudson are the only prose writers of importance that have come into recognition during his own manhood; and some sheafs of tracts, of no more than passing interest.

Arnold Bennett is a skilled craftsman of letters, able to fashion every sort of literary product save verse. Whether, could he have afforded it, every book of his since the *Old Wives' Tale* (1908) might have been as greatly conceived, is doubtful, but it is sadly certain that few of them since have been fine even in intention. Bennett has driven himself too hard. There may be by-products of genius in a busy youth given over largely to hackwork, but it is rarely that fine art results from forcing in middle years. Bennett has done plays, travels, essays and short-stories good enough to lead one to believe he could have done them better if he would. As we have him, however, it is only in the *Old Wives' Tale,* and, in part, in the Hilda Lessways trilogy that he draws near to the great novelists.

Although Wells has few of the qualities of the man of letters he has taken a fling at many literary forms. Verse, the familiar essay and the play he has avoided, but there is no form of the story with which he has not done well. Grotesques of a pseudo-scientific cast introduced him. From these he passed on to other grotesques, hazards of a future changed through applied science. Then social reform claimed him, and long books with a minimum of story and a maximum of propagandist journalism were the result. One wonders whether such writing has any value even as the record of a passing day, so colored is it with its writer's prejudiced interpretations. The novel has never swallowed more matter extraneous to literature than in *The New Machiavelli* (1910) and *The Passionate Friends* (1913). Wells has slight instinct for the novel of life as it is. He is not interested in life as it is. Indeed life as it is is so unscientifically ordered, in his estimation, that it is maddeningly repellent to him. His novels are intended by him to be agencies that will bring about a better tomorrow; they are tracts of an efficiency expert who would tidy up the world and run it according to system.

D. H. Lawrence is critic and writer on psychology, poet and playwright, as well as novelist. His plays have yet to meet success upon the stage and his verse has yet to create the taste by which it may be enjoyed. There is a quality to this verse that is its author's own and it is a pity he lacks that lilt, that magic in words, that is to poetry what melody is to music. A travel book, *Sea and Sardinia* (1922), shows that he is seeking new fields, but it would seem that it is as a story-teller he will hold the place he has won. Lawrence has made a new kind of beauty, a beauty from which cruelty and a Lamia-like un-loveliness are never far away. From the day of the publication of *Sons and Lovers* (1913) he has been a writer to reckon with, to be troubled about.

For the nearly two hundred years, then, that there has been an English novel of life as it is, many of its writers have been not novelists only but practicers of other literary forms as well. For the past century the novel has dominated all other literary forms, absorbing into itself qualities of many of them, especially qualities of drama and essay and poetry.

CHAPTER III

THE PLACE OF THE NOVEL IN ENGLISH LITERATURE

THIS book considers the English novel of the past hundred years primarily in its relation to English literature. It recognizes that the contemporary novel has been shaped partly by foreign influences, that George Moore owes much to Turgenieff and something to the De Goncourts and Zola, that Conrad owes even more to Turgenieff than does Moore, that W. L. George, passing beyond Zola as his "first influence—long discarded," has studied carefully men so different as Flaubert, Turgenieff, Tolstoi and Anatole France, that "Brinsley MacNamara" has tried to mould himself into an Irish Dostoieffsky.

In short, that the English novel of today, like English literature in other forms so often in the past, like English poetry in the Romantic Revival, or like the Elizabethan drama, has come to a certain degree under foreign tutelage. Does one therefore regard Scott or Coleridge, primarily, or at much length, in relation to German Romanticism, or Shakespeare or Fletcher primarily or at length in relation to the Italian novella? It is easy to overemphasize such influences. Scott and Coleridge in their narrative poetry and Shakespeare and Fletcher in their plays are much nearer in quality of work and in outlook to their English predecessors than to Germans or Italians. And so, for better or worse, are most of our novelists of today in their distinctive work. Hugh Walpole is little himself in *The Dark Forest* (1916), and Gilbert Cannan it was said on the publication of *Round the Corner* (1913) must have "recently read *Sanin*" (1907).

It is interesting to recall that it is Matthew Arnold, now so frequently dismissed as outmoded, who first formulated the internationalist attitude in criticism. He wrote: "The criticism which alone can much help us for the future is a criticism which regards Europe as being, for intellectual and spiritual purposes, one great confederation, bound to a joint action and working to a common result." When Arnold wrote this in *Essays in Criticism* (1865), such a statement was needed. The English point of view was strongly insular. Now that this point of view has grown so largely internationalist it is helpful again to look at literature from the racial point of view.

There is little dispute that it is by their literature and by their literature alone that the English-speaking peoples take place among the peoples that have given great art to the world. And there is equally little dispute among the critics who have read widely in all forms of English literature that it is in poetry that English literature is at its best. English poetry is the art of the English-speaking peoples at its best just as surely as the symphony is the art of the German-speaking peoples at its best.

Most of the deeply significant things said in English literature, the "readings of life," the summings up of human nature in memorable phrases, as well as most of the "natural falterings," the clarities of speech, the falling of words into lovelinesses of sound that are as haunting as old airs, are to be found in verse. Such phrases and sentences of this sort as are from prose, are, it is often contended, less frequently from the novel than from the essay. They are more prevalent in Bacon than in Bennett.

George Moore goes further than this, saying, in his *Avowals* (1903) that English prose is never at its best in the novel. Here, I think, his desire to minimize everything in the English novel that antedates his own writing has led him astray. It is true, no doubt, that many would agree that Landor and De Quincey are more finished in the externalities of style than Scott or Dickens. To some the difference would seem to be that of broadcloth and homespun. If you consider the style of the men *in toto* you may well come to the conclusion that the novelists are not so far below the essayists as Moore maintains. If style is speech or writing with the savor of personality and with distinction of utterance or expression, if style is the man himself, then Scott and Dickens are possessed of it as surely as Landor and De Quincey.

Scott gives to all of his writing, save the statement of sentiment of his lords and ladies and their dialogue, the very pith and marrow of himself. Stevenson with his "a great romantic, an idle child" has done, inadvertently, a wrong to Scott. As "mere writer" Scot, for all his hurry, is not "an idle child," but a proved master of words. Years of absorbed listening to the speech of the lower orders in Scotland and to whatever was picturesque in that of people of other orders brought the style of Scott into being. Despite the difference in his origin and in his associates from the origin and associates of Burns the two were alike in complete mastery of their native speech only. Scott could not express all of himself in the English of the center because that English had been only before his eyes, not in his ears, from boyhood. Dickens, too, made his style out of himself. Its grotesquerie, its vividness, its excess, were of the man himself.

Moore disparages the style of Thackeray, too, but his attack fails wholly here. There is no style in English prose more completely expressive of meaning and mood and atmosphere, than the style of Thackeray. Felicities of phrasing, clarities of speech, exact renderings of emotion, are so common on every page one scarcely notices them once the story has one in its grip. And at his best, in his homily in little on the death of the Duke of Hamilton in *Esmond* (1852), or at the close of that novel, there is a nobility of rhythm that has not been reached often in English. Weaknesses, mannerisms, the constant intrusions of himself that shake our belief in the reality of the story, there are, and in plenty, in his writing, but the charges against him of commonplace moralizing are hardly well taken. It is easy, looking back, to say of this moralizing that it is "old stuff." It was not "old stuff" before Thackeray made it part and parcel of our inheritance.

When one thinks of George Meredith, Hardy, Stevenson, Moore himself and D. H. Lawrence one cannot say that fine prose is not to be found in the modern novel. Yet there is a half truth in the contention that the best English prose is to be found in "historians and essayists." Landor, Pater, De Quincey, Carlyle, Newman and Ruskin—it is a formidable list that Moore marshalls against the novelists. It is, I suppose, that he may include Carlyle that Moore prefixes "historians" to essayists. He need not have done so, for Carlyle is essayist, too. Maybe he had Gibbon in the back of his mind when he coupled the two kinds of craftsmen, and then failed to throw him, too, in the face of the enemy. There are many writers of prose, other than novelists, both earlier and later than those he cites, that it would have strengthened his argument to mention, but Moore does not like to acknowledge his contemporaries and he dislikes to read seventeenth century prose.

The essay is an aristocratic form, in which, at its best, the writing is considered as carefully as the lines in a sonnet. In the very nature of things, as a dealing with life in the large, its primal appetites and emotions, its ambitions and dreams, its adventures and sufferings, the novel can seldom be as finished in detail as the essay. The novel is too big for perfection. If it were to be finished as the essay is finished three or four novels at most would be the work of a long lifetime.

The tradition, too, of the essay is that it has been written at leizure, and out of memories recovered and dreams dreamed in leizure. That it is the literature of the gentleman. The tradition of the novel is that it is written in a hurry no matter how well ripened the knowledge of life out of which it is made; that it is written to sell; that it is democratic literature, the literature for all sorts and conditions of men. The essay has belonged, traditionally, to its author, and to his like, to connoisseurs that are to be found only here and there. The novel has belonged traditionally to the reader, as well as to the author, and the reader having some rights in it, has dictated that it shall be concerned with matters vital to himself, the representative of the common interests of all men.

There is, then, an intrinsic aristocracy about the essay that restricts its appeal, and an enforced universality about the novel that broadens its appeal.

It is necessary, though, that we realize that it is only a half truth that we have followed in this discussion of the contention of Moore that the novel has not given us the best English prose. It has given us, it and its predecessors and its allied forms, as much fine prose as the essay itself and fine prose of many differing kinds. These kinds have not been of the kinds of prose Moore himself most admires, the prose of his later work with its exquisite graces, its delicacies of color, its nuances of tone. It is not often that our English novel has had such a prose as that of *The Lake*, (1905) a thing of pale blues and soft mauves, or of *The Brook Kerith* (1916), a thing of fadeaways in old rose. The prose of English fiction at its best has been of harder texture, with beauties of as varied kinds as there have been masters to write it, but not, characteristically, as much worked upon, as carefully polished as the prose of the essay.

There are, of course, unresting workmen in the novel, men who, like Conrad, are lost to their family and friends for long months through absorption in their work. Such are not, however, the rule. Jane Austen could write her stories in the sitting room, with the family talking all about her. Thackeray could write with the printer's devil waiting for his copy. Widely famed authors of today, if gossip is to be believed, never even look, after dictation, upon what they have written until it comes to them in proof.

There are weaknesses in construction, too, characteristic of the English novel. The picaresque story, one of its ancestors whose blood is still strong in our novel, was a rambling sort of affair that enhanced its interest, to many readers, by shifting from this place to that and so permitting descriptions of several places and groups of people. The ways of this picaresque story are the ways even now of many stories, and all of them upsetting to the unity of plot that is the ideal of the more artistic writers of our day.

The method of publishing novels in monthly or weekly parts, practiced by Dickens and Thackeray, was another agency that made for the discursive tendency of the novel. Serial publication even to this day often forces on a novel conditions inimical to its art. There are magazines which ask their authors to have each installment of so many pages, each complete in itself, each provocative of further reading of the story.

The miracle is that so many novels are so finely done. Genius cannot be denied, cannot be deprived of its successes, even though the form through which it works be but loosely knit. Whatever is said about the novel it cannot be denied it numbers as many great men among its writers as any prose form in English. Nor can you deny that the list of the great novelists from Richardson to Conrad is imposing even when compared with the list of the great poets.

How near to the novelists are many of those poets who, like Chaucer and Shakespeare and Browning, are presenters of character as well as kindlers of lyric ecstasy. But not only their characters force us to compare Scott and Dickens and Hardy with Chaucer and Shakespeare and Browning but their humor and the poetic intensity of emotion with which they present both character and incident.

Remember, too, that down to Scott's day the novel was a form that gentlemen felt dubious about writing. Scott's concealment of his authorship of the Waverley novels can be explained on other grounds than his feeling that to write novels was bad form for a gentleman, and yet the fact remains that he felt it was not the best of form for Scott of Abbotsford to write them. It was only when their success was an indubitable fact, only when he felt assured they in no way compromised his dignity that the secret was openly revealed.

Yet with a prejudice against it as bad form which only Scott's achievement dispelled, the novel even before his day called to its practice such a gentleman and genius as Fielding and such a gentlewoman and genius as Jane Austen. Before that day, too, it had called to its practice genius from many conditions of life. It had called Richardson and Smollett and Sterne, London printer, Scottish laird turned hack, and Yorkshire parson. It called "giants in those days" and "giants" in Scott's day, and "giants" it has called in all other days, down into our own. One reason the novel is so great is that it has called the great to write it. A form may have, traditionally, prejudice against it, and real weaknesses in itself as traditionally practiced; and another form, poetry, may be regarded traditionally, and may truly be, the best form for the expression of the genius of the race; but what do these disadvantages matter when a Scott and a Dickens, a Charlotte Brontë and a Thackeray practice that form. And even later, after the novel was greatly improved in form, its greatness was still largely the greatness of those who practiced it, George Eliot and George Meredith, Hardy and Conrad.

It is likely, as has been said, that one of the reasons the great have been drawn to the novel is that it permits of a man writing so many other literary forms than the novel itself when he is writing the novel. That, and its dominance for a century over all other literary forms, have made it irresistible. There is virtually no kind of prose writing it may not include, and it has frequently been made to include verse, too. There is no kind of reader who does not delight in it and so a wide circle of readers is always ready for it. Is it, then, any wonder that there are few writers of prose who forego the novel?

The story as story is the very root of its appeal. Each one of us, young or old, sophisticated or unsophisticated, will, the right man leading him, "dig for incident like a pig for truffles." And when there is added to this lure of the story as story the other lures of poetry and essay and drama the novel draws us one and all. Our English novel is not so fine a thing, as art, as our English poetry at its purest. The novel cannot so kindle those who delight most in literature as can poetry. The novel has not the aristocracy of the essay or the austere severity of form and the quintessentialized emotion of the drama. The novel is, though, let us never forget, at its best a fine form of art in itself, and it is, in passages, poetry and essay and drama as well. The novel is unquestionably the broadest in scope and most varied in effects of our literary forms.

CHAPTER IV

CRITICAL STANDARDS

THE novel's inclusion within itself of the qualities of many literary forms both helps and hinders our criticism of it. We have so much more to compare the novel with if it have something of poetry or essay or drama in it and the more we have to compare it with the less likely we are to err in our criticism, the more sign posts there are to keep our way straight. If a certain novel is of such material that we are forced to consider it all the way through not only as a novel but for those qualities it shares with other literary forms we are less apt to be biased for or against it by the way it smooths or ruffles our prejudices as to what a novel should be.

If this novel have achieved beauty of any kind; if it have insight and understanding and knowledge of humanity; if it have the exaltation that is the very breath of poetry; if it be quick with a personality that reveals life freshly as an essay must be; if it have those moments of tense life breaking into action that we call drama: then there is something to be said for that novel even if its story be clumsily told or its character drawing labored or uncertain. It belongs to literature, then, even if it fall short of what a novel should be. It is considerations like these that have led critics to say that George Meredith is a great writer but a novelist less than great, that Conrad is a great writer but a poor story-teller.

The inclusiveness of the novel, then, helps us to test the value of any particular novel as literature, but hinders us in our judgment of it as to what a novel should be. The trouble is that there have never been any fixed standards as to what the novel should be. So it is that George Moore, in *Avowals,* denies to Fielding and Scott, Dickens and Thackeray, any place as novelists, and allows title to greatness to Balzac and Turgenieff alone. So it is that W. L. George, in *A Novelist on Novels* (1918), can couple Wells with Conrad and Hardy as holding "without challenge the premier position among novelists."

There is, however, an approximate consensus of opinion that a novel is a long story in prose that depends for its value on portrayal of character as well as upon succession of incidents.

First and foremost, then, we ask ourselves, in our attempt to rate a novel, How is the story told? What is the fashion, what the power of narrative, of Scott or Stevenson or Dunsany? Of Thackeray or Du Maurier or De Morgan? Of Dickens or Gissing or Arthur Morrison? Of George Eliot or Hardy or Sheila Kaye-Smith? Of Meredith or "John Oliver Hobbes" or J. C. Snaith? Of George Moore or Bennett or Swinnerton? Of Conrad or Richard Curle or McFee?

If we are considering *Command* (1922), for instance, it will help us to get at the value of the story if we put its methods of presentation over against those of other novels of some power of its year, say *Sudden Love* of "Benjamin Swift" or *The Cathedral* of Walpole. It will help us still further if we put *Command* over against other "sea-stuff" of today, say of Tomlinson or Curle or Conrad; and still further again if we put it over against other books of its time that are written by Scotchmen or concerned with Levantines. Consider McFee in comparison with Rebecca West and "George Douglas" and Sir James M. Barrie, or in comparison with Gerald Cumberland and Marmaduke Pickthall and Robert Hichens.

It may not be possible, always, to find another novel of as much power as that under consideration that has to deal with the same life. If you cannot, take whatever novel you know that presents the same life. It may be that you know no other novel at all that deals with that life. Take, then, a short-story or a travel-book, or whatever presentation you can find of that same life. The important thing is to have at hand while you are considering your novel some other book that will enable you to judge of your author's knowledge of his material. Such a checking up may not be necessary but it is always helpful. By the comparisons that follow such placings of books side by side you will learn, too, of your author's principles of selection from what he has observed, of his ability to catch the genius of place, of his accuracy of description, of his interpretation of ideals.

Nor need you stop with placings of the book under consideration alongside of other books of its power and its kind in its own time. See *Command,* for instance, against the background of the literature of the sea in English on back through Clark Russell and Marryat, through Smollett and Defoe, yes, on back through "Sir Patrick Spens" and "The Sea-Farer." There is a poem of Lionel Johnson, "The Classics," in which there opens a vista into the past, through great writers Roman and Greek, to "Homer grand against the ancient morn." If you can so see the novelist you are considering in the very fore-front of a vista with the great novelists and story-tellers and presenters of character in further foreground and middle distance, with Chaucer "grand against the ancient morn" at that vista's end, you will be apt to see your contemporary in truer proportions than if you see him as a contemporary only.

Welcome with enthusiasm the newest volume in every department of literature if it kindles you in your reading of it, but see it always against the background of other writing of its kind, be that kind novel or drama, poetry or essay. See your Synge in relation to the long line of dramatists that stretch back to Marlowe; your W. H. Davies among poets of little and poignant things on back to Herrick; your W. H. Hudson as one of the wonderers at the beauty of the world of the tribe of Sir Thomas Browne; and you will be saved many blunders in your estimates of these men made the more memorable to you as men of your own time, the more interesting to interpret and to judge because they have not yet been interpreted and judged.

Talk *Command* over with your sea-faring friends, as well as with landsmen. Keep literature a daily topic of conversation.

Insist that it is not a thing aloof, sacrosanct, or for the few, that it demands no special privilege but only a considered hearing.

The power of character portrayal is as important an element, axiomatically, in a story of real life as the narrative itself. What is your novelist's power of character portrayal? is your next question of him. Can Beresford, for instance, just touch a character, just give to Jacob Stahl an allusion or two and a bit of dialogue and make him stand before you to the life as Thackeray can Sir Pitt Crawley? Or Dostoieffsky Prince Muishkin?

Many an author can tell you most completely what a character is like. We say, "Yes, Walpole has made Peter Westcott in *Fortitude* (1913) true to life. I have met a boy like that, a young man like that. What he says and does is what such a one would say and do." You can say this and yet feel you have only learnt all about Peter Westcott, that you have not met him. Yet in another story of Walpole, *The Green Mirror* (1918), you may not only know about, but meet, Mrs. Trenchard.

Characters in books differ as the people we know. This one is somebody, this one is nobody. By "somebody" and "nobody" I mean not a ranking according to social status or success in business, but a ranking by personality. A weakness of a good many novels lies just here. Their characters are so uninteresting in themselves that no presentation short of that of great genius can make them significant. Jane Austen can make colorless bores immortal. Can Virginia Woolf make them more than mildly interesting today and forgotten tomorrow? Nobodies in the social sense are legion in literature. Think how many Cuddie Headriggs and Josephs, how many Mrs. Gummidges and Silas Marners, how many Mrs. Berrys and Granfer Cantles there are in the great portrait gallery! What we ask of a character is that it shall be alive, human, as surely a fellow man as this we stop to gossip with at his gate or that we meet at corner-store.

We shall feel the surer of our novelist if he have some characters really memorable in his books, some "figures against the sky" of a solidity and distinction like those who from Chaucer on have lived and moved and had their being in narrative poem and play and novel. One wonders if a novel is really a great novel if it does not have in it some men or women to remember as we remember the Wife of Bath or Lear, Clarissa or Corporal Trim, Parson Adams or Mr. Darcy, Elspeth of the Craigburnfoot or Peggotty, Heathcliff or Becky Sharp, Cecilia Halkett or Tom Tulliver, Sergeant Troy or Heyst. Comic or tragic, either, such characters may be: but all must be of such body and breath, such a quickness of life, that we could no more forget them than we could mother or father.

There has been so much talk these last years of the necessity of objectivity in art that we forget that all great artists warm their work with themselves; illumine it with their "inner light," as the Quakers say; envelop it in the aura of their personality. So does even Shakespeare, the most impersonal of them all. And Chaucer! Who does not feel the steady glow of his personality always present in his work, a largess of refreshing heat like that of the sun some midday of late April when it fills to overflowing a cove of the hills. So, too, you feel Sterne, "exquisite, equivocal," and Scott, who can never be disassociated from "and round about him the great morning shone." What a compound he was of morning light and haunted evening hours; hearty, life giving, prodigal, incredibly romantic! They tell you, too, that Ibsen was impersonal, but the truth is he was anything but that. There blows through his every play the wind from the north the man was, cleansing, bracing, freeing.

Thackeray, Dickens, Charlotte Brontë, Meredith, Hardy, Conrad—a large part of the pleasure of reading each is derived from the personality revealed in the work, the quality of the author. As I see it, his ideas have little to do with this quality of the man in his work that we enjoy. It is the revelation of personality, what life has made of him, that counts; the color of his thought and emotion; not what he has borrowed from his time, but what he has been given through his temperament. Conrad serves best of all to illustrate the point. What do we not forgive him in the way of involutions, of wheels within wheels, of backings and fillings and indirections, because of our sense of the "authentic presence vast" of the man always at hand. In Conrad we value the story itself, but we value more still the way he feels the story; the way he tells it we value least of all.

Closely allied with this feeling we have for "the man behind the book" is the feeling we have for his attitude toward life. Thackeray could never forgive Swift for what he considered his attacks on human nature. It may be that Thackeray misinterpreted the bitter quality of the man, that Swift did not mean to indict mankind as wholly vile. Thackeray thought Swift did so indict human nature, however, and he could not refrain whenever opportunity offered from denouncing him for it. There are those who have brought a similar charge against Thackeray, but how anyone can fail to understand that the author of *Esmond* is on the side of the angels is inconceivable. Hardy, too, for all his irony and conviction of a world gone wrong, has infinite pity for human littleness. George Moore has moments of such pity, most of them in *Esther Waters,* but in his later writing he glories, or pretends to glory, in cruelty. Has there been a recrudescence in Moore of that sort of brutal selfishness he excoriated in *Mike Fletcher* (1889)? One has to be wary in interpreting Moore. "The sunny malice of a faun" lurks always in his mind; the desire of the small boy to flutter the dovecotes will not down in him even now in his patriarchal years.

The appeal of personality, in the narrower sense of personality, is sometimes as dangerous to critical judgment of literature as the appeal of personality is dangerous to judgment of our fellows in the daily relations of life. Authors who have a "way with them," like Stevenson or Barrie for instance, will lead the critic into a liking that prevents a sound estimate of them. Conversely the "way with them" may be antipathetic to other critics who will attack "the cheap optimism offensively tricked out" of the one or "the wallowing naked in sentiment" of the other. So, too, a writer who reveals cruel and morbid tendencies, like D. H. Lawrence, will alienate critics who could not but appreciate his insight and sense of beauty were they able to free their judgment of prejudice arising from the hurt effrontery with which he forces his way through his books.

The books worth reading are so many, and our leisure so little that many of us are forced to base our judgments of books on one reading of them. Such judgments often do small justice to either author or critic. It is not conceivable that W. L. George could follow George Moore and speak of "Thackeray's continual flow of sugary claptrap, the incapacity of Dickens to conceive beauty, the almost unrelieved stagey solemnity of Walter Scott" if he had read many of their books more than once. It is a little difficult, for that matter, to understand how he could say such things if he had read any but their poorest work even once. A second reading, say of *Vanity Fair* (1848) or *Bleak House* (1853) or *Old Mortality* (1816) would compel him as a candid man to revise such assertions.

The interest you have in a story as to how it is going to turn out is a legitimate interest. Those who decry it fail to recognize that a novel is always the better for plenty of story. So many novels, however, have so little story in them that it is not strange that the heresy that the story is not important should have grown up. This interest as to how the story is going to turn out is complex. It combines the kind of interest you have in the solution of a puzzle with an interest akin to that of neighborhood gossip and with an interest in the denouement as a bit of drama. The "puzzle" interest, if you have any memory worthy of the name, will not be present in your rereading of a novel, but the other kinds of interest in "How it ends" are often quickened in rereading. You know the people of the story better now and care more what happens to them; you realize more keenly the discrepancies between their ambitions and desires and the only partial realizations or the defeats of these. The drama of the story has more chance to prove poignant on a rereading.

You notice many things, obviously, on rereading that your very keenness for the development of the action kept you from noticing on first reading. You can take more delight, too, in all the many accessories that contribute so much of its richness to the novel.

Your mood, too, on second reading, has in all probability changed from what it was at the time of first reading; and if many years have intervened between the readings your experience of life has deepened; you feel and interpret many incidents of the story in another way than you did before. It may mean something very other than it meant to you before you came to realize that "with human nature what it is almost anything is possible." You come to know that you can no longer say, with Chancellor Brack, "people don't do such things."

There is a seventh consideration you must make of the novel you would criticize, a seventh question to ask of it. This "seventhly" is never for a moment to be let slip from mind. It should precede the "firstly" and it should follow the "lastly." It is the "before we begin" at the start and the "furthermore" at the end. It is, what of beauty and what kind of beauty has our author made in this novel out of his experience and dream of life? As we ask ourselves this question we must keep before us the truth that beauty is of many kinds and that there is always possible a new kind of beauty. "There is one glory of the sun, and another glory of the moon, and another glory of the stars: for one star differeth from another star in glory." Remember the words of Paul, and remember, too, words of Keats. At any moment a new planet may swim within our ken.

There is little attempt in these pages to consider the novelists in groups, or as members of "schools." What is important is not so much what one novelist shares with another or others, as what he has found of beauty and truth for himself, what reading of life he has made, what portraits he has added to the great gallery from English literature, what individual and distinguished way of telling a story he has won to.

CHAPTER V

SCOTT, ROMANCE AND THE ROMANTICS

THERE would be no author so sure of a universal welcome in the world today as a second Scott. There is a hunger for romance that goes unappeased. Should there be published any day now a book as enrapturing and refreshing to our time as *Waverley* was to 1814, the world with one voice would call its author blessed. It is not a writer of the pattern of Scott (1771-1832) whom we await but one who shall bring to us what Scott brought to our forbears, wonder, forgetfulness of self, transportation to a brighter earth than that men daily inhabit. There is much else that Scott brought, characters racy of the soil and fellowly human, rallying adventure in wild places, "the light of other days," and— for those who care for such things—moments of writing that exalt, he himself would say, as does "a solitary trumpet." These latter gifts, however, others have brought and still bring, but such a gift of romance as his no other of our writers has had to give.

Always we are on the lookout for romance. A Donn Byrne is seized upon hopefully by our generation as a bringer of romance, but, unhappily, is found little satisfying. A Dunsany contents us, maybe, for a while, with a brief play or a tale even briefer, but when he attempts a full-scope story all that he can give us is a cento of old effects. One chapter of *Don Rodriguez* (1922) reminds us of Conrad's "Inn of the Two Witches" (1916), another of all childhood's reading about crystal-gazing, another of Robin Hood, and still another of Roland's horn under the peaks that were "high and dim and far." We are glad to be carried back, but what we want is not old memories but a new romance.

Kipling gave us something of a new romance in his earlier

stories of India, inciting us to higher hopes than he could fulfill. Only those who can remember the excitement of readers when he broke upon us out of the East can realize how disappointing it was that only a *Kim* (1901) should follow the high promise of *Plain Tales from the Hills* (1888). At the outset of his career it seemed that Kipling might find a romance in the Further East of India as alluring as that which Byron had found in the Nearer East of the Levant. The spectacle of the younger author was very like the spectacle of the elder nearly three generations earlier, but Kipling was a portent for a few years only. His settling down in England, his assuming the position of prophet to the English race, an exhaustion of power—who shall say what it was—prevented him from becoming such a romantic as Byron had been.

Had William Morris been given the power of character creation he might well have been a capturer of romance to compare with Scott. But that gift was denied him, a man gifted with almost all else that any writer needs, and with gifts so many in arts other than writing that it seemed unfair one man should be so richly endowed. It was the old law of compensation no doubt that mulcted him. There is no blood in the people of his romances, no body to them. They have but two dimensions. They are flat, like knights and angels on windows of stained glass. So it is that the people of all these stories from *The Sundering Flood* (1898) on back through *The House of the Wolfings* (1889) to *Gertha's Lovers* (1856) impress you not as men and women but as pictures only, in which you can be less intimately interested.

It is deplorable that Morris lacked this power of character creation for he can tell a tale and lead you to pleasant far-off places where there is coolness and quiet and the light of a world younger than ours. Style is his, too, and the knowledge and power to recreate the background of bygone times, their organization of life, their architecture, their pageantry and their look and lay of land.

If you could identify yourself with his characters you could perhaps find more romance in these stories, but as it is you seldom come upon romance in them. It almost always evades you, is somewhere just beyond, evanescent, hovering, diffused, thinning away to nothingness. You believe an Edgar of Ravenswood loved, and was unhappy, and died in the quicksands of the Kelpie's Flow. You believe that Henry Morton braved Balfour of Burley in the cave above the black Linn of Linklater. Scott makes real *The Bride of Lammermoor* (1819) and *Old Mortality* (1816). You recall that William Morris told a tale about a boy and a girl who talked and made love across a river gorge, in *The Sundering Flood*, and that in *Gertha's Lovers* Gertha dead, with the blue speedwell against her cheek, is like a painting by Burne-Jones.

Stevenson was hailed by his generation as a true romantic, and so he was, and is. But his vein of romance was thin compared to that of Scott and death cut him off before he had little more than begun to work its richer depths. *Lorna Doone* (1869) was to its earlier time "true romance" and it is even yet a classic. Blackmore is, however, hardly a name to conjure with nowadays; he seems no more than an elder Farnol. *The Cloister and the Hearth* (1861) has retained its vitality better than any other story invested with romance of the times between Scott's day and ours. There is, though, a weight of historical data in it that presses heavily upon its romance. If you are driven to question constantly whether or not this you are reading is really true your mood is inimical to romance. Reade has not escaped the dangers to which all historical novels are subject.

There are ten men of the last hundred years, maybe, other than these I have mentioned, that have captured a little romance in their writings. There are another ten who have so aped the ways of the real romantics that their times have accepted the imitators as genuine. There is romance, and a new romance at that, in *Green Mansions* (1904) of W. H. Hudson. Rima exerts that "fascination of the unknown and the mysterious" that is of the very essence of romance. The author of *Aylwin* (1898), Theodore Watts-Dunton, is the critic of his age who has most fully analyzed romance, and his novel might well serve as an illustration of his definition. Neil Munro is a sort of Highland Stevenson, as true a romantic if not so fine a writer as his master.

No one will question that *Lavengro* (1851) admits Borrow to the company of the romantics; and *Hypatia* (1853), Kingsley; and *The Scarlet Letter* (1850), Hawthorne. The others to mention are G. K. Chesterton for *Manalive* (1912); Cunninghame-Graham for a full hundred sketches of "inland places" from the Lebanons to Argentina; Anthony Hope Hawkins for *The Prisoner of Zenda* (1894), alive and hearty though thirty years old; S. R. Crockett, Sir Gilbert Parker, Stanley Weyman, Sir Arthur Quiller-Couch, Sir Arthur Conan Doyle and Sir Henry Rider Haggard, a sextette of skilled story-tellers who have held the attention of two generations of readers, and who have been properly rewarded, all but two, with titles; Robert Buchanan and William Black, who went to that unfailing source of romance, the Highlands of Scotland; Wilkie Collins, whose *Moonstone* (1868) and *Woman in White* (1860) are still almost "best sellers" in back waters; Harrison Ainsworth, who imitated Scott at first hand and at second hand through Hugo; G. P. R. James whose "solitary horsemen" will be long unforgotten; and Bulwer-Lytton and Cooper, still classics for young years.

There are great names among these thirty I have listed, but not one of them, unless it is Hawthorne, is what Stevenson would have called "a great romantic." And I am not sure of Hawthorne's position as such. His greatest strength lay in his creation and presentation of Puritan characters. There is, it is true, romantic color always in Hawthorne, that atmosphere Motley has perfectly described as "golden gloom," and you are haunted after your reading of him by memories of strange and eerie things that we call romantic.

There is no clearer indication, surely, of Scott's preëminence as a romantic than the putting in comparison with him of these men who from his day to ours have been the first romantics. When you so place them you can pick out no one who has given us romance in any measure comparable to his. Nor did Hugo and Dumas, his disciples in France, and true romantics both in their widely differing ways, bring to the world any so great wealth of romance.

Wagner is the only man since Scott comparable to him as a bringer of romance. Through Wagner's presentation of heroes of legend, through Flying Dutchman and Lohengrin, through Tannhaeuser and Siegfried, through Tristan and Parsifal, and through the music that expresses them and reflects and accompanies their adventures, successive waves of romance have spread abroad.

Ossian (1760-1763), Matthew Arnold says, carried a "vein of piercing regret and passion like a flood of lava through Europe." That was the first great wave of romance in modern times. The second great wave came from the novels of Scott (1814-1832); the third great wave was that which was released in the eighteen-seventies when Wagner's legendary music-drama began to be a regular part of the repertoire of the opera houses of the world.

Smaller waves of romantic influence spread abroad in Mid-Victorian years from the refashioning of Arthurian legend by Tennyson and Swinburne and William Morris, and from that not unlike refashioning of old Irish legend begun about 1890 by the writers of the Celtic Renaissance. Another such romantic influence has begun to exert itself through the writing of Conrad, but whether it shall be a restricted or an extended influence it is yet too soon to determine. Conrad is, obviously, much else than a romantic, but he is a romantic through and through, and a romantic of first power. A large part of his appeal is through his presentation of the romance that always exists for a street-bred people in places at the world's end or out of the world they know. The romance of away-off and now is just as potent in charm as the romance of far-off years in familiar places. The Pacific island that is the scene of *Victory* is as far out of the world we most of us know as the Scotland of the eighteenth and seventeenth centuries. Conrad makes a wonder of the one today, Scott made a wonder of the other a hundred years ago.

Romance is easier to point out than to define. You can say of this description or of that episode in a story, "this has the air of romance about it." It is possible in the usual round of day on day to come on moments invested with romance. You are riding home under familiar mountains plum-gray in the overcast evening. Clouds lift; and the sunlight pours out through a notch in the western horizon, coloring the lonely landscape to the east with an indescribable splendor of soft purples and old rose. It lasts but a few minutes; the flooding light is cut off by the sinking of the sun, leaving the mountains mole-gray now, with a dimming aureole of gold. Something catches at your heart; there is wonder abroad; strangeness falls on the well-known road. It is as if you were living over again some moment that was of more significance than this moment is now. "Ancestral memory is awake," this man will say. "Too great beauty in the world has struck you to the heart with a realization of how short a while you have left to see beauty," says another. And a third says, simply, "Romance!"

Romance is surely closely allied to wonder and strangeness. It is suggested by certain aspects of certain places; by certain sounds: wind in the pines, with this man; the tones of a French horn, with that; breakers on the beach, with a third.

By romance I mean something a good deal other than Romanticism. "At first," says Brandes, "Romanticism was, in its essence, merely a spirited defense of localization in literature. The Romanticists . . . took as their watchword 'local coloring.' By local coloring they meant all the characteristics of foreign nations, of far-off days, of unfamiliar climes."

Romance is none of these things, but something that springs from the strangeness and wonder that are in most of them; and, say some, from a suggestion of the supernatural. The supernatural is not, however, necessary to romance. A Scott, an Arthur Machen, an Algernon Blackwood, will use a suggestion of the supernatural to attain romance and sometimes more than a suggestion of the supernatural, but it seems, except in the most expert handling, a lower, a cruder, a more primitive form of romance that is evoked. There is a suggestion of the supernatural in several episodes of *The Bride of Lammermoor;* in the prophecy quoted by Caleb Balderstone; in the apparition at the Mermaiden's Well; in the unexplained substitution of the picture of Sir Malise Ravenswood for that of Sir William Ashton's father; in the horrors of the bridal night of Lucy and Bucklaw. Scott uses the supernatural forthrightly in the appearances of the White Lady of Avenel in *The Monastery,* in her pranks in defense of the Bible of Alice of Avenel; in her conveyance of Halbert Glendinning to the underworld; in her miraculous healing of Sir Piercie Shafton after he has been run through with the sword. Scott's first readers objected to the White Lady as incredible. They would have none of her and time has failed to win her a larger share of acceptance.

It was, perhaps, this very failure of Scott to achieve what he would with the supernatural that led to Hawthorne's pawky advice to the romancer in the preface to *The House of the Seven Gables* (1851): "He will be wise . . . . to mingle the marvellous rather as a slight, delicate and evanescent flavor, than as any portion of the actual substance of the dish offered to the public."

Scott, however, seldom failed in his use of the marvellous as he did in *The Monastery.* In his Scottish novels generally he could rely on local tradition or local characters to furnish it, to memories of a Balfour of Burley who fought the devil or to stories about a strange gypsy Jean Gordon whose wild exploits were very like those of Meg Merrilees. Romance was always ready to hand in the Scotland of Scott. So unequal was the development of one section and another in the days before railroads that Scott could come upon yesterday or day before yesterday, the time of his parents or grandparents, and conditions of even older times, in the more remote moors and valleys. In the Highlands especially primitive conditions prevailed, a patriarchal civilization there preserving much that was old and bad

as well as much that was old and fine. "Ian Maclaren" has said
that Scott never really understood the Highlander, that he treated
him as a stage property and never got to the heart of him. John
Watson was partly of Highland blood and he should know, but
I have read much testimony on the other side and come upon
some among the Highlanders I have met. Hamish Bean Mac-
Tavish in *The Highland Widow* (1827) may not be a typical
Gael but he is a true one, and Robin Oig MacCombich in *The
Two Drovers* (1827) is both typical and true. Rob Roy is, of
course, the most memorable figure of a Highlander that we have
in Scott and as finely and truly rendered as those two so different
Lowlanders of the same novel, Andrew Fairservice and Bailie
Nicol Jarvie. Fergus MacIvor in *Waverley* is an argument for
Watson's contention, but let us remember, while admitting his
exaggeration and misinterpretation, that Scott quotes chapter
and text for much that seems fantastic in his behavior and in
that of his clansmen. Not only is there romance in the Highlands and the Highlanders, but there is romance in the clash of
the Gaelic civilization with that very different Saxon civilization
of the Lowlanders.

We must remember that men of the Jacobite rising of 1715
were still alive in Scott's youth and that he had himself talked
with those who had been "out" in 1745. His was a remarkable
opportunity to hear of the strange happenings of old wars and
out of the way places, and nothing that he ever heard was forgotten by him.

There is romance even in the novel of his own times that Scott
wrote, *St. Ronan's Well* (1824), romance of a kind that Kipling
would approve. Kipling has given us the romance of today at the
ends of the earth, but he would have us celebrate, too, the romance of here and now. In "The King" (1894) he upbraids
"our backward-gazing world" for not seeing that "Romance
brought up the nine-fifteen" in which the commuters came to
town. We are beginning to see that more clearly, now that elec-
trics slide quietly into our stations. "Backward-gazing," we miss

the pillar of smoke uncoiling funnelwise against the sky as the great locomotive pounds down upon us. That spectacle is romantic to us now.

The very title of *St. Ronan's Well* is suggestive of romance, though we soon learn it is but an upstart watering place with no traditions and with a sorry crew of frequenters in place of such belles and beaux as we remember so clearly from our reading of Bath. But if St. Ronan's Well is vulgar and new, just above it lies the village of St. Ronan's, old at any rate, with picturesque houses and picturesque folk in them. There is romance in the story too. Francis Tyrell and Clara Mowbray and "Lord Etherington" are lovers fated as wantonly as their more famous fellows of *The Bride of Lammermoor* and *The Ordeal of Richard Feverel*.

But though *St. Ronan's Well* is a better novel than most of the critics of Scott will allow, it is not among his best or his most romantic. *The Antiquary* (1816), the story of a time but a little earlier, the late eighteenth century, is much richer in romance. Edie Ochiltree, bluegowned beggar, has about him that "earnest of romance" that pertains to all wandering men; the digging for long-hidden treasure in the ruinous Priory of St. Ruth is romantic as treasure hunting always is; the stricken house of Glenallan, blindly stumbling into crime and its own destruction, is conceived in the very spirit of romance; and the scene of the story, the coast to the northeast of Edinburgh, is romantic in the way of rockbound coasts, with beacons and smugglers' caves and perilous passings at high tides.

There are other qualities than romance, of course, in the Scottish novels of times still earlier, but it is romance makes memorable the three whose times are nearest to the *Antiquary's*: *Waverley* (1814), of the Forty-five, and contrasts of character, Highland and Lowland; and *The Heart of Midlothian* (1818), that story of two sisters, a cowfeeder's daughters, the sin of one and the strange goodness of the other, and of their adventures among people of the roads and at the English Court; and *Rob Roy* (1818), a riotous entertainment, with its background of Jacobite plots and a family feud, with more characters that are creations, that have place in the great portrait gallery of English literature than any other novel of Scott, and yet with as great a failure, Rob Roy's wife, as Scott ever lapsed into in characterization.   In Bailie Nicol Jarvie the Lowlanders are summed up more completely than the English squirearchy in John Bull; in Helen MacGregor is the epitome of melodrama gone mad.

Of the late seventeenth century are those other Scottish stories of first power: *The Bride of Lammermoor* (1819), *The Pirate* (1821) and *Old Mortality* (1816).   In each of these are characters of Scott's best, but each is at the same time so romantic as to be a symbol of romance.

There is romance, too, in the two Scottish novels of the late sixteenth century, *The Monastery* (1820) and *The Abbot* (1820), but it is not so true a romance as that of any of the novels of Scottish life of the seventeenth and eighteenth centuries.   No story of his of times earlier than that of *The Legend of Montrose* (1819), the sixteen-forties, catches the real spirit of romance.

Woodstock (1826), a story of the England of the Revolution, has but the trappings of romance.   It delights childhood with its ghostly apparitions and its secret chambers, but in this troubled year of his loss of wife and fortune and with dramatis personæ and a scene alien to his closest interest Scott could not do his best.   Places north of the border brought to him moods quick with wonder, and memories of happenings, legendary and historic, to people of his family, or happenings of a nature that he as a Scot could thoroughly understand.   He knew there what voices spoke in the wind, what was the spirit of place, what signs and saws portended.   So the romance of these home places, Highland and Lowland, has a thrill deeper than that of mere unusualness of dress or look of country, a romance that is more than picturesqueness.

W. P. Ker has pointed out that Scott did not like "the unrest, the mystery of romance," but I am not sure that he is more than half right in his saying. The mystery of romance Scott felt at any rate, even if it was not "attractive" to him, and, feeling it, could not but convey to you, reading, his record of it. Place after place in his stories you feel this mystery: in the look of the landscape on the approach to the lonely tower of the Glendinnings; in the mien of Redgauntlet on Solway sands; in the landing that snowy day of Bertram near Ellangowan where "berlins and galleys used to lie in langsyne"; in his playing on his flageolet of the air prophetic of his fortune, of the taking up of the air by the girl at the spring, in the recognition of him by Dominie Sampson. There is no book of Scott among the Scottish novels that has not such moments, and some of them have many such moments.

That criticism is just which makes the romance of *Ivanhoe* (1819) and *The Talisman* (1825), of *The Betrothed* (1825) and *The Fair Maid of Perth* (1828), of *Quentin Durward* (1823) and *Anne of Geierstein* (1829), little more than the romance of picturesqueness. Says Carlyle, "much of the interest of these novels results from what may be called contrasts of costume. The phraseology, fashion of arms, of dress and life, belonging to one age, is brought suddenly with singular vividness before the eyes of another. A great effect this, yet by the very nature of it, an altogether temporary one." It has not turned out as Carlyle prophesied. *Ivanhoe*, for instance, is still read, though its real merits are often lost sight of in its relegation to schoolboy reading-lists. If *Ivanhoe* is not quite what Watts-Dunton calls it, "an immortal mediæval romance," it is as great a book as an historical novel can be. Unless Scott had lived a lifetime with the historical documents of Angevin England and studied them until he had completely visualized that old life, he could not have given the story the tang and savor of life. And then maybe, he had been lost in his details as is Gissing in *Veranilda* (1904). As it was, Scott made *Ivanhoe* out of Froissart, and out of his neighbors, who were much better models for Scottish characters of the eighteenth and seventeenth centuries. His success with Scottish life of the generations nearly preceding his own lay in the fact that he had learned of the folk of these generations through an oral tradition that kept them human and sharply individual, not by the dead voice of history.

And yet even in *Ivanhoe* Scott succeeded in conforming to what George Moore, in his *Confessions of a Young Man* (1888), calls "an original artistic principle of which English romance writers are either strangely ignorant or neglectful, viz., that the sublimation of dramatis personæ and the deeds in which they are involved must correspond. . . . In Scott leather jerkins, swords, horses, mountains, and castles harmonize completely and fully with food, fighting, words and visions of life; the chords are simple as Handel's, but they are as perfect." And if, in later years, in *Avowals* (1903), Moore called him "the pompous and garrulous Scott" he could not unsay the old and true praise.

Scott was wise, as has often been pointed out, in seldom making an historic character widely known, a hero or heroine of a story. In *The Abbot*, it is true, Mary and Murray are almost principals, but the story is so contrived that you are more interested in Roland Graeme and Edward Glendinning the Abbott, both fictitious characters of Scott's creation, than in the historical personages. In *Ivanhoe*, too, the historical Richard I is prominent, but not so significant as a round dozen other characters of Scott's invention, Cedric and Wilfred of Ivanhoe, Wamba the Fool and Gurth the swineherd, Brian de Bois-Guilbert and Prior Aymer, De Bracy and Front-de-Bœuf, Isaac of York and Rebecca, Rowena and Athelstane, Friar Tuck and Ulrica the Saxon. Prince John is the only character we know as an historical character until toward the close of the story, when the Black Knight is revealed as Richard the Lion-Hearted. So careful is Scott not to have a preconceived notion of a character spoil the proportions of his story that he presents Robin Hood as Will Locksley and only makes known his identity with the legendary hero when the Black Knight is revealed as the King of England.

In *Kenilworth* (1821) Scott is not able to keep us from feeling a difference of credibility between the historical characters and those of his own imagining. The story suffers, I think, from this. We all know in a general way about Amy Robsart, who is kept constantly to the forefront of the story, and though Leicester is kept pretty well in the background you have him always in your mind as the cause of Amy's misfortunes. There are scenes, too, in which he and his queen, Elizabeth, hold the stage. It is then we are too keenly aware that make-believe about history is not so palatable as make-believe pure and simple.

We do not so well know the Scottish king and the Earls of Douglas and March that are prominent in *The Fair Maid of Perth,* but they are so subordinated that even did we know them well from history they would not destroy the illusion of the picture. They are only background, like the descriptions of countryside, to Henry Gow and Conachar, Glover and Catherine, Sir John Ramorny and Father Clement, the Bonnetmaker and the Gleewoman, whose little lives momentarily so concern us.

The contrast of fact and fiction is less pronounced in *The Talisman* and *Quentin Durward* because the scenes of action of these stories take them out of a world with which we are familiar.

In all of the historical romances there is less of the glamour of true romance, as I have said, than in the Scottish stories that grew out of romance-burdened places and people whom Scott knew. In the historical romances the romance is scarcely Scott's individually but that romanticism that he discovered in young manhood in Germany, and which he shares with many writers there and in France and Italy as well as in England. The romance he found for himself, that first visited him perhaps in those early summers under Ercildoune and that was suggested by the genius and tales of a hundred places in the Border country he knew so well, was a true romance, and so pervasive and enthralling that Scotland to this day is the romantic part of Great Britain to the English-speaking peoples the world over. Even in Scott's lifetime Americans began to visit Abbotsford and to this day Tweedside and the Trossachs, Ellen's Isle and the Eildon Hills are places of pilgrimage because the Wizard made them very shrines of romance. It may be disillusioning to have a man

with a megaphone announce from a touring 'bus that this stone
by the road from Melrose to Dryburgh is that which swung open
and admitted the Queen of Elfland and Thomas the Rhymer
on their descent to the underworld. It is nevertheless, testimony
to Scott's power in the world, for, as the driver said to us as
we started on: "Isn't it queer, but none of us would be here
now if it wasn't for Sir Walter."

Come back here at twilight, when the tourists are gone, and
you find it still a place of glamour. Above are the Eildon Hills,
one of the three lower than its fellows because Michael Scott
sliced it off with his spade; to the eastward the red hill of
Ercildoune, a Scottish Venusburg; not far away a homestead in
which the succeeding generations of one family have lived for
seven centuries; and nearby Melrose Abbey, a ruin, but the most
beautiful symbol of Scotland's past that has come down to us.
In this haunted countryside, and in literally a hundred others
that he knew well, Scott found strangeness and wonder just as
surely as raciness and canniness, dourness and good-fellowship.
There is no incongruity to the Scottish mind and nature between
the hardness of reality and the glamour of romance. Both are
part of the world as the Scots find it and both to be accepted
on their own merits. Your Scot will turn romance into hard
cash and still cherish it as romance.

Is what romance is, I wonder, yet made clear? Again and
again I return to the analysis, only to find definition impossible.
Will a reference to music perhaps illustrate, if not define it? You
may be listening to a "tone-poem" or an "idyl" or a passage from
a symphony or opera,—any composition, say, that you have not
heard before. You have looked up no "programme notes" or
libretto or score before going to the concert or opera. As you
listen an oboe or English horn takes an air, or a trumpet or
French horn calls off stage a lonely clarion. What is it that
so suddenly captures you, fills you with gladness unalloyed?
What is it that thrills you with pleasurable sadness for brave
things gone on the wind? You cannot tell. You guess, perhaps,
it is the associations of the sounds that move you. You have

heard woodwind lead the shepherd's song in *Tannhaeuser;* you have heard Siegfried's horn announce his approach before he comes upon the stage. The air or call you have just heard for the first time is like an air or call you are familiar with. So you associate the present moment with the remembered one and emotions close to those of that known situation arise in consciousness, or—should we say—reawaken in you, and you are affected very much as you were when last you heard the familiar air or call. The associations or meaning of that familiar air or call you know, so you have now on hearing the unfamiliar air or call, very similar associations, a very similar, if unconscious, interpretation, present to mind.

That is one explanation. But is it the true one? Or if it is the true one in one instance, is it the true one in another? I think you cannot dogmatize. Sometimes the air or call moves you through associations or memory, but are there not other times when it moves you in a way that you cannot analyze to your satisfaction? It doesn't matter, for the purposes of illustration, whether you can explain your mood or not. The kind of mood that comes to you on hearing this air on oboe or that call on trumpet in music unheard before is a romantic mood. Romance has visited you, none the less surely that you cannot put into words just what you feel.

Listening to the Highland girl singing as she reaped by the roadside, Wordsworth queried: "Will no one tell me what she sings?" He visited "the shores of old romance" as he drank in "the plaintive numbers," but he could only guess that she told of "old, unhappy, far-off things, And battles long ago."

There is a kind of magic in certain sounds heard in certain places, in certain strange glows or slants of light in certain places, in certain feelings or half-memories that revive in certain places. It is this kind of magic that evokes romance.

You do not have to make any allowances at all for differences in the ideals of poetry of its time and of our time, for differences in the intentions of the poet then and now, in judging "The Solitary Reaper," the poem from which the preceding famous

lines are quoted. Do you have to make any allowances for the
best of Scott, the best of his prose, when you read it today, allowances you do not have to make for the best of the poetry
of Wordsworth? If I say, "Certainly not!" do I find myself
at one with the weight of critical opinion? Maybe so, but I do
not find such unanimity of opinion as I find when I ask the similar
question about Wordsworth. The reason is not far to seek.
You can dismiss nine-tenths of Wordsworth and retain as many
poems of the first degree of excellence as there are years allotted
to man. Among these seventy poems you can find at least
twenty lyrics as fine as any other twenty from any other English
poet, as fine, you might almost say, as any other twenty from
English poetry. These twenty of Wordsworth's lyrics have
"wholeness of good tissue"; there is scarcely a line in them you
would wish changed.

Scott cannot be so selected. There are novels of his, to be
sure, which are of as complete a "wholeness of good tissue" as
novels can be, and that you would hardly wish to have changed
in the way of deletion. Such are *Old Mortality* and *The Bride of
Lammermoor*. But even these do not wholly content you. Edgar
Ravenswood and Lucy Ashton, and her mother and father, speak
more "in character" than do ladies and gentlemen elsewhere in
his novels, but their dialogue has not a vigor in its sphere comparable to the vigor in its sphere of the dialogue of his peasants
and middle-class sorts and eccentric gentlefolk. Old Lady Margaret Bellenden in *Old Mortality* is eccentric, and almost always
"in character." Edith Bellenden is not eccentric; she is just
a charming young lady, and like Henry Morton, her lover, stilted
in speech.

The comparison with Wordsworth is as severe a comparison
as could be instituted. As I have explained in the introductory
chapters, the novel, because of its methods of development and
its very bulk, can hardly have the perfection of lyric or ode or
sonnet. If you would select the very best of Scott you would
have to cut even *The Bride of Lammermoor*, but to cut it very
little. *Old Mortality* would have like treatment, and you would

retain almost all of *Guy Mannering* and *The Antiquary*. A good many even of the best novels, however, would have to be cut to the quick in such a hypothetical procedure, because of Scott's inability to sustain his presentation of upper class people to the level on which they are conceived. Careless construction of story like that which mars the conclusion of *The Heart of Midlothian* would take other novels of his, too, out of the list of "best novels." But how many other novelists would not suffer a like placing of some of their books because of one glaring weakness or another.

Compare this lack of power of dialogue between upper class people in Scott with another great novelist's amazing sins of dialogue. Meredith's sins of dialogue are of a sort at the other pole from Scott's. Scott fails to energize to life the talk of his gentlemen and ladies. Meredith bestows upon all but all of them a brilliancy of repartee that was his own but which in his books should have been restricted to his Adrian Harleys and his Mrs. Mountstuarts. Admitting frankly that this habit of Meredith is a great weakness and that lack of Scott which all the world notes is a great weakness, does either weakness deny either author title to greatness? Only those who delight in belittling beautiful things a little out of fashion will say "Yes." Such should remember that what is out-of-fashion today is in fashion tomorrow, and that, in the end, all beauty is acknowledged by the world.

The power Scott has of evoking romance is not his in greater measure than the power of creating character. It is a rarer quality, and that is why it has been emphasized here. With the exception, so often noted, of his great folk, from kings and queens of "langsyne" to ladies and gentlemen of yesterday, Scott has created characters from all sorts and conditions of men with an ease and a prodigality and a surety such as only Shakespeare before his day and Dickens and Thackeray since his day have attained. Hardy, had he not given over the novel with *Jude the Obscure* (1895), had doubtless been a fifth to add to the list. Hardy has the experience of life, the knowledge of men, the vitality of imagination, the sheer creative fertility that distinguishes his four elders. The life Hardy deals with, of course, is much closer, for all his modernity of treatment, to Shakespeare's and Scott's, than is the life of Dickens. These three men alone in English literature have created wise clowns, wise clowns in whose sayings English humor is at its best—Hardy, Scott, Shakespeare.

Shakespeare was in Scott's estimation so inevitably the model for characterization that it wasn't worth while for him to say so explicitly. So he could pay compliments to Miss Edgeworth for the little he owed to her in portrayal of character as he could pay compliments to Joseph Strutt for pointing out in *Queen-hoo Hall* (1808) some methods that he might follow in his historical romances. Scott has praised, too, *The Castle of Otranto* (1764), in the preface to which Walpole acknowledges obligations to Shakespeare. It was part of the reading of Scott's youth, and he grew up in the tradition that the humor and characterization of Shakespeare, believed by Walpole to be imitated in his romance, were proper to romance.

Scott knew the great English writers of the past. There is hardly a one of any importance that he does not name and quote from. Swift and Dryden he edited, and with Chaucer he seems equally familiar. It is Shakespeare, however, that Scott refers to most often, in the pages of his stories, in his prefaces, in the fragments of verse he uses as chapter headings. That he had not followed his master in vain Francis Lord Jeffrey pointed out in *The Quarterly Review* in March, 1817, in what remains to this day the best criticism of *The Waverley Novels*. This review, based upon only the four novels *Waverley, Guy Mannering, The Antiquary,* and *Old Mortality,* not only passes thorough and illuminating judgments on these four books, but generalizes about their author's powers with what startles us as prescience of their fuller development in the Scottish novels and the romances of chivalry yet to be written. The praise is as temperate as it is just. Jeffrey is very careful to indicate that Scott's success in this "invention and delineation of character" lay within a narrower range than Shakespeare's, and that the most striking and highly colored characters are too lavish of their presence. "It was reserved for Shakespeare alone," Jeffrey goes on to say, "to leave all his characters as new and unworn as he had found them, and to carry Falstaff through the business of three several plays, and leave us as greedy of his sayings as at the moment of his first introduction. It is no light praise to the author before us, that he has sometimes reminded us of this, as well as other inimitable excellences in that most gifted of all inventors."

It was a most fortunate circumstance that Scott in the years he was learning most of Scottish life of every sort from Border to Highlands had no thought of ever using his knowledge in the prose novel. He had a passion for documentation as it was, and had he recorded all that he saw and heard that was of the nature of plots for stories, of episodes for stories, of characters for stories, and of descriptions for stories, there had been great danger that the novels would have been unendurably weighted with detail. It was much better that time had the chance to leach out of his memories what was unessential and to preserve only what was too significant to be forgotten. He went hither and yon as an antiquary and folklorist, taking down many ballads and songs from oral dictation and delighting in the copies of others his friends had collected for him. He was welcome wherever he went because of a geniality and warm-heartedness and way with him that no other man anywhere, at any time, is known to have possessed. He was welcome for his stories, too. Before he was in his teens he had held his schoolfellows in Edinburgh with his stories. And year by year until he was forty-two they were accumulating. Comparatively few had been turned to the uses of print when he sat down to finish *Waverley,* the romances in verse but tapping his great fund and leaving untouched all that part of it leavened with humor. *Waverley* had been begun as early as 1805, but it had been laid aside on the advice of a friend who thought that unless it were very successful indeed its publication might jeopardize Scott's position as a poet. He took it up again eight years later, in the fulness of his maturity, and went at it with a will. In later years he used to say that he took to prose because Byron had beat him in poetry. Whatever the reason, it was fortunate he made the experiment, for a very great deal of his vast store of anecdote and story and knowledge of men and places was unavailable for use in the kind of narrative poem he had written. There is no record of a man elsewhere who knew so thoroughly so large a countryside and one so peopled with varying conditions and races of men. Scott knew at first hand the eastern and middle Lowlands from the Border to the Highlands; the northeast coast Aberdeen awa'; and the southern and southeastern Highlands. He had sailed round Scotland from Edinburgh to the Orkneys and Shetlands and down the west coast through the Hebrides to the Clyde; and even in those parts he never grew familiar with, as Galloway to the southwest, he had correspondents who sent him all sorts of details of their localities.

A close attention to prefaces and notes is necessary to a realization of how largely indebted Scott was in the suggestions for his stories to his correspondents. In some cases, too, he borrowed from manuscript sources, following his originals, now closely, now loosely. Bailie Nicol Jarvie is as surely a "creation" as a character in a book may be, but Andrew Lang has pointed out that a speech of Jarvie's toward the end of *Rob Roy* is "lifted" from the Gartmore manuscript (1747). Dugald Dalgetty of *The Legend of Montrose*, another of Scott's most individual and striking characters, follows very closely, as Scott indicated in his preface to the story, the portrait Sir James Turner gives of himself in his *Memoirs*. After all, however, these "originals" were little more than the stimuli which set Scott working on a particular character or incident or story.

Thoreau says that "a writer, a man writing, is the scribe of all nature; he is the corn and the grass and the atmosphere writing." If we adapt that saying to Scott and declare that "Scott is the scribe of all Scotland; he is the Border and Lowlands and Highlands writing; the peasant and middle class and gentry writing" we shall not be far wrong. Born of Lowland middle class stock, Presbyterian in faith and Whig in politics, Scott became landed proprietor, Episcopalian and Tory. He was fortunately not of the temperament to be possessed by the fury of the convert. He was none the less tolerant to that from which he sprung because he had gotten away from it. In such a story as *Old Mortality,* in which questions of class and faith and politics are all the time to the fore, he holds the balance even.

There are many references by Scott in his prefaces to his attitude toward his art. He would not have called it his "art," for a man of his prejudices and traditions was "far from thinking that the novelist or romance-writer stands high in the ranks of literature." His business in the novel was, he thought, to amuse. He had no desire to be "the showman of life." He felt the story-teller in prose of his day was very much what the minstrel in hall had been in mediæval times, and therefore in a position not wholly dignified. There were stirrings in him of the joy of authorship but there was very little in him of the pride of authorship. "When I light on such a character as Bailie Jarvie, or Dalgetty, my imagination brightens," he owns, "and my conception becomes clearer at every step which I take in his company, although it leads me many a weary mile away from the regular road, and forces me to leap hedge and ditch to get back into the route again. If I resist the temptation. . . my thoughts become prosy, flat and dull." A hundred story-tellers have told this same story: when characters become real to their makers these characters take matters into their own hands and dictate what shall be the course of the action.

So it was, maybe, with the ending of some of his stories. *The Surgeon's Daughter* (1827) does not end with wedding bells, though you feel that Scott would have liked so to end it. Wilfred, in *Ivanhoe,* does not marry Rebecca. Why not, Scott tells us. It was, partly, that such a union could not be in the twelfth century. Partly, it was that the author "thinks a character of a highly virtuous and lofty stamp is degraded rather than exalted by an attempt to reward virtue with temporal prosperity." These are strange words from the man who can admit that he raised

Athelstane from the dead on the "vehement entreaties of his friend and printer." Sir Walter, it would seem, was of one mind now and of another mind again. Or it may be that at one time he could control his characters and make them do what he would, and that another time they ran away with the story as did the Bailie and Dalgetty.

There are moments in Scott, moments of direct and rapid narration, like that of the fight in *The Two Drovers,* when his style is as simple and unadorned as Swift's. And there are other moments when his style is incredibly careless. He wrote in a great hurry, out of a towering vitality, a dammed up reservoir of memories of living and of observation of life; the story pressed hard on him, and must be gotten out quickly, even if anyhow.

There are other moments in his descriptions of the pageantry of the chase or the battle, when his style runs swift and clear as a trout stream. So it runs in the description of the foxhunt on Otterscope-scaurs in *Guy Mannering* and in the battle of Drumclog in *Old Mortality.* There is movement in these scenes, the shifting to and fro of men singly and of bands of men, but no warm color such as you crave as a relief from brown moor or mountainside reaching up under the gray northern sky. In the foxhunt white mists roll away from the hills and "silver threads" of water trickle down their sides. There are but cold colors here, and as cold are those of the bloody skirmish in the bog. As the cavalry of Claverhouse climb the ascent opposite that on which the Covenanters are waiting their attack, the horses and men can be distinguished from a drift of black cattle only by the glitter of arms.

This little attention to color in landscape is, I think, a sin of omission on the part of Scott but it is partly the fault of his times. They had not learned then to see the purples and blues so easy for us to pick out now that we have studied them in so many modern paintings and prints. The tournament of Ashby-de-la-Zouche in *Ivanhoe* has more color, particularly in matters of detail. Rebecca is gorgeous in a "turban of yellow silk" and a "simarre of the richest Persian silk exhibiting flowers in their

natural colors embossed upon a purple ground." Sir Piercie
Shafton lolls proud as a pie and even more gayly hued about the
dark tower of Glendearg, "in a carnation velvet doublet slashed
and puffed out with cloth of silver." Richness of color in dress
compels Scott to more vivid description than do the wintry
colors of the North but he is not so happy, I think, in such description as in that of the sombre scenes he knew so well and
loved so wholly.

It is in the speech of his peasants, as I have said, that Scott
reaches his greatest distinction of style. The talk of the three
old hags in *The Bride of Lammermoor,* like their characterization,
is Scott at his best, a master of style and drama. As finely wild,
yet more exalted, is the speech of Meg Merrilies; and Edie Ochiltree's, though often on a lower note, is extremely varied and
rich. The lament of Meg over her lost shieling in Derncleugh;
her blessing on young Ellangowan; her warning to Hazlewood—
these are not all of equal inspiration or beauty of execution, but
all are as surely lyrics in prose as the most prized passages of
De Quincey or Carlyle or Ruskin.

Since Scott wrote as one who held his rôle to be that of entertainer, it is not to be expected that he would often attempt
to read the riddle of things. But as all the great emotions find
place in his stories it is only natural that now and then he would
say his say on time and change and the little lives of men. He
will so comment both directly and indirectly. Speaking as the
story-teller omniscient in all that pertains to his characters, he
says in *Ivanhoe,* of the knights who fought in the tournament:
"Their escutcheons have long mouldered from the walls of their
castles. Their castles themselves are but green mounds and
shattered ruins—the place that once knew them, knows them no
more—nay, many a race since theirs has died out and been forgotten in the very land which they occupied, with all the authority
of feudal proprietors and feudal lords." It is interesting to note
that this passage, which falls into a rhythm so close to that of
Ossian, is suggested by lines of Coleridge.

Indirectly, Scott comments through his characters, often

through the lowliest of them, his Edies, his Megs, his Caleb Bal-
derstones.   Once he does it superbly well through Graham of
Claverhouse in his homily on death after the Battle of Bothwell Brig in *Old Mortality*.   Here Scott has found a rhythm in
English of a fineness comparable to that more often to be found
in his native Scotch.   The Antiquary expatiates largely on his
philosophy of life but we are not expected to take him too
seriously.   He is like Scott himself in many ways, in his weaknesses and in his benevolence, though the eccentricities of speech
and manner are those of another original.   You cannot identify
him with Scott when he refers to a "trumpery whirligig world."
The world was not that to Scott in 1816.   Even after the loss
of his wife and his fortune Scott met life with a smile, and in his
early years at Abbotsford, when *The Antiquary* had been written,
nothing could quench his optimism, if we are to take his books
as the expression of his feelings.   Troubling things he could
ignore or forget.   As has been often noted, he writes as if there
had never been a French Revolution, as if the constitution of
things as they are had never been questioned.   So it is that there
is in his stories even to this day that balm for sore hearts that
literature so seldom affords.   You can go to Scott for the easing
of heartache as you would to a gallop in wind and sun.   You can
go to him when the world weighs too heavily upon you, as if to
some loved place that has proved before now a well of healing.

We all know the varying criticism of Scott in the past,—that
Carlyle held him cheap and that Ruskin held him beyond price;
that he bored Thackeray and held Hugo captive; that Goethe
praised *The Fair Maid of Perth,* and that Turgenieff paid homage
to him in the pilgrimage to Abbotsford on the occasion of the
centennial of his birth in 1871.

We all know the varying criticism of today.   Whatever is said
pro or con proves that Scott is still very much to reckon with.
He remains a great figure among the English novelists and an
influence in the world.   Only recently an American scholar, James
Taft Hatfield, traced the Ku Klux Klan of reconstruction days
to the secret brotherhood of *Anne of Geierstein.*   Few characters

are used oftener in speech than his to designate the qualities of Tom, Dick or Harry. Tom is told not to be a Flibbertigibbet; Dick that he's a Dominie Sampson; and Harry that he is just the Antiquary over again. In a corner of New Hampshire that I know, the store-keeper is Walter Scott Blank and a baby born in 1922 was christened Rowena.

Such use of his characters speaks his universality today. Not quite so long ago as yesterday I had a more telling proof. We were walking to a little town under low mountains. It was in the long twilight of August in Northern Scotland. It was a Saturday night. We were in quest of minced collops and other provender to tide us over the Sabbath we were to spend with our friends. We had fallen upon them without warning and the house was stocked insufficiently for two more in family and that two company. The daughter of the house who was our guide said suddenly, after a pause in the conversation, "My engagement was broken, you know, just before we were to be married. He was a MacGregor. You are never certain what one of them will do, but whatever it is will make trouble. Oh, but why am I telling you that! You know what they are. It's all in *Rob Roy!*" What drove her to confide in the Americans so unexpectedly thrust upon her people I do not know. It was, perhaps, youth responding to youth. Or maybe it was that we all three had just been stirred by bagpipes from the bare hillside above us. A sickle moon hung ahead of us over the dark mass of a castle that had once been prison to Mary Queen of Scots. The noise of burns running full asserted itself when the skirl of the pipes died away. There was much of Scotland in the scene, in the hour, in the story,—bagpipes, and memories of Mary, and the MacGregors still what their neighbors have always held them to be. But more memorable to me, if not so moving at the time, was the faith the girl had that all the world had read *Rob Roy*. There could be no testimony so conclusive of the universality of Scott as this of the girl off-guard in a moment of emotion and thoughtless of all but her own trouble.

CHAPTER VI

DICKENS AND THE FOLK-IMAGINATION

It is an old custom of criticism to write down Dickens (1812-1870) as English of the English. Think of anything essentially English, says such criticism, and Dickens comes to mind. Think of Christmas, and memories of the *Carol* (1843) follow fast on the thought. Think of stage-coaches, and incidents of the road from his stories gather together, this one from *Pickwick* (1837), that from *Nicholas Nickleby* (1839), a third from *A Tale of Two Cities* (1859)—too many of them, indeed, to keep track of. Think of hearts of oak, and scores of characters crowd forward, mothering women and trusty men, Toodles and Peggotty and Little Dorrit, Gabriel Varden and Mark Tapley and Joe Gargery prominent among them.

There is no doubt that Dickens did so come to mind whenever Victorians thought of Christmas and stage-coaches and hearts of oak, and no doubt either but Dickens does often so come to mind when Georgians think of these things. May not such an association of ideas, however, indicate something else than that Dickens is essentially English? It certainly indicates that Dickens was read very widely and is still read widely.

Nor are Christmas and stage-coaches and hearts of oak by any means all of Dickens. To make up the rest of him go many characteristics that are of the Londoner rather than of the Englishman. The high spirits of the man, his mercurial temperament, his turn for play-acting, a something in him that was not far from instability—these are certainly not of Hodge or Lob-Lie-by-the-Fire or John Bull. And can you call his humor traditionally English? Are the ways and sayings of his Sam Wellers and Sim Tappertits the right clowning we are used to in Fielding or Scott

63

or Hardy? Scarcely, I think. Such affinities as this humor has with the humor of older writers are with certain antics of the Vices in morality plays, with the "humors" of Ben Jonson, and with the oddities of Smollett.

There is often something of the simplicity of a folk imagination in the story-telling of Dickens. Item on item might be cited to bear out this statement, but more confirmatory of it than any item is the fact that this story-telling has been taken to heart by so many of his country and of his tongue outside of his country. There is little in his stories that requires a second reading to be understood. Dickens tells all as clearly as if he were speaking, and therefore of a necessity to be apprehended completely on a first hearing.

The incidents in him, the murders and mysteries, the robberies and riots, the meanness and trickery of cheaply evil men and the ruthlessness of hard men, are paralleled in the lowliest experience. The ultimate triumph of the less fortunate or the downtrodden over the more fortunate or the oppressor, wins the response which the triumph the man of the people has won ever since the days of *Reynard the Fox*. What happens to the heroes of Dickens might happen to any mother's son of us. Their successes can be hugged to heart as dream-come-true by the humblest of readers.

The characters of his stories, each character so strongly marked and so vivid and so simple, are many of them like those of the folktale. Such are Mr. Pickwick and Sam Weller, Oliver Twist, Little Nell and Martin Chuzzlewit, and such, for whiles, even David and Pip, realistic as are the stories they dominate. Like the folktales, too, the stories of Dickens send their heroes on the road. Nicholas Nickleby tramps to Portsmouth, and meets adventures by the way as surprising for Victorian times as those of Jack-the-Giantkiller for ages more naïve. Barnaby whirls a delirious round as madly as any gossoon of them all. The Christmas stories are confessedly fairy tales. Codlin and Short are of the brotherhood of the hardy tramps who are the protagonists alike of rogue-story and folktale. Carker on horseback ranges about like the falsest of false knights. Quilp is but the ogre up-to-date; Fagin a more modern version of the necromancer of old tales; and Mr. Jarndyce a reincarnation of the good fairy that delights to aid a deserving hero.

The magician's wand, too, is potent in Dickens. Nothing in nature would account for the change in character he accomplishes in Scrooge and Tackleton and Mr. Dombey, but he knows the heartsease of the happy ending, and he cannot deny it to us. He waves his wand of rowan, and hard men become kind. That is the very way of the fairy-tale.

The phantasmagoric quality of Dickens, too, is like that of the folktales, as it is like, in a way, the procession of distorted figures through the novels of Dostoieffsky. Dickens has his little dabs of color here and there, but he lacks the vividness and harlequin plenitude of color of the folktales, their reds and golds and royal purples. Gray skies and gray rain, the blackness of night on sodden roads, winds moaning wolf-like about old gables, are the constant accompaniment of his stories and not the sunbursts and magic lights that entrance the primitive mind because they are so different from the somberness it is daily aware of.

In saying that Dickens lacks color I do not wish to imply that he lacks warmth. He does not. There is red blood in these stories, and kindliness, and good cheer, but no such riots of bright hues as make splendid the folktales.

So folklike are the marvels, the kaleidoscopic changes, the distorted figures, of these early stories of Dickens, and so folk-like the temperament and many of the characteristics of the man who made them that one wonders if the blood of the little dark people who are the substratum of London's population was not strong in his veins. If he was not, for all his blue eyes, an Iberian? There is nothing of "the dull and creeping Saxon" in him, and little of the visioned Celt. Forster, his biographer, is silent about his father's people, and follows his mother's, the Barrows, but a generation back of her. That Dickens was cockney in blood is half a guess, that he was cockney in temperament and character is a surety. The love of the city was as deep-rooted in him as it was in Charles Lamb: he could not be happy, he could not write, if he were long away from London. France, Italy and Switzerland he knew through vacations, and America through two tours of hard reading, but there was no real sympathy in him for any of these countries or their peoples. He was the most provincial kind of narrowly insular Briton, a Londoner of Londoners. And such a one, despite his devotion to Christmas and stage-coaches and hearts of oak, may not be a typical Englishman. London may be, after all, no more truly representative of England than Paris is of France.

The more keenly you realize the isolation of Dickens among English writers the more forthrightly you will own the originality of the man. Matthew Arnold has told us of the Hebraism and Hellenism of English civilization. Taking the words in a sense at once narrower and larger than he intended they designate most clearly two of the dominant traditions of English literature, the tradition of the Bible and the tradition of the Classics. There is little influence of the one and no influence of the other on Dickens. Another dominant influence in English literature is that of the romances, an influence partly French, partly Celtic, in origin. There are great moments of romance in Dickens, like that of Rudge galloping wildly through the wet night to London, but such romance is not of the sort that makes glamorous the old romances. There is the great main line of English tradition in English literature, the tradition that comes down unbroken to us through Chaucer and Shakespeare and Scott and Hardy. It had little to do with the making of Dickens.

In *David Copperfield* (1850), avowedly largely a biographical novel, Dickens lists the books that David read in boyhood. No one has challenged the claim that these were the books that most influenced Dickens. Smollett heads the list with *Roderick Random* (1748), *Peregrine Pickle* (1751) and *Humphrey Clinker* (1771). There follow Fielding, Goldsmith and Defoe, with but one book each, *Tom Jones* (1749), *The Vicar of Wakefield* (1766), and *Robinson Crusoe* (1719). The three other books mentioned as among David's reading in boyhood are foreign, *Don Quixote, Gil Blas* and *The Arabian Nights.*

No plays are listed here, but with the exception of Smollett, and perhaps Defoe, what Dickens owes to the past he owes to a theatrical tradition rather than to the tradition of the novel. Nor does he owe anything to the poets. His writing reveals little reading of them, and though he has his moments of ecstasy they are nearly all presented theatrically rather than lyrically.

It is easy to overstate the debt of Dickens to the theater. The truth is there is no great man of letters in all English literature so wholly sui generis as Dickens. A hint of Ben Jonson, a hint of Defoe, a strong hint of Smollett, and something more than a hint of the London stage of his youth—that is all there is of Dickens that is not original. We need not, of course, postulate that originality is wholly a good thing. If it is subdued to the purposes of beauty, it is; if not so subdued it may be simply "new commonness . . . hanging its paper flowers from post to post." A large part of what is original in Whitman, for instance, is either "new commonness" or new ugliness, and dross whether one or the other. A lesser part is beauty of a new sort and a joy forever.

There is dross in plenty in Dickens, the whole business of the Maylies, both in conception and execution in *Oliver Twist* (1839), and that queen of pseudo-tragedy, Edith Granger, of *Dombey and Son* (1848), for instance. The greatness of the man lies in his prodigal power of character-creation; in his folk-like imagination; in the sweep and verve of his writing; in his humor.

The testimony of those who should have special knowledge is conflicting as to whether the eccentric people of Dickens are caricatures or realities. Many English critics who know the lower middle classes of London hold these eccentrics caricatures. Gissing and Kipling, authorities of first importance, think the eccentrics real people. Gissing is very explicit on this point in his *Charles Dickens: A Critical Study* (1898). He calls them "true, lifelike, finely presented." The testimony of Kipling is no less unequivocal. It occurs in *A Diversity of Creatures* (1917), in the story "The Village that Voted the Earth was Flat:" "'I don't dive after Dickens,' said Ollyett to Bat and me by the window, 'but every time I get into a row I notice the police-court always fills up with his characters'." Kipling unquestionably knows human nature; and London, and the country environing London, with which the story is concerned.

Is it true, then, that Dickens is not a caricaturist, but that he has a predilection for writing of odd and distorted people, caricatures by the processes of nature, eccentrics, "characters." That he has such a predilection is, of course, true, but it is just as true that he loves the method of caricature in presenting character. The metallic quality of Miss Murdstone so constantly harped on, the flying off of Peggotty's buttons stressed again and again, the "Barkis is willin'" insisted on time after time, are certainly the ways of caricature.

Hogarth and Cruikshank have been suggested as original and encourager of this practice of Dickens. The vagaries of character delineation in the novels of Theodore Hook (1788-1841) have been held partly responsible by other critics. An original for the grotesquerie of Dickens has been found in the stage-ways and sayings of Sam Vale (1797-1848), a low comedian popular in London in pre-Pickwickian days. Sam Vale is said to have suggested Sam Weller, his name, his tricks, his talk. And this same influence, if admitted in Sam Weller, may be followed much further through the kith and kin of Sam that abound in all the novels.

There are undoubted likenesses here and there between character and incident in Jonson and Dickens. Zeal-of-the-Land Busy of *Bartholomew Fair* (1614) is possibly the spiritual progenitor of Stiggins in *Pickwick*. The "fine pump" the stage-keeper refers to in the introduction to this same play is very like the property pump that delighted Mr. Vincent Crummles of *Nicholas Nickleby*. No bit of gossip about Dickens is more familiar than his gusto in playing Captain Bobadill. Nor did his familiarity with Jonson end with *Everyman in His Humour* (1598) and *Bartholomew Fair*. Dickens knew his Jonson, apparently, as he knew his Smollett. This familiarity has naturally strengthened belief in the old contention that his caricatures hark back to the "humors" of the Elizabethan. If they do the debt is not a large one. The whole matter has been overemphasized. For all his slight affiliations with what has gone before Dickens is, as I have said, more original, less dominated by tradition, than any other great English novelist.

Caricatures or character-portrayals, the people of Dickens were for two generations household words throughout the English speaking world. It is not so very long ago that the gentleman-of-the-old-school in America would describe any "lone lorn creetur" as a Mrs. Gummidge, just as he would refer to "left-overs" from feasts as "funeral baked meats" and to a skilful and tidy cook as a "neat-handed Phillis." He had forgiven the Master, for his genius, *American Notes* (1842) and *Martin Chuzzlewit* (1844), and forgetting their slanders of his country-men, owned Dickens a peer of Shakespeare and Milton. The day's talk could hardly be accomplished without quotations from the three of them. In such practice and belief he would bring up his family, who would no more question the greatness of any one of the three than they would the truth of any fundamental convention.

There were hundreds of such fathers in America, men who had bought the succeeding volumes of Dickens as they appeared, and had read and reread them as faithfully as their Bibles. There were thousands of such fathers throughout the English-speaking world. Only Burns of all British authors has been such a house-hold institution as Dickens. And Burns, because of his medium, is not largely known through his characters. There are the cotter and Tam O'Shanter, and a few others, but not the hundreds of Dickens that were from 1840 to 1900 the familiars of thousands on thousands of all sorts and conditions of the race.

Many of these people of Dickens were cherished not as great portraits in the gallery of the race, but as amusing caricatures,

oddities whose development, in the monthly parts of their publication, was looked forward to as are the gambols of the "fun-
nies" in the newspapers today. The relation between Dickens
and the great mass of his readers was never just that which exists between an artist and the admirers of his art. It had in it
an element of artistic appreciation, but it was more personal
and more intimate. It was more like the bond between star
of the music-hall or of the playing field and the followers of her
or his particular kind of "turn" or sport. There was, however,
always a fervor in the admiration of Dickens that raised it to
a higher plane than that usual to such admiration, something of
the fervor that men ·feel for a leader of their party or their
faith. Dickens was to them not only the teller of tales, "the
inimitable" as they called him in his lifetime: Dickens was not
only the humorist as omnipotent with words and situations as
ever a forward with dribble or shoot, or a "slugger" with drive
or wallop: Dickens was also prophet of glad tidings of great
joy and leader of the masses out of the bondage of monotonous
and cramped living. Optimist, humorist, maker of magic, tri-
umphant asserter of the genius of democracy, Dickens was hailed
by his generation, and, as such, was supported his life through
with an acclaim so general that both he and his audience thought
there could be no dimming of his fame.

Yet the fame of Dickens has dimmed, the more rapidly perhaps
because his stories are deeply concerned with issues of the hour,
or because his characters fall more and more without the common experience as the narrowing of the world irons out the
oddities into the flatness of the common human.

There is no question that the queerness of the names of his
characters is one item in their growing alienation from the affections of the younger generation. It is almost as difficult, says
the Georgian intelligentsia, to be interested in a Flopson or a
Pocket, a Pirrip or a Pumblechook, a Wopsle or a Jaggers, as
in an M or an N, an X or a Y, a Z or an &. The contention
is not wholly well-taken. You might as well object, from another
point of view, to the Marall and Overreach of Massinger, the

Lumpkin and Languish of Goldsmith, the Hillcrest and Horn-blower of Galsworthy, though you could not urge that these descriptive names are as ugly to eye and ear as the odd names beloved of Dickens.

There are those who defend his choice of names, saying that it is part and parcel of a grotesquerie that runs all through his art. That grotesquerie is a forte of Dickens is true, but I am not at all sure that his choice of names always ministers to its success. It is a little difficult for a character to live up to the name of Wopsle or Pumblechook. Nor am I sure that his grotesquerie, though so characteristic, always ministers to the betterment of his art. There is surely an overplus of it. There is no questioning, though, the fact that many of his most success-ful characters are grotesque, his Weller père, his Mrs. Gamp, his Betsey Trotwood, his Durdles, but he would be a hardy man who would say they were better done than those characters who are only a little awkward or uncouth, like Tom Pinch or John Browdie, Joe Gargery or Solomon Gills; or such everyday people as that fool woman Mrs. Nickleby, or Jarvis Lorry, or William Dorrit or Biddy. There is no questioning, either, that his ec-centrics are the majority among his characters you recall readily as you summon the novels one by one before your mind's eye. Jingle, Bill Sykes, Newman Noggs, Mrs. Jarley, Barnaby Rudge, Pecksniff, Captain Cuttle, Uriah Heep, Skimpole, Sissy Jupe, Jeremiah Flintwinch, Jerry Cruncher, John Wemmick, Mr. Venus, and Luke Honeythunder are of the strange characters that pop up and pass by on such summoning. In their wake follow the villains of less eccentric ways, the Ralph Nicklebys and Tulkinghorns and Jaspers, remembered not more for their char-acterization than for the wrong they do.

In the earlier Dickens, the characters, strange as they are, are generally more believable than the events in which they have a part. Even in his later period he seldom told a wholly plaus-ible tale, only in *Great Expectations* (1861), one in which every detail is subordinated to its proper place in the progress of the story. It is a pity of pities that he, against his own better judgment, took the advice of Bulwer-Lytton and brought Pip and Estella together in the end.   Up to this point event had followed event with seeming inevitability.   The note of loneliness and infruition is struck at the very outset of the story.   Everything prepares the reader for the ultimate defeat of the dearest hopes of Pip, and so it should have come to pass.   The happy ending strikes a false note.   No story Dickens wrote is so tightly knit together; no other one has so unifying or so romantic a background.   You meet Pip first on the marshes by the great river. They are the scene of crises of his life.   Their wide expanse and the tidal flats beyond them, their lonely stretches fading into the river mists beyond them, color all his life.   The marshes minimize London and all the febrile life of London that involves the boy over whom they cast their spell in infancy.   Here, had Pip but known it, was the home in which he might have been happy; here duty called him when youth called more strongly "away!"

It has been said that Dickens mastered his art of story-telling only when he had exhausted his freshest and most vital material. As a matter of fact he never mastered the art of story-telling, but he grew steadily in power of presentation of life as he grew older.   *David Copperfield* (1850), *Bleak House* (1853), *Little Dorrit* (1857), *Great Expectations* (1861), and *Our Mutual Friend* (1865) are the stories we can call measurably believable. These stories may be considered as belonging to realistic literature, the earlier stories being all more or less unbelievable but all memorable for characterization, for humor, for scenes of intense life, for a vitality of imagination like that of folk-literature.

There are many admirers of Dickens who hold him greatest for *Pickwick*.   They, perhaps, are the true-blue Dickensians, for *Pickwick* is certainly Dickens most characteristically himself. My heartiest admiration, on the other hand, is for those novels from *David Copperfield* to *Edwin Drood* (1870), in which he has worked away from the grotesque to the true.   I would not question the existence of such people as those with whom he crowds these earlier stories.   I think we must follow Gissing and Kipling in their acceptance of the reality of his people.   I do, however, believe that Dickens has excluded from these earlier stories so large a proportion of usual people from the walks of life he drew upon, as to give his readers a one-sided picture of the lower middle class London life of his day. A glance at even so Dickensian a novel as *Thyrza* (1887) will reveal how much more realistic a presentation Gissing makes from like material. There is no element of the grotesque in Gissing's presentation, and he has not exaggerated the element of the grotesque in his material by limiting his story to characters dominantly grotesque or by emphasizing the grotesque side that may be found in almost any character.

Pickwick, Dickens tells us, was "designed for the introduction of diverting characters and incidents." Originally the diversion was intended to be at the expense of Mr. Pickwick, but as the story progressed, Dickens came to have a soft side for him, and ended by whole-heartedly admiring the benevolent old boy into which he had developed his butt. So much does he love a simple, honest man, with unselfishness and fellowliness strong in him, that such characters are repeated from book to book. The Cheeryble brothers are less eccentric than Mr. Pickwick, but very like him, and Mr. Jarndyce and Mr. Meagles are of the same stock.

Oliver Twist (1837) is as good and as bad as Dickens can be. Bumble and Noah Claypole, all, indeed, who figure in the scenes at the poorhouse and at undertaker Sowerberry's, are admirably done. So are Fagin, and the Artful Dodger, Bill Sykes and his dog. Monks and the Maylies are nearly as impossible as Edith Granger and her dual revenge on Mr. Dombey and Carker, his mastering man. Dickens always excelled in description of queer places, and the poorhouse and Sowerberry's and Fagin's rooms are all rendered so as to be remembered. He was too, a master of episode, and the flight of Sykes and his leap to death cannot be bettered in their kind.

Theatricalism might be found in the chronicle of these desperate last hours of Sykes. It might be said that what Dickens intended as tragedy had the air of melodrama about it. Whether you find the situation melodramatic or tragic will depend largely on your sympathy with the methods of its portrayer. There is always something of the theater about Dickens, often something of the swagger of the "heavy" about him in his moments of intensity. That swagger was long accepted as a convention of the stage and its parallel in Dickens similarly accepted. Each one of us will judge by his taste. There is one way of Bernhardt and another way of Duse. I happen to prefer the way of Duse to that of Bernhardt but that does not drive me to perjure myself and refuse to own I have been thrilled by Bernhardt, even in a *Gismonda* (1894). Likewise I own I have been thrilled by the death of Sykes, and that I call it tragedy.

Nicholas Nickleby (1839) is a mixture of picaresque story, story with a moral purpose, and realistic story. It reveals that contradictory characteristic of Dickens, his artistic sympathy at its fullest with the characters for whom he has the most reprobation from the standpoint of morality. He lavishes all his art on Ralph Nickleby, who is what Dickens considers humanity at its worst. There are more than a hundred characters in this book, at least a quarter of them full-length portraits. Of such a fulness of life are most of his stories, fifty to a hundred characters not unusually appearing in them. The people of *Nicholas Nickleby* are from many conditions of life, too, Crummles and his players, Squeers and his pupils, Ralph Nickleby and his tools and dupes, the impossible Mantalinis, the delectable Kenwigs, and those Cheerybles whose goodness brings tears to the eyes and has made the world think better of all shipping merchants and warehousemen for their sakes.

Little Nell, unfortunately, dominates *The Old Curiosity Shop* (1841), leading Dickens to an even more "incredible excess" of pathos than does Paul Dombey. Of all the many who have found fault with Dickens for this book Andrew Lang has put the case most strongly. The indictment will be found in *Letters to Dead Authors* (1893). "To draw tears by gloating over a child's death-bed, was it worthy of you," he asks. Lang can find but one answer, and Lang is a thoroughgoing admirer of

Dickens, one who can be so forthright as to say "Every English-man who can read, unless he be an Ass, is a reader the more for you." But in compensation for Little Nell are all the delightful people of the roads, Codlin and Short, Mrs. Jarley and George, Grinder's lot and Jerry, Mr. Vuffin and Sweet William; and Dick Swiveller and the Marchionness, Sampson Brass and Sally Brass, Kit and Quilp's boy, Quilp and Mrs. Jiniwin. Exceptional people all of these are, but none, unless Quilp, exceptional to ab-normality.

There is more romance in *Barnaby Rudge* (1841) than in any other story of Dickens. There is the romance of the roads here that there is in *The Old Curiosity Shop* and in *A Tale of Two Cities* notably;—and there is the romance of an old house fallen on evil days, a romance that Dickens, being the man he was, so seldom found appealing. There are here, too, mob scenes vividly handled; and once in a while a touch of the poetry of place, so large a part of the beauty of English literature and so rare in Dickens. Of all out-of-door scenes glimpses of marshes and broad waters most appealed to him; and sheep-bells are almost the only quiet sounds of the countryside that he seems to have noticed. He makes mention of sheep-bells in books so far apart in time as *Nicholas Nickleby* and *Great Expectations*. In the latter book, too, he once speaks of "the breath of the beans and clover," and the allusion comes to you with all the sweetness of a simple air in a modern concert.

Martin Chuzzlewit (1844) is a heavy handicap to Dickens in more ways than one. It is not only that Americans even at this late day still resent its presentation of the aspects of American life he here chooses to write about, but that its so manifestly false picture undermines their trust in Dickens as a faithful presenter of English life. If he could be so untrue to facts as he is so often in the American scenes, and if he could so exaggerate when he has hit upon facts, one is driven to wonder if he is habitually untrue or exaggerated in his scenes of English life. We have the word of Gissing and Kipling that such lower class people as his are still to be found in and about London; so we shift our ground to that of supposing he perhaps just exaggerated, or that he distorted those phases of English life that he knew little of or that ran counter to his prejudices.

Certainly much that he came across in America in his trip of 1842 ran counter to his prejudices. We would not accept his views on international copyright; we were still maintaining negro slavery; we had land companies that were little better than swindling concerns, if not so many such as he indicated; we delighted in chewing tobacco, but not so universally as he represented; and we ran after literary lions, though not so many of us as he chose to believe.

Our worst sins, in his estimation, were those intrusions upon his privacy, his right to do as he would with his own time that the Englishman has always fought for as an inalienable right. Judging from his writings, some of us assumed so democratically minded a man would like democratic ways, but even his London blood and bringing up did not save Dickens from being in this respect deeply dyed with Englishness. He did not like democratic ways, an unliking perhaps a little inconsistent in one who could not help disparaging the gentleman. Only Mr. Crisparkle in *The Mystery of Edwin Drood* (1870), of all his gentlemen by birth, seems to have his admiration. And one wonders if Mr. Crisparkle has it perhaps only because he is not a great gentleman. Lord Dedlock is the most sympathetically rendered of his great gentlemen, but the characteristic gentleman, greater or lesser, of Dickens, is a Sir Mulberry Hawk or a Steerforth.

Dickens had always a penchant for the gloomy and a penchant for the lurid. He indulges both in *Dombey and Son* (1848). That novel might, indeed, be symbolized as a fire by night, smoulderings breaking into flame under a pall of heavy darkness. The moods of content that came to Dickens might, too, be symbolized by fire and darkness, but by fire controlled and tamed, safe in the fireplace by which a family is gathered, snug indoors from the darkness of night outside. Fireside ease and cheer, home, lovers brought to the security of the hearth after

wanderings in untoward and perilous places—all such domesticities were much celebrated by this man who had failed to make
his wife an ally to bring these into his own life. There was a
streak of Bohemianism in Dickens, an almost gypsy propensity
to flit from place to place, but this might not have developed to
the extent it did had he and his wife been congenial.

The pathetic is as constant to *Dombey and Son* as the lurid
and the gloomy. His own "childhood thrown away," his apprenticeship to hard work at tender years, affected his portrayal
of children all his life through. The Paul Dombey of this book,
Little Nell, the step-fathering of little David Copperfield, the mis-
education of the Gradgrinds, the boyhood of Arthur Clennam,
are all the work of a "born sobber" whose memories of his own
youthful unhappiness were assuaged by rehearsing the miseries
of young years.

All the world knows it is his own story Dickens told in *David
Copperfield*, his own story in the scenes of David's maturity, as
well as in the scenes of David's childhood. The original of Dora
in real life need not have been less than a saint to object against
being killed off in fiction that David might marry another
woman. *David Copperfield* is a story one may accept as life as
it is. The Dickens who was teller of modern folktales in *Pickwick*
is realistic novelist in *David Copperfield*. Realistic, too, is Dickens in *Bleak House,* despite the super-Frenchiness of the maid
Hortense and the going up into spontaneous combustion of
Krook, the junk dealer. It can match Mrs. Gummidge and
Peggotty, Micawber and Uriah Heep, Betsey Trotwood and Dr.
Strong of *David Copperfield* with Boythorn and Skimpole, Mrs.
Jellyby and Mr. Bucket, Mr. Chadband and Miss Flite. *David
Copperfield*, too, has its unrealistic characters, its Rosa Dartle
and its Littimer for two. So it is with most of even these later
realistic novels. Only in *Great Expectations* can Dickens rid
himself of most of his habitual dozen people hard to swallow.

Hard Times (1854) is, in material, the least cockney of the
novels of Dickens; it is, on the whole, the least effective, too.

Perhaps the provincial background took him out of his element, perhaps it was the illness he suffered while writing it that lessened his power.

Little Dorrit (1857) is somehow the least talked of and written about of the novels of Dickens. One wonders if it is also the least read. If that is so it may be because it has in it, for all its parade of mysteriousness, its wicked step-mother, and its foreign villain, not a great deal of story. It returns to the old themes so often favored by Dickens, a neglected childhood, a neglectful upper class, illegitimate birth, jail. Characters familiar from the earlier Dickens reappear: the volcanic woman, here in two manisfestations, Tattycoram and Miss Wade; the benevolent old gentleman, here Mr. Meagles; and the rather colorless young hero of middling station, here Arthur Clennam.

There is not a great deal of such falling into types in Dickens. No novelist has builded his characters on a greater number of originals. Dickens had an eye for people. All he met he remembered, without effort of will it would seem and without notes. Ever afterward they were somewhere in the back of his mind ready to be called at his need into a fuller life than that of actuality.

A Tale of Two Cities (1859) has divided those who admire Dickens into two camps. Some think it a great historical novel and regret that it and *Barnaby Rudge* are the only incursions of the novelist into this field. Other Dickensians hate to think that the master has backslid into the story of adventure. George Moore cannot understand a hero being sent to Paris to be hanged. His own precious prodigals are sent there for quite other purposes. The real trouble with the book is that it is largely worked-up "stuff." Such are all its Paris scenes. Dickens could not write them, as he could nearly all else he presented, out of hearsay of his elders, out of his vivid reliving of all that came to him by gossip and newspapers, and out of his own rich experience of life, an experience larger than that of most men of his years, for it reached back into his early childhood, to years when most children have little experience of anything beyond play. This beginning of experience just past infancy accounts partly for his early maturity. *Pickwick* (1837), for all its qualities of the folk, is laden with a heavy knowledge of life for a man of twenty-five.

Our Mutual Friend (1865), a book teeming with life, was his last great effort before he turned from writing to public reading. He intended greatly in this book, planned it as a story of sweeping scope, of a London penetrated thrillingly by the great river that made any wonder possible on its banks or bosom. The characters run to sixty and number among them some of his most memorable eccentrics as well as some of his most intolerable caricatures. In some of these latter he cheaply exulted in lampooning the kinds of people he loathed. Jesse Hexam, fisher of dead men; Mr. Venus, taxidermist; and Silas Wegg, ballad monger, are as picturesque a trio as you will find anywhere in the English novel. On the other hand the Podsnaps, the Veneerings, and Lord Snigsworth are as shoddy in conception as Dickens held them to be in quality. Eugene Wrayburn is another one of his creator's many failures in delineating quasi-gentlemen, and it is difficult to believe in the reality of his co-hero Handford-Rokesmith-Harmon. As so often with Dickens the story has proved too much for him and forced him to warp his characters to fit it. Warp them, however, for the warping's sake, he does, too, in this story, as in so many stories else.

If it were not for *Great Expectations* one might doubt if any labor and any standard of values could have brought the stories of Dickens, in artistry and truth to life, to an equality with their sheer imaginative power and prodigality of character and humor. The man wrote to please, as Scott did before him, and would have been totally unable to understand a teller of tales, writing, as Robert Frost owns in *New Hampshire* (1923) he has written, "several books against the world in general." Dickens was deeply concerned when the miscellany *Master Humphrey's Clock* failed to please, and quickly developed *The Old Curiosity Shop* out of it into a continued story. The idea of making something beautiful to please himself never occurred to him. Indeed, the novel, but recently emerged into a status of respectability at that time, was not generally subjected to those tests which the more aristocratic forms of the art of letters, poetry and the essay, were asked to judge themselves by.

Dickens was absorbed wholly in his writing, but rather as an actor in a part than as a poet in a thing of beauty. His humor especially delighted him, and most of all as it was revealed in his humorous characters. The best of his humor is here, in the series of portraits from Mr. Pickwick and the Wellers, father and son; Mr. Crummles and his troupe; old Willett and his cronies at the Maypole; on through Tom Pinch and Mark Tapley and Sarah Gamp; and Skimpole and Mr. Guppy and Mrs. Jellyby; to Durdles and Grewgious and Honeythunder. Well enough in their several ways are the screaming farces of Dickens, his uproarious exuberance of spirits over the ordinary delights of daily existence, his grotesque fantasy. These are even good things; the humorous portraitures are great things.

It is in the creation of these portraits I have mentioned, and of the legion of their fellows that Dickens finds his chief distinction. Together they make the greatest group of low-comedy figures since Shakespeare.

His contemporaries valued him as highly as reformer as humorist. But the battles of the reformer of one age are dead issues in another, and all that Dickens fought for is of yesterday. England loved greatly Dickens the radical, as it has loved greatly all its faultfinders, whether they speak with the thunder tones of a Carlyle or scold in the acrid voice of a Shaw. The surprising thing is that with all his concern over the questions of the hour the writing of Dickens is so little clogged with their debris.

Dickens the weaver of entrancing tales, Dickens the humorist, Dickens the reformer—these were the aspects of him his own age most honored. And indeed he lacked many powers that have gone to the making of our English novelists. There is little of the poet in him, nothing comparable to what there is of poet in a Scott or a Meredith. The style of Dickens is not one of the memorable styles of our tongue, not the style of a Thackeray.

There is reading of life in Dickens, but not a great deal of it, and what there is not always the most profound. In *Great Expectations* he can discover: "Our worst weaknesses and meannesses are usually committed for the sake of the people whom we most despise." In *Dombey and Son* it turns out, as Mr. Morfin says, that the inordinate pride of Mr. Dombey is close to a virtue in the circumstances of his failure. Pondering the situation, Dickens sees "that vices are sometimes only virtues carried to excess." It is as comforter rather than as seer, that he speaks in *Nicholas Nickleby,* when he tells us: "Things that are changed or gone will come back as they used to be, thank God, in sleep."

Two generations of journalists took their way of writing largely from Dickens,—and Macaulay. As great a writer as Meredith is given to ways of Dickens at times, especially in *Evan Harrington* (1861). The very George Moore who mocks him so often could not have done the scenes in the home of Esther Waters as he did them had not Dickens labored with like material before him. Gissing and Wells and Swinnerton re-echo Dickens. Barrie, Burke and Neil Lyons have all gone to school to him. Arthur Morrison and De Morgan and "Oliver Onions" show his influence in parallel incident or parallel character or parallel method.

It is hardly too much to say that all English story-tellers since his day who have succumbed to the spell of London have succumbed to the spell of Dickens. I have forborne to lengthen the list but from Robert Buchanan to Chesterton there are many more whose writing proves their allegiance to him in this way or that. The febrile conditions of life in the great city that account at least in part for his theatricality and luridness and distortion of character, and not Dickens himself, may in some instances have led to, in the successors of Dickens, what they led to in him. In other words, it may be London and not Dickens that has made certain younger writers like Dickens. Dickens is, however, so individual, so strongly marked, so idiosyncratic, that in most cases of such resemblances we are likely to believe them direct followings.

Library and bookshop both bear testimony to the sustained appeal of Dickens to readers. He continues to be read very widely though relatively not so widely as a generation ago. Critics may rate him less highly than they do Fielding or Scott or Thackeray, but he still has the applause of the crowd. It is very difficult to judge of such matters, but if the references in writing and daily talk are evidence, a greater number of his books are known to the man in the street than of any other of the novelists the years have made "classic." And it is the earlier novels that are most familiar, the books down through *David Copperfield*. Our cited generation is still faithful to the man who found London as full of wonders as the Bagdad of the *Arabian Nights*. The folk are still faithful to the foremost teller of modern folktales.

CHAPTER VII

THACKERAY

THERE are many English writers who have put the very quality of England into their writing. There are few who are typically English—not a matter for wonder surely. The artist, in the nature of things, is seldom representative of his country, the English artist very seldom. For all its rigorous discipline of form, Art speaks out, confesses itself, declares its faith and joy in beauty, practices repellent to the typical Englishman, who fears above everything else to give himself away. So Thackeray (1811-1863) feared to give himself away, but, being artist, could not help doing it, and was ill at ease, conscious of bad form, self-contemptuous, in the process.

With the greatest natural endowment of any English novelist, Thackeray restricted his use of his powers, when such use seemed to him to run counter to his conception of what an English gentleman should write. A man of keen and just sentiments, he repressed those sentiments time and again, and the ironies, in revenge, ordained that when he could not but let himself go, sentimentality should sometimes result. Had he practiced more often the expression of his deepest emotions Thackeray had perhaps learned to express them in a way to content his dignity, to avoid those weaknesses of sentimentality that beset him.

A simple Victorian at heart, a simple Colonial Victorian of middle-class origin, Thackeray had allowed his imagination to be mastered by the eighteenth century ideal of the English gentleman, a gentleman of broad acres in the country and of *bel air* in town. His wife's illness and enforced absence from home took the very heart out of his life and drove an inveterately domestic husband and father into something of a clubman. The spectacles of other writers abandoning themselves to their speculations and emotions, the spectacle of Bulwer-Lytton as "Poet-Philosopher" and the spectacle of Dickens as "sobber," were painful to Thackeray, and scared him away often from readings of life and lyric passages and dramatic scenes that the progress of incidents in his stories leads you to expect.

So it came about that Thackeray, a practitioner of the art that is largely a chronicle of mating and of the approaches to mating, could write in *The Adventures of Philip* (1862): "It is not only wrong to kiss and tell, but to tell about kisses." Were some of our latter day novelists, George Moore for one, sentenced to obey this dictum it would be a blessing; but the world is the poorer that Thackeray, who knew more of the human heart than any novelist of his generation, deliberately avoided telling us the half he knew. What he has presented of that store has more appeal to our sense of truth, our sympathies and our appreciation of art than the full telling of all his knowledge by any other novelist. At his best, in *Barry Lyndon* (1844), in *Vanity Fair* (1848), in *Pendennis* (1850) and in *Henry Esmond* (1852), he is the master of all in the long line from Chaucer to our day.

And why is Thackeray, who did not speak out fully, master of them all? It is because of reasons that run from firstly to nthly, very many, indeed, and the best of them very needful to discuss; but not more than a half dozen of them can find place here. Firstly: Thackeray is "the showman of life" of first power among those English writers who have used the novel as the means of telling us about the outwardness and inwardness of things in our world.

Secondly: Thackeray is the greatest master of English prose among our novelists. Thirdly: Thackeray has created more characters we accept as wholly true to life than any other novelist. Fourthly: Thackeray has given us the story that is the finest creation of the art of fiction in English, a book of perfect proportion, of wholeness of good tissue, a snatching of a romantic beauty from "the remorseless rush of time" that is as memorable in the art of the novel as "New Year's Eve" in the essay, as "The Twa Corbies" in the ballad, as "O Sweet Content" in the song, as "Loveliest of Trees" in the lyric, as *Lear* in the drama. I refer, of course, to *Henry Esmond*.

As one puts *Henry Esmond* in this high company one realizes at once the richness of material and the shortcomings of form of the English novel at its best. The English novel is incomparably richer in material than any other form in English literature except the drama. The novel is hardly, save for a few exceptions, in the same category as an "object of art" with lyric or essay, and, obviously, in proportion and finish, save for hardly more exceptions, of a lesser perfecton than song or ballad. Perfect as the short story may be in form it cannot vie with the novel, as there is a sketchiness about it, an incompleteness of realization almost necessary to its brevity, as well as an absence from it of those memorable sayings, those perfectly phrased revelations of truth that give its inner life to all literature. Why the essay should have these sayings, should have sentences like "Men fear death as children fear to go in the dark" or "The world meets nobody half way" and the short story be all but wanting in them is not easy to explain. Hunt through the short stories for such "readings of life," however, and you will find they are so far to seek as to be almost impossible to find.

Fifthly: Thackeray is master of them all because he comes to the presentation of life with less prejudice, more tolerance and more sympathy, than any other novelist. He has no axe to grind. Charlotte Brontë, misled by his sharp presentation of wrong in privileged places, thought that Thackeray would be a reformer, and she was disappointed in him when she found that he but revealed things as he saw them. Thackeray had so keen an insight into the blacknesses of the best of us that he could not be intolerant of the blacknesses of the weakest. His keenness of vision gave him knowledge of life as it is, his comparative exemption from bias enabled him, with his mastery of words, to present it very nearly as it is. He was often not happy, of course, over what he saw, he does not always make us happy by his presentation of it. "Is it best," he cries, in that Christmas Book, *Mrs. Perkin's Ball*, "Is it best to be laughing mad, or crying mad, in the world?" Mad in some fashion he feels that man must be if he shall endure his knowledge of the inwardness of things, if he allows himself to know them as they are. It is better perhaps Thackeray conjectures, not to think, but just to work without thought at honest daily labor, to scrub the steps like Betty the housemaid.

Yes, work is the panacea; work will cure all the ills of the heart and spirit, work and—time. Yet, before work and time have brought solace, there is suffering to be borne as best one may, but always with as brave a front and as complete a repression of one's feelings as one can attain to. Clive Newcome very humanly and in a fashion un-English, talked much to the Arthur Pendennises about his troubles. With them, in the home of his friends, he was off guard; and so was his creator at moments. Thackeray is really off guard oftener than he admits, for many times when he turns "cynical" in his comment he is but crying out that he is hurt by things as they are.

True Englishman that he is, Thackeray hates babbling and effusiveness and heroics, and would keep his mouth shut if he could. With many of his characters, too, "Mum's the word." Never does that little puss, Elizabeth Prior, betray what is in her heart, or hardly that she has a heart at all. Miss Prior has not her due, by the bye, from the critics of Thackeray. She is as inimitable as Becky herself, another lady that can keep a tight rein on her tongue when she will.

It is more than a little troubling to explain just how, with this so slight revelation of themselves by the characters, we get to know them so intimately. But is it not thus that we get to know our neighbors? We know them well even when they do not give themselves away in moments of confession. Never, of course, do we come to know them as well as we know ourselves. And yet, to know all the characters of a book as well as we know ourselves is often what we demand of an author. That sort of knowledge we rarely acquire of the characters of Thackeray, perhaps only of Henry Esmond, aided by the intimacies of his journal.

But, after all, we do get to know well a great host of them, their appearance and the charts by which they steer, their temperaments and personalities. We know them as fellow men and women, but unlike those mortals, blessedly unchangeable down the years.

How often have they trooped by me these thirty years: Catherine and John Hayes; Barry Lyndon and the Chevalier de Balibari; Becky and Amelia, Jos Sedley and George Osborne, Dobbin and Steyne, Rawdon Crawley and Sir Pitt; Helen Pendennis, the Fotheringay, Blanche Amory, Fanny Bolton, Laura Bell; Arthur and Warrington, Captain Costigan, Foker, Major Pendennis, Mr. Morgan; Henry Esmond and Frank, Castlewood and Mohun, Father Holt and Tom Tusher, Hamilton and the Pretender, Lady Castlewood and Beatrix; Ethel Newcome and Rosey and the Old Campaigner, Madame de Florac and Lady Kew, the Colonel and Clive, Sir Brian and Hobson, Barnes and James Binnie, Ridley and Fred Bayham, Charles Honeyman and Mr. Sherrick! That is nearly fifty, unforgetable men and women, and not all such listed; and four books more from which to summon people quick with life!

Madame Esmond Warrington must be added to this rare gallery of portraits; and that demure chit Elizabeth Prior, who consoled Lovel in his widowerhood; and Dr. Firmin, at least, from *Philip* (1862); and a half score from the few chapters of *Denis Duval* (1864) Thackeray lived to write, chapters that showed him, at the end of his career, recovered from the slump that visited him in *Philip* and well under way in a novel that promised to be of his best. Here we have Denis and Madame Duval, the Count de Saverne and Monsieur de la Motte, Agnes and Mr. Joseph Weston, Dr. Barnard and Captain Pearson, Miss Sukey and Mr. Rudge.

Among these characters are to be found all sorts and conditions of men, from servants to scions of royalty, and from times as early as the age of Anne on to Thackeray's Victorian day. English and Scotch, Irish and French, Colonials from India and Virginia have place in his pages, with incidental Germans and Hindustani and half-castes, all recalled from the wide experience always as of yesterday to this man of unfading memories, and all reborn into the world of his imagining.

There is little running to type among these characters, although his heroes, writing men and painters and soldiers most of them, are alike in being pretty fellows and a bit dandiacal, of moderate attainments and of as moderate success in life, and unfortunate or inconstant in love. A Pendennis or a Clive or a Philip, individualized as each is, might any one of them be taken as representative of the Victorian dandy, a type as symbolic of the age as could be hit upon, though not so dominant in the mid-nineteenth century as Squire Western in the early eighteenth century.

Today the country squire lingers with us in the novels of J. C. Snaith and Archibald Marshall, but he is, after all, a survival. The truth is John Bull is John Bull no longer. The country squire is not today typical of England. Sport is still a something akin to religion in the hearts of many Britons, but red coat and white trousers, top boots and riding crop have ceased to spell its ritual. No other figure, either of "flannelled fool at the wicket or muddied oaf at the goal" has taken his place as symbol of England. There is too much diversity now in sport and avocation alike for any one figure to be largely representative of England at work or at play. The professional footballer of Bennett and the draper's clerk of Wells, the racing man of Moore and the school-teacher of Gissing, a Conrad seaman and a Hardy farmer, even if fused into one would not give us a composite portrait typical of the England of the century's close.

Nor has any representative figure emerged from the welter of the World War. It is perhaps as well for the novelists that such a one has not appeared, for a character typical of a time is a dubious asset to the novelist, however valuable it may be to the historian. An individual may now and then be completely typical of his time, but if he is, he is dangerously near to a caricature or to a pawn or to a mouthpiece, with too little savor of reality to make us believe in him.

It is the individual always that interests Thackeray. And for himself, and not as a representative of his class or time. In this attitude, too, Thackeray is staunchly English. Not all the levelling of modern industrialism, with its bias toward communism, has materially abated the individualism the Englishman has fostered as essential to his well-being.

Thackeray is English, too, in his admiration of the temperament and point of view, the code and standard of values of the group of his countrymen dominant in his time. He quarrels with certain ways of this group, certain elements of their code, certain of the outworn institutions they cling to, but what is best in them is to him the hope of the world. If you doubt the truth of this reading of Thackeray, recalling his repeated castigations of social use, the marriage of convenience for instance, recall, too, his satisfaction in the gentility of Esmond, his tribute to Lord Kew of *The Newcomes* (1853) his easy way with Lord Ringwood of *Philip* because he is a great gentleman. Thackeray is no more unwilling to render unto Cæsar the things that are Cæsar's than to render unto God the things that are God's.

Thackeray is at one with Burns and Pope in believing that "an honest man's the noblest work of God." Witness Dobbin and Colonel Newcome, honest men both and nature's noblemen. Both lived their lives by the gentleman's code. Both were gentlemen in spirit and conduct. And yet even those who loved them felt they were not quite the mode, and to be ashamed of, a little, because of slight lapses and gaucheries that showed them not to the manner born.

And yet, ridiculous though both may be in little things that count large in life, we admire Colonel Newcome and Major Dobbin more, do we not, than the Barnes Newcome who overreaches the one or the George Osborne who trifles with the beloved of the other! But would we so feel toward the two in the contacts of daily life? Would not the Colonel be a bit of a bore and Dobbin "a chuckle-headed fool" with the gift of irritation? Let us hope that we are so appreciative of innate and essential goodness that it compensates us for all shortcomings of tact and personality in our friends. Thackeray doubts that it does so compensate us, owning in the benediction that closes Pendennis:

"If Mr. Pen's works have procured him more reputation than has been acquired by his abler friend, whom no one knows, George lives contented without the fame. If the best men do not draw the great prizes in life, we know it has been so settled by the ordainer of the lottery. We own, and see daily, how the false and worthless live and prosper, while the good are called away, and the dear and young perish untimely,—we perceive in every man's life the maimed happiness, the frequent falling, the bootless endeavor, the struggle of Right and Wrong, in which the strong often succumb and the swift fail: we see flowers of good blooming in foul places, as, in the most lofty and splendid fortunes, flaws of vice and meanness, and stains of evil; and, knowing how mean the best of us is, let us give a hand of charity to Arthur Pendennis, with all his faults and short-comings, who does not claim to be a hero, but only a man and a brother."

Personality, ability and fortunate birth, Thackeray does not hesitate to admit, and not goodness and endeavor, are what make a man's way through the world easy to his feet. "A young nobleman, full of life and spirits, generous of his money, jovial in his humor, ready with his sword, frank, handsome, prodigal, courageous, always finds favor. Young Scapegrace rides a steeple-chase or beats a bargeman, and the crowd applauds him. Sages and seniors shake their heads and look at him not unkindly; even stern old female moralists are disarmed at the sight of youth, and gallantry, and beauty. I know very well that Charles Surface is a sad dog, and Tom Jones no better than he should be; but in spite of such critics as Dr. Johnson and Colonel Newcome, most of us have a sneaking regard for honest Tom, and hope Sophia will be happy, and Tom will end well at last."

This is acquiescence, surely, in the way of the world, and not a troubled acquiescence. The disappointment of Charlotte Brontë in him as a critic of society was well taken. She might admit with him that only one who deceived himself could see things otherwise than Thackeray saw them, but she might yet demand a note of indignation in his owning of the truth. He would have had to have a streak of the Puritan in him to have felt such indignation, and there was nothing Puritan in him at all. He could not pretend an indignation that he did not feel. Hypocrisy, indeed, was particularly abhorrent to him, a vice that offended him more, as it did Fielding, than other vices which bring more sorrow into the world.

The points so far elaborated in the contention that Thackeray is the first of our English novelists are those least likely to be opposed. There will be more quarrel with the statement that he is the greatest master of prose among our novelists, and more quarrel still with my sixthly, the claim that he is of the poets as surely as are Meredith and Conrad, with lyric passages that would find place in any anthology of poetry in prose. And there are more than a few of these passages, surprisingly many, indeed, when we keep in mind his repression of much that he felt.

Thackeray might have been a greater poet in prose than he is had he not been afraid to be. Lyric mood carries those it possesses perilously close to the shores of romance, where are to be heard songs as seductive as any the sirens sung. Such a carrying Thackeray, willy-nilly, fought against, but if unsuccessfully, he, like that canny man of old he was so unlike in all else but wisdom and discretion, deafened with wax the rebellious crew of his emotions, and so won through in safety.

All poetry, it is to be remembered, is not the poetry of romance, of strangeness, of wonder, of things thrilled with the unknown. There is the poetry of familiar things, things too good to be true, but true nevertheless in their littleness or greatness. This is the kind of poetry in which that century so dear to Thackeray, the eighteenth of happy memory, so decorously delighted. One almost hesitates to speak of "decorous delight" in this day which is so prone to hold all that is decorous to be near to the stilted or artificial. The decorous is not necessarily so any more than the abandoned is necessarily artistic or sincere. There may be decorousness not cut-and-dried or pompous.

There is no doubt about the devotion of Thackeray to poetry. Hear him give it place with love and religion among the great things of life, in *Esmond,* in the Colonel's acknowledgment in old age of what Beatrix had been to him: "Such a past is always present to a man; such a passion once felt forms a part of his own being, and cannot be separated from it; it becomes a portion of the man of today, just as any great faith or conviction, the discovery of poetry, the awakening of religion, ever afterwards influence him."

That declaration establishes the certainty of his belief in the high importance of poetry. Whether he was himself a poet is, of course, another matter. The eternal themes of poetry are his, in season and out of season,—love and parting and death, the quick falling of bloom, the vanity of human wishes, lyric places and lyric people. Can he sing these in lyric prose, invest them with lyric mood? Listen, and judge for yourself, first from this bit of landscape in *Esmond:* "a fine prospect of sunset and the great darkling woods with a cloud of rooks returning." Then from these lines about music, the onset of a passage too long to quote in full: "She plays old music of Handel and Haydn, and the little chamber anon swells into a cathedral, and he who listens beholds altars lighted, priests ministering, fair children swingings censers, great oriel windows gleaming in the sunset, and seen through arched columns and avenues of twilight marble." Listen, too, to this lyric of parting: "The night is falling: we have talked enough, over our wine: and it is time to go home! Good night. Good night, friends, old and young! The night will fall: the stories must end: and the best friends must part." Listen to the lilt, and heart's-cry old as life itself, in this passage on death, sudden death, the sudden death in a duel of the great Duke of Hamilton who was betrothed to Beatrix; and how little it was to many and how world-altering to a few: "The sun was shining though 'twas November: he had seen the market-carts rolling into London, the guard relieved at the palace, the laborers trudging to their work in the gardens between Kensington and the City—the wandering merchants and hawkers filling the air with their cries. The world was going to its business again, though dukes lay dead and ladies mourned for them; and kings, very likely, lost their chances. So night and day pass away, and tomorrow comes, and our place knows us not. Esmond thought of the courier, now galloping on the North Road to inform him, who was Earl of Arran yesterday, that he was Duke of Hamilton today, and of a thousand great schemes, hopes, ambitions, that were alive in the gallant heart, beating a few hours since, and now in a little dust quiescent."

That, I submit, is not only English prose at its best, but as surely poetry as "Lycidas" or "Adonais" or "The Scholar-Gipsy." With the other passages quoted, it seems to me to write Q. E. D. to my secondly and sixthly, that Thackeray is a master of prose and a poet.

When I began my enumeration of reasons for the greatness of Thackeray I had intended to elaborate the first half dozen of them and so have done. If he is great in these six ways, I argued, he is great indeed, and no more need be said. But a seventhly calls insistently for a place. Seventhly, then, in the accounting for the greatness of Thackeray, is his power of drama, his great dramatic moments. Stevenson thought the surprisal of Becky and Steyne by Rawdon Crawley "pure Dumas, only better." There are many fellows to it: the war of wits of Chevalier de Magny and Barry Lyndon; the triumph of Major Pendennis over Morgan; the rescue of Beatrix from the Pretender; the meeting of Henry Esmond's grandson and Baroness Bernstein; Dr. Barnard's facing of the mob, of *Denis Duval;* and the parting of Ethel Newcome and Clive in the Hotel de Florac.

It is an old axiom that all significant drama springs from character. It is what the people are that makes their conflicts of moment to us. And yet there are situations interesting to all of us and absorbing to some of us, from the very nature of the emotions involved and the hazards run, even when those who suffer these emotions and hazards are hardly more than automatons. The reductio ad absurdum, by burlesque, of this sort of thing, is found in *The Rose and the Ring* (1855). Here you have Thackeray the incomparable farceur. In *Catherine* (1840) he had developed another sort of burlesque, a mordant burlesque with a moral purpose. Outraged by the much glorification of vice in stories of the late thirties, stories that celebrated highwaymen and other criminals, Thackeray went the authors of such books one better by presently realistically, and with moral indignation subdued until the end, the career of Miss Catherine Hall to its culmination in murder. He had found the type of such work in *Jonathan Wild* (1743) but he used the methods of Fielding after his own fashion and for the end that "no man shall allow a single sentiment of pity or admiration to enter his bosom for any character in the piece."

In *Barry Lyndon* (1844) Thackeray is again working after the manner of *Jonathan Wild*. Redmond Barry tells his own story, approving of all his nefarious doings as ingrate, soldier of fortune, gambler, blackmailer and murderer, and carrying off all with an air. The people Barry meets are most of them so little better than himself, that the reader does not object to Barry's victories over them. Maybe you would not object anyway, for sympathy with the rogue is deep-seated in human nature, and it has been ministered to by rogue stories for so many generations that more *Catherines* and *Barry Lyndons* than Thackeray could write would scarcely free us from its domination. Charles Lamb's defence of the Restoration comedy comes to mind, that its immoral characters are after all but puppets, not human beings, and as such their wickednesses do not greatly concern us and leave our moral standards unharmed. But Barry Lyndon is human, as human as Falstaff or Fagin, and we refer all his actions to the everyday standards by which we judge ourselves and our friends. Thackeray uses Barry as the means by which to attack all the many vices of which that worthy is compact, but so full of life is he that his creator's moral purpose is partly defeated. So vital a figure cannot help being interesting, so real a figure cannot help appealing to us, for all his want of principle and his cruelty, as a fellow human. And after all Barry was gallant, and as Thackeray himself owned, much is forgiven to a man of gallantry.

So it is in the great scene with De Magny, you do not cry "Devil take the hindmost," but want Barry to win, and rejoice when he does win. It is only when you have escaped from the unquestionable charm of this hardened ruffian, it is only when you contemplate his career after the book is closed that it can convey to you the moral preachment that Thackeray intended. Then you can become aware of it as a scathing indictment of the criminal hero of the fiction of its time. Finer in its art by many degrees, it is not so efficient a tract as *Catherine*. *Barry Lyndon* is all of a piece, perfect in proportion and detail, a high accomplishment of the art of letters. Yet for it to achieve what its author intended it to achieve, its hero would have had to be a man as repellent in his personality as in his character. The flesh is weak and responds to pleasantness of personality more readily than to goodness. And yet, to those who have the experience and the insight that enables them truly to estimate values in life *Barry Lyndon* can point the lesson Thackeray intended. The trouble is so few have that experience and that insight. To those less well equipped, *Barry Lyndon* remains but a brave rogue story.

Catherine and *Barry Lyndon* are the most considerable of the early work of Thackeray. They are, in a fashion, representative of all of it, in that they are largely satiric in purpose. Thackeray came to the novel by way of satire, the only story-teller of his day who so approached his life work. A little later Meredith was to come to *Richard Feverel* (1859) after *The Shaving of Shagpat* (1855) and *Farina* (1857), but he came not only by way of these two but by way, too, of "Love in the Valley" (1851) and many another poem. Dickens, Reade, Kingsley, the Brontës and George Eliot tried other forms, sketch and play and poem, before they came to the novel, but there was little satire in their early work.

In approaching a high form of art such as the novel by way of a lesser art like satire Thackeray was again characteristically English. It may have been the better market in *Fraser's Magazine* and *Punch* for satiric writing than for other sorts that was partly the cause of his addiction to it, but it was in the nature of Thackeray the young Englishman as well as in the nature of Thackeray the individual to choose satire as what to write when write he must for a living. Gentlemen of his day did not look upon writing as a serious vocation, as gentlemen of times later than his and on into ours have not so looked upon it, but it was permissible in Thackeray's time, as it still is, for gentlemen to penny-a-line as journalists to tide themselves over hard times. Thackeray did not really commit himself to the art of letters by writing satire. Much, indeed, of that satire might be regarded as a belittlement of letters. There is snobbishness, if you like to so call it, in such an attitude, but it is partly a kind of defense for a young man trying letters without a great confidence in himself. Thackeray knew well that the art of the novel was a difficult art and it is hardly to be wondered that he, an Englishman, did not like to own whole-hearted allegiance to an art before he was sure he would succeed in it. If a man attempt that which has not social sanction, his position is doubly deplorable if he cannot do that unsanctioned thing well.

All sorts of writing that we are glad to have from Thackeray came into being by this way of journalism, among it *The Yellowplush Papers* (1838), *The Book of Snobs* (1847), light verse of many sorts and the essays of *Roundabout Papers* (1863). He tried his hand at nearly every literary form and took his material from nearly all walks of life. So skilled a craftsman of letters as he, did well even in forms not particularly suited to his genius, such as serious verse and the play. One cannot speak with enthusiasm of "The Chronicle of the Drum" or of "The Wolves and the Lamb," but there is some title in every other form he essayed that one cannot only speak of with enthusiasm but can call great after its kind. No man since Dryden has been able to do more kinds of writing supremely well than Thackeray.

Thackeray was content, apparently, with one trial at the drama in "The Wolves and the Lamb." Certainly its plot, fashioned forth later as *Lovel the Widower* (1861), does far better service in the novel than it did in the play. This play was a failure just as dramatizations of his novels have been most of them failures. It is not that his stories lack dramatic moments or dramatic characters or dramatic themes, but that, perhaps, one does not welcome in the communal spirit that is abroad in the playhouse that philosophy of life with which one cries agreement under the lamp. *Esmond* might perhaps have been recast into a telling stage play, but its adapter must have succumbed to the temptation to make Beatrix marry Henry. Our sentimental audiences would never be content to see a man marry the mother of his beloved. Yet so to marry Beatrix and Henry is wholly to transform the story Thackeray wrote. *Vanity Fair* has been fairly successful as a play but like the dramatizations of most great novels a disappointment to admirers of the original. *The Rose and the Ring* (1855), as irony would demand, has been the most successfully dramatized of them all. As pantomime presented by marionettes it is just such a show as its author would have delighted to see.

It is not to be wondered, as I have already intimated, that Thackeray so long delayed trying his hand at a full-scope novel. Again and again he had laughed at romance, again and again he had satirized all the stock situations of the novel. If he attempted a story of the traditional sort such as Dickens wrote, Thackeray must present seriously just such situations as he had been in the habit of satirizing.

Then, too, there was Mrs. Grundy to be reckoned with. "Since the author of Tom Jones was buried," he writes in the preface to *Pendennis* (1850), "no writer of fiction among us has been permitted to depict to his utmost power a MAN."

Another explanation of the slowness of Thackeray's approach to the novel was that suggested by Trollope—that Thackeray was a bit lazy. That explanation has lost weight with the years, the publication in 1867 of the careful notes to *Denis Duval* helping to lay it away.   There was little truth in Trollope's contention. Thackeray had not the vitality, week in and week out, of his thick-bodied little rival Dickens.   Nor had Thackeray the industrious habit of Trollope, with his so many words an hour, his so many hours a day, his so many days a week.   Thackeray had not always finished a story when its publication was begun; but there were many of his day who shared this failing with him, even Trollope himself in two instances.   Thackeray rambled about, he failed to keep to the point, he asked advice of his readers, but such practices were a part of his conception of his kind of story, which, he said, involved "a sort of confidential talk between writer and reader."   These practices were not the result of laziness or indecision or indefiniteness of aim.   He changed episodes arranged in a first mental draft of a story when he came to the writing of it, sometimes even the plan of a story after it was well begun; but there would be few novels brought to an end were they brought to an end exactly as they were first intended.

The scope, the abundance of incident, the intensity of feeling, the sweep of life of *Vanity Fair* (1848), all bear testimony to the seriousness of its intention.   Thackeray girded up his loins for the battle the writing of this book was, but so does every writer of parts have to gird up his loins to fight his way through a great book.   The theme of it had been with him since his Cambridge days, maturing in his mind for more than fifteen years before he put pen to paper.   A ripe man keenly remembering his youth is revealed in it, that rich compound of experience and insight and pity and wisdom and joy in truth and love of beauty that was Thackeray.   All of the man is put for the first time into his writing, the poet as well as Mr. Worldly Wiseman, the friend of humanity as well as the sage.   In none of his books is there a fuller revelation of life, in none a weightier commentary upon life. *Vanity Fair* has not the balanced proportions of a *Barry Lyndon* or an *Esmond,* a story published in numbers and so long could hardly be symmetrical in form.   *Pendennis* and *The Newcomes,* likewise published in numbers, are of like looseness of structure.

Vanity Fair is the characteristic Thackeray book, that which seems most typical of the man when you have read all of him and thought of him through long years and argued on him a hundred times with your friends. And as *Vanity Fair* is the characteristic Thackeray book Becky Sharp is the characteristic Thackeray character, her career the epitome of what man has made of man, as Thackeray sees it. I, for one, have a high admiration for her fight against fate, her triumph over fate, her winning of a place of comparative security for herself after that so long struggle against great odds. So human is she that you forget that her name was given her to indicate her qualities. It does its worst, but that worst in vain, to make you think her a caricature, as the name of Dobbin does its worst to make you think the honest Major but a reflex in human guise of the plodding farm horse, a caricature or an abstraction. As you read, Dobbin emerges as much else, a man after your heart, a man who keeps the faith and is staunch.

Pendennis is a fellow in all good qualities to *Vanity Fair*, but a mellower book. In it we have Thackeray depicting "to his utmost power a man" from the point of view of a man older and more at one with inevitable things than was the author of *Vanity Fair*. If no character in *Pendennis* is so universal as Becky, let us reflect that but few characters could be. Major Pendennis is, perhaps, nearest to such universality. How vivid he is, of what a personal savor, of how devastating a fidelity to human nature! And the crowning moment of his old age, a putting of a valet into his proper place! Is that not just the touch to indicate the real importance of the man? We are back again, as always in Thackeray, to the old cry that all is vanity.

Esmond gives us the most fascinating character in Thackeray, as *Vanity Fair* gives the most characteristic, Beatrix, of course, a Meredithian woman created before Meredith began a novel. There is no need to say more of her than to repeat Colonel Esmond's words about his own thoughts, in old age, of what she was and is to him: "As he thinks of her, he who writes feels young again, and remembers a paragon." Esmond was what his creator would be, "Pray God, a gentleman." And if Esmond was, as Trollope says Thackeray said to him, a prig, the in-evitable comment is, "Then God send there may be more prigs in the world!" Always Thackeray was afraid that his heroes should be too good, or too romantic, that they should approach somewhat to Amadis of Gaul or Sir Charles Grandison. In the end, however, Thackeray became wholly reconciled to Esmond as he had conceived him, and made Beatrix in old age refer to him as the finest gentleman she had met in all her wide experience of the world.

The Newcomes is not quite of the power of *Esmond* or *Pendennis* or *Vanity Fair*. There are two heroes, the Colonel and Clive, and the story goes to pieces after the death of the Colonel. Thackeray runs away from the bringing together of Clive and Ethel. And yet it is surely a great novel, with the Colonel the third of Thackeray's great characters. Becky, Beatrix and Colonel Newcome are as distinguished portraits as we have in English literature. There are those that find the Colonel a little too good for credibility, who say his death is a scene sentimental-ized. Let those who so believe so believe. Let those with an-other experience of life believe it a scene of true and deep senti-ment. For myself I can only say that I find the Colonel's "adsum" believable and profoundly affecting.

Thackeray always assumes that you, his reader, have made with him all of his discoveries about life, all of his readings of the riddle of things. There is nothing pontifical about him; he never orates at you, takes you into a temple, plagues you with ritual; his revelations are casually made, as if you were sitting by him in tavern or study, and he leaned over and said: "You feel as I do about this, don't you, 'that occasion is the father of most that is good in us,' or 'what is victory over such a fellow? One gives a chimney sweep the wall'."

All sorts of heroics, of assumptions of dignity, of aloofness, of the hierophantic, were obnoxious to Thackeray. "If Mr. Clive," he writes in *The Newcomes*, "If Mr. Clive is not a Michael Angelo or a Beethoven, if his genius is not gloomy, solitary, gigantic, shining alone, like a lighthouse, a storm round about him, I cannot help myself: he is as heaven made him, brave, honest, gay, and friendly, and persons of a gloomy turn must not look on him as a hero."

Those who must have their artists of "temperament," and "gloomy, solitary, shining alone" are apt to miss the significance of Thackeray, to find him too temperate, too repressed, too English in short. Those who know our race, our habit of speaking, whatever our emotions, in unraised voice and by silences, understand him fully and write him down first of our "showmen of life" who are novelists. Those whose ears are familiar with the great cadences of our language, who know "both the bird-voice and the blast of our omniloquent tongue," write him down master of English prose. Those who have read the great stories of the world who know the great characters of literature of all times, write down Becky Sharp and Beatrix and Colonel Newcome as fellows of the greatest of these figures. Those who subscribe to this threefold declaration write down Thackeray as the greatest of English novelists.

CHAPTER VIII

THE SPECTACLE OF THE BRONTËS

THEY do not always matter, these stories that we cannot put down until their last page is finished. It is a common experience that, after we have satisfied the puzzle interest they arouse, we are through with them. We have sat up all night with *Jane Eyre* (1847) and *Wuthering Heights* (1847) to find out how they ended, but we have not been through with them then. Three generations of us now have followed the fortunes of the strange people of these stories, and many of each generation have returned to them for a further reading. Their wildness, their passionateness, the heart's-cries breaking out in them, the bleakness of their setting—one or the other of these qualities draws us back. We like a something northern in them, a something unreasonable and unreasoning; we find in them what we find in certain of the Icelandic tales, *The Lay of Helgi* for one.

The Irish and Cornish blood in the sisters has led the critics to discover Celtic qualities in their writing, but if such qualities are there it seems to me they are found rather as they are transmuted in the Scandinavian tales, than as they are in the Celtic originals. The Scandinavian characteristics of the people of Yorkshire and the austerities of the landscape about Haworth were greater influences on the sisters than their ancestry. The moors had more to do with their making than Brontë or Branwell blood.

Though we read *Jane Eyre* or *Wuthering Heights* first as a story, on our subsequent readings of either we read for the intensity of the personal and poignant emotion it expresses. We read both books, too, because of the unusualness of the lives of their makers. As Thackeray says: "What a story is that of that

102

family of poets in their solitude yonder on the gloomy northern moors." These words, first printed in *The Cornhill Magazine* in April, 1860, in an article that introduced Charlotte's *Emma,* have ever since haunted all who care for letters. They make one of the sentences of our tongue we cannot read but aloud. They put the spectacle of the Brontës before us so we may never forget it, and a good deal of what the Brontës are, is the spectacle of the Brontës. I am not forgetting one jot or tittle of their power when I say this. I am but calling attention to the truth that we read all they wrote in the light of their tragic lives. "What a story is that of that family of poets in their solitude yonder on the gloomy northern moors!"

Today much that the Brontës wrote is outmoded or valuable principally for its influence on the progress of the novel, or of civilization. Charlotte Brontë (1816-1855) struck stoutly for the woman's right to write frankly as a woman, and not merely in accordance with the convention of what it was proper for a woman to write. She did not want the man's license. That Mrs. Behn had arrogated to herself. Charlotte Brontë wanted the human right to be openly and honestly the woman as man had had the human right to be openly and honestly the man. There may be those of an old-fashioned sort among us who think the frankness she practiced has been carried further than need be these last years. It is a question into which taste enters. There is one frankness of the lady, another of the midwife, another of the sex-ridden neurasthenic. The frankness of Charlotte Brontë was that of a woman of "passionate honor," who wrote in early Victorian days, and who was a lady.

There are passages in all three of Charlotte's novels, in *Jane Eyre* (1847) and *Shirley* (1849) and *Villette* (1852) that retain their power through the years, and Emily's *Wuthering Heights* (1847) is written out of so dramatic an intensity and enveloped in an atmosphere so eerie that its survival as a classic is assured despite its burden of absurdities that would long since have sunk a story that was a horror and nothing more. We must always remember, though, we who admire this novel of Emily Brontë

(1818-1848) and her verse; and the three novels of Charlotte
Brontë; and have a word of praise for *Agnes Grey* (1847) and
The Tenant of Wildfell Hall (1848) of Anne Brontë (1820-
1849): that all of this writing is made more significant by the
fates of the three sisters and the legend that has grown up about
them. No writers of their power in all English literature have
been so bewritten by biographers and critics. It is all but impossible for one now to judge of them by what they wrote and by
that alone.

If one tries to judge by what they wrote and by that alone
one can only say that Charlotte is the greatest of the family;
but the weight of words in current criticism assigns that position
to Emily. It is not on *Wuthering Heights* that the claim is based
but on her poems. The enthusiasm over the discovery of certain new poems, and the satisfaction of differing with hitherto
accepted opinion, have led many critics, together with the high
intention of all the verse and the many intimations of greatness
in it, to a crying up of this poetry of Emily Brontë not at all
justified by what is actually accomplished in it. There are
stanzas completely realized here and there, but no poem of
"wholeness of good tissue." At her best she can write:

> "He comes with Western winds, with evening's wandering airs,
> With that clear dusk of heaven that brings the thickest stars:
> Winds take a pensive tone and stars a tender fire,
> And visions rise, and change, that kill me with desire."

There is another passage as haunting in "It was the autumn of
the year," and a perfect stanza in "Honor's Martyr," but the
bulk of the verse remains verse, with the spirit of poetry investing
it but now and then. It does not compare in richness, for instance, with that treasure of halfworked gold, the verse of Emily
Dickinson.

It is on *Wuthering Heights* that Emily Brontë must depend
for fame. There are characters in the story which are hard to
forget, Heathcliff most impossible of all ultra-romantic lovers
though he be, and Catherine Earnshaw, compound of tenderness

and wildness, of innocence and passion, that must be a close reproduction of certain phases of her maker. And there is Hindley Earnshaw, less impossible but as brutal as Heathcliff. Heathcliff indeed could hardly have been as brutal as he was without being a beast, too, but that the fiery purity of Emily could not allow him to be, even if it could so conceive him. And there is Hareton Earnshaw, the third of this trio of brutalized men and the only one of them for whom their author saw a regeneration during life. Does she show us Hareton humanized by love because so the story came to her, or because she felt there must be in the end some compensation to the reader for all the horrors of the earlier parts? And there are Joseph, the old farmhand, a Puritan of Puritans, seemingly sincere in his cant; and Nelly Dean, the faithful servant, almost the only wholesome human among all the people of the book. The Lintons, save Catherine, are abstractions, and she, save for a differentiating spitefulness, is but a reflection of Catherine Earnshaw, her mother. It is not the characters of the story that are the best of it, but the passion with which it is imagined and the passion with which it is told, a passion that raises certain passages of it to a lyric abandon that had not been in the novel before she and her sister Charlotte had written. You must turn to the great passages of lyric prose that distinguish the essay to find parallels, to Sir Thomas Browne, to Carlyle and to Emerson.

As a child Emily Brontë had heard from servants in her father's rectory stories of hard and reckless doings among the people of the moors. Such stories haunted her. She had read, too, as had her sisters, attempts by local writers of little note to put such stories into books. Poorly done as they were these stories, too, haunted her. She had the will to write, to write about the little she had lived, the somewhat more of life she had heard of, the great deal she had dreamed. She cared so much to write that, being of the blood she was, she was enabled to write. Her so great longings could not be denied. Is there elsewhere than in these sisters any other such phenomenon, two women gaining the power to write as largely out of the great desire they had to write, as out of innate ability to write? Does it help explain to say that such a passion to write as they both had is an attribute of genius? Not very much, I am afraid. Thousands have had such desires, been possessed by them as strongly as human beings can be possessed by desires, and have been visited by no such attainment. Emily Brontë cared so greatly to write *Wuthering Heights,* to write a wildly romantic story of hard lives against the bleakness of the West Ridings, that she won somehow to do what she wished.

There are moments in *Wuthering Heights* that for eeriness are unsurpassed in English literature since certain of the ballads, "The Wife of Usher's Well" and "Clerk Saunders" and "The Demon Lover"; and there is a tenderness along with this eeriness that, in the nature of things, is unknown to the ballads. The cry of the wandering soul of Catherine Linton who was Catherine Earnshaw, heard by Lockwood in his nightmare that winter's night at Wuthering Heights, the cry of that "little exquisite ghost" and "the little ice-cold hand" that his fingers closed upon outside the casement, and the child's face looking in at him—these make one of such moments, a moment of almost intolerable pathos. Another of these eerie moments is of a quieter mood. It occurs at the close of the story, when Heathcliff has joined Catherine Linton in death. Nelly Dean, to whom is assigned the task of telling those parts of the story that Lockwood does not tell us directly, relates the incident, Lockwood recording it in words which Nelly herself could not have used:

"I was going to the Grange one evening—a dark evening threatening thunder—and, just at the turn of the Heights, I encountered a little boy with a sheep and two lambs before him. He was crying terribly, and I supposed the lambs were skittish, and would not be guided.

" 'What is the matter, my little man?' I asked.

" 'They's Heathcliff, and a woman yonder, under t'nab,' he blubbered, 'un' aw darnut pass 'em.'

"I saw nothing; but neither the sheep nor he would go on,

so I bid him take the road lower down. He probably raised the phantoms from thinking, as he traversed the moors alone, on the nonsense he had heard his parents and companions repeat; yet, still, I don't like being out in the dark now, and I don't like being left by myself in this grim house."

Emily Brontë explains away, if you like, the apparitions that appeared to the boy, but she is careful not to explain why the sheep would not pass on. It is animals that, traditionally, best know the distinction between the quick and the dead. And, though their spirits thus walk, Nelly, somehow, believes that Catherine and Heathcliff are at peace. At peace their creator leaves them, with a benediction not unlike that Masefield uses to bring *The Everlasting Mercy* (1911) to a quiet close. Lockwood is in the graveyard where are the graves of Catherine Linton and Edgar Linton and Heathcliff: "I lingered round them, under that benign sky; watched the moths fluttering among the heath and harebells; listened to the soft wind breathing through the grass; and wondered how any one could ever imagine unquiet slumbers for the sleepers in that quiet earth."

This passage is, of course, descriptive of nature in a measure, but here, as almost always in *Wuthering Heights*, attuned to some mood or circumstance of one or another character. It is in the description of the old house that gives title to the story and of its wild and lonely surroundings, that the description has to do solely with objective things. At the very outset she defines her title, and rather badly at that: " 'Wuthering' being a significant provincial adjective descriptive of the atmospheric tumult to which its station is exposed in stormy weather." And from such turgidity as that she can pass, a sentence further on, to "one may guess the power of the north wind blowing over the hedge, by the excessive slant of a few stunted firs at the end of the house; and by a range of gaunt thorns all stretching their limbs one way." So it is often in Emily, simplicity on turgidity, fresh phrasing after rhetoric. On the whole Emily is not so great a sinner in this respect as Charlotte, nor is Anne either. You are always a little uncomfortable, when you feel Charlotte's intensity increasing, lest she may pile up her figures too thickly.

Emily is characteristically herself in her description of certain moments when Linton Heathcliff and Catherine Linton were almost happy together. As Catherine recalls them, she says: "One time, however, we were near quarrelling. He said the pleasantest manner of spending a hot July day was lying from morning till evening on a bank of heath in the middle of the moors, with the bees humming dreamily about among the bloom, and the larks singing high up over head, and the blue sky, and bright sun shining steadily and cloudlessly. That was his most perfect idea of heaven's happiness—mine was rocking in a rustling green tree, with a west wind blowing, and bright, white clouds flitting rapidly above; and not only larks, but throstles, and blackbirds, and linnets, and cuckoos pouring out music on every side, and the moors seen at a distance, broken into cool dusky dells; but close by great swells of long grass undulating in waves to the breeze; and woods and sounding water, and the whole world awake and wild with joy. He wanted all to lie in an ecstasy of peace; I wanted all to sparkle and dance in a glorious jubilee."

There are rich cadences in this prose, cadences most fully savored when read aloud. It is ornate at times but at its best it resolves itself into clarities to which it is a delight to listen. "Gimmerton chapel bells were still ringing; and the full, mellow flow of the beck in the valley came soothingly on the ear. It was a sweet substitute for the yet absent murmur of the summer foliage, which drowned that music about the grange when the trees were in leaf. At Wuthering Heights it always sounded on quiet days, following a great thaw, or a season of steady rain—and of Wuthering Heights Catherine was thinking, as she listened; that is, if she thought or listened at all; but she had the vague, distant look I mentioned before, which expressed no recognition of material things either by ear or eye."

It is such lyric passages that give us much of the joy we have on rereadings of *Wuthering Heights*. The brutalities of the men of the story that had so fearful a delight for their creator lose in significance with every reading. It is not that, say, the brutality of Heathcliff is in itself unbelievable, but that such a brutality should exist along with the chivalry of a kind the man displays in his dealings with Catherine after her marriage to Linton. Denying the possibility of such restraint in a man of his nature the reader comes to ignore that phase of him and to recall only his great love for Catherine as it is revealed at her death, at the time of Lockwood's nightmare, and as Heathcliff himself is about to die. We go back to the book for moments of wildness and terror, for other moments of pure lyricism, for pictures of lonely moorland, for the characterization of Joseph and Nelly, for the wonder there is in the love of Heathcliff and Catherine Earnshaw.

It is George Moore, of course, with his love of being contrary, who comes forth to champion Anne as the greatest of the Brontës. Poor Branwell has long had his advocates; and it is easy to foresee that some devotee of Anne more sociological than Moore, will find deep social significance in Mrs. Huntingdon's defiance of her husband in *The Tenant of Wildfell Hall*. Such a one will say this is an anticipation of what the future was to bring about in the marital relationship, that it makes her a prophet and therefore the most important of the Brontës. Was it not "advanced" for a wife to say in 1848: "I must contrive to bear with you . . . for as long as I discharge my functions of steward and housekeeper so conscientiously and well, without pay, and without thanks, you cannot afford to part with me. I shall therefore remit these duties when my bondage becomes intolerable"? Her "brutal insensibility," as Mr. Huntingdon calls it, had already led her to deny he had any rights as her husband. "I was infatuated once, with a foolish, besotted affection, that clung to him in spite of his unworthiness, but it is fairly gone now—wholly crushed and withered away; and he has none but himself and his vices to thank for it."

It was her own brother Branwell whom she studied for the presentation of Mr. Huntingdon's decline under drink. It was her own experiences as nursery governess that gave her the material for *Agnes Grey*, only no dear delightful curate came into her life as did Mr. Weston into that of her heroine. There are pleasant descriptions of houses and landscapes in these stories, an aspect of character caught now and then, a bit of insight through that power of clairvoyance shared by all the family. There is no great portraiture in either book. It is doubtful whether either would be read now if Anne were not the sister of Charlotte and Emily.

Depth of feeling and not breadth of scope is what distinguishes the novels of these two important Brontës. Yet it is to be noted that what there is of breadth of scope is Charlotte's and not Emily's. The outstanding power of *Jane Eyre* and *Villette* alike is in their intensity and sincerity of self revelation. Both are written out of the experience as boarding-school pupil and governess and pupil-teacher of Charlotte Brontë. Those experiences were, indeed, the half of her life. Her other experiences, almost all of them, until her "arrival" as the author of *Jane Eyre*, were experiences at Haworth. It was a dreary home, this rectory on the moors, with its graveyard under the windows and "disease and death's irremediable doom" hanging always over the inmates of the house. There was little intimate contact between the daughters of the rectory and the people of consequence in the neighborhood, the kind of people the sisters were to write of in their stories. So it was that their school friends, and the families of their school friends, the employers of Charlotte and Anne when they "went out" as nursery governess, and the villagers in Haworth were those they knew best.

Charlotte tried hard to get away from herself in *Shirley*. She made her sister Emily her heroine, but an Emily reborn to a well-being that had always been far from Emily Brontë. It is a strangely pathetic attempt at an assuagement, after her death, of the privations of a girl's life, this rebirth of her, in a story, into affluence, and health, and a bright beauty that was but suggested by the real girl.

In *Villette* Charlotte returns to her own story again, to the theme of her first attempt at a novel, *The Professor,* which the publishers would have none of when she sent it the rounds in 1846, and which was not published until 1857, two years after her death. *Villette* is made chiefly out of her two years in Brussels, 1842-44, but some of its scenes, like the description of Rachel, were based on experiences in London, and some of the characters, Dr. John for one, based on people she met in London, following the publication of her earlier books.

There is a very great deal of diversity of opinion about the merits of the three books *Jane Eyre, Shirley,* and *Villette.* Perhaps just because there are only three of her stories that count a great many people have read all that is significant in Charlotte Brontë. Most of these have read *Wuthering Heights* too. In my experience there is another and very much larger group that has read only *Jane Eyre.* Does this mean that *Jane Eyre* has a universality of appeal denied to *Shirley* or *Villette,* or, for that matter, to *Wuthering Heights?* Or it it just chance that has won *Jane Eyre* such general recognition? It is, I think, that element of the mystery story in *Jane Eyre* that accounts for its popularity. If it were a mystery story and that only it would have passed as the stories of Lippard have passed with their passage on passage of passionate self-revelation; but its lyric joy in the beauty of the world, and the great portrait of Jane, of sombre tone quickened by wild light, have made it proof against the years. There is "flaming heart" in *Jane Eyre,* and "flaming heart" the world has never ignored in an artist. Do not the great lines of Crashaw telling of the attributes of Saint Teresa describe, too, both Jane Eyre and her creator?

> "O thou undaunted daughter of desires!
> By all thy dower of lights and fires,
> By all the eagle in thee, all the dove,
> By all thy lives and deaths of love,
> By thy large draughts of intellectual day."

Read those four initial "by's" each a "with," and you have Charlotte Brontë. She was indeed an "undaunted daughter of desires," with "dower of lights and fires," with "eagle" in her

and "dove," who had known in imagination many "lives and
deaths of love," and whose "large draughts of intellectual day"
have had no small part in the liberation of woman from her early
Victorian trammels. I have often wondered if Arnold Bennett
did not create his Hilda Lessways as much out of Jane Eyre as out
of Crashaw's Saint Teresa and some sly girl of the pottery towns.
Charlotte Brontë is before him with such a characterization.
She has anticipated him, too, in *Shirley*, in finding romance in
mills. That anticipation occurs in a talk between Shirley and
the old Cossack of a clergyman, Mr. Helstone. Shirley speaks
first:

> " 'I like that romantic Hollow with all my heart.'
> 'Romantic—with a mill in it?'
> 'Romantic with a mill in it. The old mill and the white cottage are
> each admirable in its way.'
> 'And the counting-house, Mr. Keeldar?'
> 'The counting-house is better than my bloom-colored drawing room;
> I adore the counting-house.'
> 'And the trade? The cloth—the greasy wool—the polluting dyeing-
> vats?'
> 'The trade is to be thoroughly respected.' "

This is a new point of view, and there are many new points
of view in Charlotte Brontë. Her presentation of life, too, is
new, and the note she strikes is new, as new as the note of
Poe. *Jane Eyre* is like no novel that preceded it. *Shirley* is like
no novel that preceded it. *Villette* is like no novel that preceded
it save *Jane Eyre*. Charlotte Brontë had not read Jane Austen
when she began to write, and when she did read her she found
nothing there to profit her own art of fiction. She had read
Scott, and in her youth, had written: "All novels after his are
worthless." There is something, perhaps, of Edgar Ravenswood
in Mr. Rochester, but if there is, the debt is slight, and nowhere
else in her, save in her description of landscape, is there any influence of Scott. Thackeray she came to admire only short of
idolatry, but he was in no sense her master. From their mention
in her writing we know that she had read *Gulliver* (1726)

Pamela (1740) and *Rasselas* (1759) but none of these books influenced her any more than the *Bewick's British Birds* (1804) she had likewise, as she would say, "perused." Her affiliations are with the poets rather than the novelists, and with the essayists who have risen to lyric prose. She harks back to *Ossian* and Carlyle; she foreshadows Meredith. Has not the famous description of Rachel, whom she called Vashti, the very accent of Meredith? "A great and new planet. . . . She rose at nine that December night: above the horizon I saw her come. She could shine yet with pale grandeur and steady might, but the star verged already on its judgment day. See near it was chaos—hollow, half-consumed—an orb perished or perishing—half lava, half glow." And does not the passage echo both Carlyle and MacPherson?

Yet most of Charlotte Brontë, ninety per cent of her, is of Haworth and her little experience of life and her native genius. It was on the moors she found the symbol of what Jane Eyre was in childhood. "A ridge of lighted heath, alive, glancing, devouring, would have been a meet emblem of my mind when I accused and menaced Mrs. Reed; the same ridge, black and blasted after the flames are dead, would have represented as meetly my subsequent condition, when half an hour's silence and reflection had shown me the madness of my conduct, and the dreariness of my hatred and hating position." All her short life Charlotte Brontë was "a ridge of lighted heath, alive, glancing, devouring," and her writing, being the very pith and marrow of herself was, too, "a ridge of lighted heath, alive, glancing, devouring."

She was cut off before fate could have its will of her and leave her "black and blasted." Perhaps her marriage would have had that fell end, for the Rev. Arthur Bell Nicholls, considerate as he was in some ways, was only the best of the curates her father had and not a man of any largeness. It is told of him that he said he had married Charlotte Brontë and not "Currer Bell." It was "Currer Bell," of course, that she had called herself in that ill-fated volume of verse she had published with

Emily and Anne in 1846 as *Poems* by Currer, Ellis and Acton Bell, and it was as Currer Bell she had won her great success with *Jane Eyre*.

There is much that is not fine in *Jane Eyre*. Thackeray was amused at the thrillingness to Jane of the fragrance of Mr. Rochester's cigar, "the trail of Havana incense," and he perplexed Miss Brontë with pleasantry on the subject. No doubt he smiled, too, at much else in this so palpably woman's man, as all men who have met Mr. Rochester since that day have smiled. Yet Mr. Rochester is not to be smiled away. Strip him of the feminine Byronics and you have a man there, a man of mettle and hard intent. There is much that is impossible in the story. Jane could not but have known there was a mad woman in the house. But these impossibilities, like those of *Wuthering Heights* do not, somehow, matter much. And that mad woman's prowlings about the house furnish their share of drama to the story. As a child I was haunted by that scene of Jane's awakening in the night to see the maniac's face peering into her own; and forty years afterwards that scene scores with me as of old.

What delights me most now in *Jane Eyre* is the revelation of Jane, a woman not perfect, but "nobly planned," of that "passionate honor" Thackeray saw in Charlotte Brontë, and that Charlotte Brontë was able to transfer to Jane Eyre. What else most delights me now is the wealth of lyric passages in the story, capturings of mood, flashes of insight, descriptions of the countryside. This one moves me somewhat in the way the "Toys" of Coventry Patmore moves me: "I covered my head and arms with the skirt of my frock, and went out to walk in a part of the plantation that was quite sequestered. . . . I leaned against a gate, and looked into an empty field in which no sheep were feeding, where the short grass was nipped and blanched. It was a very gray day; a most opaque sky 'onding on snaw,' canopied all; thence flakes fell at intervals, which settled on the hard path and on the hoary lea without melting. I stood, a wretched child enough, whispering to myself over and over again, 'What shall I do?'—'What shall I do?'"

There is more joy in Mr. Rochester's tribute to a gray day at Thornfield, though it ends, as so much in *Jane Eyre* ends, on a note of bitterness and aversion: "I like this day; I like that sky of steel; I like the sternness and stillness of the world under frost. I like Thornfield; its antiquity; its retirement; its old crow-trees and thorn-trees; its gray façade, and lines of dark windows reflecting the metal welkin; and yet how long have I abhorred the very thought of it; shunned it like a great plague-house."

That "metal welkin," and the "hoary lea" of the former passage are rhetoric that one cannot explain away as symptomatic of the age. They persist in memory and hurt on every reading. Yet despite them how memorable are the passages! There is a slight blemish, too, in the following passage, but how finely Puritan it is, with a stoical joy in it of the order you find in the winter-studies of Redfield and Frost: "The ground was hard, the air was still, my road was lonely; I walked fast till I got warm, and then I walked slowly to enjoy and analyze the species of pleasure brooding for me in the hour and situation. It was three o'clock; the church bell tolled as I passed under the belfry; the charm of the hour lay in its approaching dimness, in the low-gliding and pale-beaming sun. I was a mile from Thornfield, in a lane noted for wild roses in summer, for nuts and blackberries in autumn, and even now possessing a few coral treasures in hips and haws, but whose best winter delights lay in its utter solitude and leafless repose. If a breath of air stirred, it made no sound here; for there was not a holly, not an evergreen to rustle, and the stripped hawthorn and hazel bushes were as still as the white, worn stones which causewayed the middle of the path. Far and wide, on each side, there were only fields where no cattle now browsed; and the little brown birds, which stirred occasionally in the hedge looked like single russet leaves that had forgotten to drop."

Charlotte Brontë was of her time in some respects just as she

was far ahead of it in others. She dared to represent Jane Eyre
owning to her love for Mr. Rochester before his for her was
declared, a very unorthodox procedure for an early Victorian
lady, but the cardinal conventions of duty and virtue and faith
in God she accepted as cheerfully as she accepted the change of
the seasons. This "night-piece" from the wanderings of Jane
Eyre is just as typical of the eighteen-forties as Angel Clare's
owning of his agnosticism is typical of the eighteen-eighties.
There is in it, however, what is far from mere spirit of the age,
an augustness of rhythm and a sweep of imagination that have
too seldom marked the prose of our novelists: "I touched the
heath; it was dry, and yet warm with the heat of the summer
day. I looked at the sky; it was pure. A kindly star sparkled
just above the chasm ridge. The dew fell, but with propitious
softness; no breeze whispered. Nature seemed to be benign and
good; I thought she loved me, outcast as I was; and I who
from man could anticipate only mistrust, rejection, insult, clung
to her with filial fondness. . . .

"Worn out with this torture of thought, I rose to my knees.
Night was come, and her planets were risen—a safe still night, too
serene for the companionship of fear. We know that God is
everywhere; but certainly we feel His presence most when His
works are on the grandest scale spread before us; and it is in the
unclouded night-sky, where His worlds wheel their silent course,
that we read clearest His infinitude, His omnipotence, His omni-
presence. I had risen to my knees to pray for Mr. Rochester.
Looking up, I, with tear-dimmed eyes, saw the mighty Milky
Way. Remembering what it was—what countless systems there
swept space like a soft trace of light—I felt the might and
strength of God."

There are not nearly so many impassioned passages in *Shirley*
as there are in *Jane Eyre,* the more objective treatment of the
former story giving less opportunity for them. In *Villette,* with
its return to autobiography, they are again found in plenty, and
are, many of them, lyrics of the north country, catchings of rapt
mood in wild weather or under auroral skies, that one remembers

as one remembers similar passages from the poets. Lucy Snowe is speaking in this one: "As for me the tempest took hold of me with tyranny: I was roughly roused and obliged to live. I got up and dressed myself, and creeping outside the casement close by my bed, sat on its ledge, with my feet on the roof of a lower adjoining building. It was wet, it was wild, it was pitch dark. Within the dormitory they gathered about the night-lamp in consternation, praying loud. I could not go in: too resistless was the delight of staying with the wild hour, black and full of thunder, pealing out such an ode as language never delivered to man—too terribly glorious, the spectacle of clouds, split and pierced, by white and blinding bolts."

More northern even than such a rejoicing in tempest is this lyric of auroral lights:

"The air of the night was very still, but dim with a peculiar mist, which changed the moonlight into a luminous haze. In this air, or this mist, there was some quality—electrical perhaps —which acted in strange sort upon me. I felt then as I had felt a year ago in England—on a night when the aurora borealis was streaming and sweeping round heaven, when, belated in lonely fields, I had paused to watch that mustering of an army with banners—that quivering of serried lances—that swift ascent of messengers from below the north star to the dark, high keystone of heaven's arch. I felt, not happy, far otherwise, but strong with reenforced strength."

There is space, sweep, contours of half a continent, in this description of hard weather: "The keen, still cold of the morning was succeeded, later in the day, by a sharp breathing from Russian wastes; the cold zone sighed over the temperate zone and froze it fast. A heavy firmament, dull and thick with snow sailed up from the north, and settled over expectant Europe."

Such passages as these do not arrest us on a first reading. They may even be skipped when our interest is the incident. When we read *Jane Eyre* the first time we are eager to find out how things are to go, as she grows up, with this passionate little girl, whose fortunes have so interested us from the moment of our meeting. The interest we have in her deepens with every change in her life. We are interested in her at Gateshead Hall; we are more interested in her at Lowood, though these school scenes are too long-drawn out; we are on tenter-hooks as to her fate at Thornfield. And when the marriage of Jane and Mr. Rochester is forbidden at the altar! Will it be "all for love and the world well lost"? Will Jane go with Mr. Rochester though she cannot be his wife? The old, old struggle between duty and desire is again presented, but we who know Jane have never a doubt. Country rectories had not yet been liberalized by *The Woman Who Did* (1895) and *Ann Veronica* (1909). Jane Eyre, like Charlotte Brontë, was a woman of "passionate honor." Yet the situation is dramatic, tense, almost agonizing. Her flight from Thornfield is finely told; the recital of her reduction to starvation a remarkable achievement for a writer who had no personal experiences of a like sort to serve as guide; and her return to Mr. Rochester, free but blind, at his call of need heard by her inward ear across the half of England, an admirably conceived short cut to a happy ending.

Though *Shirley* is a far more objective story than *Jane Eyre* it, too, is full of Charlotte Brontë. It starts out bravely as a tale whose background is to be the anti-machinery riots of the early nineteenth century, and through that background and through its characters it intends to keep its author away from autobiography. And in a sense it continues to do what it starts out to do. It keeps away from a reciting of incidents of Charlotte Brontë's life, but it does not avoid self-revelation. She based the character of Caroline Helstone on that of her friend Ellen Nussey, but who doubts the words put into her mouth express Charlotte's belief about herself? "Why should anybody have told me? Have I not an instinct? Can I not divine by analogy? . . . The voice we hear in solitude told me all I know in these matters."

So she accounts for her clairvoyance, but in *Shirley*, generally, she uses her experience rather than her intuitions. She presents the story, too, in what for her is a realistic fashion. Her men, even the curates, are more human than Mr. Rochester and St. John Rivers. They are flesh and blood, not figments of fancy, Robert and Louis Moore, Mr. Yorke, Mr. Helstone, Joe Scott, Moses Barraclough, William Farren. All of these characters had originals among the men Charltote Brontë knew, and the curates were so close to theirs the originals grew famous in their own despite.

Shirley herself is a creation, of other clay entirely than troubled Jane. She was, indeed, dark like Jane, but distinguished, of features "fins, gracieux, spirituels." She was, in a way, boyish; she was daring, splendid, of a glad confidence. I have always resented that "sister of the spotted, bright, quick, fiery leopard" that Louis Moore wrote her down in the unpardonable lingo of his diary. Only in her grace and brightness was she in any way leopard-like.

Shirley has its moments of excitement, but no such crises as *Jane Eyre*. All's well with its lovers, too, in the end; and with the lovers in *Villette*. It would seem it was as much the sorrow and death about her that drove Charlotte to the happy ending as it was the convention of the time. There does not seem to me to be the freshness and spontaneity about *Villette* that there is, in their differing ways, about both *Jane Eyre* and *Shirley*. There are many who regard it, however, as her best book. It was written, say some of these admirers, out of memories of a great passion, out of her love for that schoolmaster of Brussels who in the story is M. Paul Emanuel. The children of Professor Constantin Heger presented to the British Museum in 1913 four letters of Charlotte's to their father. These ought to settle the question of the nature of her attitude to him, but I am not sure that they do. From these letters she might be interpreted to be in love with him, and he discouraging her, but it is hard to tell whether her attitude is love, or only a sort of pathetically delayed schoolgirl "crush." She was past twenty-eight when she was writing them, and lonely at Haworth, and with her dreams of authorship still unfulfilled.

There had been men in her life before M. Heger but she had

not cared for them. It was, indeed, difficult for her, with her standards, to find a man to love, and one wonders, if she did love M. Heger, how she found it in her heart to love such a one. He was far from a romantic figure. Perhaps it was only after she returned to Haworth that distance lent the enchantment her letters seem to reveal. If she really loved him once one wonders how she had the heart to transform him into the humorous reality of the M. Emanuel Lucy Snowe loved in *Villette*. That story was published nine years after Charlotte had seen M. Heger, time enough for her recovery from any passion; but would any length of time turn love into humorous tolerance?   Dr. John was too nice for Lucy Snowe, so Lucy was married off to M. Emanuel. A Charlotte Brontë would hardly have so belittled one who had awakened in her a great passion. But there are the letters!

The adventures of Lucy Snowe in the Belgian boarding-school are far more true to life than the adventures of Jane Eyre in Thornfield. The characters in *Villette* are all of them believable. The writing is better, with few of the lapses into rhetoric of *Jane Eyre*. The proportions of the story are better. Charlotte Brontë was maturing in her art. But *Villette,* better planned, better written, a more completely realized intention than *Jane Eyre,* has not the "first fine careless rapture" and the richness of passion that make *Jane Eyre* a thing of lonely splendor in English letters.

Charlotte Brontë recognized her limitations. She realized her lack of experience. She knew that she was, as Mr. Rochester told Jane Eyre, a neophyte who had "not passed the porch of life," and was "absolutely unacquainted with its mysteries," at least from the standpoint of experience. And though "the voice we hear in solitude" told her much of life she was not going to take what it told her as a basis for generalizations about life. What her clairvoyance revealed to her was that her power lay in the poetical presentation of character. "There is nothing really valuable, in this world," she cries in *Shirley*, "there is nothing glorious in the world to come, that is not poetry."   It was denied her to write poetry in verse, but out of her great desire to write poetry it was given her to write poetry in prose. A hundred lyric passages attest that power in her; four great portraits in them, Jane Eyre and Shirley, Lucy Snowe and M. Paul Emanuel, prove her a peer of the great portrait painters of our novel; and a crude but arresting gift of narrative has survived many changes of taste in the forms of fiction. There is a surety of continuing appeal in such story-telling and portraiture and poetry.

CHAPTER IX

THE FELLOWS OF SCOTT AND THE EARLIER VICTORIANS

OF the novelists who began to be recognized while Scott was writing Galt has best stood the test of time. The fine thinness of Peacock's art has worn scarcely thinner with the years, but it was never substantial enough to be a thing of delight to many. Bulwer-Lytton has still popularity of a kind, a popularity that distresses the fastidious, but he is all but rejected of the powers-that-be in criticism. Disraeli, despite *Coningsby* (1844), has fewer and fewer readers; and Theodore Hook (1788-1841), whom he satirized as Lucien Gay in that novel, almost no readers at all. The stories of Hook have still a factitious reputation, but the only book of his now in print is *The Choice Humorous Works*. And this, it is to be feared, survives only as a sort of assistant to after dinner speakers. At that the edition of 1902 suffices to meet the demand.

Miss Ferrier, though a compeer of Miss Edgeworth and Miss Austen, is but a name to most readers; and Maryatt has been relegated to the position of an outmoded writer of boys' books. They will tell you at the old-book stores that Bulwer is the only one of the seven that is often asked for, but that there are a few collectors of Peacock. Disraeli (1804-1881), these booksellers say, will slowly disappear from their shelves, volume by volume, but I once watched a thick book about him, in good condition, lie unsold on the fifty cent table for several weeks, and then descend to the side-walk table of twenty-five cent books, from which I bought it, hardly more shopworn than on its first appearance inside the store. This *Disraeli in Outline* (1890) represents the revival of interest in the novels of the Earl of Beaconsfield that followed upon his death in 1881. It is contemporaneous with

Froude's *Lord Beaconsfield*, but owes its biographical passages not to him but to Hitchman (1881) and the *Letters* (1887) edited by Ralph Disraeli. There was another little flare-up of interest in Disraeli on the centenary of his birth, in honor of which appeared a biography by Wilfred Meynell and a reissue of his works.

DISRAELI

With all this to-do about Disraeli there was very little impetus given to the reading of his novels. There was some attempt to make much of him as a writer because he had been a Tory premier of England, but most of the interest excited was in Disraeli as a statesman and as a picturesque figure in Victorian life. A poor play with him as hero was very popular, but even this stimulus did not drive many to his books. The truth is, of course, that he was unable to put much of the vivid intensity of his nature into his writing. He could write about himself and he could "invent," but he had not the power to give his characters an existence of their own. He had no real imagination and so all he could do, at first hand, was autobiography of a kind. His "invention," of course, was but a compound of memories of the writing of his predecessors, or a rather pinchbeck reporting of the celebrities of his day. Some of his admirers have compared his rendering of the Marquis of Hertford as the Marquis of Monmouth in *Coningsby* with Thackeray's rendering of that same worthy as the Marquis of Steyne, an unfortunate comparison. The latter, of course, is one of the great portraits of all literature, the former hardly more than a pretentious wax-work.

We quote often the best of the sayings of Disraeli. "On the side of the angels" is as much a part of our speech as is any proverb. We shrug our shoulders at his description of Gladstone as "a sophistical rhetorician inebriated with the exuberance of his own verbosity," and, shrugging, we recognize it as true, almost, of its creator as of W. E. G. Out of his own mouth he has condemned himself. Admitting that *Coningsby* (1844) and

Sybil (1845) and *Tancred* (1847) are of historical value as records of early Victorian times, we cannot place them among the great novels, or even among the novels a little less than great. The indictment by Thackeray of the pretentiousness and splurge and Orientalism of Disraeli was well taken. "Codlingsby" is the best of *Novels by Eminent Hands* and the truest criticism of Disraeli yet set down.

BULWER-LYTTON

It was Hawthorne who put Edward George Earle Lytton Bulwer-Lytton (1803-1873) in his place with that damning phrase, "the very pimple of the age's humbug." I have always balked at the phrase, but since it is, and is true, it must be quoted. It is ugly, perhaps worse than ugly. It arouses resentment, too. No one who remembers his childhood but is grateful to Bulwer for *The Last Days of Pompeii* (1834). It is one of the books that in those days seemed worthy of a place by *The Arabian Nights, The Odyssey, Robinson Crusoe, Swiss Family Robinson* and *Tom Sawyer*. That is an uncritical listing of the classics of childhood, or perhaps an admission that the classics of childhood are as subject to mistaken preference as the classics of maturity. *Tom Sawyer* is obviously a better book than *The Swiss Family Robinson, Tom Sawyer* is almost a fellow of *Robinson Crusoe. The Arabian Nights* is first of its kind, but it falls far short of *The Odyssey*. These so different books are dear to childhood for the strangeness and wonder common to them all. *The Swiss Family Robinson* is artless. Than *The Odyssey* there is no finer art. One must be twelve before one begins to see the five are things of differing values. And one must not be more than twelve if one is to get what one has a right to get out of *The Last Days of Pompeii*. In those youngest years we are utterly won by it. Geography and history have made the material of the story familiar to us. Volcano and Rome are words to conjure with. Lives in bloom stilled by a lava-flood will awe even the most unfeeling child, and haunt the sensitive one of nights.

To Bulwer it would seem the cruelest of ironies that he should survive as the author of a child's book. He thought his intention the highest an author could have. He believed *Pelham* (1828) for all its persiflage, a proud and regal accomplishment; *Harold* (1848), a perfect compound of philosophy and noble sentiment; and the trilogy of *The Caxtons* (1849), *My Novel* (1853) and *What Will He Do With It* (1858) a complete exposition of all that was best in English life. It was, too, a good deal to have Wagner find in one's novel an inspiration for an opera. *Rienzi* (1835) may be but 'prentice-work among the music drama of the master, but it was surely a high compliment to Bulwer to have his *Rienzi* singled out as the one modern story that compelled a musical setting by the great composer. It is something, too, to be called "richly and glowingly intellectual" by Poe, and, as a novelist, "unsurpassed by any writer living or dead." And, after such praise, to be judged by posterity as at best a child's classic! Better than that the hard words of a Thackeray in "Epistles to the Literati" of Yellowplush and "George de Barnwell" in *Novels by Eminent Hands,* or even Tennyson's retort to "The New Timon" (1845). And yet do not the very words of Tennyson half foretell the fate that has come to him:

> "Who killed the girls and thrilled the boys
> With dandy pathos when you wrote:
> 'O Lion, you that made a noise,
> And shook a mane *en papillotes!*' "

In 1866, when Peacock died, a poet and satirist of a restricted reputation, Bulwer was a literary celebrity of the first water. Now, two generations later, Peacock has the securer place in English letters. There is so much writing to the credit of Bulwer that his celebrity has dwindled slowly. Those nearly seventy titles of his, those one hundred and ten volumes, contain a good deal of writing that was important to their day. One aspect of Victorian times is there presented, an aspect that reveals shoddiness and ugliness and pretense, along with a sort of tawdry splendor. It will be long remembered that Bulwer established the black swallowtail as the correct evening dress for men; it will be long remembered that he wrote novels that were regarded as fine by many early and mid-Victorians; and it will be long remembered that three plays of his, *The Lady of Lyons, Richelieu* and *Money*, were regarded as even finer than the novels by many early and mid and late Victorians. Indeed, so imposing is Bulwer, judged by what Matthew Arnold calls the historical estimate in criticism, that there are still those who believe he must be a great author judged by the absolute estimate.

It is only by keeping always in mind "the truly great" in literature, and by putting the work of all writers to the test of comparison with the work of "the truly great" that we can see men like Bulwer and Disraeli in proper relation to, say, Scott and Thackeray. And it is only by putting the lesser men like Galt and Peacock over against these "truly great" that we can see how sterling is their work. Important in the social history of their time Bulwer and Disraeli were; accomplished, perhaps, in the art of life; accomplished certainly in the artifices of life that brought them to the attention of the public. Wilde and Shaw have gone to school to them for certain effects in the artifices of publicity. Compared to Scott and Thackeray, Bulwer and Disraeli ring false. Compared to Scott and Thackeray, Peacock and Galt ring true, but thin.

THOMAS LOVE PEACOCK

There has been a cult of Peacock (1785-1866) for a hundred years now, but despite comparatively frequent republications of his novels the numbers of the cult do not greatly increase. That is perhaps as it should be, for he is a minor novelist, if a novelist at all. Of his seven so-called novels five at least are as largely satire of contemporary personages and manners, or familiar essays cast in the form of dialogues, as they are stories. *Maid Marian* (1822) and *The Misfortunes of Elphin* (1829) may pass for romances, but *Headlong Hall* (1816), *Melincourt* (1817), *Night-*

mare Abbey (1818), *Crochet Castle* (1831) and *Gryll Grange* (1860) are rambles around a subject in the pleasant company of Peacock, with satirical attacks, in season and out of season, on what offended his prejudices. There is an element of fantasia in them, and good verse of a bacchanal sort, or of that borderland between lyric and society verse in which our literature is so rich. There is nothing in all Bulwer and Disraeli so likely to keep their memories green as "Love and Age," that lyric of his later years. Its verses, a lucky seven, are arch and charming, wistful and mellow. They sing themselves into your memory and will not out of it.

What I care for in Peacock is not the satire of manners or the stories; nor, very much, the characters; but the songs, and the wit, and the personality of the man. It is wit in the full sense of the word, in the old sense and in the modern sense. "The fastidious in old wine are a race that does not decay" is of the best of these sayings. Of a less personal and more sententious sort, with an eighteenth century savor, are "Men are easily cured of unfashionable virtues, but never of fashionable vices." So, too, is "The world will never suppose a good motive where it can suppose a bad one." There are moments of his dialogue that point the way to Meredith's. Such a passage is that in *Nightmare Abbey* on the departure of Mr. Cypress from England. The capping of epigrams here ends with Mr. Hilary's "The inscription '*Hic non bibitur*' will suit nothing but a tombstone." And Meredith owes not a little to the championship by Peacock of the intellectual woman.

Nightmare Abbey is generally said to be the most read of the books of Peacock. If this is so, it is perhaps because of its satiric presentations of Shelley as Scythrop and of Byron as Cypress. There is pretty fooling with the Shelleyan triangle in the loves of Marionetta and Celinda for Scythrop, and an admirable travesty of Byron in

> "There is a fever of the spirit,
> The brand of Cain's unresting doom."

Gryll Grange is to me, however, his book of books. In Dr. Opi-
mian there are suavity and ripeness of wisdom you will have to
turn back to Lamb to find equalled.

JOHN GALT

The lowland Scot is quintessentialized in the picture of Auldbiggings in *The Last of the Lairds* (1825) as I have not found
him elsewhere. The village busybody into whose mouth John
Galt (1779-1839) puts the story is on his way to the home of
Mailings when he meets the Laird's man Jock "sitting in a niche
of golden broom." Before the caller has a chance to speak Jack
volunteers:

"Ye'll fin' the Laird a busy man."

"Indeed! and what is he doing?"

"Doing? What should he be doing, but sitting on his ain
louping-on stane, glowring frae him?"

Do we not all know the Lowlander that is "glowring frae him,"
not only in meditation as is the Laird, but in many other moods,
in kirk, in court, in but and ben, in shop and mine and fishing
boat? It is a ruling passion, this "glowring frae him"

Auldbiggings, on the whole, however, is not so complete a creation as Mrs. Soorocks, and those so characteristic sisters, Miss
Sooshie and Miss Girsie. There is humor in their delineations,
and pathos, too, but a tight hold is kept always on pathos by
Galt, even in *The Annals of the Parish* (1821), where there is
every chance to let it run loose in the many misfortunes chronicled by the Reverend Micah Balwhidder. Mr. Balwhidder is,
indeed, with his clishmaclavers, the ancestor of the pathetic oldsters who stray about in the kailyarders of a generation ago, Sir
James and the Reverend Doctors Watson and Crockett.

It is in the realistic sketches of his native Ayrshire that Galt
has done lasting work. *The Ayrshire Legatees* (1820), *The Annals of the Parish* (1821), *Sir Andrew Wylie* (1822), *The Pro-
vost* (1822), *The Entail* (1824), and *The Last of the Lairds*
(1826), what may be called his west country series, are about all

that survive of Galt, as the Barchester series are nearly all that survive of Trollope. They are all, indeed, unless that "Canadian Boat-Song" which was printed in the *Noctes Ambrosianæ* in *Blackwood's Magazine* for 1829 should happen to be Galt's:

> "From the lone shieling on the distant island
>   Mountains divide us and the waste of seas;
> Yet still the blood is strong, the heart is Highland,
>   And we in dreams behold the Hebrides."

Whether Galt was capable of such a rhythm as that is a question, but there is no question that he could attain to a real beauty of rhythm in prose. Listen to these words spoken by Mad Meg in *The Annals of the Parish:*

"Come awa', sir. This is an altered house: they're gane that keepit it bein; but, sir, we maun a' come to this, we maun pay the debt o' nature. Death is a grim creditor, and a doctor but brittle bail when the hour of reckoning's at han'! What a pity it is, mother, that you're now dead, for here's the minister come to see you. Oh, sir! but she would have had a proud heart to see you in her dwelling, for she had a genteel turn, and would not let me, her only daughter, mess or mell wi' the lathron lasses of the clachan. Ay, ay: she brought me up with care, and edicated me for a lady; nae coarse wark darkened my lily-white hands. But I maun work now: I maun dree the penalty of man."

The irony of that, intentional or unintentional on the part of the girl, adds to the impressiveness of it, and that irony does not destroy the beauty of the lyric that the passage is, as irony so often destroys lyricism.

There is not one of these six stories of the west country folk that does not have characters to remember, and of them Micah Balwhidder and Mrs. Soorocks have "the relish of eternity." Always in this series there is the "birr and smeddum" to his writing that he liked in books; always in this series he is sincere; all but always he is patiently realistic; often and often there is a rhythm to delight in and the arresting phrase. Such a sentence as this is no rarity: "It was between the day and dark, when the shuttle stands still till the lamp is lighted." John Galt is a better writer than the world has as yet owned him to be.

DAVID MACBETH MOIR

David Macbeth Moir (1798-1851) is still remembered in Scotland for the *Autobiography of Mansie Wauch* (1828), and read, at least in this one book. Not only is he read but read aloud, and with laughter slow to die down. It is his humor that keeps Moir alive, a humor unstaled by a hundred years. There is more than humor in him, however. There is a faithfulness to low life that makes him, like Galt, a forerunner of George MacDonald and the Kailyard School. *Mansie Wauch* may be a forerunner, too, of that other autobiography of a tailor, *Alton Locke* (1850), of Charles Kingsley. Mansie is, indeed, a hardy character, a character completely done. He is a douce and pawky man, very human. Though a pattern of respectability, he can grow genial in his cups, or as he would say "a wee tozy-mozy."

MISS FERRIER

The three novels of Susan Edmonstone Ferrier (1782-1854) are named after three institutions held fundamental in Scotland, *Marriage* (1818), *Inheritance* (1824) and *Destiny* (1831). All three, marriage, inheritance and destiny, are, in Scotland, contributory to the welfare of the family,—necessary, indeed, to its continuance. It is obvious that marriage and the inheritance of position and property are necessary to the family. It is not so obvious, though it is true, that a triumphing sense of the dignity of being fated, of being chosen by God for a particular and a high destiny, is necessary to keep family pride as family pride should be. And without family pride there can be no Family with a capital F. Miss Ferrier believed in this sort of Family. She vindicated it, whether Highland or Lowland, against the aristocratic ideals of Southrons. They, great county folk though they be, are shown to be possessed of gentility in lesser measure than the Scottish provincials.

Marriage and *Destiny* approximate rather closely in their themes. In both much of the action springs from the unhappiness of Englishwomen brought as brides to lonely Highland homes. There is a rough plenty and a sufficiency of company at Glenfern and Glenroy but not the luxuries or. the suave society the ladies are used to in England, and Highland pride can brook no criticism of Highland deportment and ways of living. In both stories there is a heroine of the patient Grizel type, which was not at all the kind of girl Miss Ferrier had been or the kind of woman that she developed into. She believed in the authority of parents; she was a good daughter and sister; but she was not one to turn the other cheek as was her Mary, and, to only a less degree, her Edith. For all her gentility, her position as granddaughter of a baronet and friend of Argyll's niece, Miss Ferrier was as forthright in her satire as if she were of the masses. She had "the thick Scots wit that fells you like a mace" that Henley found in "The Staff-Nurse: Old Style," he writes of in his "In Hospital." She uses it to the disadvantage of Lady Elizabeth Waldegrave, that vulgar English patrician of *Destiny*. She makes that lady resent talk of her position as widow and grandmother: "Grandmothers and widows! Coarse and gross! Who ever hears of such things in good society."

Miss Ferrier is even more outspoken in the delineation of character and in the dialogue of Lady Maclaughlan and Mrs. Macshake, terrible old hectorers redeemed by humor. She delights so in caricatures of militant ladies it is a pity she could not have lived to meet Mrs. Proudie. She caricatures her old men, too, Sir Sampson, and the Laird of Glenfern, but Glenroy, for all his typical Highlandness, is himself, an individual, a personality. The young girls her heroines, Mary and Gertrude and Edith, have a quiet strength, but their young men are not much more differentiated than Scott's lovers. They are just pleasant lads, with good looks and breeding.

There is more plot in *Inheritance,* and less Scots bite than in

Marriage and *Destiny*. Rossville, the scene of its action, is apparently in the western lowlands, and you would expect Miss Ferrier, though an Edinburgh woman, to know the west country too. She may know it, but she does not write so racily of it as of the highlands. She spent much time in Argylshire and therefore knew well the western highlands and their men and women. She loves the countryside, but she acknowledges its loneliness and long days of bad weather; she loves its people, but she laughs at the particular forms human weakness takes on hereabouts. Thus she sings Gaelic greatness at the opening of *Destiny:*

"All the world knows there is nothing on earth to be compared to a Highland Chief. He has his loch and his islands, his mountains and his cattle, his piper and his tartan, his forests and his deer, his thousands of acres of untrodden heath, and his tens of thousands of black-faced sheep, and his bands of bonneted clansmen with claymores, and Gaelic and hot blood, and dirks."

Miss Ferrier does her lowlanders only less well, the memorable characterizations of them being in *Inheritance,* with Miss Becky Duguid and Uncle Adam most memorable of all. There is a happy ending to this story, as to both the others, the girls getting not only good husbands but a competence with them.

Miss Ferrier can be stilted and Ossianic in her pictures of landscape, but there are many passages and innumerable touches that are all her own and of the very color of place. I had just the thrill when I came upon her "purple moor with its grey stones" that I had when I first came upon that coloring in a landscape in oils thirty years ago. She wrote good prose because she was always reading good poetry. You will find her quoting all the poets from Sophocles to Byron in chapter headings and text. Dante, Chaucer, Spenser, Shakespeare, Milton, Racine, Dryden, Pope, Burns, Wordsworth—it is a noble roll she makes of them. Nor are the minors forgotten. Herrick is there, all of a little lyric. Miss Ferrier was a learned writer, but she wore her learning lightly. She had a deeper insight into life than she chose to reveal in her stories. Read her description of Scott stricken, with his stricken grandson by his side at table in Abbotsford, if you wish to know this side of her art. Read her novels if you care, in material, for Scotland in old times and kindly gentry and good-hearted gawks, and, if you care, in manner of writing, for sprightliness, and satire in heroic doses, bitter and bracing.

MARRYAT

Frederick Marryat (1792-1848) survives by virtue of rereadings by oldish men who enjoyed his stories when they were boys. He has, of course, a few new readers year by year, chiefly men attracted to him because of his material. Navy men read him because he writes of naval engagements, and some other seamen because they have heard of him as England's first sea-novelist of yesterday. He has still a certain vogue, too, through his early stories, as a boy's novelist, and some slight appeal, through his later stories, as an author of tales for younger youngsters, boys and girls both. *The Children of the New Forest* (1847) is on current lists of school reading; *Mr. Midshipman Easy* (1836) does not gather dust on all library shelves; and five other of his stories than these two are to be had in cheap editions of recent date.

There are men among us who delight in *Peter Simple* (1834), *Snarleyyow* (1837), and *The Phantom Ship* (1839), and try to convert those of us who cannot share that delight to their way of feeling. I would say, theoretically, that no landlubber could have that delight in full measure, but it is a matter of fact that one of my acquaintances who rereads his Marryat is a cloistered scholar of sixty knowing little of the sea. To him Vanderdecken and Schriften are of the very essence of romance. The old legend of *The Flying Dutchman* is in itself undoubtedly romantic, but whether Marryat has made his version, in *The Phantom Ship,* romantic, is another question.

Snarleyyow, or the Dog Fiend, does not live up to its title, though there are caricatures of seamen in it you remember for a while, Obadiah Coble, Jansen, Dick Short and Jemmy Ducks, and one scene at least that, once read, you cannot forget. This is the parting of Vanslyperken and his dog as the two are about to be hanged from opposite yard-arms of the cutter Yungfrau. It may sound laughable in the retelling. In the telling there is a pathos that has its will of the reader despite the welter of farcical fun and boisterousness and cruelty that riots through the story.

Marryat knows a little more about the widow Vanderloosh, the beloved of Vanslyperken, than about the "elegant ladies" he chooses oftenest as heroines, but only a little more. His lack of knowledge of women is proverbial and in this instance what is proverbial is true. Patience in *The Children of the New Forest* has some substance and some personality, and Amine in *The Phantom Ship* at least constancy of purpose to mark her, but most of his women are not individualized at all. They are not even types, but the thinnest of shadows.

Once in a while Marryat takes a fling at current fads, as in his satire of equality in *Mr. Midshipman Easy*. There is little interest for us today, however, in such flings. There is a certain value, perhaps, in them as records of the talk of the time. The mere chronicling of the round of sea life of the early nineteenth century has its historical value, too, but such a chronicling is in itself of no literary value.

If there is any literary power of a high order in Marryat it is vigor, vigor of expression, vigor of feeling, vigor of movement. There is deep knowledge of seamanship revealed in his writing, the experts tell us, in his description of the handling of ships in storms and in fights. There are few memorable characters, almost none to put beside the seamen of Smollett. Coxswain Swinburne and boatswain Chucks in *Peter Simple* are perhaps comparable to Trunnion and Hatchway and their fellows, but there are not many such in the score of Marryat's stories. There is straight-forwardness in his narrative; there is effectiveness in his descriptive passages; but there is no real strength and no grace of style in him anywhere; there is no reading of life; there is no appreciation of beauty; there is no lyric feeling. And yet there is something about him that distinguishes him in kind from such writers of boys' books as Mayne Reid and R. M. Ballantyne. The man was a forceful personality to his shipmates, to all the circles in which he moved; and, somehow, in a manner hard to define, the forcefulness found its way into his writing. Almost all the power that was in him, however, was in Smollett before him, in the Smollett of *Roderick Random* (1748). Marryat was a more modern and a more moral Smollett, but a lesser novelist.

Tom Cringle's Log (1836) by Michael Scott (1789-1835) was as famous in its day as any story of Marryat. To-day it is shrinking toward the value of an *Ocean Tragedy* of Clark Russell (1844-1911), or a *Castaways* (1916) of W. W. Jacobs (1868-   ). Scott delighted in West Indian nights, obi, sea-fights and the clash of races. He has no style, but he writes with his eye on the object.

It was the spectacle of Miss Edgeworth, perhaps, that set so many Irish ladies to writing in the early years of the last century. If she were so great a success in her presentation of Irish people and institutions and places, why should not other women of position in Ireland try their hand at like attempts? If Sir Walter Scott could go to school to her, as he owned, why not they? Lady Morgan, The Countess of Blessington, Mrs. S. C. Hall and Mrs. Caroline Norton all were publishing before *Traits and Stories of the Irish Peasantry* of Carleton began, in 1830, to make known to the English-speaking world Irish Ireland, peasant Ireland, from the standpoint of the Irish peasant himself.

Lady Morgan was of the people, though alienated from them somewhat by her theatrical associations and her social progress; the Countess of Blessington was the daughter of a Tipperary squireen; Mrs. Hall was a gentleman's daughter; and Mrs. Norton was of the famous house of Sheridan. Not one of the four is important as an artist but Lady Morgan and Mrs. Hall at least are important historically. In the verve and extravagance of *The Wild Irish Girl* (1806) of Lady Morgan (1777-1859) is foretold the work of W. Hamilton Maxwell (1792-1850), his *O'Hara* (1825), and *Wild Sports of the West* (1832). In the work of Maxwell is foretold the work of Lever.

In the *Sketches of Irish Character* (1829) there is writing about life seen at first hand by Mrs. Hall (1800-1881) in County Wexford. Her countryside, in appearance, is like a corner of Southern England rather than the bare Ireland of most of the story-tellers; and, in the well-being and contentment of its people, close to Arcadia. Bannow is a land of plenty and of peace, or what passes for peace in Ireland. There are fights, but they are with smugglers or riff-raff; there are bullying police and wild gentry, but they are kept in the background; on the whole it seems to be a community of hard working farmers prospering under an indulgent and stay-at-home landlord.

The copy of *Sketches of Irish Character* that I read is so beautiful a piece of book-making that I hate to acknowledge its stories are uninspired and dullish. They are not short-stories but tales that might well have been expanded to the length of her subsequent novels, *The Whiteboy* (1845) and *The Fight of Faith* (1869). Maclise has given to the *Sketches* several charming pictures of Irish girls; MacManus a spirited portrait of Mrs. Hall; and other distinguished hands are responsible for a series of figures and interiors and landscapes that summon before us many of the aspects of Irish life. Cruikshank is represented by one engraving; Gilbert by two; Weigall by several.

The Countess of Blessington (1789-1849) wrote on Ireland in *Grace Cassidy* (1833), recalling her girlhood in Clonmel. It is not a story of much interest of any kind. Both the Countess and Mrs. Norton hold a more important place for their command of the art of life than for their command of the art of letters.

My Irish friends are at one in saying that *Knockagow* (1879) will be found in almost every house in Ireland that boasts any novels at all. It is my own experience that every reading Irishman knows the book. It is a kind of homelier and less well-written *Cranford* (1853), a series of sketches of a village rather than the novel it professes to be. It reaches in some scenes all the way across the sea to America. The characters are not strongly individualized; they are close to the types we all know; but they are none of them too formal or too extravagant to be accepted as real people. *Knockagow* has the hold it has because it is a faithful picture of everyday Irish life; because it is about familiar emotions and situations; because it is warm-hearted. Charles Joseph Kickham (1826-1882) did another book that passes for a novel, *Sally Kavanagh* (1869), but it has never had the appeal of *Knockagow,* partly, perhaps, because it is a sad story.

CHARLES LEVER

The Irish novel was slow to develop even to such realism as there is in *Knockagow.* There is in the whole pageant of it, indeed, from Miss Edgeworth to George Moore, no more personable figures than those of Kickham and Lever, and no better writers. Charles Lever (1806-1872) is the best known Irish novelist to the English-speaking world. There are still two readers of *Harry Lorrequer* (1837) to one of *The Lake* (1905). It is not only the stuff out of which he makes his stories and the high spirits of their presentation that send people to them, but the illustrations of Hablot Browne and Cruikshank. A collected edition of thirty-seven volumes, 1897-1899, with the famous cuts, testifies to the continued appeal of Lever.

I never fell into the habit of reading Lever in boyhood, but he was everything to the boy across the way. And through all the thirty years and more that have passed since, that neighbor of mine has remained faithful to Lever. "The time devouring nightingale" sings for him whenever he sits down to *Charles O'Malley* (1841) and *Tom Burke of "Ours"* (1844). Lever is to him the most lighthearted, the most heart-easing, the most world-banishing of romancers. That admirer, American-born of Scotch-Irish parents, thinks that the best side of Irish life is its humor and sporting dash, and he believes that Lever has done Irish Ireland and the world a service of lasting value by catching these qualities in full swing.

Landlords, soldiers, travelers in quest of adventure, hunting folk of all sorts from squires to grooms, and bevies of beauties swarm in his pages. Such a diversity of material should perhaps tend to banish dullness, but dullness is inevitable where everything is either rattle-pated or second-rate or worse. Lever is as definitely second-rate as Trollope, but without the Englishman's consistent wholeness of tissue. Trollope has few ups and downs; Lever has downs from the second-rate and ups again to its level; but like Trollope he never transcends the second-rate. Trollope is plodding, prosaic, unromantic, faithful to a commonplace sort of characterization. Lever is mercurial, up to snuff, romantic after the way of the footlights, a caricaturist.

It was a grievance to Lever in his later years that he was not ranked with his great contemporaries. He discussed his ways of writing and his purposes in his prefaces, and he thought that some of the work of his maturity was major art. He was surest of *The Dodd Family Abroad* (1854). If nothing of his writing was major art, it was at least certain that his Irish novels were the medium through which England, and a good part else of the world, judged Ireland and the Irish. The Irish writers of today of strong nationalist purpose scold Lever for having made the Irish peasant into a buffoon or a jarvey or a "stage Irishman." The stage Irishmen of the several varieties that were popular a generation ago are, however, as much the creation of Boucicault as of Lever. Boucicault cheapened everything that he touched. He took, for instance, a creditable story, *The Collegians* (1829), of Gerald Griffin (1803-1840), and made it into a very shoddy play, *The Colleen Bawn* (1866).

Lever did not know the peasant on the land or in the fishing boat; he knew the peasant chiefly as servant, or village "character," or sunk into the condition of wanderer on the roads. And although the experiences of Lever as a doctor brought him into some contact with what of a middle class there was in his time in Irish Ireland, he was not largely concerned with such people in his novels unless they were eccentrics or those set apart by fate as very different from their fellows. His Mickey Free and

Darby the Blast owe something perhaps to the hands that created
Eddie Ochiltree and Sam Weller, but they owe more to that
witty man of the people so prevalent in Ireland. This character
is already described by folklore in "man Jack" whom you meet in
the tales about Dean Swift.

It was the Irish upper middle class and the gentry that Lever
generally presented, though his hero was often an English soldier stationed in Ireland, or an English idler traveling there. It
was the hard-riding, hard-drinking set, men quick to take offense
and delighting in duels, that he affected. His portraits of such
people, and, indeed, all of his Irish portraits, were drawn from
the life, and they were often recognized by those who, without
their knowledge, had sat to him. Historically, Lever will always
be valuable as a portrayer of a past era in Ireland, but the world
has now found out that as an artist he has never had more
standing than was left him after Thackeray published "Phil
Fogarty: A Tale of the Fighting Onety-Oneth. By Harry Rol-
licker." If you call that burlesque cruel, remember that all art
that counts outlasts any and all ridicule.

JAMES GRANT

Of second consequence though Lever be, there is a marked and
easily measured step down from his level to that of James Grant
(1822-1887), his follower in the novel of military life. The
stories of Grant have all the old and well-worn paraphernalia of
romance, historical backgrounds rather carefully done, and descriptions of landscape designed to please a rhetorical taste.
There are no characters really created, no experience of life recorded, few moments of intensity save of the stock sort. *The
Adventures of an Aide-de-Camp* (1848) is a fair sample of them.
It is readable after a fashion, but lacking any savor at all, almost
the only book by a Scot without tang that I ever read. Yet
Grant is reprinted, a long shelf of him, and the library cards in
the volumes show that he is still on modest demand.

Samuel Lover (1797-1868) is a lesser figure as a novelist than Lever. *Rory O'More* (1837) and *Handy Andy* (1842) were well-known books in their day and down to mid-Victorian times; and they still have their readers, *Handy Andy* the more. Neither of them is really a novel, but a series of incidents strung together in the picaresque manner, by the participation of the hero in all of them. It is a topsy-turvey Ireland they present, with caricatures instead of characters playing the principal parts. *Rory O'More* might be called a historical picaresque; *Handy Andy* a merry-go-round of everything extravagant and wild in the Ireland of its day. In *Handy Andy* you meet tinkers and beggars, jockeys and squires, priest and hedge schoolmaster, gentry and rag-tag and bobtail. And always you have with you the blundering hero. It is what its author owned it to be, "one of those easy trifles which afford a laugh," but it has its serious truth, too.

MICHAEL BANIM AND JOHN BANIM

Michael Banim (1796-1874) and John Banim (1798-1842) have more claim to be considered as faithful portrayers of the Ireland of their day. They collaborated in the three series of *Tales by the O'Hara Family* (1825-1827). These tales are of an avowed purpose, written to show England "the causes of Irish discontent and to insinuate also that if crime were consequent on discontent, it was no great wonder." They are of little more than historical interest. This same criticism holds true of almost all the writing of both brothers. The Banims give a rather gloomy picture of Irish life in their realistic stories of their own time, and they fail to get away from the obvious in their historical stories. *The Boyne Water* (1826) of John is, though, a book of large intention and of a great canvas. The stories of the Banims have even today something of a circulation among reading Irishmen, but such readers, in my experience, read them from a sense of duty rather than with delight. The Banims are little read elsewhere.

WILLIAM CARLETON

William Carleton (1794-1869) is a man of altogether greater parts than the Banims. He was just short of being a man of genius. He knew Ireland as no other man of his time knew it. He inherited a great store of folk-tales and folk-songs from his father and mother. His boyhood on a northern farm was rich in experience and his wanderings in youth had so added to that experience that when he published *Traits and Stories of the Irish Peasantry* (1830) the book was accepted as an epitome of Irish life. He had inherited, too, from his father the art of the shannachie, and he was able to retain a good deal of that oral art in the written word. Could he have retained all of it he would have been a great novelist. But he could not. The legends and the words of the shannachie are there and his knowledge of character, but not his tones of voice, his facial expression, his power of dialogue, his command of exact mimicry, his personality. The stuff of his tales is true, his fidelity to life never failing, his intention high, his architectonics good for an Irishman, but he lacks the ability to get into his writing those intimate qualities of the shannachie that make the telling of a tale a something beyond what all but the greatest actors can attain to in the reading of a part. I have always the feeling as I am reading Carleton that had I himself or his father there telling the tale I would have what my expectations lead me to hope for on the next page, but that I never find there in the perfection art demands.

Traits and Stories of the Irish Peasantry had not just those qualities that have made Irish novels lastingly popular abroad. There was a good deal that was hard in them, and the humor was not light-hearted. Then, too, they were tales, these stories, and not a novel, and the tale has never been so popular in England as the novel. So it is that for one reason and another they dwindled in significance with the years. *Fardorougha the Miser* (1838) and *Rody the Rover* (1845) are solid work but they are hardly so good in their kind as "The Poor Scholar" and "The Hedge Schoolmaster" of *Traits and Stories* in theirs.

There is intensity in "The Poor Scholar" and humor in "The Hedge-Schoolmaster," but there is not great characterization in either, nor is there great style. Even when Carleton comes upon a fundamental truth of Irish nature the words he finds to express it are not worthy of the discovery. "Of all the characters," he says in "The Poor Scholar," "of all the people of all nations on this habitable globe, I verily believe that that of the Irish is the most profound and unfathomable, and the most difficult on which to form a system, either social, moral, or religious." All the world will agree with the latter half of this statement, but no one is likely to maintain that it is put with distinction. Carleton had not the audience to draw out the best that was in him. There was not, in his lifetime, a large reading public of good taste in Ireland, and not many people outside of Ireland were interested in stories so wholly national in quality as his. In Ireland *Willy Reilly and His Dear Colleen Bawn* (1855) was his most popular, novel, possibly because it was founded on the most familiar of Irish ballads. It is far from his best.

LE FANU

Joseph Sheridan LeFanu (1814-1873), a grand-nephew of Richard Brinsley Sheridan started, as did Lever, as a member of the group that contributed to the *Dublin University Magazine*. His novels began in 1845, when he published *The Cock and Anchor,* though those that were best liked date from the sixties. These are tales of terror of eighteenth century lineage. *The House by the Churchyard* (1863), the first of this group, has still a kind of half-life, about like that of *The Fatal Revenge* (1807) of Maturin. From that day until our own, in which we have Matthew Phipps Sheil (1865-   ), there have always been Irishmen writing tales of terror. Not the least memorable of them is Bram Stoker (1847-1912) whose *Dracula* (1897) has hardly withered with the years. Were all its chapters as good as those first few about that castle in Transylvania, vampire haunted, it would be about the best of its kind in English. There is beauty as well as terror in this first part of the book. One remembers the wealth of fruit blossom about the hurrying coach, the contrast of the white of plum blow and the black of fir, and the still further contrast of all this softness of spring with the howling of wolves and the feline cruelty of the sinister Count.

MISS MITFORD

There were many women story-tellers busy with their art from the time of Scott to the time of Meredith, from the time of Miss Ferrier to the time of Miss Braddon. After the Brontës and George Eliot, Miss Mitford and Mrs. Gaskell were the most important of these, though Mrs. Charles Gore loomed larger in her day and generation. Mary Russell Mitford (1787-1855) did in *Our Village* (1824-1832) a series of "Sketches of Rural Character and Scenery" in which story and familiar essay blend delightfully. *Our Village* is in its lesser way as surely a classic as *The Essays of Elia*. It has an atmosphere and a tone, a quiet light of happiness, a cheerful stillness peculiar to itself. Though the interest does not center in any characters of first power yet you remember that stout farmer Miss Sally and Tom Cordery the poacher as you remember Tom Tipp of "The South-Sea House" or Sir Roger or Overbury's Milkmaid. Owing something itself to Crabbe and Miss Austen it, in its turn, influenced many other writers. Mrs. Hall owed as much to it for her method in *Sketches of Irish Character* (1829) as she did to Miss Edgeworth, and *Cranford* (1853) would not be the *Cranford* it is without *Our Village* to furnish precept and example.

MRS. CHARLES GORE

Mrs. Charles Gore (1799-1861), with seventy odd books to her credit, was a household word in America as well as in England. Many of her novels were reprinted here as soon as the first editions arrived from England. She came into her own with *The Manners of the Day, or Women as They Are* (1830). She was still enough of a person in 1847 for Thackeray to satirize her in *Novels by Eminent Hands*. It was perhaps *Mothers and Daughters* (1831) that led him to call his burlesque " 'Lords and Liveries.' By the Authoress of 'Dukes and Diamonds,' 'Marchionesses and Milliners,' etc., etc." Those titles indicate very fairly the content and emphasis of her work. Society in the exclusive sense was her concern, society and its smartness, and its intrigue and its wickedness. So much of a person was she in early Victorian times that she was thus praised by one of the collaborators in *A New Spirit of the Age* (1844): "As a painter of society, possessing knowledge of human nature, she leaves the Richardsons and Brookes far behind. The elasticity of her manner is perfectly unrivalled. If she rarely reaches the quiet humor of Madame D'Arblay, and never realizes the Dutch fidelity of Miss Austen, she preserves, upon the whole, a more sustained flight than either." And though the extravagance of this praise drives Richard Hengist Horne, as editor, to a qualifying footnote, the presence of such praise in such a seat of the mighty as *A New Spirit of the Age* proves what a figure she was in her own time.

FRANCES TROLLOPE

We hear more today of Frances Trollope (1780-1863) than we do of Mrs. Gore. That is for two reasons: that she was the mother of Anthony Trollope, and that she was the author of *Domestic Manners of the Americans* (1832). She followed this attack on our ways of living and extravagances and vagaries with a novel, *The Refugee in America* (1832), and the "States were mad clean through." The books of Mrs. Trollope were not more unjust in their ways than the *American Notes* (1842) and *Martin Chuzzlewit* (1844) in theirs. Mrs. Trollope was, as those she so adversely criticized would say, "apt and smart," but aptness and smartness and industry make up the most of her equipment as a novelist. She had unquestionably the knack of hitting the popular taste and her age gave her a good living for her writing. Her eldest son, Thomas Adolphus Trollope (1810-1892) was the author of a number of novels, now forgotten, as was, too, his second wife Frances Eleanor Trollope.

GRACE AGUILAR

A curious posthumous success as a novelist was that of Grace Aguilar (1815-1847), only one of whose stories *Home Influence, A Tale for Mothers and Daughters* (1847) was published in her lifetime. It ran through thirty editions before its first impetus was spent and it has still a quiet and steady circulation. You do not hear it much spoken of, but the cards in the library copies show it is still going the rounds. Miss Aguilar was, in her own words, "brought before the public principally as the author of Jewish works, and as an explainer of the Hebrew faith." Her first novel, however, religious and sentimental as it is, is not preoccupied with matters of race or faith, but with tractual exhibits of the fruits of good and bad home influence. It has little literary quality.

MRS. GASKELL

Mrs. Elizabeth Gaskell (1810-1865) is not, like Miss Mitford, the author of but one book that counts. There are fellows to *Cranford* (1853), if no equals. As in *Our Village* the appeal is in the spirit of the writing rather than in the characterization. You do not forget, of course, Captain Brown and his two so different daughters, or Miss Matty, or Martha and Jem, but they are at best but black and white sketches washed with watercolor. What you most delight in is the kindliness, the caring so much for little things of Mrs. Gaskell, the gentle gentility of it all, the fragrance as of wall-flowers about it, the blessed humanity that warms you to a glow as you read, the something like a benediction that is over you as you finish the last of its still pages. It is impeccably written, too, of a wholeness of silken tissue from start to close. One hesitates to speak of other books of Mrs. Gaskell, for none of them is of a class with *Cranford*. Everybody who knows the Brontës knows her as the biographer of Charlotte, and a great many people have been attracted by two so differing novels of hers as *Mary Barton* (1848) and *Sylvia's Lovers* (1863). Neither is in a mode really congenial to her. *Mary Barton* is a study of a Manchester workingman and *Sylvia's Lovers* a sensational yarn turning on the operations of the press-gang on the coast of Yorkshire late in the eighteenth century.

DINAH MARIA MULOCK CRAIK

Mrs. Dinah Maria Mulock Craik (1826-1887) is another author best remembered by one book, but that is a book that has a place in social history rather than in literature. *John Halifax, Gentleman* (1856) has been taken as almost spiritual fare by two generations of the folk who regard literature as a servant of morality. Yet it was disturbing to its own time, as disturbing as were to a later time such tracts as *The Autobiography of Mark Rutherford* (1881) of William Hale White (1831-1913), *The Silence of Dean Maitland* (1886) of Miss M. G. Tuttiett and *Robert Elsmere* (1888) of Mrs. Humphry Ward (1851-1922).

G. P. R. JAMES

They blame it on Thackeray that he is known as "solitary horseman James." It is not, however, the fault of "Barbazure," which doesn't use the phrase, but the fault of James himself that he is so known and that so he will be known as long as he is known at all. The "solitary horseman" was to him the very symbol of romance, and, romance being his business in all his scores of novels, he must use that figure to be at his best. It is often at the outset of the story, or at the opening of the second chapter, that we meet the "solitary horseman," or his doubling into "two horsemen," or his multiplication into "the cavalcade." And again, we do not meet him until far into the book, on the ninety-first page in *The Robber* (1838), and on the one hundred and twenty-third in *The Ancient Regime* (1841). In *The Robber* there is undoubtedly something of romance in our meeting with the hero. The counters are all old, it is true, but they are none the less effective in their undistinguished way—"solitary horseman," "moor," "mist," "bird of night," "stillness," "the western gleam in the water," "phosphoric lights," "feudal hold."

The stories of James (1801-1860) are still readable. You will follow interestedly the fortunes of the two boys, Hugh and Albert, who divide your sympathies in *Mary of Burgundy* (1833); you will grow curious about Richelieu old in *Richelieu* (1829) and Richelieu young in *Lord Montague's Page* (1858), his earliest novel and almost his latest; and you will track out all the intricacies of the plot of *The Robber*, and take to heart its fights, its imprisonments, its hair-breadth escapes, its burning castle, stock stuff though it all is. You will read them, however, with an interest hardly more than the interest of "seeing how it ends," and you will never want to read any one of them more than once, no matter how hard put you may be to kill time.

There is a marvellous boy, a page, in many of the novels of James, a Master Ned, a Jocelyn or a "Little Ball o' Fire." This character is as constant to him, almost, as his "solitary horseman," or as the breeched girl who masquerades as a boy is to one type of the Elizabethan drama. In *Lord Montague's Page, The Robber,* and *John Marston Hall* (1834) the page is the most romantic character of all.

The narrative of James runs easily, but it has no surprises; his characterization is of the faintest, and only clearly realizable when it parallels Scott's; his descriptions are of a stereotyped sort; his situation and dialogue are alike without humor; his style is without Style. Admirable human being that he was, James was as a writer but a fashioner of automata. There is no glint of distinction in him. He is not even a minor novelist. He is barely a third-rater. There is between James and such a typical second-

rate novelist as Stevenson that difference of quality that separates
that which is literature from that which is not.

When one thinks of the first-rate in literature, of how much
there is of that which is little regarded, one does not wonder that
James is but a name. What one does wonder is that he should
have been considered for so long and by so many people the successor of Scott. There are such people with us still, perfervid
admirers of his, or one time admirers at least. So much was
James to the boyhood of a man I know well that he rubbed his
hands together with delight at mention of "G. P. R." and said,
with a catch in his voice: "When I was young I was thrilled
through with expectation each time I sat down to a new book of
James. And he never disappointed me. No, sir. Never! I
don't know how it would be if I went back to him now. But
forty years ago I'd ride gladly all the nine miles into Ithaca to
get a book of his out of the library."

What shall we say in the face of such testimony as this? Just
this: Sentiment is a weak ally of any work of art. Only its
own perfection of conception and execution can keep it undimmed
down the years. The stories of James are not art at all. There
was that in his historical matter and in his presentation of it that
appealed to good men and true and intelligent. Critics of mid-
Victorian times contemporary to James saw his failings, R. H.
Horne in England and E. P. Whipple in America. They were
right in their severe judgments. Time has proved that. There
is little reading of him now. "Into the night go one and all"
of the third-raters when the generation whose taste they gauge
has been succeeded by another. They may have a half-life in
out of the way corners where the tastes of the older day persist, but sixty years after their heyday they are known only by
the antiquarians.

HARRISON AINSWORTH

It is Thackeray who is credited with having said of *Jack Shep-
pard* (1839): "Mr. Cruikshank really created the tale, and Mr.

Ainsworth, as it were, only put words to it." If that saying is not ten-tenths true it is at least nine-tenths true. And equally true it is to say today that what appeal there is still in the volumes of William Harrison Ainsworth (1805-1882) is there because of their illustrators, Cruikshank, or Hablot Browne. In the latest list that has come to me from London I find *"Old Saint Paul's, a Tale of the Plague and the Fire* (1841), engraved title and front by H. K. Browne, 1847"; and *"The Miser's Daughter, a Tale* (1842), illustrated by George Cruikshank, first 8vo edition 1848, cloth, re-cased and back neatly repaired," and *"The Lord Mayor of London,* or city life in the last century, first edition 1862, three vols., cr. 8vo, cloth, ex library copy, covers soiled;" and, *"Crichton; a romance* (1837), engraved title and plates by H. K. Browne, third edition 1849, revised, 8vo, cloth, fine copy."

The prices on these books range from £3 10s to £1 1s, the lowest being that volume which cannot boast either Browne or Cruikshank as illustrator, though it alone of the four is a first edition.

There is no question but that the stories of Ainsworth merit the oblivion into which they have fallen. The avowed object of their author when he began with *Rookwood* (1834) was "a story in the bygone style of Mrs. Radcliffe," but what he was really trying to do was to apply the methods of Scott to a portrayal of scenes from English history. Scott made now this part of Scotland, and now that, the background of his story. Ainsworth did this, too, to some degree, with his native Lancashire and other sections of northern England, but he cannily devised the practice of fitting a story to a place or building that was a national memorial like St. Paul's or the Tower of London. He loved to celebrate highwaymen, making a merit that it was their escapes he emphasized and not their robberies. There is really very little difference in the quality of his writing from that of the dime novels of a later period. There is a certain dignity, sometimes, in the historical material that he works into his stories, and he had the good fortune of illustrators of first rank and of good book-making, print, paper and binding. In his incident, however, he is as crude as any concocter of dime novels, in the architectonics of his story incredibly clumsy, and in his writing at its worst as stilted and banal as correctly written English has ever been. "Hence reptile" is a typical retort to an "abject minion of the law." He had no power of characterization at all, the nearest approach to it he could accomplish being a copy of Scott, whose Glosson he adapts from *Guy Mannering* for Potts in *The Lancashire Witches* (1848); or a borrowing of a character from history, such as Dick Turpin with whom, as Jack Palmer, you associate in *Rookwood* for quite a time before you discover him to be the noted outlaw. The show scene from *Rookwood* is the ride of Dick Turpin on Black Bess from London to York; but it is no better done than the escape of Luke Bradley from the keepers of Rookwood. There is no tale more often retold than that of the run of a gallant horse to its death; but perhaps even more typically English is the fight between keepers and poachers. Ainsworth writes here as well as he can write; your blood is stirred, as it has been so often by similar fights in story on story down to Richard Jefferies and Eden Phillpotts.

Ainsworth found himself on his native heath with *The Lancashire Witches*. It is a romance of Pendle Forest, most carefully studied from old documents and antiquarian records and local lore and visits to the scenes of the story. With all the pains that went to its making it ought to be a better thing than it is. Scores of characters jostle each other in it; fight after fight occurs; there is a sensation in every chapter: it is a precious brew. All the old ingredients of witchcraft are to be found here, omens, apparitions, pictures that fall from the walls, poison, swimming tests, wax-figures stuck with pins, burning at the stake. And despite all these, romance escapes him. Ainsworth was wise to invite comparison with Mrs. Radcliffe rather than with Scott. It is Scott, though, that he tried to imitate. Imagine if you can a Scott without power of character creation, and without humor and without romance, and you have some approximation, but no more than an approximation, to the littleness of Ainsworth.

GEORGE BORROW

No other English story-teller has been so completely identified with one subject as George Borrow (1803-1881). You can say of no one else that he is the writer about this or that as you can say of Borrow that he is the writer about gypsies. Such a restriction of a man to a subject would be too narrowing in one instance, as if you were to say of Dickens that he is the writer about cockneys. Or such an identification of a writer with a subject would give it too exclusively to one and one only, as if you were to say of Olive Schreiner that she is the writer about South Africa. Bret Harte comes nearer to such an exact identification with a subject than anybody else than Borrow. Harte is only a little other than the writer about the gold-rush in California.

There was writing about the gypsies earlier than Borrow, and, in Scott, good writing about them, or about their kind, notably in *Guy Mannering*. There was not, however, earlier than *The Zincali: or An Account of the Gypsies in Spain* (1841), any intimately informed writing about the true gypsies that was art of a high order. Those experts who write of Borrow's presentation of the gypsies have all some fault to find with it, but none of them much fault. All own his deep knowledge of the gypsies and their ways, Charles Godfrey Leland, Francis Hindes Groome, Theodore Watts-Dunton, John Sampson.

The Zincali was followed by four other compounds of autobiography and dream, *The Bible in Spain* (1843), *Lavengro* (1851) *The Romany Rye* (1857) and *Wild Wales* (1862), all but the last with much in them about the gypsies. Borrow boasted of world wandering, but all five of these books are made out of experiences either in Spain or Great Britain. Though there is much else than experiences with gypsies recorded in the four earlier books, the gypsy episodes dominate in all. He left the gypsies out of *Wild Wales,* perhaps because he had no intimate association with them on the trip from which the book grew. His wife and stepdaughter were with him in Wales and he had no such opportunities of hobnobbing with the Petulengros and their pals as when he had a free foot.

Watts-Dunton tells us that he once asked Borrow what he thought were the distinguishing characteristics of the gypsies and that Borrow replied: "Simplicity—frankness." It is these characteristics and the love of freedom and of wild places that inform the greatest passages about the gypsies in Borrow. One such is the famous passage about the "wind on the heath" in *Lavengro,* and another the passage about the cuckoo and the gypsy in *The Romany Rye.* Jasper Petulengro is the speaker in both passages. There are a hundred passages only less memorable that should be named. Many of them, indeed, call aloud for quotation, records of wild moments in Spain; the incident of the viper he tamed before he was three years old, that viper that was "a line of golden light"; pictures of the flare of a cross-roads forge through the night, and of a thunder-storm with livid glows of green and orange; of Stonehenge and drifts of sheep; of a bright night with moonlit Jupiter large among a million stars.

There is a gusto in wild living, and an exaltation, in some of such scenes, that you will not find together again in English literature until you come to Synge. Cunninghame-Graham has the gusto and W. H. Hudson the exaltation, but neither of the two, the two qualities together in anything like the degree of Borrow and Synge. Yet strange as it is in one who can kindle you as Borrow does there is an initial repulsion in the man that you have to overcome before you can enjoy his writing. There is something in his personality that affronts and alienates you, that all but disgusts you. Borrow makes a splendid spectacle of himself but it is repellent for all its splendor. The man was cold and selfish, difficult always, and of an intolerable pride. Candid he was, too, in his writing, so all these qualities confront you from the moment you begin to read him. Then there is the, episodic manner of his narrative to contend with, and the very varying interest of the incidents he relates, and the very varying worth of his writing. There are cheap passages and stilted passages and obvious passages along with the moments of beauty.

The best thing Borrow ever wrote, the story of Isopel Berners, is cheek by jowl with trumpery stuff about "The Man in Black." Gypsying with tinker's kit in his pony-cart, Borrow meets Isopel traveling with "The Flaming Tinman" and his mort. The men fight, the tinman loses, and Isopel stays in the dingle with Borrow. He half falls in love with her, a girl born in a workhouse, but now a Brynhild of the roads. He has no pride in her, however, in what of love he has for her, so she leaves him to go to America lest he marry her and be sorry. There is a pathos and a splendor in this story that makes it one of the great love-stories. There is a simplicity and a dignity and a bravery of endurance that allies it to the Icelandic tales. And strange as it may seem to our day it is a story of passion curbed and held. The beauty of Isopel was to Borrow something more than the beauty of a tree in flower, as was the beauty of Stangerd to Cormac, but in more ways than one the story of Isopel Berners recalls the Cormac saga. Borrow builded better than he knew, in these last chapters of *Lavengro* and these first chapters of *The Romany Rye*. To him, apparently, it was but an episode of that low life he delighted to exalt, this story that bridges the two books. It is but one of many chance romances of all sorts he found among farriers and horse-traders, among criminals, among prize-fighters, among the people of the roads.

There are a hundred silhouettes of people in Borrow, but few portraits full-length and detailed. Of this latter sort are his portrait of himself, of heroic mould and romanticized; and that of his pal, Jasper Petulengro; and that of the old harridan, Mrs. Herne; and most memorable of all that of Isopel Berners, that blonde giantess so stout-hearted and heavy handed, so tender and true.

ROBERT SMITH SURTEES

You will find Robert Smith Surtees (1803-1864), in new editions as well as in old, on the tables of certain country houses. Those who ride cross-country, those who love horses and dogs and fox-hunting, like to turn to remembered passages of his, and to look at pictures by John Leech of episodes in the Jorrocks saga. The escape of the hare at the very outset of *Handley Cross* (1843) is recounted nowadays when some unfortunate cottontail is gotten up by the Huntingdon Valley hounds; the Squire's son gives his dad as Christmas present the nineteen hundred and plus edition of *Mr. Sponge's Sporting Tour* (1853), with cuts of riders redfaced and redcoated, and horses and dogs galore; and the current biography of Surtees brings, one after another, a baker's dozen of generously plaided gentlemen to the corner of the bookstore where it is displayed, and the little pyramid of the big books, properly bound in scarlet, disappears within a fortnight.

Whether Surtees has other readers than the fox-hunters I do not know. Kipling has a pungent reference to his "Dickens-and-horsedung characters" in "My Son's Wife." I have tried the name of Surtees on other novelists of our day with varying results. Masefield knew him, but Masefield is of the hunting guild, as all who have read *Reynard the Fox* (1919) are aware; and James Stephens knew him, but Stephens comes from Ireland, where, until yesterday, as in England, the fox was a sacred animal. Other distinguished writers, however, made no comment when the name of Surtees came up in conversation. Divided into those who know Surtees and those who know him not are, too, the gentlemen who make their living by talking or writing about literature. I have met few "average readers" familiar with him, though the library records show a slight demand for all of his books from *Jorrocks's Jaunts* (1838) to *Mr. Facey Romford's Hounds,* published posthumously in 1865. And wherever you come upon *Handley Cross,* in home, in old bookshop, in public library, it is apt to be dogeared or broken backed.

There is no universality of appeal in the man, though there is always in his writing that hurly-burly and that helter-skelter precipitancy of incident on incident that are supposed to drive away dullness and the blues. He is humble enough about his stories, telling us in the preface to *Handley Cross* that "the work merely professes to be a tale, and does not aspire to the dignity of a novel." Though it was not written, as were those opening chapters of *Pickwick* it somewhat resembles, to provide letter-press for sporting cuts, it reads often as if that had been its purpose. Surtees is, as Kipling points out with over-emphasis, a kind of sporting Dickens. Mr. Jorrocks, his chief creation, is the cockney tradesman become master of hounds. He is, of course, a caricature, but there is a certain reality underlying the caricature. The members of his hunt and their retainers, and their women-kind, are caricatured, too. Caricature is, indeed, the way of his art in all of his books. There is little freshness in the caricaturing, the figures being of the old type, and his incident, tumultuous and hurried, is of the sort conventional in the rough and tumble story from the time of Smollett.

What is best in Surtees is a sort of racy Britishness. He is strongly prejudiced and proud of his prejudices. "The fox is the thing. . . . 'Unting exemplifies wot the grammarians call the three degrees of comparison:—stag-'unting is positively bad, 'are-'unting superlatively so." He loves old England, the old ways, the old blood, the color of the life of old times. He likes the fowls of yesterday, peacocks and white dorkings; he likes the baying of hounds in kennel, and a good song with a rollicking chorus, like "Cappy's the dog"; he likes game-pie and black puddings; he likes wines with body, no "claretty stuff," and brandy; he likes chimney pots and old walls deep with ivy; he likes wide-spreading oaks and firm turf to gallop upon; he likes, in short, what he was born to as a north-country gentleman. He is no snob; the cockney is understood and accepted by him, and the vulgar everywhere forgiven much for the humanity there is in them. He can sympathize even with him who because he "understands 'osses rayther too well" can overreach his friend in a horse deal. No writer is more hail fellow well met than Surtees. His hearty slogan is "where there's ceremony there's no frindship." But always, in all moods, he is "the good old English gentleman."

It is the custom to bracket G. J. Whyte-Melville (1821-1878) with Surtees. Both were gentlemen riders and both wrote of the hunting field. Surtees lost his nerve toward sixty and left off riding to the hounds; Whyte-Melville kept his, and it cost him his life at fifty-seven. He was found stone-dead in a plowed field just at the start of a hunt. The explanation of Sir Herbert Maxwell is that "the good horse must have crossed his legs and fallen on his rider." A fine man in all ways, Whyte-Melville was unlucky in many ways. His soldiering in the Crimea went well with him; but his marriage was unhappy. He was unlucky, too, in that he had few writing friends against whom to measure himself; and unlucky, too, in that he, somehow, missed Leech as illustrator of his stories. Several other third-rate novelists have acquired the longer life of the second-rate through their illustrators.

Nor was he fortunate in the selection of illustrators for the collected edition of his works in twenty-eight volumes under the editorship of Maxwell in 1898-1902. A racier art than that of Thomson, or Brock, or Caldwell, or Jalland, is needed for *Riding Recollections* (1875), for *Digby Grand* (1853), for *The Gladiators* (1863), for *Katerfelto* (1875). Whyte-Melville has had to stand on his own merits as a writer. Those merits are considerable, but no more than considerable. He is an artist of a kind, a better writer than Ainsworth or G. P. R. James, but with only a little more gift of characterization. His range is far wider than that of Surtees, though he lacks the pungency of the Yorkshireman, and wider, too, than that of "Nimrod" (Charles James Apperley, 1779-1843).

First and last and always Whyte-Melville was the gentleman, to the manner born, chivalrous, punctilious as to the minutiæ of his code. Fond as he was of horses there was nothing horsey about him. Good soldier that he was there was little of the martinet in him and no pride of brass buttons. His writing was a hobby to him, a hobby second only to his riding to his hounds.

He had a private fortune and so he could give away to good causes what he made by his pen.

In the novel he never wrote a better book than *Digby Grand,* with which he began, in 1853. It is a hollow-hearted book, a story of a life that came to little. No one reading it is deceived by the happy ending. That is forced, unbelievable. In many ways it is a parallel study to *Pendennis* (1850), but of aristocratic life. It has plenty of variety, with scenes of English county life, of army life at home and in Canada, of horse-racing, of the stage, of the usual round of the young man of fashion. There is a "star" chapter, "The Great Haverley Run," about as well done as the cross-country of Kingsley, almost as well done as the fox hunts in Somerville and Ross.

It may be that Whyte-Melville owes what place he has today to the cross-country folk who collect him, but there are other books of his than the hunting sort that have a place in the affections of men. One of these is *The Gladiators.* This has been accepted as what it was intended to be, a proud story of imperial sweep, ranging in its scenes from a Rome of luxury and pomp and cruelty to a Judea of fanaticism and sounding arms. There is a splendid Briton in it, Esca; and a still more splendid patrician lady of Rome, Valeria, who turns amazon and fights in golden armor; and a gentle Jewish girl converted to Christianity, who marries Esca after all the toil and trouble in the world.

Cerise (1866) was much loved a generation ago, especially in America, as its reprintings here show, and, apparently, by other than sporting people. It has in it Louis le Grand, and obi and a rising of negroes in the West Indies, and Jacobite plotting in England and a happy ending. *Katerfelto* has good hunting in it, stag-hunting; and gypsies, in whom Whyte-Melville was keenly interested; and a charlatan of towering temper.

In *The Interpreter* (1858) the scene shifts as often as it does in a picaresque story. Now it is Hungary we have to do with, and Austrian officers and gypsies; now school in Somersetshire, and poaching adventures, and manor-houses; now it is Hungary again, an old chateau and princes; now war in Wallachia, with men of many countries involved, Russian, Turkish, Hungarian, Belockee, English; then Vienna with masked ball and broken hearts; then Constantinople, and beauties of the harem, and horrors; and then the Crimea. There our hero loses by a shot a black retriever that had been his companion in all these wanderings. The dog's death is almost the end. There is Hungary again and a tragedy in a boar-hunt, the return to England, and a hint of a happy ending.

In none of these novels do you find a rich revelation of human nature. All that is set down sounds true enough, but you enter into no such intimacy with the characters as you do in the books of the great novelists. His comment in the novels is seldom more profound than that of the seasoned clubman. It is the product of a conventionalized worldly wisdom, disillusioned and weary, but redeemed just a little by the ingrained chivalry of the man.

In *Bones and I* (1868) and *Riding Recollections* (1875) is better stuff, discoveries about life from deeper soundings than those of the novels. Yet he is not a proved essayist either. Always in Whyte-Melville there is a falling short of high intentions. You cannot call him an amateur, but there is always something of the amateur about him. He never learned to realize the possibilities of what was in him as does the master of an art.

CHARLES READE

It is not easy for the respecter of tradition to hold in little appreciation what has been once of large importance to the world. It is not easy for one whose *Peg Woffington* (1853) and *Christie Johnstone* (1853) are the first editions of those books bought by his father on publication to have to say that time has been just in its belittlement of Charles Reade (1814-1884). It is the usual thing to except *The Cloister and the Hearth* (1861) from the inevitable shrinkage that has come alike upon his plays and novels. And yet if the truth is to be told it must be said that even this great panorama of the Europe of the fifteenth century retains what life it has almost solely as a transcript of history. There are rushes of narrative in it so well sustained for a while that you call them epical, and then will come such a collapse as brings the whole episode down in ruins. Such a collapse is that occasioned by his description of the fight with the bear in the wayfaring of Gerard and Denys; so extravagantly absurd is this that it reads like a travesty of a romance of chivalry.

Again and again what were once regarded as his great "show" passages are fallen to poor things enough now; what were once regarded as moments of high tragedy now disclose themselves as no more than melodrama. Parts of all writing, even of writing of the highest power, may be outmoded by time, but other parts of such writing, the great situations that are inevitable, and nobly felt, and grandly fashioned; the readings of life that show insight and vision; the store of wisdom that is come of years of rich experience and deep sympathy with men; the characters that are vital, that are no mere compounds of manners and eccentricities—these are still ours whether it was Solomon or Sappho originated them, Æschylus or Shakespeare, Cervantes or Goethe, Ibsen or Hardy. Art of such sort stands foursquare against the years; and even slighter things, whose makers' names are lost, like "The Twa Corbies" and "Edward," are indestructible. There must be, always, power of the highest order in writing, if it is to survive. It is just this power of the highest order that Reade lacks. After his gift of epical narrative his greatest gift is in the presentation of women in their bloom. There is a graciousness, a freshness, a warm sympathy, a very breath and glow of womanliness about Nance Oldfield and Christie Johnstone when we first meet them in the pages of Reade. The pity is he cannot keep them before us, throughout the story, with the vitality with which he first presents them.

What of natural genius he had in story-telling was for the short novel. He could fail in that, too, witness *Clouds and Sun-*

shine; but in *Peg Woffington,* the *Masks and Faces* of himself and Tom Taylor turned into a novel, and in *Christie Johnstone,* he is at his best. That best, however, was clearly short of the best of the great novelists. There was no real richness of experience in the man for him to draw upon. For all the incident he manufactures for his tales and long novels, they are of a meager humanity. The characters are apt to be types, the situations stock, the writing careless, the comment of the writer on the actions of his puppets conventional or platitudinous.

There is a group of his stories that are unequivocally novels with a purpose. *It is Never Too Late to Mend* (1856) attacks the abuses of the prisons of its day; *Hard Cash* (1863) attacks mad-houses; *Foul Play* (1869) attacks ship-knackers; and *Put Yourself in His Place* (1870) attacks trades-unions. He justifies this practice of the tractual story. "I have taken," he says, "a few undeniable truths out of many, and have labored to make my readers realize those appalling facts of the day which most men know, but not one in a thousand comprehends, and not one in an hundred-thousand realizes, until fiction—which, whatever you may have been told to the contrary, is the highest, widest, noblest, and greatest of the arts—comes to his aid, studies, penetrates, digests the hard facts of chronicles and blue-books, and makes the dry bones live."

It was not, unfortunately, a long life that he was able to give the dry bones he set about vitalizing in these stories. They lasted just about a generation. In boyhood I followed eagerly the exciting machinery he made to carry the heavy weight of purpose in these stories, but on turning to them now all looks perfunctory, a little cheap, obvious, distorted, or melodramatic. *Griffith Gaunt* (1866) I missed somehow in those old days, so I looked forward to reading it with an expectation very other than one can bring to a re-reading of any story, no matter how loved in some by-gone period of life. There was no danger with this book, previously unread, of finding a one-time treasure tarnished by the years. I could resign myself to it with no memories of my own to trouble me, and no preconceived prejudices, for

I had heard scant talk about it, and written criticism of an unread book makes little impression on one. I wanted to like *Griffith Gaunt,* but I could not. It bored me; I did not care for the characters; I had a very moderate interest as to whether things turned out well or ill for the heroine and hero. I had hoped to have another pleasant association with Charles Reade to store away alongside of my memory of Christie Johnstone on her first meeting with Ipsden; and my memory of Ellen Terry as Nance Oldfield, whose Nance was the very woman that Reade created in *Art: A Dramatic Tale,* back in 1855. I had to forego that third association. I had to content myself with the portraits of those two so gracious women of long ago.

ANTHONY TROLLOPE

It is ironical that *An Autobiography* (1883) should be today the best known book of Anthony Trollope (1815-1882). It is more ironical that it should be among writers and students of literature that an author once so popular with the general public now wins his most interested readers. There is no means of finding out what is his most read book. That may be one of the Barsetshire cycle—*The Warden* (1855), or *Barchester Towers* (1857), or *Doctor Thorne* (1858), or *Framley Parsonage* (1861), or *The Small House at Allington* (1864), or *The Last Chronicle of Barset* (1867); or *Orley Farm* (1862), the affinities of which to a detective story help to keep it going the rounds; or *Phineas Finn* (1869), much talked of and quoted in the seventies and eighties.

There is no doubt, however, that there is now more discussion in print about *An Autobiography* than about any other book of Trollope, and that that discussion is largely occasioned by his frank acknowledgment of his mechanical methods of writing, of his so many words an hour, his so many pages a day. His average productivity in his best years was ten thousand words a week. So general is the knowledge of these methods of his that all criticism of him is written with them in mind. Such criticism is, perhaps, prejudiced, but I do not think, in the long run, it has worked to the limiting of his readers. What the critics say may help a writer to a public, but when a novelist is once established it is what Beth says to Sue that keeps his books read. Marie Corelli and Mrs. Florence Barclay, once known to the public, needed middlemen no longer.

Trollope did not delude himself into the belief that he was a man of genius. Again and again in his autobiography he owns his limitations, claiming only for himself that he is a hardworking and faithful and moral writer. He is a craftsman proud of his skill and convinced that he is worthy of his hire. Of all the many gifts that go to the making of greatness in literature he had none in full power. And whatever theories may be held as to what makes a writer of first rank, it is a fact that no English novelist has been judged of such rank unless he has been of first power in some of his gifts.

Trollope is not a master of narrative. He has created no characters to rank with Cressida or Mistress Quickley, with Parson Adams or Sir Charles Grandison, with Emma Woodhouse or Davie Deans, with Harry Foker or Lord Jim. Mrs. Proudie is his nearest approximation to such a figure, but she is a half-caricature. Mr. Crawley and Mr. Slope are true enough to life but they are not fully realized, and not of any distinction. Trollope himself thought Chaffinbrass in *The Three Clerks* (1858) and Lucy Robarts in *Framley Parsonage* were as good work as he had done in characterization, and that *The Last Chronicle of Barset* was, as a whole, his best novel. There is a great flaw in the plot of this last novel, however, and another flaw in the characterization of Mr. Crawley, who is, too, involved in situations not unlike those of Mr. Slope in *Barchester Towers*.

Trollope has no moments of great drama. He has no real humor, but only a pleasant suggestion of humor. There is no lyricism in him, no kindling descriptions of landscape or pageantry, no flashes of insight that lay bare the secrets of the heart, no distinction of style. In the last analysis of any work of art we ask ourselves: what new beauty is here? Ask that question of a lyric of Herrick or of an essay of Lamb and the answer will be that though either may be called minor, there is in it new beauty, a perfection of art. Ask that question of an *Old Mortality* or a *Tess* and the answer will be that though either may have dull chapters there is in both stories "the authentic presence vast" of genius. Ask this question of Trollope, and you must answer there is no new beauty in his writing. Such powers as he has are all of them of the second order, or of an order less than second.

No word of Trollope brings to you a more vivid sense of his shortcomings than his statement that it was a visit to Salisbury that suggested to him *The Warden*. You think of the great cathedral, the glory of it rose-red in the sunset, the lush green of its walled close, the lift of its spires, the symbolism of its windows and pinnacles, its centuried association with the daily lives of men; and then you appraise the beef and ale and Yorkshire pudding of his novels. Hawthorne intended his characterization of them as lumps of earth, giant-hewn, to be commendatory, but he intended it, I think, to be belittling too.

There is gossip of the cathedral close in *The Warden* and the rest of the Barsetshire series; there is gossip of the cathedral town; there is gossip of the countryside round about the cathedral; but there is nothing at all of the wonders of the great pile in them, and nothing at all of the wonders of the plain it looks out upon, that plain that bears on its broad folds the great temple of Stonehenge and its hundreds of prehistoric barrows.

It is one aspect, chiefly, of the English that we find in this series, that aspect that led their Welsh neighbors to call the English "dull and creeping Saxons." The material of the series is English, the politics of the close, the snobbishness, the social conventionalities, the hunting, the pride of cellar and of place. And the method of presentation is English, too. The traditional form of the novel is followed; moral suasion is attempted; the Latin tags crop out as they do in the conversation of the clergy.

So Trollope intended it to be. Of *Framley Parsonage* he says: "The story was thoroughly English. There was a little fox-hunting and a little tuft-hunting; some Christian virtue and some Christian cant. There was no heroism and no villainy. There was much Church, but more love-making. And it was downright honest love, in which there was no pretence on the part of the lady that she was too ethereal to be fond of a man, no half-and-half inclination on the part of the man to pay a certain price and no more for a pretty toy."

Trollope is particularly English in such glorying as this in the absence of hypocrisy and in the honest earthiness of love. And he is just as English, but this time Puritanly English in the complacent morality of his boast: "I do believe that no girl has risen from the reading of my pages less modest than she was before, and that some may have learned from them that modesty is a charm well worth preserving. I think that no youth has been taught that in falseness and flashness is to be found real manliness but some may perhaps have learned from me that it is to be found in truth and a high but gentle spirit." Such a passage, little as it has to do with art, reveals a pleasanter state of mind in the writer than that parallel passage of Arnold Bennett in which he tells of the books of a later generation that broke down the morality of Carlotta.

Time dealt pretty justly with the novels of Trollope during his lifetime. It sifted out his less important work and left the Barsetshire series and *Orley Farm,* and *Phineas Finn* (1869) and *Phineas Redux* (1873) as the nine books that counted out of three score then published. That was pretty much the valuation of Trollope to which I was brought up by my father, though he rejected the two *Phineas Finns.* That, exactly, was the valuation of Frederic Harrison in 1895, and that is pretty much the valuation as arrived at by the consensus of critical opinion today.

There has been a recent attempt to bring about a revival of Trollope. Two books about him by skilled propagandists attest to his continuing appeal to literary men. That he will return, however, to anything like his Victorian reputation is problematical. He will be valuable, historically, for his pictures of English life during the third quarter of the nineteenth century, and equally valuable, historically, for his pictures of Irish life of a slightly earlier period. Because of a special concern with English literature in Ireland I have read gladly his earliest novels, *The Macdermots of Ballycloran* (1847) and *The Kellys and the O'Kellys* (1848), but I doubt if they have much appeal today to anyone not particularly interested in their subject-matter. As a boy I heard some talk from other boys about *Phineas Finn,* but neither the philandering nor the political intrigue appealed to me as have, more recently, the pictures of Irish life in his earliest novels.

Orley Farm I found harder to reread at fifty than it had been to read at twenty-five. My joy in Trollope, indeed, has never been more than moderate, and it grows more moderate with the years. I like, to a degree only short of sentimentality, the Victorian life he describes. I like his ideals of conduct and of sport, and my politics are not very far from his. Despite those prejudices, however, I am driven to own him of a lower order of ability than the greater novelists. Just as surely he is on a plane above the lesser, above Bulwer and Disraeli. He is prosy but readable, creeping but never wholly dull, a consistent second-rater who is always safe and sound.

CHARLES KINGSLEY

Charles Kingsley (1819-1875) meant a great deal to his own time; he means comparatively little to ours. To mid-Victorian England, and, in only a less degree, to English-speaking people everywhere in the mid-years of last century, he was a very Titan. He was novelist, maker of fairy-tales, song-writer, interpreter of natural science, champion of the underdog, defender of the faith, and prophet. Above all, and despite the fact he was little-traveled, he was the very personification of English England, of that imperialistic England that owed, he thought, its world conquering to its seamen of Scandinavian ancestry, to vikings, to Elizabethan sea-rovers, to Nelson and his peers, to the men who manned the ships through all the seven seas in Kingsley's own day.

A boys' book, and two or three songs, and a couple of lyrics, all just short of the best of their kind, is what Kingsley is valued for by the English-speaking world today. There are better things in him, perhaps, than these. There is *At Last* (1871), his record of travel in those West Indies that all his life he had looked forward to visiting, that he believed so surely the Earthly Paradise. That book holds a more honored place among books of travel than any novel of his in the long list of novels of power. It is not so great as *Arabia Deserta* (1888) of Doughty, or as *The Bible in Spain* (1843) of Borrow, but look back through all the long vista from Tomlinson's *Tidemarks* (1924) to *Coryat's Crudities* (1611) and you will find few of its fellows that will hold your attention more closely. There are *Hereward the Wake* (1866) and *Hypatia* (1853), in many ways the best of his novels. It is by none of these, however, that he is best known: but by *Westward Ho!* (1855); "The Sands of Dee" and "The Three Fishers" and "Young and Old"; and "The Last Buccanier" and "Airly Beacon."

The fen country of East Anglia, which is the background of many of the scenes of *Hereward,* made more of an appeal to his imagination than any other corner of England save Devon, and he knew it better than he knew Devon. The fens were a fresher field, too, than Devon, less written about, more his own than the gentlemen adventurers and their outfittings for Eldorado. He had not a specialist's knowledge of the vikings, but he had found their gear in the fens, and he had visualized them sharply in places he knew well. A part of his boyhood had been passed in the fens, and his college days in Cambridge close to them. The story of *Hereward* had grown slowly in his mind all his young and middle years. Given to the world when he was forty-seven, it had not about it the signs of hurry that all the other stories show so openly. It has ease, and spaciousness, and inevitability. You know from the start, because of what you know of history, that the hero, for all his prowess, will be overcome in the end by fate. And his nature, as Kingsley interprets it, is bound to undo him. You know Hereward more intimately than you do any other of Kingsley's heroes, even when, as in *Yeast* (1848), the hero is much more the author himself. Hereward has, of course, the impetuosities, the mad moments, the gusts of passion of his maker, as he has his gift of song, but Hereward is, in the main, faithfully presented from the records that have come down to us of the historical Hereward. We are unfortunately reminded here and there, by footnotes and by references in the text of the story, that it is partly made out of material read up for the purpose of writing it. *Hereward* did not come from so full a store of old knowledge as do the historical novels of Scott that are made out of the past of Scotland, *The Abbot*, for instance, and *The Fair Maid of Perth*. It is, for all that, the most unified and the most completely realized story of Kingsley.

Westward Ho! was, too, partly of material that came to him by oral tradition and by his own knowledge of Devon. A Barbadoan grandfather had told him much of the West Indies and had made real to him sea-fighting there in the late eighteenth century and older engagements the memories of which had not died out in the islands.

There was, of course, more first-hand material in his novels of the England of his own time than in the historical novels, *Hypatia, Westward Ho!* and *Hereward*. All his shortcomings are more apparent, however, in *Yeast* (1848) and *Alton Locke* (1850) and *Two Years Ago* (1857) than in the romances. There are realities known to us all in the life depicted here by which to measure the truth of their action. In such stories of a society not unlike that we know well, we will not give the author the rope that Hawthorne says we must give him in the romance. *Yeast* and *Alton Locke* are both amateurish and crude, and *Two Years Ago* an unassimilated hodge-podge of adventure and Christian Socialism and American Slavery and satire of English conventions. He is concerned with the agricultural poor in *Yeast* and with the poor of city slums in *Alton Locke;* the running amuck of the mob in *Hypatia;* and the shipwreck in *Two Years Ago.* These scenes are all vividly done. They are his writing at its best, they and his descriptions of landscape.

There are few real creations of character in Kingsley. His protagonists are types like Tom Thurnall; or symbols like Amyas Leigh; or rebodyings of heroes out of old legend like Hereward. You remember, as more true to life, certain men of humble station, like Tregarva, Saunders Mackaye, Salvation Yeo, and Martin Lightfoot. You remember, too, certain intellectuals with a queer twist to their natures, like Aben-Ezra and Elsley Vavasour.

Kingsley labors hard to present ideal women as his heroines, but they have little of the savor and tang of life. They are a boy's women rather than a man's. Indeed, boyishness is to be found in all his ways and works. It is winning in itself but it is not transmuted into fine art. It has won to him many boys who had the itch to write, as well as many more boys who had the itch to see the world. It won to him Noyes, who remains boyish-minded in his maturity, and it won to him Kipling, who has developed the tradition he received from Kingsley into something far finer than Kingsley could make of it. For what he was to his time, and for his influence on later writers of the English England school Kingsley is to be remembered. As a novelist he is steadily losing place. Time is righteously cruel to all but the great.

WILKIE COLLINS

What pretensions Wilkie Collins (1824-1889) has to a place in English letters rest in his mastery of plot. In plot and plot alone, of all the qualifications of the novelist, has he succeeded in a high degree. Count Fosco, of *The Woman in White* (1860) is thought by his admirers to be a great character. Certain it is that he has bred many others of his ilk in the fiction of the years subsequent to his appearance, notably the hero of

Maugham's *Magician* (1908). Fosco is, however, what Carlyle called "deceptively enacted" rather than created.

It is difficult for the seasoned reader to believe in such a monster of cold wickedness even while the book is being read. It is impossible for such a reader to believe in Fosco after the book is laid aside. Fosco may even become in memory, not a far remove from the " 'sdeath villain" type of the stage. Melodrama, indeed, is what these stories of Collins all are essentially, melodrama with a secret to be discovered, a mystery to be cleared up. You read them, if you read them at all, for the satisfaction of the puzzle interest that is in all men; and you like, not more than mildly, a thrilling fight or a murdering fire you meet by the way. Collins believed the novel should have as rigidly designed a structure as the melodrama, that the novel was but a kind of play written out in greater detail than was possible in the three hours allotted to a piece on the stage. He would have damned with fervor, had he read it, that passage in Trollope's *Autobiography* in which Trollope expressed his belief as to what it should be. Collins had, save plot, none of the attributes his senior thought the novel should have. Says Trollope: "A novel should give a picture of common life enlivened by humor and sweetened by pathos. To make that picture worthy of attention the canvas should be crowded with real portraits, not of individuals known to the world, or to the author, but of created personages impregnated with traits of character which are known. To my thinking, the plot is but the vehicle for all this; and when you have the vehicle without the passengers, a story of mystery, in which the agents never spring to life, you have but a wooden show."

That is what Collins is mostly, just "a wooden show" with marionettes pulled about by wires that jingle and ring. The stage itself comes into much of his writing, into stories of as different sorts as that Christmas tale, *The Stolen Mask*, and as that long novel, *The New Magdalen* (1873). Collins dramatizes easily, and four of his novels, *The Woman in White*, *No Name* (1862), *Armadale* (1866) and *The New Magdalen*, he himself turned into stage pieces that lived as long as did most stage pieces of their time. I knew Mercy Merrick from flamboyant billboards I gaped at in childhood, before I read of her sorrows and her redemption in *The New Magdalen*. Mercy is not so wholly a lay figure as is the heroine of *The Woman in White*. If Laura Fairlie were flesh and blood we could hardly stand her degradation in her marriage with Sir Percival Glyde. It is just as well to have wooden figures, or figures of lath and plaster, in tales of such violence as these of Collins.

In the eighteen-eighties, when I began to read widely, *The Moonstone* (1868) was still a much-loved book. It interested me then, for the one reading a detective story can hope for, but it disappointed me, even then, for the lack of fascination in the jewel itself. The yellow diamond did not make me visualize it as did certain jewels of *The Arabian Nights*, and it fell far below the romance and beauty of the stone from the serpent's head that flashes out of *The Shaving of Shagpat* (1856). So, too, by the bye, does the idol's eye of Dunsany. *A Night at an Inn* (1916), however, does not ring so hollow as *The Moonstone*. You are, of course, interested to find out who is the thief, or rather to find out who Collins made the thief, for you never have a sense of inevitability in the story. You have little interest in what happens to most of the characters.

Now that a new kind of mystery story, that of Conan Doyle, has come and gone, and a still newer sort, that of Algernon Blackwood, has pleased and is passing, even the unsophisticated find Collins but dull to mildly interesting. Readers nowadays must be caught very young to care for his marvels. Save for his plots he is but a sort of washed out Dickens, of faint characterizations, styleless, posturing, ultra-melodramatic. Collins has not even the gift of story-telling. He arranges the sequence of his incidents most skilfully; he varies the scene frequently; he keeps you guessing; but he has not the bright vividness of personality of a Kipling, for instance, that holds you spellbound as the tale is unfolded, or those changes of pace and tone of writing, that preserve the qualities and ways of the speaking voice always present in the born story-teller. Wilkie Collins was a nine days' wonder of day before yesterday. Today he is just about what you would expect a nine days' wonder of day before yesterday to be.

CHAPTER X

THE HIGHER PROVINCIALISM OF GEORGE ELIOT

THE genius of George Eliot (1819-1880) was an unaccountable sport from the grave and brooding nature of Marian Evans. Those who knew Miss Evans of Griff House as neighbor and those who knew Miss Evans of Coventry as friend could recognize her in the translator of Strauss's *Leben Jesu* (1846) and in the writer of the descriptive passages of the novels of George Eliot, but they could not understand how the young woman they had known could have created Mrs. Poyser and Mr. Tulliver or have attained to such humor and racy reality as mark the dialogue of *Adam Bede* (1859) and *The Mill on the Floss* (1860). Some one from their corner of the Midlands must have written *Scenes from Clerical Life* (1857) and *Adam Bede,* for episodes the neighborhood remembered were embodied in them. That Marian Evans had been a writer from girlhood they knew, but they never suspected her of the gifts of story-telling and dramatic power. George Eliot was of a nature richer than they had been able to discern in Robert Evans's youngest child.

Nor did the most of those about her in her first years in London (1851-1856) look to a future for her in creative writing. They were few of them artists themselves, the greater number being middlemen who dispensed current ideas and newly discovered scientific facts to the growing public interested in intellectual things. Two of them alone showed appreciation of her potential powers. Herbert Spencer, the man of first importance among the group, was one of these. It was not to be expected that one of his interests should discover the artist in Marian Evans, yet he guessed it was there and suggested to her that she write a novel; nor was it to be expected that the man who did discover the artist in her, George Henry Lewes, was possessed of such insight. One does not look for powers of divination in a jack of all trades.

Lewes had no certainty, though, that she would succeed in the experiment of fiction. It was worth her while to try, he felt, and try she did, and had luck with her trial. *The Sad Fortunes of the Rev. Amos Barton* (1856) happened to hit the fancy of many mid-Victorians. It was no such success as *Pickwick* had been but it interested so many people that John Blackwood, in whose magazine it had appeared, welcomed another story from her.

Marian Evans and Lewes, fellow hacks, had been writing side by side for two years when *Amos Barton* was begun. They had talked over the chances of her success with fiction again and again, as those who live by writing must talk over any possible new line of endeavor. And, indeed, even as far back as her Coventry days, that is prior to 1851, she had considered writing a novel. That she had given a great deal of thought to the subject just previous to the undertaking of *Amos Barton* is apparent from her article in "The Westminster Review" of July, 1856, "The Natural History of German Life." The memorable passages of this article are all out of her observation of Midlands life and her thought upon it. There is no influence of Lewes in these passages, and it may be that his rôle in her development as a story-teller was but that of encourager. Yet it may be, too, that she had never written stories at all without his encouragement.

They both mistrusted her powers of imagination, of invention, of drama. And, indeed, for better and for worse, she had little of such powers. What she had was the gift of story-telling, the gift of character creation, humor, a deep if narrow experience of certain phases of Midlands life, a memory that retained with astonishing accuracy remarks and speeches and dialogues she had heard, and an impulsive and warm-hearted sympathy with human weakness. So scant was her experience of life that she was soon written out. After the fresh and pleasing 'prentice work of the *Scenes from Clerical Life* she achieved two master-pieces in *Adam Bede* and *The Mill on the Floss*, both books made almost wholly out of her own individual experiences and the experiences of her family.   There followed the half-beautiful, half-prettified *Silas Marner* (1861), and four "invented" novels, *Romola* (1863), *Felix Holt* (1866), *Middlemarch* (1872), and *Daniel Deronda* (1876).

In the talk about the "objectivity" of great writing it is often assumed that the material of this great writing is "objective," as well as the method of the presentation of that material.   That is, that the writer not only keeps himself out of the presentation of the story, but portrays in the story a life in which he has not had a share, a life outside of his experience, a life perhaps not even observed by him, but imagined by him—in short, "in-vented."   There is ample testimony that a writer may be so possessed by the children of his brain that they come to have an existence apart from him, actions that he cannot dictate, tem-peraments that he cannot change.   Such characters may have their origins in people the writer has met, but they grow in his imagination into something very other than their originals.   Char-acters so created may be the most vital and lasting, but writers that cannot be dismissed as minor often borrow characters from life.   And such characters are often those we cannot forget, a Dalgetty, a Skimpole, a Great Mel.

Of such origin are all the successes of George Eliot; Milly Barton and Mrs. Hackit; Adam Bede and Mr. Poyser, Bartle Massey and Dinah Morris, Seth Bede and Mrs. Bede; Mr. Tulliver and Luke his man, Mrs. Tulliver and her sisters Deane and Pullett and Glegg, Mrs. Moss, Maggie and Tom; the patrons of "The Rainbow"; Mrs. Holt and Harold Transome; Dorothea and Mr. Casaubon and Caleb Garth.   There was enough of Marian Evans for her to fashion herself into so differing charac-ters as Dinah Morris and Maggie Tulliver, Dorothea Brooke and Romola.   Mrs. Hackit and Mrs. Poyser are studies after her mother.   Adam Bede and Caleb Garth are aspects of her father in youth and age.   Dinah Morris had in her something of an aunt as well as much of herself. Her brother Isaac was the original of Tom Tulliver, and Mr. Poyser and Mr. Tulliver were recognizable by readers in Coventry as family portraits.

Like Scott, George Eliot was less successful with her portraits of the gentry than of the commonalty. Even when she knew well those who suggested her ladies and gentlemen, as in the case of the patron of her father of whom Arthur Donnithorne is the reflex, she could not give such a character the body and personality of her farmers and artisans. Mrs. Transome in *Felix Holt* is almost the only exception.

There is seldom an element of caricature in her presentation of character. She did not believe in presenting people as other than they were. And if caricature was the result of a presentation, as it perhaps was in the case of Mr. Lyon, it was an accident, not what she intended. She had not been able to tolerate either caricature or idealization to heroic mould in the novels she read before she herself took to writing novels. Just what she wished to do in her writing she has told us several times and always with clarity. Her intention was always realism. She had found her way to this creed as early as the article referred to above, which she contributed to "The Westminster Review" in July, 1856, "The Natural History of German Life." She is here quarreling with the usual unrealistic portraiture of English fiction:

"Our social novels profess to represent the people as they are, and the unreality of their representations is a grave evil. The greatest benefit we owe to the artist, whether painter, poet, or novelist, is the extension of our sympathies. . . . A picture of human life such as a great artist can give, surprises even the trivial and the selfish into that attention to what is apart from themselves, which may be called the raw material of moral sentiment. When Scott takes us into Luckie Mucklebackit's cottage, or tells the story of *The Two Drovers*—when Wordsworth sings to us the reverie of 'Poor Susan'—when Kingsley shows us Alton Locke gazing yearningly over the gate which leads from the highway into the first wood he ever saw,—when Hornung paints a group of chimney sweepers,—more is done towards linking the higher classes with the lower, towards obliterating the vulgarity of exclusiveness, than by hundreds of sermons and philosophical dissertations. Art is the nearest thing to life; it is a mode of amplifying experience and extending our contact with our fellow men beyond the bounds of our personal lot. All the more sacred is the task of the artist when he undertakes the life of the People."

This passage, written when she was thirty-seven, just before she began her first story, *Amos Barton,* shows the part of her that was artist still fast in the clutches of that other part of her that was moralist. Realism was to be the servant of morality. And although her success as an artist weakened, for a few years, the hold that the moralist had on her, the moralist reasserted its power as soon as she had used up her little fund of country experience, the only kind of experience she could fashion into art.

In *Amos Barton* she justifies the kind of art she is here following. She supposes some lady finding the hero "an utterly uninteresting character." To her she replies:

"But, my dear madam, it is so very large a majority of your fellow-countrymen that are of this insignificant stamp. At least eighty out of a hundred of your adult male fellow-Britons returned in the last census are neither extraordinarily silly, nor extraordinarily wicked, nor extraordinarily wise; their eyes are neither deep and liquid with sentiment, nor sparkling with suppressed witticisms; they have probably had no hairbreadth escapes or thrilling adventures; their brains are certainly not pregnant with genius, and their passions have not manifested themselves at all after the fashion of a volcano. They are simply men of complexions more or less muddy, whose conversation is more or less bald and disjointed—yet these commonplace people,—many of them—bear a conscience and have felt the sublime prompting to do the painful right; they have their unspoken sorrows, and their sacred joys; their hearts have perhaps gone out towards their first-born, and they have mourned over the irreclaimable dead. Nay, is there not a pathos in their very insignificance—in our comparison of their dim and narrow existence with the glorious possibilities of that human nature which they share?"

The theory of her art is still more fully developed in that famous first chapter of the second book of *Adam Bede,* Chapter XVII of the novel. Here she turns essayist for half the chapter's pages, and discusses, as did Fielding before her, the kind of writing proper to the kind of novel she is attempting. She here epitomized her art as an effort "to give a faithful account of men and things as they have mirrored themselves in my mind. . . . I feel as much bound to tell you precisely as I can what that reflection is, as if I were in the witness-box narrating my experience on oath."

The five pages in which she elaborates the theory here advanced are so familiar they need not be largely quoted. Let her summing up suffice:

"In this world there are so many of these common coarse people, who have no picturesque sentimental wretchedness! It is so needful we should remember their existence, else we may happen to leave them quite out of our religion and philosophy, and frame lofty theories which only fit a world of extremes. Therefore let Art always remind us of them; therefore let us always have men ready to give the loving pains of a life to the faithful representing of commonplace things—men who see beauty in these commonplace things, and delight in showing how kindly the light of heaven falls on them."

Her girlhood's experience of country life would not, unaided, have brought her to this theory of art, and to the later practice of it. It needed masters to accomplish this, masters like the Scott and Wordsworth she acknowledges, to show her the true values of that life, both in itself and as the material of art. It needed, too, the theory and practice of an earlier Warwickshire writer to develop her appreciation of those values into the creed of realism that she avows. Her figure of the mirror is obviously borrowed from Shakespeare. To him, too, she went for ways and forms of country conversation, and caught some far echo of his dialogue in the chatter of her Poysers and Dodsons.

All her writing in which there is joy and beauty is based on this same experience of life on a Warwickshire farm, an experience that came to an end on her father's retirement from business in 1841, and his removal from Griff House to Coventry. Her father was, as an agent of great estates, a good deal else than a farmer, but none of the great houses of the neighborhood, save that of the Newdigates, Astley Castle, meant much in the life of his daughter Marian. She knew best farm homes, and the homes of artisans, and the homes of merchants in little towns. She knew very few other homes in her impressionable years. Church had its place in her world, and chapel too, and she was acquainted with country doctors and lawyers and school-teachers. A school-teacher or two are among her successful portraits, but no minister save Mr. Barton, and no lawyer or doctor at all. Tryan and Irvine, Dempster and Jermyn, Pilgrim and Lydgate are but minor achievements, lavish as she has been of effort to put them clearly before us. It was given her to do her best only with farmers and artisans and their fellows in the lower middle class.

In her heart of hearts George Eliot always knew this was her proper material, though in her later London days her acceptance as a kind of prophetess made her feel it was her duty to present the whole range of English life. One with her obligations must not confine her consideration of life to any particular class. "The most fortunate Britons," she writes in *The Impressions of Theophrastus Such* (1879), "are those whose experience has given them a practical share in many aspects of the national lot." Yet she is quick to add: "who have lived long among the mixed commonalty, roughing it with them under difficulties, knowing how their food tastes to them, and getting acquainted with their notions and motives not by inference from traditional types in literature or from philosophical theories, but from daily fellowship and observation."

Her keenest sympathies are always with the lowly. She, of course, regarded herself as an intellectual, but she was in many ways still close to the folk and she could laugh at learning with Mr. Glegg in shrewd provincial fashion as he sing-songed:

> "When land is gone, and money spent,
> Then learning is most excellent."

It was characteristic of her Saxon slowness of nature that she chose so generally to write about experiences that were long past. The experiences that she wrote about in *Adam Bede,* published when she was forty, and in *The Mill on the Floss,* published when she was forty-one, were experiences of her life on the farm, which ended when she was twenty-two. Eighteen years or more were necessary for the mellowing of those memories of youth into fit material for art. It was not until 1869 that she began to write in *Middlemarch,* which was published in 1872, about the life of Coventry she had quitted for London eighteen years before. She had been in London for twenty-five years when *Daniel Deronda* was published, in 1876, not, indeed, a novel of London life, but a novel to the making of which went many experiences she had had after coming to London.

She herself was conscious of this habit of hers. Writing to Madame Bodichon in 1859 she says: "At present my mind works with the most freedom and the keenest sense of poetry in my remotest past, and there are many strata to be worked through before I can begin to use, artistically, any material I may gather in the present." It is a good thing to let Time have its will with facts before making them the material of art. It is true, too, as Crockett points out in his introduction to Galt's *Annals of the Parish,* that we can hardly ever again get to know any life so well as that we get to know before we are twenty.

Though George Eliot has left on record that "the germ of *Adam Bede* was an anecdote told me by my Methodist Aunt Samuel" it is likely that Hetty owes something of her being to another original than the poor girl Mrs. Samuel Evans rode with in the cart to the place of execution. The wife of Lewes was a volatile little beauty, in some ways not unlike Hetty, and one is driven to wonder if George Eliot did not use what she had come to learn of Mrs. Lewes when she bodied forth the girl. Nothing of Lewes went to the making of Adam Bede, but the relation of Adam to Hetty and Dinah was in some ways like that of Lewes to Mrs. Lewes and George Eliot. And though Dinah is modelled after the Methodist Aunt, there was a conscientiousness like that of George Eliot at the basis of her character, and the Methodist phase of George Eliot's development to lend sympathy to the presentation of Dinah's Methodism.

On that side of her with which Marian Evans faced the world there was no humor, and there was none in Dinah, and Dinah was as Saxon as her maker, and as painful in her preaching as that maker was to become later in hers. There was, too, under this outward frigidity of restraint, a like warm sympathy for human weakness in the character and her creator.

Maggie Tulliver is, we all know, much more like Marian Evans than is Dinah. In temperament Maggie was Marian Evans, and in bodily perfections what Marian Evans would have liked to be. She was, like Maggie, brown as a gypsy, impulsive to a fault, and, in her youth, of stifled emotions. Romola was physically another sort of apotheosis of Marian Evans, and very like her in her devotion to an exacting father. Dorothea Brooke is another one of her dreams of herself, an idealization of herself done tolerantly and with laughter, and Lewes is again used in the make-up of Ladislaw.

Although George Eliot has put so much of herself into so many of her heroines no one of them is very like another. There is no running to type. What does repeat from story to story is a certain relation of heroine to hero. Perhaps because she was herself, for all her intellectual independence, a woman who must cling to some man, her brother, her father, Lewes, Cross,—she shows you often a woman with a weakness depending on a strong man. There are the cases of Janet and Tryan, Romola and Savonarola, Esther and Felix Holt, Gwendolen Harleth and Daniel Deronda. And there are other dependencies of a like sort, though not all of a pattern.

There is no case of such dependency in *Adam Bede*. Indeed it is in many ways very different from its fellows, as it is surely distiguished above them.   There is no other of all the ten stories one may call major that is at once so freshly felt, so close-packed with keen observations on life, so wholly of fine tissue. There is no other of them, either, save *The Mill on the Floss,* that can boast so memorable characters.   If you are in the habit of marking the good things in your books you will find no other novel of hers so ticked or lined as *Adam Bede*.   And these ticks and lines as you look them over will tell you that your discoveries were not all made at one reading.   These marked passages belong to your last reading, these others in a fainter pencilling to your first.

There is no moment of drama in *Adam Bede,* or for that matter in any other of her stories, so intense as that, in *The Mill on the Floss,* in which Maggie parts from Stephen Guest.   The fight between Adam Bede and Arthur Donnithorne is but artfully con-trived and the reprieve of Hetty at the scaffold is but one of many such scenes in English fiction, quickly accomplished, arrest-ing, moving, but hardly more than the stock situation of its kind.

It is said that Lewes had much to do with George Eliot's scenes of heightened action.   That may be so, but one wonders if it were necessarily he who taught her even so much as the tricks of her trade.   He was himself an undistinguished novelist, and she a good journeyman of letters before she found her way to great writing in the novel.   It is quite possible she taught herself her craft in her following of the novelists she called master.   She learned that craft only in her middle years, and only after much painstaking and heavily Teutonic endeavor, but when she had learned it it bore the unquestioned hallmark of her own personality and experience.

It was only in the novel that her work was masterly.   Her verse was indeed competent, but it had few felicities; her essays in *Theophrastus Such* and elsewhere are often platitudinous and almost always overlong and doughy; her criticism is painstaking but full of false values, largely because of her insistence on the moral rather than the artistic standpoint.

In fiction her range was wide for one of so limited an experience in her formative years. That she was not without power in the short-story *The Lifted Veil* (1859) is proof, lacking in unity though it is. The short novels of *Silas Marner* and *Scenes from Clerical Life* are as good examples of their class as we have from any writer who has essayed both this form and the full scope novel. And within the full scope novel she has written stories of farm and mill and village; of provincial towns, and in part, of London;—stories spanning the four score years from the last decade of the eighteenth century to the threshold of the last quarter of the nineteenth. And outside of this field there is *Romola*, a historical novel of Italy in the days of Savonarola.

George Eliot is fully at her ease only in *Adam Bede*. In no other of her novels does the story move so smoothly and unerringly to its large close. There are those who find an unharmonious note in the coming together of Adam and Dinah; there are others who go further and say their marriage is anticlimax. Its seems to me to be in perfect accord with what has gone before; it seems to me to be not anticlimax but simply a compensation such as life often brings to those who suffer much. It seems to me to be the highest realism, an inevitable outcome of the situation with which we are concerned. One demands in art, as in life, rest after unrest, such a peace as is the Sabbath's, as an assuagement to the strife and wearing labor of the week.

There are earlier moments of *Adam Bede* of a quality like that of the close, moments of stillness that bring us a feeling of late afternoon light, of a world suffused with an amber glow, like that of Sunday eves in an autumn long gone. Walks after Sunday School in boyhood took one reader of George Eliot by both farms and homes of mill-workers; and in the nights after such walks George Eliot was approved reading. So it has come about that his thoughts turn as inevitably to George Eliot on afternoons of late autumn amber-toned and still as they do to Whittier on winter nights when the wind is up and the snow sifting against the panes.

The Mill on the Floss is another mellow-toned book, with the greatest of its maker's characters dominating it as surely as does Henchard *The Mayor of Casterbridge* (1886). Mr. Tulliver, too, is of the children of Lear. Henchard could say with his elder and duller fellow: "This world's been too much for me." And if you substitute "Henchard" for "Tulliver" and delete the "dimly lighted" of the lines that follow of Tulliver's death they would be equally true of Henchard's death in the loneliness of Egdon Heath: "Poor Tulliver's dimly lighted soul had for ever ceased to be vexed with the painful riddle of this world." And you would not have to delete the "dimly lighted" if you would not extend it beyond the "soul" to will and intellect, as you most surely are prone to do. Both Tulliver and Henchard were true-blue Englishmen, both honest fellows at war with the world. Both had bad luck with their womenkind. To both in the defeat of hopes a daughter became all in all. *The Mill on the Floss* is hurried toward the close, and a tragic ending forced on the story. Its faults amount almost to a distortion of form, destroying the effect of a noble plan.

It is almost a tradition to praise *Silas Marner* as perfect after its kind. It is certainly all of a tone, a study in grays and old blues. That is perhaps the trouble—the figures are a little dimmed by the texture of their setting, as figures on old coverlets are apt to be. The finding of Eppie, of the golden hair, by Silas just upon his loss of his hoard of golden guineas, is of the very stuff of which fables are made, and, as such, is not to be taken to heart so closely as an episode unequivocally human. Humanized, of course, *Silas Marner* is, but it remains more than half fairy tale. We do not know any of the characters, even Silas himself or Nancy Lammeter, as we know the principals of *The Mill on the Floss* and *Adam Bede*.

Romola (1863) was, George Eliot confessed, hard work in the writing. It is now hard work, now easy work, in the reading.

Except for enthusiasts over Florence the long passages about Florentine art and politics and religion are heavy going. But though *Romola* is heavy in places it is not dull. No story involving a man-hunt can be dull, and the pursuit of Tito by Baldassarre is as primitive a man-hunt as any that delights the patrons of the movies. *Romola's* main shortcomings are all owing to its being written not out of memories, but out of material worked up for the purpose of writing an historical novel of Savonarola and his time.

Romola and her father are decorations, beautiful in a cold still way, but with only the semblance of life. Savonarola we already know. Our interest in him here is not as a character in a story but as the interpretation of an historical figure. There is more life in Tito, who has in him something of the mercurial quality of Lewes, one or another side of whose nature was to creep into so many of the men of her later novels. Another aspect of Lewes is presented, as I have said, in Ladislaw; and he reappears, idealized all but unrecognizably, in Daniel Deronda.

Felix Holt (1866) has its moments of power, and two or three characters to remember. Mrs. Transome is George Eliot's most successful gentlewoman, Tommy Trounsem of the lineage of great clowns, and Harold Transome very real in his hardness and soft repulsiveness. Jermyn, like Grandcourt in *Daniel Deronda*, is of the stage stagey. Esther Lyon is rendered tenderly and without envy, as is that other girl of April-like bloom, Nancy Lammeter in *Silas Marner*. It is not every homely woman that can draw her lovely sisters with delight in their beauty and with the kindliest affection for their selves. Esther and Nancy alike, however, remain sketches rather than finished portraits.

The wise son who does not know his own father and who would hunt him down as a rascal is an old theme, a variant of the Sohrab and Rustum story. It is not very successfully handled in *Felix Holt* with Harold Transome and Jermyn as the antagonists. Chance, too, has too large a part in the story, as in the finding of Christian's wallet by Felix Holt and its passing into the hands of Mr. Lyon, the man most affected of anyone in the world by its contents. What is well done in the story, like the riot and the humble characters in tavern and servants' hall, is done out of memories of the young womanhood of George Eliot in Warwickshire. *Felix Holt* is else of a caliber much less than that of the two great novels.

Middlemarch (1872) is George Eliot's story of greatest intention. It aims to be a microcosm of the life of a provincial city of the Midlands. A dozen characters of the first magnitude are attempted, and from many classes of society. A number of themes that were of outstanding importance to that day and generation are introduced into the story. Foremost among these, of course, is the question of the freedom of women. Of this topic and of its companion topics George Eliot had command, as she had of the life of Coventry out of which she made her people and plot, but somehow or other the story limps and drags. She does not visualize the characters and the scenes for us as she does the characters and the scenes of *Adam Bede* and *The Mill on the Floss*. There is, since it is George Eliot writing, good work in *Middlemarch*. Dorothea Brooke is a memorable portrait, and Casaubon, a kind of embodiment of the masculine side of George Eliot herself with her intellect left out, is a notable and repellant portrait. Caleb Garth is still another success. *Middlemarch* is unquestionably, too, an "informing" book, but as a whole dull as well as heavy, and soddenly Teutonic.

Daniel Deronda (1876) is what its author called "another big book." There is very little of it a record of a living in which George Eliot had part in her youth, the only kind of living that she could artistically reshape into a story. She had, of course, met many Jews, but the most of what she has here to tell us about them is what she had read up; that kind of worked up material she had not the power to vitalize. Mordecai and Daniel are pale abstractions, repudiated alike by the people of whom they are intended to be flattering symbols, and by the world at large. There are, of course, Jews who rejoice in *Daniel Deronda* as a tract to advance Zionism, but they are not a majority of the many Jews who from the time of Mathilde Blind have put into print their admiration of George Eliot.

There are admirers of the portrayal of Grandcourt, critics who hold him to be the beau-ideal of the gentlemanly villain. To me he does not seem real at all, but a theatricalized mannikin strayed out of Bulwer.

The character of Gwendolen Harleth has been as carefully studied as her name. The rhythm of that is an echo from Pre-Raphaelite writing, which was much given to the composition of names that should be "sweet symphonies." All that could be done to make her live, by such invention as George Eliot had, has been done, but she is always just a little short of believable. The writing that first presents her is almost precious: "The Nereid in sea-green robes and silver ornaments, with a pale sea-green feather fastened in silver falling backward over her green hat and light-brown hair was Gwendolen Harleth." That is not the kind of writing in which George Eliot excels. Except when writing about homely folk, and about the villages and countryside which they and their ancestors have colored with their ways of farming and handicraft and worship, she is seldom at her best.

From the villagers and farming people of Warwickshire she has collected a rich treasure of good sayings, and in contemplation of these same people she has made discovery upon discovery about life. One could make a long list of such adages as these few I quote:

"There's many a good bit o' work done with a sad heart."

"Thee allays makes a peck of thy own words out o' a pint o' the Bible's."

"College mostly makes people like bladders—just good for nothing but to hold the stuff as is poured into 'em."

"You make but a poor trap to catch luck if you go and bait it wi' wickedness."

"The smell o' the bread's sweet to everybody but the baker."

"I shall feel as uneasy as a new-sheared sheep when she's gone from me."

"Men are mostly so tongue-tied you're forced partly to guess what they mean, as you do wi' the dumb creatures."

And not content with this last fling at the enemy George Eliot gives to Mrs. Poyser these words that silence once and for all man's assumption of superior knowledge:

"However, I'm not deniyin' the women are foolish: God Almighty made 'em to match the men."

Less pungent, but of more serious import, is that statement of Mrs. Poyser about the hard lot of the farmer: "As for farming, it's putting money into your pocket wi' your right hand and fetching it out wi' your left.   As far as I can see it's raising victual for other folks and just getting a mouthful for yourself and your children as you go along."

I have heard virtually these same words from small farmers from Somerset and Mayo; from a crofter "Oban awa'" and a New Zealand sheepman; from a California orchardist sierra-ward of the San Joaquin Valley and a Pennsylvania hillman on the slopes above Broadhead's Creek.

Of more limited application but just as true is what she has to say of the service to the world of such humble lives as that of Adam Bede: "Their lives have no discernible echo beyond the neighborhood where they dwelt, but you are sure to find there some good piece of road, some building, some application of mineral produce, some improvement in farming practice, some reform of parish abuses, with which their names are associated by one or two generations after them."   It must be that many of us have thought gratefully of such a man, whose very name, in a neighborhood four or five generations old, is now lost, for the road he built past our door that is dry in the spring thaws, or for the old walls about us that turn the wind as well tonight as they did a hundred years ago.

These shrewd observations upon life and these discoveries of truth are not always, though generally, given to those who speak in dialect.   When they are phrased in Queen's English they lose something of their relish, though none of their wisdom.   We all recognize that it is a common attitude towards things that

Gwendolen Harleth reveals when she says: "I think I dislike what I dislike more than I like what I like."   That is, too, her negative character in a nutshell.   Again, George Eliot will make such observations as the direct comment of the narrator upon the course of events in the story.   It is in this way that she tells us in Adam Bede: "It is better sometimes not to follow great reformers of abuses beyond the threshold of their homes."

Such discoveries are not all of one sort.   Now it is her observation of nature that leads her to say: "There is always a stronger sense of life when the sun is brilliant after rain."   Oftener they are discoveries about human traits.   Such are: "Secrets leave no lines in young faces"; "There's nothing but what's bearable as long as a man can work"; "Our highest thoughts and our best deeds are all given to us"; and "We are apt to be kinder to the brutes that love us than to the women that love us.   Is it because the brutes are dumb?"

This last discovery is written "in character," from the angle of masculine thought that she had to assume because George Eliot was supposed to be a man.   Here that assumption leads to no insincerity, but there are places in her writing in which it results in what is very nearly insincerity, and it often warps what she has to say.   Feminine as she was in all essential ways she was in rebellion against the limitations of being a woman.   "You may try," says the Princess Hahn-Eberstein to her son Daniel Deronda, "You may try, but you can never imagine what it is to have a man's force of genius in you, and yet to suffer the slavery of being a girl."

Womanly as she remained to the end in her social relations George Eliot could boast of a completely liberated intelligence early in her writing years.   She was never the thrall of sex in her writing.   So free was she of such trammels that critics of the highest discernment, Thackeray among them, thought that George Eliot was a man.   Others, like Dickens, were sure George Eliot was a woman, and it happened that they were right.   There is evidence in the stories in support of either contention.

It was in 1861, on the publication of *The Mill on the Floss,* that it was disclosed that George Eliot was Marian Evans. It seems to us now that had not the announcement been made everyone who read the story would have known that none but a woman could have created Maggie. Yet it might very well have been that many would not have so believed. Even in our own day the man-like attitude of Sheila Kaye-Smith has led certain critics to wonder whether the author of the books so signed was not a man writing under a woman's name. And William Sharp, despite much suspicion as to his identity with Fiona Macleod, kept the readers of his books, issued under that name, uncertain of their authorship to the day of his death.

His way was to dramatize the feminine side of himself into a sort of second self and let the second self write about Highland themes and sign itself Fiona Macleod. The way of George Eliot was to write from the standpoint of a high humanity untrammeled by sex. There need be, after all, only moments in most stories where what is written is dependent on the writer being man or woman, though of course, all that is written may easily betray masculine or feminine bias. The statement, "that hard rind of truth which is discerned by unimaginative unsympathetic minds," is not in any way dependent upon the sex of the writer. Nor is this: "There are faces which nature charges with a meaning and pathos not belonging to the single human soul that flutters beneath them, but speaking the joys and sorrows of foregone generations—eyes that tell of deep love which doubtless has been and is somewhere, but not paired with those eyes—perhaps paired with pale eyes that can say nothing; just as a national language may be instinct with poetry unfelt by the lips that use it."

There is no passage in all George Eliot that has given me such pause as this. It is a flash of an insight that is rare in her writing, of a kind that is more common in Conrad. It shows her aware of the generations on generations of men that have lived in a countryside, that the present moment and mood are dependent on moods and moments long gone on the wind. It is in such a revelation as this that she proved herself a true pythoness, and not in her cryptic and supposedly sacrosanct utterances to her devotees at the Priory.

Despite her close association with a number of Positivists George Eliot never owed full allegiance to Comtism or aimed herself at being a philosopher of any allied school. We may take it that she does not wholly disagree with Piero di Cosimo when he says in *Romola:* "A philosopher is the last sort of animal I should choose to resemble. I find it enough to live, without spinning lies to account for life." A staunch moralist she was always, deeply interested in a regeneration of the social order through a general acceptance of scientific truth. Comte's application of his theories to contemporary society she could not wholly accept, but a good deal of his theory was much to her liking. After she was sure of her following, as she was from the time of *Silas Marner,* she reproduced some of this Positivist thought in her writing, where it added to the burden of preachment that already over-weighted the stories, and lessened their value as works of art. Her wisdom at its best, in *Scenes from Clerical Life, Adam Bede* and *The Mill on the Floss,* is a wisdom as far from a systematic philosophy of life on the one hand as from worldly wisdom on the other. Her wisdom at its best is rather a sublimation of the wisdom of the folk, but leavened a little with the perfervidness of the Methodism she was so close to for a while. Her wisdom, like that of the folk, was the accumulation of the experience of a countryside through immemorial years.

It would be a pleasant pastime to develop the relation of the later work of George Eliot to the philosophy of Comte but it would hardly help to further our appreciation of her writing as art. This later work is of first importance, perhaps, in sociology, but certainly not in letters. The literature of life is the only realistic literature of power, the literature of ideas is but literature of knowledge. The distinction is as true today as when DeQuincey formulated it, and it would be well for the standards of taste of our day were it more insistently present in the minds of our critics.

Unquestionably there are relations between the teaching of Comte and that of George Eliot, as there are relations between the teaching of Schopenhauer and that of Hardy, and as there are relations between the teaching of Nietzsche and that of Phillpotts. It is always to be remembered, however, that the teaching of artists is but a by-product of their art. In realistic art it is the picture of life that counts.

The masters of George Eliot in her art of the novel are obvious enough from the form and content of her work, but we have her own word, too, as to who they are. Scott she mentions oftenest, and with the greatest admiration. Fielding gave her something of her form, and Richardson something of her analysis of motive and emotion. Jane Austen she calls first within her scope among English novelists, but she owed little to her. George Eliot preferred Thackeray to Dickens, but there are closer similarities between certain of her characters, the Dodsons for instance, and certain of those of Dickens, than between any of her characters and Thackeray's. The one close approximation to Thackeray is in her observation apropos of Arthur Donnithorne: "We don't inquire too closely into character in the case of a handsome generous fellow, who will have property enough to support numerous peccadilloes." Put this side by side with the passage about the "young nobleman" in Chapter X of *The Newcomes* (1853), which is quoted previously in the chapter on Thackeray, and the similarity of thought will be readily noticed.

George Eliot is in the great tradition of the English novel. She received that tradition from the past, a great inheritance, and she handed it on, not only unimpaired, but a richer legacy, to those who came after her. From her the succession is to Hardy, from Hardy to Phillpotts, from Phillpotts to Sheila Kaye-Smith. The very name of Wessex, now the sign-manual of Hardy's novels, is to be found in *Daniel Deronda*. It would seem to be a borrowing by the elder from the younger novelist. Hardy first used the name of "Wessex" for what he calls his "realistic dream-country" in *Far from the Madding Crowd* when that novel was first published in the *Cornhill Magazine* in 1874.

As *Daniel Deronda* was not published until 1876 Hardy has clearly the priority in publication. Yet *Daniel Deronda* was begun late in 1873, and it may be that the passage in Chapter III in which she sends Gwendolen to "Wessex" was written before the appearance of Chapter L of *Far from the Madding Crowd,* where the name occurs, which was late in 1874. If George Eliot happened upon the name independently it is as curious a coincidence of the kind as there has been in English literature. Whichever hit upon it earlier there is no doubt but that it is Hardy's now, as is all else he inherited from the writers of the main line of the English novel from Fielding down, and continued in his own work.

That emphasis on the presentation of his characters at their work that is so characteristic of Hardy is not characteristic of George Eliot, but there are scenes of labor in her stories. We recall Adam Bede in his carpenter's shop, Silas Marner at his loom, and Felix Holt at his teaching. There are scenes, too, of haying that suggest themselves as possible originals of similar scenes in Hardy, for, as in Hardy, the idyllic note is always tempered by touches of realism. "The jocose talk of haymakers," she writes in *Adam Bede,* "is best at a distance; like those clumsy bells round the cows' necks, it has rather a coarse sound when it comes close, and may even grate on your ears painfully; but heard from far off, it mingles very prettily with the other joyous sounds of nature. Men's muscles move better when their souls are making merry music, though their merriment is of a poor blundering sort, not at all like the merriment of birds."

Such passages as these are memories of her girlhood in Warwickshire, "our north-midland county of Loamshire," as she calls it in her novels. It is a "rich land tilled with . . . much care, the woods rolling down the gentle slopes to the green meadows." There still lingered here and there in this countryside, even down to her own time, something of that Merry England that seems so fabulous today. There was jollity in the church music, in which the peasantry had a share with bassoon and serpent as well as with voices; the old dances were still stepped at social gatherings; and there were high jinks at harvestings and fairings. She shows us Methodism at war with such levity, which was a weakness of church people who lived on the land. The dissenting people of the looms and coal-pits had, in general, put away such worldliness under the exhortations of their preachers and of the wandering evangelists. There is an unctuousness in her portrayal of the folk in their hours of relaxation or abandon that is not wholly in keeping with her Puritan prejudices. Her tavern talk is of the earth earthy; its humor of a sort that the Wife of Bath would understand.

It is only literature that has given us the full flavor of the English folk. There are no really great paintings or really great music of the quality of the "clown" passages in Chaucer and Shakespeare, in George Eliot and Hardy. Compared to these how faint and thin seems even such a gallant attempt to present the folk musically as the *Pastoral Symphony* of Vaughan Williams. And what painting at all is half as successful in its kind as this symphony?

It is said that in her later years George Eliot thought the pine hills of the south country, in Hampshire and in Surrey, the most beautiful part of England, but it was the flat lands of Warwickshire that spelt home to her and that forced her to make them the background of her most intimate writing. In *Daniel Deronda* she expresses her belief that "a human life . . . should be well rooted in some spot of a native land, where it may get the love of tender kinship for the face of earth, for the labors men go forth to, for the sounds and accents that haunt it, for whatever will give that early home a familiar unmistakable difference amid the future widening of knowledge; a spot where the definiteness of early memories may be inwrought with affection, and kindly acquaintance with all neighbors, even to the dogs and donkeys, may spread not by sentimental effort and reflection, but as a sweet habit of the blood."

That passage breathes the faith that has animated much of the great writing in English literature, in verse and prose both, that celebrates the beauty of the English countryside. One thinks of Overbury and Walton, of Gilbert White and W. H. Hudson, as one reads and lets one's memory have free play. This doctrine of attachment to place has long been a part of the code of a large body of Englishmen, unlettered as well as lettered. Even among those whose love of the sea and adventure have made them wanderers to the ends of the earth there has been a renewal of the old doctrine in the place that has finally stayed their steps. They have written of Australian bush and Alpine valleys in Canada with all the love their stay-at-home fellows have declared for Westmoreland or Sussex.

In George Eliot the description of a countryside is seldom introduced for its own sake alone, through sheer joy in out-of-doors. The description is almost always interwoven with some mood of the character or with some chorusing of the author on the ways of mankind. It is thus that we come by this lyric in *The Mill on the Floss:*

"The wood I walk in on this mild May day, with the young yellow-brown foliage of the oaks between me and the blue sky, the white star-flowers, and the blue-eyed speedwell, and the ground-ivy at my feet—what grove of tropic palms, what strange ferns or splendid broad-petaled blossoms, could ever thrill such deep and delicate fibres within me as this home-scene? These familiar flowers, these well-remembered bird-notes, this sky with its fitful brightness, these furrowed and grassy fields, each with a sort of personality given to it by the capricious hedgerows— such things as these are the mother tongue of our imagination, the language that is laden with all the subtle inextricable associations the fleeting hours of our childhood left behind them. Our delight in the sunshine on the deep-bladed grass today might be no more than the faint perception of wearied souls, if it were not for the sunshine and the grass in the far-off years, which still live in us, and transform our perception into love."

The style of George Eliot speaks for itself in this passage, as in the several passages previously quoted. Her "Queen's English" is at its best in description. Her narrative moves rapidly enough, but one feels it would run more easily were it in dialect.

She is surer of distinction in dialect than in the traditional English of the novel.   In her analytical passages she has a tendency to overuse scientific terminology, but when her people of the farm and the shop are once at the give and take of conversation we have a dialogue of real power.   It is racy, always to the point, and often hard-hitting.   It is very English.

For all her Welsh surname, and the origin of her father's people in Flintshire, George Eliot is a Saxon of the Saxons, of a stock in which the Teutonic element is paramount.   With her broad, gypsy face and gypsy brownness of skin she did not look the Saxon Englishwoman.   That she was, however, through and through.   Self-centered, home-loving, deeply concerned with morality, oppressed with that sense of duty that bears down hard on all Puritans, she was very typical of Mid-Victorian England. And all that she was she gave full expression to in her novels.

Fortunately she was an artist, too, and in the two great novels of her late heyday her art mastered her and held her moral bias in abeyance.   Unfortunately the two all but exhausted her rather narrow knowledge of life.   Then, her store of experience emptied, at least that store of experience of country life that alone of all her experience she could fashion into art, she turned to "ideas," Positivist ideas.   Henceforth there came from her studies of life profoundly interesting to people preoccupied with current problems, but never again the glad art of *Adam Bede* and *The Mill on the Floss*.

CHAPTER XI

GEORGE MEREDITH AND HIS READING OF LIFE

George Meredith was accepted as a peer by the great Victorian writers on the publication of *Modern Love* in 1862. That acceptance was of the writer as artist, for the lyric beauty and power of analysis of his sonnet-sequence. George Meredith was accepted as a great writer by the English-speaking world in the mid-eighties. That acceptance was of the novelist who, now that George Eliot and Trollope were dead, remained, with Hardy, the last of the great Victorians. *Diana of the Crossways* (1885) made a stir that would not down, and the first collected edition of the novels (1885-87) brought about a general realization that here was one who could no longer be denied a place among the great portrayers of English life. It was an acceptance of Meredith as an artist in literature, but as other than that, too. In many places his "readings of life" were taken as those of a philosopher, and in some quarters he was hailed as a prophet.

As a prophet Meredith was forgiven those obscurities of style and those cryptic interpretations of life that had long been a bar to his appeal to the general reader. The people expect dark sayings and a fine frenzy in a prophet. Had not they taken the trouble to understand Emerson and Carlyle and Browning? Each of these three had made his contribution to the general thought of the race, and each had outlined his hope for the morrow, when Meredith began to be listened to by the people at large. Those who were attentive to his "readings of life" formulated them into a code to follow, and knew a rapture of the forward view that has not forsaken them even in these so changed times.

The analysis of love in the novels of Meredith, for one thing, helped largely to a more enlightened attitude on the part of the English-speaking civilization toward the relations of the sexes and was an element in forwarding a saner feminism. In his first prose work, *The Shaving of Shagpat* (1855), in the story of "Bhanavar the Beautiful," Meredith made his heroine the mistress of her fate, and from that time on he delighted to present heroines who fronted life bravely and tried to make their way in the world as if they were as directly responsible for the advancement of civilization as the men. He thought they were so responsible and what they needed to meet their responsibilities was education, training, insight and knowledge. Hardly ever does he allow propaganda to dominate the story; it is generally kept in its place as what might be said by this or that character at that moment. He will introduce a character, however, as he does Dr. Julius von Karsteg in *The Adventures of Harry Richmond* (1871), that this character may preach the evangel, but Meredith never makes a character act other than he would by nature to score a point for what his creator is advocating. That woman must be free is a note sounded again and again, in *Evan Harrington* (1860), in *Rhoda Fleming* (1865), in *Beauchamp's Career* (1875), in *The Egoist* (1879), and, most pronouncedly, in *Diana of the Crossways* (1885). It was generally known, by the time of this last-named book, that Meredith himself had suffered deep unhappiness in his first marriage, from this very freedom for woman he so stoutly advocated. There was, of course, his happy second marriage to point to as an illustration that what he plead for had been tried and not found wanting in his own experience. *Diana of the Crossways* speaks again and again the importance of love to the man as well as to the woman. This is his record of how the love of Redworth for Diana remade the man: "She gave him comprehension of the meaning of love: a word in many mouths, not often explained. With her, wound in his idea of her, he perceived it to signify a new start in our existence, a finer shoot of the tree stoutly planted in good gross earth; the senses running their live sap, and the minds companioned, and the spirits made one by the whole-natured con-

junction. In sooth, a happy prospect for the sons and daughters
of Earth, divinely indicating more than happiness: the speeding
of us, compact of what we are, between the ascetic rocks and the
sensual whirlpools, to the creation of certain nobler races, now
very dimly imagined."

One would like to believe that the truth here preached was
now part of the inherited culture of the race. Perhaps it is;
certainly a good many of his preachments have had permanent
effect; and some of his prophecies have been fulfilled. With that
fulfillment the passages concerned with the exposition of his doc-
trines become outmoded, as must in the end all that belong to
what De Quincey calls "the literature of knowledge" and fall
short of "the literature of power," of pure art.

From the outset of his career Meredith had been told that
he was hard to follow. It was not generally understood that
The Shaving of Shagpat was an allegory on humbug. There
were those who delighted in its "oriental manner," in its reminiscences of *The Arabian Nights,* but even to such readers it was
a puzzle. George Eliot was one who welcomed it warmly, but
she made less of *Farina: a Legend of Cologne* (1857), which is
an extravaganza with a satiric purpose. It exults in the beauty
of landscape and the German Romanticism that Meredith grew
to know in his schooldays on the Rhine but it at the same time
satirizes certain aspects of romance with which Kingsley, for one,
had been preoccupied, particularly in *Westward Ho!* (1855).

It is incomprehensible as we read *The Ordeal of Richard
Feverel* today that it was not accepted generally as great writing
on its publication in 1859. The critics appreciated it, quoting
largely from its memorable passages, but it made little appeal to
the public that was eagerly accepting *Adam Bede* as the novel of
the year. George Eliot, of course, wrote on the note of the time;
and Meredith wrote to appease his heart's hunger for beauty;
and to deaden, by his anger at a ruinous system, the heartache
that a kindred one had helped to bring into his own life.

With so heavy a thesis weighing upon *The Ordeal of Richard
Feverel* it is to be wondered that Meredith attained to so many

scenes of clear beauty in it. First of them all are those that constitute that idyl of first love, the meeting of Lucy and Richard, in the two chapters "Ferdinand and Miranda" and "A Diversion played on a Penny Whistle." Of this idyl it is but the simple truth to say that it is English prose at its utmost of lyric beauty. No man has made our speech move to a blither rhythm than this. Steeped in poetry as the idyl is, its prose remains prose, romantic, unrestrained, almost luscious, in perfect harmony with the emotion it expresses.

Meredith was to probe deeper into human experience than he did in *The Ordeal of Richard Feverel* (1859); he was to write *The Egoist* (1879) and *Diana of the Crossways* (1885). He was to shape a novel of better proportions; he was to write *Rhoda Fleming* (1865). He was never, however, to write another book of so fresh and appealing a beauty, never to do character more completely than in Mrs. Berry or Lady Blandish or Lucy, or in Farmer Blaize or Adrian Harley or Richard. All told there are nearly thirty characters of parts in the book, a prodigality of creation that proves Meredith a novelist of the old order that had time to meet men in their hundreds and to get the savor and tang of each.

Evan Harrington (1861), though it has more of autobiography in it than any other of Meredith's novels, is the least Meredithian of them all. That is, perhaps, because it conforms somewhat to the characteristics of the fiction dominant in its day. The way of Dickens is followed in the presentation of Raikes and Tom Cogglesby, and the presentation of the Countess de Saldar has more than chance resemblance to Thackeray's methods. Meredith, too, is trying to hold in check his difficult and symbolic ways of speech, and succeeding, at least partially, in being simple and direct and quickly intelligible. So it comes about that we have in *Evan Harrington* the easiest to read and the most completely understantable of Meredith's novels. Again, we have hosts of characters; and, again, several done directly from life. As Adrian Harley was based on Maurice Fitzgerald, nephew of the author of *Omar Khayyam* (1859), so Rose Jocelyn was based on Janet Duff Gordon, and Rose's parents on Janet's parents. Evan is, of course, largely Meredith himself.

There seems to be no doubt at all that Meredith labored to make *Evan Harrington* easy of apprehension. An artist with an audience is hardly human if he does not respond, now and then, to what is expected of him by the best, at least, of that audience. It is right that he should so respond, if he can without sacrifice of his art. There is clear evidence in *Emilia in England* (1864), the story that followed *Evan Harrington,* that he understood the relation in which he stood to his readers. Emilia sings to English villagers at a feast a song they do not know. They applaud the singing but they do not love the song. It is impossible, they should, explains Meredith, for "poor people, yokels, clods, cannot love what is incomprehensible to them. An idol must have their attributes: a king must show his face now and then: a song must appeal to their intelligence, to subdue them quite. This, as we know, is not the case in the higher circles." Farmer Wilson asks her for "something plain and flat on the surface." She gives them a simple song that they have always known. They rise to it as one man, "half-dancing, half-chorusing."

In *Evan Harrington* Meredith had shown his disposition to do just what Emilia did. He could not, however, do it as she did, without irony. He must have his fling at "the higher circles" who are not, of course, different from "yokels" or any other human beings in not loving "what is incomprehensible to them." Nothing makes a reader angrier with an author than an inability to understand him. If the author so writes that the reader has difficulty with him it follows that either he writes ill or that his reader is stupid. The reader will fume, if in self-respect he does not choose the former alternative. Meredith knew this well enough but he could not always so accommodate himself as he did in *Evan Harrington*. The compromise that he made in almost all of his subsequent stories was little indeed. He found, perhaps, that he was no more liked for *Evan Harrington,* in which he had forborne to be wholly himself than he had been in *The Ordeal of Richard Feverel,* in which he was George Meredith unreservedly.

Potboiling Meredith refers to in his letters, but there is no evidence that any of his novels were potboilers. His suburban journalism; and his writing for London newspapers and magazines, at least in part, was potboiling; and his reading of manuscript as literary adviser to Chapman and Hall might fall under that designation. Arnold Bennett would like to believe that Meredith, like himself, had written potboiling novels, but the facts are against him. Certainly no man as closely in touch with what the public wants as a publisher's reader could have expected the success as potboilers of any of his novels from *Sandra Belloni* (1864) to *The Amazing Marriage* (1895).

It would seem that, after *Evan Harrington* (1860), Meredith felt it wisest to be himself, and to trust that writing done with high intention and recognized as true art by his fellow-craftsmen and the critics, would come in time to be appreciated by some part of the public. Carlyle, with his "wind in the orchard" style; and Browning, with his introspection and his elliptical utterance, helped to prepare an audience for the novels of Meredith in so far as writing in less popular forms than the novel can prepare an audience for the novel. Meredith had to find an audience for his novels among readers of history and the essay and poetry, or else to create the taste among the so-called novel-reading public by which he was to be enjoyed. It is probable that his audience was recruited from both groups.

Meredith felt keenly the slowness with which he made his way. In a letter of 1881 he refers to himself as "an unpopular author," and in another of that same year to his son, he sets down bitterly, "as for me, I have failed." It was America that first began to buy his novels at all freely, when his collected edition came out from 1885 to 1887. Even as late as the latter year he could write, "in England I am encouraged but by a few enthusiasts." Yet then, for a full quarter of a century, his novels had found place in such leading magazines as *Once a Week, The Fortnightly Review,* and *The Cornhill Magazine.* It was not always easy placing them there, however. Friendship with editors helped him in some instances in placing them, but almost always the stories had to be cut down. In other cases the stories went the rounds and had finally to be placed not where he wished them but where they would be taken. Their serial appearance, however prominent, did not, unfortunately, ensure large sales when they came to be put out in volume form. It was more than a little ironic in a time when Stevenson and Hardy and Barrie were making pilgrimage to his home in Surrey, Box Hill near Dorking, that Meredith was still troubled about the "placing" of his stories.

The old note of "many years of inadequate recognition" is sounded even in the memorial presented to him by "some comrades in letters" on his seventieth birthday in 1898. By now, however, Meredith was generally recognized not only throughout the English-speaking world, but in France and Italy as well. German recognition came more slowly, but in 1904 a complete translation of the novels was begun in Berlin. The novels that Meredith wrote after his general acceptation by the English-speaking countries in the mid-eighties are none of them masterpieces. They are remarkably young-hearted for a man past sixty, all three of them, *One of Our Conquerors* (1891), *Lord Ormont and His Aminta* (1894), and *The Amazing Marriage* (1895), but the characters remain people you are hearing stories about, whom you meet only at moments. Indeed, from *The Ordeal of Richard Feverel* (1859) on, Meredith had always a tendency to get between his characters and the reader or to leave his characters unexplained. To the former practice his greatest weakness is contributory, that of making so many of his people speak his own witty and highly colored speech, when to be in character their dialogue should be dull or obvious. In this practice, as in almost all of those practices that detract from his effectiveness Meredith seems to be sinning with his eyes wide open to his sin. What Richmond Roy says to his son Harry about repartee shows that Meredith was aware of the artificiality of his dialogue: " 'As to repartee, you must have it. Wait for that, too. Do not,' he groaned, 'do not force it! Bless my soul, what is there in the world so bad?' And rising to the upper notes of his groan: 'Ignorance, density, total imbecility, is better; I would rather any day of my life sit and carve for guests—the grossest of human trials—a detestable dinner, than be doomed to hear some wretched fellow—and you hear the old as well as the young—excrutiate feelings which, where they exist, cannot but be exquisitely delicate. Goodness gracious me! to see the man pumping up his wit! For me, my visage is of an unalterable gravity whenever I am present at one of these exhibitions. I care not if I offend. Let them say I wish to revolutionize society —I declare to you Richie boy, delightful to my heart though I find your keen stroke of repartee, still your fellow who takes the thrust gracefully, knows when he is traversed by a masterstroke, and yields sign of it, instead of plunging like a spitted buffalo and asking us to admire his agility—you follow me?—I say I hold that man—and I delight vastly in ready wit; it is the wine of language!—I regard that man as the superior being. True, he is not so entertaining."

Yet, seeing this, Meredith can make the little German princess Ottilia in *The Adventures of Harry Richmond* talk exactly as he himself writes in his lecture *An Essay on Comedy and the Uses of the Comic Spirit* (1877), and Robert Eccles, the downright farmer of *Rhoda Fleming,* unlimber in a like strain.

There are other reasons, too, why we do not get to know all of Meredith's characters as intimately as we should like. There is seldom any trouble in seeing them. They are generally pictured clearly as to externals, men and women alike, the women with a gusto that puts them before us in the flesh. What a gallery of portraits they make, Lucy, Rose and the Countess de Saldar, Emilia, Rhoda and Dahlia and Margaret Lovell, Janet and Kiomi and Ottilia, Cecilia and Rénée and Jenny, Laetitia and Clara, Diana, Aminta and Carinthia! What they do is what their mostly stubborn selves might well do; yet with at least every other one of them we are not in confidence, but apart from them, watching, wondering what may be their secrets. Meredith is often more interested, once he has us in love with them, to cite what they do as illustrative of human nature feminine, than to explain the whys and wherefores of what they do.

The men, though not generally so fully presented as the women, we get to know better; but whether because of our knowledge of our own sex, from which we may supply fully what Meredith only hints of, or to his power of presentation, is a question. Richmond Roy and Sir Willoughby Patterne are his most brilliant portraitures, among his men surely, and I think we may go further and say, without such reservation, his most brilliant characterizations, among men and women both. They are taken at a pitch a little higher than that of the common human; they have about them a little of the air of the artificial comedy of the Restoration, but they live and move and have their being as surely as Petruchio or Major Dobbin.

It is easy to forget that the art of Meredith is a very composite art, so thoroughly fused is all that goes to its making into a new and original way of his own. Stop and consider this character and this and this, and you will find analogies between Meredith and *The Arabian Nights,* the Border ballads, Shakespeare, Donne, Molière, Congreve, Fielding, Scott, Peacock, Hugo, Carlyle, Dickens, Browning and Thackeray.

There is a like fusion of gentleman and honest man and scholar and wit in the artist that shapes and uses this composite art. And yet this man so thoroughly himself is many-sided as the repertoire of a great actor. How strangely unlike are the Tinker, Laxley, Wilfrid Pole, Mr. Pericles, Squire Beltham, Captain Welsh, Dr. Shrapnel, Blackburn Tuckham, Dr. Middleton, Vernon Whitford, Beau Beamish, Dacier and Redworth!

How different are the novels themselves, their scenes of action, their stories, the kinds of people with which they are concerned! *Sandra Belloni* brings foreign musicians to mix with social climbers of the new rich in suburban London, and upper class folk and villagers that represent the countryside these outer suburbs are displacing. Swinburne appears in the story as Runningbrooke, as Stevenson was to appear later in *The Amazing Marriage* as Woodseer. In *Vittoria* (1867), the sequel to *Sandra*

Belloni, Welshmen and Englishmen make part of the scores of characters that figure in the war of Italy against Austria. The canvas of *Vittoria* is the greatest Meredith has attempted to fill; it is a panorama as vast, and painted in fuller detail, than that of any English book between *The Cloister and the Hearth* (1861) and *The Dynasts* (1903-08).

Rhoda Fleming is a cross-section of all social orders in the countryside of Kent. There are farm laborers, yeoman farmers, a bank porter from London, squires, and troubling womenkind of all degrees; there are scenes on farms, in London lodgings, on the hunting field, in manor-houses. The theme is the frustration, by Rhoda, because of jealousy and a fierce pride of sex, of the conventional righting of the wrong done her sister Dahlia by Edward Blancove. The young squire would marry the farmer's daughter, but Rhoda steps between, mistakenly, and to the ultimate reduction of her sister to a "woman with a dead soul." Here, too, is the story of Margaret Lovell, which Meredith never makes quite clear to us, coming perilously near to that sentimentality he jeers at so consistently.

The Adventures of Harry Richmond is, in form, the old picaresque story. The scene shifts from a country-house on the Hampshire heaths, to London lodgings, to a farmhouse, to a boy's school, to wanderings with tinkers, to a sailing ship, to the court of a German princeling, to a yachting trip on North Sea and Channel, to a parliamentary election, to a gypsy tent, to the country-house again, to a southshore watering place, and, in the end, to the country-house in flames and doomed to destruction.

Richmond Roy, and not Harry Richmond his son, from whom the story takes title, is really the hero. All the action of the story springs from the efforts of Richmond Roy to establish his claim and that of his son to the throne of England. Underlying the story is the historic fact of a left-handed marriage of George IV. Richmond Roy is imagined the son of such a union. He is your inveterate playboy, the son of the actress, posturing, irresponsible, generous, quixotic, his loved son's worst enemy.

Characters crowd the story, all clearly differentiated, but only about half of them really explained by their actions or by the author's comment upon them. Janet, for instance, whom Harry has finally the luck to marry, is inexplicable in more than one crisis. In the early version of the story there was some comment on what she did, but Meredith cut much of this out in the revised later versions, to the further perplexity of his readers. He has followed a similar practice in other revisions, almost always to the detriment of the story. Gradually I am picking up the novels in the first collected edition of 1885-87. It is in that I prefer to read them.

Beauchamp's Career is the story of a young Radical broken by his aristocratic family lest he disgrace them by success on the wrong side in politics. Incidentally it is the story of his love-affairs; of the marriage of the right girl for him to a staunch Tory lest Beauchamp reason her away from her inherited ideals; of his marriage to a wrong girl, largely because he mistakenly thinks her a Radical; and of the useless sacrifice of his life. The story presents that stirring spectacle of the fight of a brave man against great odds for what he believes right. You follow his fortunes eagerly, so winning is his personality and so honest and unselfish his purposes. There is propaganda in the story, but it is kept well in hand, so the story has lost less with the passing of the years than might have been expected. There are people in it that haunt you, Everard, Rosamund, Rénée, Cecilia, Nevil Beauchamp himself. And scenes, too, most of all that chapter, "Morning at Sea under the Alps," that is comparable to "By Wilming Weir" in *Sandra Belloni,* and to the famous "Ferdinand and Miranda" chapter of *The Ordeal of Richard Feverel.* Meredith tried another such love scene in "A Marine Duet" of *Lord Ormont and His Aminta,* but it was not as the great three. The spirit is there, but not the old surety of words.

The Egoist is the most famous novel of all the great twelve of Meredith, for the reason perhaps that its hero, Sir Willoughby Patterne, stands as symbol of the selfishness of the man as lover. No candid man reading this book but feels his face slapped smartly in chapter after chapter. It is to men what *Vanity Fair*

speedily embrace Philosophy in fiction, the Art is doomed to extinction, under the shining multitude of its professors. They are fast capping the candle. Instead, therefore, of objurgating the timid intrusions of Philosophy, invoke her presence, I pray you. History without her is the skeleton map of events: Fiction a picture of figures modeled on no skeleton anatomy. But each, with Philosophy in aid, blooms, and is humanly shapely. To demand of us truth to nature, excluding Philosophy, is really to bid a bumpkin caper. As much as legs are wanted for the dance, Philosophy is required to make our human nature credible and acceptable."

In all these quotations there is in evidence the resolute optimism of Meredith. Insisting on looking on things as things are, seeing the inwardness of them, he is still of high heart, still cheerful, still comforted. All is not right with the world, but it is still morning, with time enough to better things before night falls. He respects what he calls Hardy's "twilight view of life," but it "afflicts" him. His own philosophy of life is evident enough in his novels but it is more succinctly expressed in his verse. Life must be lived thoroughly in all its phases, animal, intellectual and spiritual. He sums up his doctrine in "The Woods of Westermain:"

> "Blood, brain and spirit, three
> (Say the deepest gnomes of earth)
> Join for true felicity."

Novel after novel illustrates that truth, *Diana of the Crossways* most fully, but not more emphatically than the last word on the subject in *The Amazing Marriage*. One man or woman alone, he believes, can do much for the happiness of others, sometimes just by being himself or herself. Carinthia, for instance, had "the effect on the general mind of a lofty crag-castle with a history."

There's a lift in that sentence, a lift in its optimism, a lift in its art. The man can write. Consider the many and various sorts of effects of which he is master. Where in English prose is description more beautiful than "Morning at Sea Under the Alps?" Where drama more tense than the parting of Percy Waring and Margaret Lovell? Where narrative clearer than the wayfaring of Harry Richmond and Kiomi? Where character presentation more complete than that of Sir Willoughby or Richmond Roy? Where analysis more illuminating than that of love, toward the end of *Diana of the Crossways?* Where else, save in the master of masters, such a humor, ranging all the way from the laughter "broad as a thousand beeves at pasture" of old Mel to "the sunny malice of a faun" that twitches the corners of the mouth of that wise youth Adrian?

Consider, too, the knowledge of life of Meredith, and his cosmopolitan outlook. Here is a man as far from insular as man may be, a man more than Englander, more than Briton, one who is seer for all who speak the English tongue, and for many, too, of what he calls "the grand romantic continent." Men and women of many classes and many countries have place in his novels, and none are conceived with prejudice, and only the Welsh with sentimentality.

Had Meredith been plain-spoken there would be no question of his place among the great novelists of our tongue, plain-spoken all other of them from Richardson to Hardy. Ellipsis and symbolic language have had so little place in them that there has arisen a belief such qualities are out of place in the novel. In poetry, in the essay, they have always been in place. Recall Donne and Browning, Carlyle and Doughty, if you have your doubts. Must it be with these that we rank Meredith, rather than with the novelists? I should say, not only with these, but with the novelists, too. No novelists we accept as of first power have given us characters greater than a score of his greatest, or more moments of a dramatic power that makes us tremble to its will.

CHAPTER XII

THE MASTERY OF THOMAS HARDY

THERE is a richer record of the common lot of mankind in Hardy than in any other of our novelists. His writing discloses a completer understanding and interpretation of an English community than does that of any other of them all from Richardson to Sheila Kaye-Smith. It reveals a greater knowledge of the everyday experience of men and women, of what happens to them, of what they feel, of what they hope. Hardy knows the life of Wessex as only Scott before him had known the life of a whole countryside, and Hardy has the power to present all the phases of that life, low and high, town and farm, as Scott had not.

It is true, of course, that the chief concern of Hardy is with the peasantry and farming folk and the tradesmen of villages and country towns, but he can give us a Lady Viviette or a Lord Mountclere without stiltedness or caricature, as Scott could not. There are not so many characters in Hardy as in Scott, or as in Dickens; or such an accumulation of worldly wisdom as in Fielding or in Thackeray; or such a plumbing of the depths of human nature as in Meredith: yet Scott alone of our great novelists had seen and heard and made a part of himself as many incidents and moments of emotion and of drama from the lives of others as Hardy.

Hardy is a part of a community as Fielding, Dickens, Thackeray and Meredith, each a member of a set or a class, could never be. The family of Hardy, long resident in Dorset, handed on to him its traditions; the neighborhood yielded to the sympathetic listener much of its inheritance of stories; a hint or a suggestion spoke volumes to his realizing mind; his memory retained every scrap of local lore, and his imagination gave significance to all his memory retained. In time, that imagination reshaped, for this story or that, what was essential to it from the great mass of facts, and gave those selected facts, in their refashioned or transmuted form, an intensity and a unity they had not as mere bits of actuality. As he built up his stories all that had come to Hardy in any way grew to have a new existence in a new world, yet no matter how great the refashioning or the transmutation the stories retained what he himself calls "the fresh originality of living fact." Always we feel, with Hardy, our feet firmly planted on the ground, on "good gross earth."

The experiences of a whole neighborhood and not merely the experience of one artist alone inform the novels of Hardy. It is this objectivity of his that gives such breadth to his work, that widens his sympathies, that endows him with large tolerance for the mistakes and false steps to which instinct and human weakness lead his people.

These people are of many sorts. They are peasants as simple as Tess when we first meet her; artists as introspective as Jocelyn Pierston after his twenty years of the centers of Europe; ladies as worldly as Mrs. Charmond. With notable exceptions, such as that of Pierston, these people meet life eagerly, seize it with both hands, are instinct with the will to live. The women particularly surrender quickly to impulse, responding to the first brisk wooer that comes their way, especially if he be a pretty thing in pink and white. They have not the insight that tells which men are steady and true, or if they have, they have been so sadly schooled in love by their elders, or so wholly unschooled in it, that they do not choose in accordance with that insight, but allow themselves to be dominated by mere mating sense.

Ethelberta does, indeed, attempt to educate her younger sister Picotee in such matters, telling her that "love-making and dishonesty are inseparable as coupled hounds." Ethelberta, however, is a cool hand, very unlike most of Hardy's heroines, and her beauty had early led her to much experience with men. Elfride, of *A Pair of Blue Eyes* (1873); Bathsheba, of *Far from the Madding Crowd* (1874); Grace Melbury, of *The Wood-landers* (1887); and Tess, of *Tess of the D'Urbervilles* (1891); are the typical Hardy women. Good girls all of them, they succumb almost at once to the wooing of cheap or flashy suitors, Bathsheba and Grace when they have already known the devotion of Gabriel Oak and Giles Winterborne, true men and doers of the world's work.

These girls are all inexperienced, it is true, but according to popular belief they should be guarded by that instinct fabled of women that enables them to distinguish between the good and the bad. Hardy has no faith, evidently, in their possession of such an instinct, but he is keenly aware of their possession of that much more primitive one of mating. The conduct of his women is often something of an irritation to women readers of Hardy but nothing of an irritation compared to that which Thackeray's women provoke. Women are apt to maintain, too, that Hardy is fairer to his men than to his women, and seize eagerly on the declaration of Bathsheba that: "It is difficult for a woman to define her feelings in language which is chiefly made by men to express theirs." If they could so express their feelings, perhaps we could understand why Bathsheba did not respond to Gabriel Oak on his first wooing, and Grace to Giles Winterborne. Perhaps we can understand anyway. The contention is, of course, that a better case for the behavior of the girls could be made out in language made by women to express their feelings.

The impulsiveness, the instability, the inconstancy, the poor judgment of the women of these Wessex novels are their most patent characteristics. The general reader will comment on this bias of Hardy; or on his pessimism, often considered as a cognate topic; or on his descriptions of countryside. To such a reader Hardy is that fellow who has such a beautiful setting for things going wrong through the cussedness of women. Such a reader feels outraged by tragedy against an idyllic background as he would feel outraged by unfortunate happenings on a holiday in golden weather, a poor meal maybe, or a missed train. That is about as seriously as the general reader can be expected to take his novels. I have dwelt a little on the attitude of those who take their novels as they take their "movies," as amusement, because it is not every author regarded by the thoughtful among his contemporaries as a classic who is at the same time popular, as Hardy is. The novels of Hardy, from *Far from the Madding Crowd* (1874) on, were welcomed by the public as were those of Blackmore and William Black, and regarded by the critics as worthy of comparison with those of George Eliot and Trollope.

Of what other English novelist can it be said that he was recognized for a half century of his own lifetime as one of the institutions of his country and of that wider country of his language. Meredith was undoubtedly a writer of great achievement for an even longer period, but his recognition was slow and never so universal as that of Hardy. Milton and Wordsworth, Emerson and Carlyle, Tennyson and Browning, had honor through long years, but not one of them greater honor than Hardy has had. In such company, the company of poets and prophets, Hardy belongs through his verse, as surely as in the company of the great novelists through his mastery of characterization, and thrilling drama, and epic sweep of story.

No man of all of England's great in literature is more thoroughly English than Hardy. There are those who see in him the influence of German philosophy. No doubt he knows his Schopenhauer, but the most careful parallel study of the two yields no proof of more than likeness of thinking on certain subjects. Nor do the architectonics of Hardy's stories owe more to French fiction than his thought to German philosophy. Hardy took the novel as George Eliot had developed it from the comic epic in prose of Fielding and developed it still further as an essentially English form. Greek tragedy Hardy knows well, and Elizabethan drama, and the whole poetical inheritance of his country. These good things he had paid heed to, as have most of the great English writers, but his stories and verses are as wholly his own as ever were any man's. So it has been from the start in English literature. Chaucer made all his borrowings English and his own; and Shakespeare; and Milton; and Scott; and Wordsworth. What was French or Italian or Greek or Roman or German in incident or form or cast of thought suffered in coming to England that change into something rare and strange and English that is so evident and so hard to explain.

That the novelists of the younger generation who have gone to Russia for their methods have not been able to English their borrowings so thoroughly does not necessarily mean that those borrowings were too un-English to be assimilated. It may mean only a lack of power of assimilation on the part of Cannan and Walpole and Lawrence. Methods of great art of the centers have long been used in shaping the material of the provinces into art. They were thus used by Spenser in *The Shepherd's Calendar* (1579); by Fielding in *Joseph Andrews* (1742); and by George Moore in *A Drama in Muslin* (1886).

Hardy is resolutely the presenter of a province. His Wessex is that section of southern England that corresponds roughly with the old kingdom of the West Saxons. The scenes of most of the stories are laid in Dorset itself, the center of his Wessex and his own home county. The counties contiguous to Dorset, Hants, Wilts, Somerset and Devon, are background for certain stories or parts of stories; and in *A Pair of Blue Eyes* he reaches west into Cornwall, and in *Jude the Obscure* (1895) northeast-ward into Oxford. Once in a while he will send a character overseas, as Stephen Smith to India; but except in *A Laodicean* (1881) there are few scenes in the novels outside of Wessex, except those in London, which, as is natural, the Wessex folk often visit on business or pleasure.

Nor are there many people of other than Wessex origin in the stories of Hardy. Eustacia Vye had Belgian blood in her veins; Baron Xanten had a German father; Sergeant Troy had a French mother; Donald Farfrae is a Scot; parvenus like the Stoke-D'Urbervilles sometimes try to establish themselves as a county family by migration into Wessex, but even they were Wessex folk expatriated by residence for a generation in London.

Hardy himself knows his Paris and Rome, his Switzerland and Rhine, but from his writing you would not judge him a man who has been much abroad. That he is a student of European history, however, especially of the Napoleonic era, is very evident, not only from *The Dynasts* (1903-1908), but from many other writings of his. This interest in the Napoleonic wars is but an outgrowth of his interest in his home country. Wessex was the part of England most threatened by Napoleon's proposed invasion, and Hardy has told us of family legends concerned with the expectancy of a descent of the French on the Dorset coast.

All cultivation is called upon by Hardy to put this beloved land of his clearly before us. Maryann Money, of Bathsheba's household, is described as having the mellow hue of a Nicholas Pouissin; a procession of drunkards is like a Flaxman group; an inn interior shows "Rembrandt effects"; and a landscape was like "landscapes of Ruysdael and Hobbema." As painting is called upon so are philosophy and history and the classics and the poetry of England. The folklore and local songs of Wessex enrich his writing; the dance music and rural sports are studied that his presentation of Wessex ways shall bring the full life of the land before the reader; you are sure he treasures the stories of homestead after homestead along the roads that radiate from Dorchester, and has tested the truth of what he writes of some by what he knows of many. The birds and shrubs, the crops and grazings, the plantations and contours of this and that stretch of upland and vale are known to him; the geological formations that underlie the landscape and the archaeology that underlies the history of Wessex. Hardy knows his Wessex in every aspect of its social economy and history and landscape. He is keenly sensitive to the spirit of place and very faithful and fortunate ,in rendering it in words.

The people of Hardy are what they are because of their environment and ancestry. He uses the scientific knowledge that the Victorian era discovered to account for and to explain his people, just as he uses all artistic culture to picture them for

us. Charles Kingsley before him had found very remote ancestors of Tregarva in that Cornishman's lineaments. So Hardy,
in *The Pursuit of The Well Beloved* (1892), following the
method of *Yeast* (1848), finds in the personal peculiarities and
odd customs of the quarrymen of Portland Bill elements of the
Astarte worship existent there in Phoenician times and handed
down, in modified form, even well into the nineteenth century.

   The Well Beloved (1897), from a certain point of view, seems
almost a travesty of its author's art. Its stressing of coincidence
even though the coincidence makes for bitter irony, might be
taken as satire of his frequent dependence upon this device in
his earlier and greater novels. There have been great writers
whose candor compelled them to gird at themselves. Ibsen
satirized himself in *When We Dead Awaken,* the last of his
plays, in which as in *The Well Beloved,* a sculptor is the hero.
It may well be that Hardy, the great English ironist of our age,
has here turned his irony upon himself. Certain it is that Hardy
up to the end of his career as a novelist in 1895 had been devoted
to one type of art, as Pierston to one type of woman's face.
And as Pierston, on the threshold of old age, turned from the
type of Avice Caro that had lured him from youth on, to
Marcia Bencombe, so Hardy turned from the novels he had
followed so whole-heartedly for a quarter of a century to the
poetry in verse he was not known to have pursued. One need
not strive to find an allegory in *The Well Beloved,* or even
symbolism there, however, to believe it ironic of its author's
ways of writing. Nor need one take it for anything more than
fantasia pure and simple, extravagant as that fantasia is with its
wooing by the hero, at intervals of twenty years, of three girls
in three successive generations of one family, mother, daughter
and granddaughter.

   Desperate Remedies (1871), at the very outset of his career,
presents all of Hardy's faults at their crudest, and so it, too,
in its way, serves as a travesty. There are no very memorable
characters here, and such as have some body seem like sketches
for the completed portraits of later books. One is otherwise,

Æneas Manston, who is very like an exaggeration, for purposes of burlesque, of a Hardy villain. The writer's interest in the details of architecture that betrays his first calling is distinctly in evidence, and his interest in landscape and country ways. Coincidence is rife, things go wrong seemingly out of wantonness, the past refuses to keep its dead buried.

And then, that so often recurrent miracle in the history of the English novel, right upon the heels of 'prentice-work, a book of perfected art! Hardy has no other novel more wholly of one tone and texture than *Under the Greenwood Tree* (1872). He classifies it with his "novels of character and environment," with *Far from the Madding Crowd, The Return of the Native* (1878), *The Mayor of Casterbridge, The Woodlanders, Tess of the D'Urbervilles* and *Jude the Obscure*. And despite a certain slightness *Under the Greenwood Tree* is of this great septenary, and not of that lesser group of seven, the "novels of ingenuity" and the "romances and fantasies." Fancy Day and Dick Dewy, Shiner and Mr. Maybold, are not of the most memorable of Hardy's characters but they are all solidly done. The choir, when once together, is unforgettable, though this member or that by himself, or in his lay capacity, does not count for much. Hardy has made it, as he intended, "a painting of the Dutch School," but it is more than that, a complete reincarnation of a yesterday for ever gone. The humorous and the picturesque are so blended in its presentation that one is not aware which prevails. The very thought of it is soothing, heart-easing, mellowing; the conjuring of it up, man and instrument by man and instrument, one of the supreme delights of retrospection.

A Pair of Blue Eyes (1873) has an interest for the student of Hardy other than that of its tragic story in certain autobiographical disclosures it makes of its author's youth. It has been said that Thackeray divided himself in two in *Pendennis* (1850), making the weaker half of him into Arthur and the stronger half into Warrington. In like fashion it might be said that Hardy had based the character of Knight on the harder side of his own nature and that he had made the circumstances of the birth and position in early life of Stephen Smith not very unlike his own. Hardy was born in Upper Bockhampton, the Upper Mellstock of the novels, a village a couple of miles outside of Dorchester, in 1840. His father, like Stephen Smith's, was a builder, and like many another builder's son the world over Hardy was set to studying architecture. Adventures of his while he was articled to an ecclesiastical architect in Dorchester and while he was a student in London, where he went to be under Blomfield, are the substratum of the parts of *Desperate Remedies* and *A Laodicean* that have to do with architects. It is only in these lighter stories, however, that you find close correspondences between his own life and that of any hero of his.

Far from the Madding Crowd is the only novel of the fourteen of Hardy, other than *Under the Greenwood Tree,* that ends well. There are trials and tribulations on the way to this happy ending, practically all of them caused by the inability of Bathsheba Everdene to know a good man when she sees one. Her heart was free when she first met Gabriel Oak, but he did not strike her fancy, and he was, moreover, in her estimation, as a small farmer, not quite good enough for her. There was to her nothing thrilling or romantic about him. He had not the glamour of position that there was about Boldwood, or that strong farmer's gentlemanly mien. Nor had Gabriel the cheap Jack gallantry or tinselled good looks of Sergeant Troy. Oak wooed Bathsheba as a friend when what she wanted was to be stormed by a masterful man. The fearful joy of being so mastered turned quickly to disillusionment under Troy's lack of consideration and neglect of her interests. So his abandonment of her within a year of their marriage was a happy relief. Even now, however, she had not the perspicuity to favor Gabriel but was drifting into an engagement with Boldwood, when Troy, who was thought drowned, made his reappearance and claimed her. The shooting of Troy by Boldwood cleared the way for Gabriel, who alone of her wooers was now left, Boldwood being off overseas to penal servitude. And yet we know that this marriage arrived at by so unromantic a process of elimination of lovers is going to be a happy one, for it is real love that is between Bathsheba and Gabriel. Their love is a something more than passion, a something very other than mere infatuation, a something of which respect and affection and similarity of interests are a large share: "Theirs was that substantial affection which arises, if any arises at all, when the two who are thrown together begin first by knowing the rougher sides of each other's character, and not the best till further on; the romance growing up in the interstices of a mass of hard prosaic reality. This good-fellowship, camaraderie, usually occurring through similarity of pursuits, is unfortunately seldom superadded to love between the sexes, because men and women associate not in their labors but in their pleasures merely. Where, however, happy circumstance permits its development, the compounded feeling proves itself to be the only love which many waters cannot quench, nor the floods drown; beside which the passion usually called by the name is evanescent as steam."

Far from the Madding Crowd is a great story, firm in plot, of well-balanced characterization, with moving dramatic movements, and lyrical interbreathings of Arcadian freshness. The clowns that form the chorus, Joseph Poorgrass at their head, are, literally, Shakespearian. And Bathsheba and Gabriel and Sergeant Troy have permanent place in the great portrait gallery of English fiction.

The Hand of Ethelberta (1876) is a slight comedy, bright, bitter, disillusionizing and saved from the revolting only by the hardness of fiber of poor Ethelberta herself. It has, beside Ethelberta, two memorable characters. There is that redoubtable old roué whom she tames, Lord Mountclere, who might easily have been a caricature, but who is not. There is, too, the inimitable Chickerel, butler beyond compare and parent of Shaw's waiter in *You Never Can Tell* (1896) and of the Admirable Crichton of Barrie. Much that appeared first in Hardy reappears in the playwrights and novelists that come after him. The plight in which Hilda Lessways finds herself after her engagement to

Edwin Clayhanger, is like that in which Cytherea Bradleigh found herself in *Desperate Remedies,* a book forty years older than *Hilda Lessways* (1911).   And the three wooings of Mark Lennan in *The Dark Flower* (1913) of Galsworthy had already been foreshadowed in the three wooings of Jocelyn Pierston in *The Well Beloved* (1897).

The Return of the Native (1878) is the third great story of Hardy, a greater in conception, if not in execution, than either *Under the Greenwood Tree* or *Far from the Madding Crowd.* Eustacia Vye is your queen of tragedy, a companion figure to Zenobia in *The Blithedale Romance* (1852) of Hawthorne and demanding dramatization into a part such as Siddons and Cushman delighted to play.   Lonely, unlovable, splendid, caught in the net of her temperament, Eustacia needs no pity or love or pardon.   What is most to be deplored about her is that her unhappiness involved Clym Yeobright, a good man, in unhappiness. In the end Eustacia paid for her stoop to folly with her life and her lover's too, when he attempted to save her from the pool into which she threw herself.   All is in harmony in *The Return of the Native,* story, moments of drama, characters, scene.   It is splendidly somber from the awed opening, on Midsummer Night, with the fires above Egdon, to the stilled close that leaves Clym Yeobright defeated, yet struggling, to live out his years alone on the desolate heath.   Thomasin and Diggory Venn lend a little of the meliorating charm of hominess to the harrowing story, but they cannot counterbalance the tragedy Eustacia draws down on herself, her lover and her husband.

Hardy has never written better than in *The Return of the Native*.   His description of Eustacia, beginning: "She had Pagan eyes, full of nocturnal mysteries" reveals him for the moment anyway "a lord of language."   It bears out, as fully as *Tess of the D'Urbervilles* itself, the truth of that dictum of its maker that "The crash of broken commandments is as necessary an accompaniment to the catastrophe of a tragedy as the noise of drum and cymbals to a triumphal march."

Hardy is not a man always at his best, either in the choice

and arrangement of incident or in the style of his stories. As he can overstress coincidence and strain our credulity, so he can write turgidly at times, become involved, grow heavily Latinical, lose his sense of rhythm. It is not often so in the greatest of his books, *The Return of the Native*, *The Mayor of Casterbridge*, and *The Woodlanders*. In description, in narrative, and in analysis of character his writing is almost always clear, well balanced and rhythmical. It is in his earlier work, or in his latest novels, when he is burdened by a thesis, as in *Tess of the D'Urbervilles* or *Jude the Obscure,* that the style stumbles and drags.

Noting that his style is always at its best when Hardy is writing dialect one thinks of what he said of Gabriel Oak, that he looked his best in his working suit. So it was always with Scott. His Sunday clothes of English never fitted as did his working clothes of Scotch. Speaking of Hardy in like metaphor one should say that when Hardy dons English he is not quite so comfortable as when his wear is Wessex but he can always look his best if he walks circumspectly in his clothes of London cut. The stiffness of his verse, for instance, is apt to fall away, when he turns to dialect. That may be, however, because of the emotion of the moment as much as the dialect. It may be the feeling that makes the lines flow clear, rather than the familiar speech. In dialect, too, is the lament of Marty South over Winterborne, but here, again, it may be the emotion that gives this *liebestod* its great distinction.

Rhetoric is not so apt to creep into the dialect, or exact but ugly words of no associations. That rhetoric mars even some of his passages admitted to be great is a charge that has been brought against him. The description of Eustacia, for instance, is said to be too ornate. That is not my feeling about it, but that it is a noble use of our tongue in the tradition of Sir Thomas Browne and De Quincey. It is easy for one averse to ornateness to confuse it with rhetoric and so rule it incontinently out of court.

The Trumpet Major (1880), *A Laodicean* and *Two on a*

Tower (1882) Hardy has himself minimized by listing them
outside of his "novels of character and environment." Yet *Two
on a Tower* has moments of unsurpassable irony and certain
descriptions of the heavens that are equal to any writing Hardy
has done. No English writer has been more aware of the skies
at night than Hardy, not even Milton. The stars that hold
their courses over Wessex are to him as much a part of it as
the sea that walls it to the south or the downs that give it its
sense of space and freedom.

In *The Mayor of Casterbridge* (1886) the tragic figure is the
man Michael Henchard, like Eustacia, the worker of his own
woe. If there is a character anywhere in the whole range of
the English novel that can be compared to Lear it is Michael.
He is almost all of the significance of the story, dwarfing the
other characters, his wife and Elizabeth Jane, Farfrae and Lu-
cetta, so that they count hardly at all. From his sale of his
wife as the book opens to his death on Egdon Heath at its
close Michael is all your concern, save for a few moments only.

The Woodlanders (1887) has in it no such dominating figure.
Winterborne, Grace Melbury and Marty, Fitzpiers and Mrs.
Charmond, once you have read the book, are your familiars for
ever, but no one of them overshadows the rest as Michael does
in *The Mayor of Casterbridge*. Marty is Hardy's staunchest
woman, the true mate for Winterborne, could he only have seen
it. Had fate been kind Tess had perhaps been such another.
There are likenesses between the two girls, just as there are likenesses between Winterborne and Gabriel Oak.

Tess of the D'Urbervilles has been the most widely read and
the most discussed book of Hardy, largely, no doubt because
of the challenge on its title page, "a pure woman faithfully presented." Yet too much significance may easily be attributed to
the controversial nature of the story. There is no doubt of its
power, just as a story, to move us, to harass us, to break our
hearts. Yet we cannot help realizing its tractual quality, that
the fate of Tess is made to point a moral, the unhappiness that
man has made for man through moral laws that clash with

natural instinct. So great, however, is Hardy's power over our emotions that we forget the thesis in following the sufferings of the driven girl. The humor, however intended, fails as comic relief, because we foresee that Sir John, the source of most of it, is going to be his daughter's nemesis.

Jude the Obscure, I have never been able to take on its merits as a novel, for it has always seemed to me, from my first reading of it on publication, the statement of a pathological case in Sue Bridehead and the statement of an all but pathological case in Jude himself. Nowadays so many novels present "cases" that Jude seems quite a usual sort of story, but I am still of the opinion I held in 1895, that "cases" are for the alienist rather than the novelist, for science rather than for art. No book has ever hurt me as has *Jude the Obscure* because no other novelist who has written a book of this kind can make me care so much what happens to his characters. Dostoieffsky had potentially the power so to hurt but since the Russians expect to have things go wrong with them and do not struggle against fate the wrecking of their lives does not deeply affect me. There cannot be great tragedy if the protagonists do not struggle against the fate that threatens them.

Hardy admits that he is a pessimist, but he contends that his "practical philosophy is distinctly meliorist," that "his books are a plea against man's inhumanity to man." He objects to all the declarations in his poems being regarded as his personal beliefs. Many of his poems are wholly dramatic, being the expressions of people whose point of view he captures for the moment. Others are but the reflections of transient moods of his and not his settled convictions. If we were to believe he would answer "yes" to the question asked in "Nature's Questioning" we would hold him black pessimist indeed:

> "Has some Vast Imbecility
>   Mighty to build and blend,
>   But impotent to tend,
> Framed us in jest, and left us now
>   to hazardry?"

The question asked here certainly represents his attitude at moments, and moments that have persistently recurred in the writing of his maturity. At the end of *The Dynasts* (Vol. III, 1908) he reveals that he has had moments when he was almost persuaded out of his pessimism:

> "You almost charm my long philosophy
>   Out of my strong-built thoughts and
>   bear me back
> To when I thanksgave thus. . . . . . ay,
>   start not shades;
> In the Foregone I knew what dreaming
>   was,
> And could let rapture rule! But
>   not so now.
> Yea, I psalmed thus and thus . . But not
>   so now!"

There is just a glint of hope in *The Dynasts* that the "Vast Imbecility," the Unconscious Will that controls the world and all that in it is, may some day develop a conscious design toward good and the ability to further that design's realization.

Hardy's is, like Donne's, "a naked thinking heart that makes no show," an insight that records exactly what it sees. It sees more of evil than of good, but the resulting pessimism "does not involve the assumption that the world is going to the dogs." The vivid life that forms so much of both poems and novels precludes any such conclusion. The writer may philosophize as gloomily as he chooses but the people that he writes about are full of zest for life. The pessimism of Hardy is a matter of temperament. He was born with a Novembry cast of mind, and his experience and observation of life have deepened his natural bias.

Hardy has labored hard to tell the truth about life as he sees it. And he has labored equally hard to make the telling of that truth beautiful. In the preface to *Jude the Obscure* he tells us of the slow growth to completion of that novel: "The scheme was jotted down in 1890, from notes made in 1887 and onward, some of the circumstances being suggested by the death of a woman in the former year. The scenes were revisited in October, 1892; the narrative was written in outline in 1892 and the spring of 1893, and at full length, as it now appears, from August, 1893, onward into the next year; the whole, with the exception of a few chapters, being in the hands of the publisher by the end of 1894." Seven years the story was in the making, and two in the actual writing. That is unhurried work, but not more unhurried than that of several of its predecessors, if one may judge by the long intervals between them.

Hardy has never told us the reasons involved in his giving up of the novel with *Jude the Obscure* in 1895. *The Well Beloved* that followed in 1897 had already appeared serially as *The Pursuit of the Well Beloved* in 1892, and though it is substantially revised in book form it is essentially the old story. Whatever happened to make it his last word in the novel, *Jude the Obscure* is that last word. The *Changed Man* volume of 1913 does not count. Most of it was written before 1895 and what was written afterwards throws no light on why he stopped with *Jude the Obscure*. It was undoubtedly a shock to many confirmed Hardians, and it may well be that Hardy did not wish to hurt a public that had long followed him by further presentations of "the fret and fever, derision and disaster that may press in the wake of the strongest passion known to humanity." Or it may be that he was so sore at heart over the reception accorded the book he would not venture another that might be similarly received. Another guess is that the completion of a philosophy of life seemed more important to him now than anything else and that this could best be accomplished in forms other than the novel. Still another guess is that he wished to return to his first love, poetry in verse.

Whatever the motive that took Hardy again to verse we cannot but rejoice in the fact that he did return to it, for had he not we should be without a very significant part of the poetry of the past quarter of a century. It is unlikely that Hardy had he gone on with stories would have written any more as great as those from *Far from the Madding Crowd* to *The Woodlanders*, and further *Tesses* and *Judes,* valuable as they must have been as works by Hardy, would not have compensated us for the poetry which they would have cost us.

Nor would we have had him, if we could, give us more volumes of tales, condensed novels, short-stories, sketches and the like of the order of *Wessex Tales* (1888), *A Group of Noble Dames* (1891) and *Life's Little Ironies* (1894). Of fine stuff many of these are, but the forms he here uses are not often those most congenial to him. There is no "Julie-Jane" or *Mayor of Casterbridge* among these shorter stories.

Nor am I sure of *The Dynasts*. There are Hardians who acclaim it the greatest of his works, but what its value as art is is not clear to me. It is, I confess, too much for me. I cannot keep all its vast panorama in sight at once, or feel that all the stupendous mass of it is necessary to reveal what seems to be the meaning. I can understand how fascinating a task it was to Hardy so to complete a reading of life long half expressed in novels and verse. Its effect on the reader is another matter entirely. There have been times in the reading of it, when, doubtless because I do not know my history well enough, I have felt like a man in a maze and hopeless of ever finding my way out.

The Hardy that is assuredly great is he who tells stories better than any man of his generation and who has more stories to tell than any. Scores of his verses are stories condensed into a few stanzas but capable of presentation, had he so wished, as full scope novels. There is simply no end to his stores of stories, to his knowledge of what has happened to men, to his understanding of their motives and thoughts. Characters he may repeat from story to story, but situations and moods are strikingly different each from each. It is by the richness of his experience, as I said at the beginning, that Hardy is set apart from all English novelists of his time. His way of acquiring that experience his followers find difficult to learn, but they have readily enough schooled themselves in his methods of laying out and building a story.

They are already a large group, these followers of his, with Phillpotts, "Zack," "John Trevenna," Shan Bullock, Charles Lee and Sheila Kaye-Smith prominent among them. These are out and out disciples, but those who have learned largely of their craft from him include very many others of the two generations of novelists that have come into being since he began to write.

There is a fable of frequent repetition in the temples of criticism to the effect that Hardy came into general recognition only when English writers, grown aware of the Russians, began to hunt for an English novelist fit to be mentioned in the same breath with Tolstoi and Dostoieffsky. The troubled critics could find equals to Turgenieff, but no Englishman to place with the great humanitarians. Then it was, shortly after 1900, that they discovered Hardy worthy to be placed beside Tolstoi and Dostoieffsky. All the truth in the story is that a coterie which had not realized how great Hardy was suddenly awakened to the fact. The weight of critical opinion in England and in America alike, from 1874 on, had been that Hardy was of the immortals. Lionel Johnson in so recognizing him in his *Art of Thomas Hardy* (1894) was but repeating the opinion held orthodox from the publication of *Far from the Madding Crowd* (1874). Hardy has been a classic for a half century.

As a matter of fact Hardy has little in common with Tolstoi, except a vast knowledge of humanity. This, too, he has in common with Dostoieffsky, and an infinite pity for the little lives of men. Hardy is an artist, a lover of severity of form, a practicer of selection and of restraint, the maker of a beauty in words that was not before he wrote. It is not, however, a beauty of a new kind, but of a kind long familiar in English literature. Through his characterization, his dramatic power, his humor, his pictures of the countryside, Hardy proves himself of the stock of Scott and Shakespeare and Chaucer.

CHAPTER XIII

STEVENSON AND THE OLD QUESTION OF STYLE

THERE are those who are pleased to say, apropos of Stevenson, that a man cannot live by style alone. One wonders if there is any considerable reading of his books under the witticism. There can scarcely be, for so much else than style is to be found in Stevenson, even on a casual looking into him. Yet is style alone a little thing? Those who say it is are proved by their saying believers in the false assumption that style is a something plastered on writing, added to "a piece of literature," like stucco to a house, after it is next to finished. His confession of playing "sedulous ape" to this author and that has confirmed many in the largely held belief that Stevenson so regarded style. This practice of imitation is, as a matter of fact, but a phase that almost every writer goes through until he finds his way to the style that most fully expresses not only what he has to say but himself as he says it. Style is, of course, the very essence of the man writing, the quality of himself he puts into what he writes.

Stevenson, questing here and there in the eagerness of youth, tried the way of Hazlitt and of Lamb, of Wordsworth and of Obermann, of Montaigne and of Sir Thomas Browne, of Defoe and of Hawthorne, until he came to maturity with his own way. That way, he wrote to Barrie, within a year of his death, was most influenced by the Covenanting writers. He had read them in childhood, he says, and he had returned to them now. He was laying out a story of them to be called *The Killing Time* which, however, like *The Young Chevalier* and *Sophia Scarlett* and *Canonmills,* never got well under way.

It is very definite, this owning of obligations to "Woodrow

Walker, Shields, etc. . . . . My style is from the Covenanting writers." It would be preposterous to deny that an author knows best who his masters are, but it must be remembered that in a statement of this kind the author is not on the witness stand owning the whole truth. Stevenson fell under the influence of other writers than these above mentioned, writers as different as Sterne and George Meredith, and took from them what he needed. As we have his style in its full maturity, in *Weir of Hermiston,* it is the perfect medium for the telling of that story; it is of the color of the "cold old huddle of grey hills" of the Border that is the story's background; it is of the very essence of the man telling it, a thing of clarities, austere and pure.

And, beyond the style, what is there in Stevenson?

There are: essays that are, with Hudson's, the best of their time; travels that are almost as good in their kind as the essays in theirs; verses that, save those of *A Child's Garden* (1885), are not yet rated generally at their true worth; short-stories like "Thrawn Janet" and "Will o' the Mill"; incomparable farce like that of *The Wrong Box* (1889); fantasia like *Prince Otto* (1885); tales of adventure like *Treasure Island* (1883), *The Wrecker* (1892) and *The Ebb-Tide* (1894); historical romances like *Kidnapped* (1886) and *David Balfour* (1893); and romantic novels like *The Master of Ballantrae* (1889) and *Weir of Hermiston* (1896).

To put it in another way. There are in Stevenson a hundred moments of arresting writing, "character, thought or emotion" embodied "in some act or attitude . . . remarkably striking to the mind's eye," in essay, travel-book, play, short-story, tale of adventure and romantic novel. There are a dozen stories, short and long, that cannot easily be forgotten. There are twenty characters that find place, five or six of them prominent place, in the great portrait gallery of English fiction. There is a spirit of romance as authentic and pervasive as that of Hawthorne.

Of these moments let three stand as typical: the passage in

the essay "Old Mortality," in which he commemorates that friend of his youth who "had gone to ruin with kingly abandon"; the terror of blind Pew in *Admiral Guinea,* when, feeling about in a room, his hand passes through a candle flame and he knows himself helpless before an enemy; and the scene between Kirstie and Archie with which *Weir of Hermiston* breaks off, when Archie "saw for the first time the ambiguous face of woman as she is," the scene Stevenson wrote on the very day of his death.

Of the dozen stories I have already mentioned eleven, "Thrawn Janet" and "Will o' the Mill," *The Wrong Box, Treasure Island, The Wrecker, The Ebb-Tide, Prince Otto, Kidnapped* and *David Balfour, The Master of Ballantrae* and *Weir of Hermiston.* I would not like to be pinned down to the twelfth. It might be "The Beach of Falesá," or "A Lodging for the Night," or "The Merry Men," or "The Bottle Imp," or "Markheim," or "The Sire de Malétroit's Door," or *Dr. Jekyll and Mr. Hyde.*

The twenty characters one is sure to remember from Stevenson are, I think, more easily pointed out. No one will question John Silver, who is as real to the world as Captain Kidd, and not many blind Pew. Prince Otto is, perhaps, the only original portrait in the book, to which he gives title, although its author stood up stoutly for the Countess of Rosen, who with Madam Desprez in "The Treasure of Franchard," pleased him alone among the women he had portrayed up to 1890. Alan Breck Stewart and David Balfour and David's uncle Ebenezer emerge as real people from the many adventures of *Kidnapped,* and Miss Grant and Prestongrange and James MacGregor, at any rate, from its sequel *David Balfour.* There are the Master and Mackellar surely in *The Master of Ballantrae,* Alison Graeme and Mr. Henry, less surely. In *The Wrecker* I cannot believe in Loudon Dodd, but Pinkerton and Nares have personality as well as body. Captain Davis of *The Ebb-Tide* seems to me to be a man known and realized. In *Weir of Hermiston* there are five people certainly creations, Old Weir and Archie; Frank Innes, "the fool advocate," and the two Kirsties. Kirstie the elder, there are some to say, gives the lie to the often repeated criticism that Stevenson had never created a real woman. Others point to her as the damning exception that proves the rule. Stevenson clung so wistfully to Dickon Crookback of *The Black Arrow* (1888), that one wants to list him as the twentieth character of parts from the long shelf of books. It is a scant list from so many stories. There are almost as many from one novel of Scott as from all these stories of Stevenson.

We know the originals of most of these characters, so informing is the Stevensoniana that has accumulated in the period since his death. It was the maimed strength of Henley that suggested John Silver; R. A. M. Stevenson, the first cousin of Louis, who suggested Prince Otto; and Willie Traquair, David Balfour, "though that was dashed with Hugh Wilson." At the very end, when he was working at *Weir of Hermiston*, Stevenson was developing a greater power of portraiture than he had yet possessed. Though he had been away from Scotland for years he was able to recover, from hidden memories and experience, a greater knowledge of Scottish life than his middle years had known. That is often the way of it. Men busy with the life about them in manhood pay less heed to what they heard and saw in their young years than they do as they grow older.

From almost the start of his writing Stevenson had clearly in mind the principles of certain forms of story he wished to write, just as almost from the start he had known the kind of style he wanted to express himself. Not even in the letters of his maturity is he clearer as to what he would achieve than in "A Gossip on Romance" (1882). Play-actor that he was by nature, he wanted to be eloquent, he wanted words that should run "in our ears like the noise of breakers," and a story that should "repeat itself in a thousand colored pictures to the eye." It is in this essay, too, that he reveals that the basis of a large part of his writing is place, the spirit of place, the spirit of romance there is about a haunting place. "Many of the happiest hours of life fleet by us in a vain attendance on the genius of the place and moment. It is thus that tracts of young fir, and low rocks that reach into deep soundings, particularly torture and delight me. Something must have happened in such places, and perhaps ages back, to members of my race; and when I was a child I tried in vain to invent appropriate games for them, as I still try, just as vainly, to fit them with the proper story."

This passage illuminates another tenet of Stevenson, that he regards his stories as, in a sense, games, play. As he says later of the reader's attitude to fiction, "Fiction is to the grown man what play is to the child." And yet Stevenson sticks to this attitude neither in his criticism of fiction nor in his performance of it. That is but one kind of fiction which is play to writer or reader. He practiced other kinds, too. From the writer's point of view he knew many of his stories not play at all, but the hardest kind of hard work. He girds at Scott for taking his stories only as play. "Of the pleasures of his art he tasted fully; but of its toils and vigils and distresses never man knew less." The reverse of this is truer of Stevenson than the original of Scott. Of the toils and vigils and distresses of his art never man knew more than Stevenson. He tried to make not only each short-story but each long story, a perfect whole. He did not always succeed, sometimes because his material got the better of him, as in *The Wrecker*. The Paris scenes of this tale have no place in the development of its plot; they sadly spoil its proportions.

It is in "A Gossip on Romance," too, that Stevenson makes his studied declaration of faith as to what is the "plastic art of literature: to embody character, thought, or emotion in some act or attitude that shall be remarkably striking to the mind's eye." It is a far cry from this declaration, which he has practiced so consistently, in situation on situation, to the presentation of the subconscious self that delights a Sherwood Anderson. Stevenson died before the world was troubled by Freud, but had his life been prolonged to see what issues are current in the novel today he would have been driven to whole-hearted disgust of many such issues. "A Portrait" would have been followed, perhaps, by other sets of stanzas as frank in disapproval as that memorable five.

His great task was happiness; his creed to write only of those things that could be turned to hearty entertainment or to beauty or to nobility. Of squalid beachcombers stricken with influenza, he can write, and even of the lepers of Molokai, but always with the cleanly accuracy of a physician. He hated the exultant horror of the amateur pathologist over such matters, going George Meredith one better in his denunciation of such ultra-realism. In such a realist, he tells us in "The Lantern-bearers" (1892), "we find a picture of life in so far as it consists of mud and old iron, cheap desires and cheap fears, that which we are ashamed to remember and that which we are careless whether we forget; but of the note of that time-de-vouring nightingale we hear no news." Such realists, he goes on to say, "fill the globe with volumes, whose cleverness inspires me with despairing admiration, and whose consistent falsity to all I care to call existence, with despairing wrath. . . . The true realism always and everywhere, is that of the poets: to find out where joy resides, and give it a voice beyond singing."

It was not given to Stevenson to practice often what he here preaches. It is only now and then that the world and all its troubles fall away from us as we read him, that we are "rapt clean out of ourselves," that we hear "the time-devouring night-ingale," and know ambrosian nights. Such service *Treasure Island* did us in "the bright, untroubled period of boyhood," but there is no book of his that is to us now what that was then. In another way, the way of the romantic novel of real life, *Weir of Hermiston* promised to be another such triumph, but its maker was cut down just when he had struck his stride.

There is no hint anywhere in Stevenson that he avoided reality. He was willing to

"see things bare to the buff
And up to the buttocks in mire,"

but such a sight of them did not mean to him that he must tell what he saw. He believed there are "sights that cannot be told" and "stories that cannot be repeated." In that belief though the times are against him, Time may be with him. There is little profit in discussion of such matters. We can only wait. Our children's children shall see.

In the lesser matter of pleasantness, it is very much with authors as it is with neighbors. If a man is your friend and his friendship means much to you you will put up with a good deal of unpleasantness from him. If he cannot be more to you than an acquaintance you will not put up with his un-pleasantness. Only the greatest insight and the greatest art, only the power of a Shakespeare or a Donne, a Swift or a Thackeray, an Ibsen or a Hardy, can make worthwhile the revelation of hideous truth. The little fellows cannot make such revelations beautiful as art or helpful to morality. If less than the great must work in such material let it be in the laboratory or the hospital, and let the records of their discoveries remain filed away among the arcana of science. There the specialists who should know may find them, and, thereby, the rest of us be spared that knowledge.

Stevenson knew, with the self-knowledge of the Scot, that he was not of the Titans. His attitude is very like that Robert Bridges explains of himself in his "Invitation to the Country." Stevenson, too, is

> "content, denied
> The best, in choosing right"

If he could not

> "play
> With hidden things, and lay
> New realms of nature bare"

he could make beautiful the new phases of old issues that he was permitted to see. He could, and did repeat old effects, largely effects from Scott, on the note of a new temperament, his own temperament. And if anyone says this is the way of the minor rather than the major writer, the truth of his saying must be admitted. Stevenson is as surely a minor novelist as Herrick is a minor poet. There is story-telling ability of the first power in him, but no great prodigality of portraiture, no great revelations about life, not more than one story of epic proportions, and it but a fragment. Stevenson is of the authors who are loved as much as they are admired, of the company of Goldsmith and Lamb and Jane Austen and Barrie, minors all, but none the less sure for that of readers down the years.

The life of Stevenson was vivid rather than broad, all the more vivid because he never knew how much of it was left him to live. The playboy in him, the play-actor, the "deal of Ariel," the "just a streak of Puck," shut him off as it does Barrie from a really rich life. The Scott type, with whom all men feel at ease, the eager listener, rather than the eager talker, is generally he who learns most of his fellows. To Stevenson, of course, talk was the half of life, and so brilliant his own and so taking, that many of those who knew both his conversation and his writing thought him halt when he took pen in hand.

There was a great deal of talk in his life, talk with many conditions of men in many places here and there about the world. It was profitable, too, when he would hear and heed as well as play listener. When he did drink in what he heard he would sharply visualize and remember the experience of the talkers. Then their experience became a part of him as surely as if it had been his own.

There was, too, a great deal of talk of another sort in his life, a kind that told even more in his writing. This was the talk in the home of his youth, and the talk of later years with both father and mother. Alison Cunningham, his nurse, gave him her own experiences and the traditions of her family, in his nursery days, and then and later there came to him from mother and father the family traditions of Balfours and Stevensons, both stocks that had been long at the "height and summit of affairs" in Scotland. And there was a great deal of reading, both of literature and of history, particularly the history of his country, and, more particularly still, the history of his own folk, the Covenanters.

Though Stevenson was "valiant in velvet," with a tendency all his life to unconventionality in attire, he was always Puritan at heart, as Puritan as Hawthorne. Both men were in revolt against the forbidding conventions of Puritanism, both were worshippers of beauty, but neither could escape and neither, I believe, really wished to escape, from the dominance of the Puritan morality. Though there may have been years in Edinburgh and Paris when Stevenson was free of its restraints, the ways and practices and disciplines of Puritanism came back to him in the last years in Samoa.

There was something of play-acting as well as of Puritanism in the family prayers, with the whole large household assembled in the great hall, an attitude that would seem to indicate a Highland chieftain somewhere among his ancestors, who reappeared in Tusitala and demanded ceremonial and the fealty of clansmen. Stevenson was very evidently a believer in ancestral memory. He refers to it in a passage I quoted above from "A Gossip on Romance," and again, in the dedication to *David Balfour*. Here he says: "I see like a vision the youth of my father, and of his father, and the whole stream of lives flowing down there, far in the north, with the sound of laughter and tears, to cast me out in the end, as by a sudden freshet, on these ultimate islands. And I admire and bow my head before the romance of destiny."

"The romance of destiny!" In that phrase are packed close the Presbyterian and the romantic. Destiny made sport with Stevenson, it might have been ironically, but he made it be romantically. That is the secret of Stevenson. He turned all he touched to romance just as did that other Puritan of an older generation in New England. They are strangely comparable, these two romantics so different in temperament, Hawthorne and Stevenson. Though both have given us memorable characters, both are more memorable for atmosphere than for portraiture. Both are deeply concerned with the sins of the fathers that the children must pay for so dearly. Both led rather narrow lives and both have restricted themselves to this narrow experience in their writing. Their books are of like scope, with romance in both the most distinguishing possession. You think of the romance of Hawthorne and, sooner or later, you come on Salem and the old days of the witches and the ships from the world's end. You think of the romance of Stevenson, and you come in the end to the Lothians, that countryside to him of all places in the world most haunted by romance. To the end he longed for "the vacant wine-red moor" with curlews and lapwings crying "about the graves of the martyrs." That is the symbol of the man, staunch Covenanter and true romantic all his short years.

CHAPTER XIV

THE CREED OF GEORGE GISSING

IN *The Private Papers of Henry Ryecroft* (1903) Gissing (1857-1903) defines art as "an expression, satisfying and abiding, of the zest of life." It is an illuminating saying and as true as any so sweeping dictum may be. It was a courageous saying, too, for Gissing to write down, for he saw his own work dispassionately enough to know that no matter "how satisfying and abiding" his expression might be his concern was often with material that had little "zest of life" in it, and that he, writing, had only certain moments of gusto. If we view his books in the light of this saying, only one, *By the Ionian Sea* (1901), will pass muster as such art as he is defining. It is a honey-toned thing, this study of Greek Italy, mellow as old marble lying warm in the sun after the weathering of centuries.

An Author at Grass, the title under which *The Private Papers of Henry Ryecroft* was published in *The Fortnightly Review,* is symbolic of a tired hack that could recuperate only when turned out to pasture. That title would seem to predicate that only a second order of zest would be possible to these papers, the zest of peace, of freedom from a galling round, of leisure to do what a worn jade had longed for. There are zests of these kinds in *Ryecroft,* but there is, too, that greater zest of life, that ruddy joy in living, that Gissing finds basic to art of all kinds. The book is that sort of journal that affords its maker opportunity to practice all the many forms of the essay. In it Gissing is now familiar, now sententious, now appreciative of the country-side, and now critical.

There is just a trifle of pose in this journalizing. He was not writing out of a leisure that was infinite, as he pretended;

he was still busy rehashing old material in *Will Warburton* (1905) and other stories for which people would pay. It was a leisure, however, larger than any he had known since childhood, and he for the first time enjoyed a measure of that bookish ease that he had always thought the best of life. The style, too, of *Ryecroft* is touched with artificiality, but not more of artificiality than is consonant with the slight pose of the writer's attitude. Perhaps these are too emphatic expressions, "pose" and "artificiality"; perhaps one should say only that the prose of *Ryecroft* is mannered in a way that the prose of *By the Ionian Sea* is not. It fits the hand that fashions *Ryecroft* like the proverbial glove. His betters and his peers have been guilty of as great shiftings from themselves at their simplest. Lamb played at being Browne when the subject permitted; Carlyle indulged himself in lamentations more Job-like than there was need for; and Stevenson and Richard Jefferies labored so long over artifices that these became in the end second nature to them.

Of the twenty novels of Gissing there is none without moments of gusto, but only three with a zest that is true joy. These are *Thyrza* (1887), *Born in Exile* (1892) and *Eve's Ransom* (1895). Three others, *Demos* (1886), *The Nether World* (1889) and *New Grub Street* (1891), have an intensity of feeling in them that might pass for zest, but if it does, it is a zest of indictment, not the zest of life that is gusto. It is ironic that *Veranilda* (1904) does not have gusto, for it was for years a labor of love to the Latinist in Gissing. It was not a tale of the Rome he knew best, the pre-Christian Rome of the poets, but of sixth century Rome, Christian Rome, Gothic and Byzantine Rome; and it may be this later time, less familiar and less congenial to him, that accounts for the absence of that intimacy you are led to expect because of his devotion to Greek and Latin culture.

The preoccupation of Gissing with the classics is revealed in all sorts of places, likely and unlikely, in his writing. Somehow it keeps itself out of *Charles Dickens: A Critical Study* (1898) but it finds its way even into the dialogue of his novels. Wilfred Athel of *A Life's Morning* (1888) is but one of several of his heroes who discusses the Classics with his friends and loves. In *Ryecroft* this preoccupation finds frequent utterance and in *By the Ionian Sea* it is in full cry. The fox was in sight when he wrote this; he was in Naples on his way to Magna Græcia: "Every man has his intellectual desire; mine is to escape life as I know it and dream myself into that old world which was the imaginative delight of my boyhood. The names of Greece and Italy draw me as no others; they make me young again, and restore the keen impressions of that time when every new page of Greek or Latin was a new perception of things beautiful. The world of the Greeks and Romans is my land of romance; a quotation in either language thrills me strangely, and there are passages of Greek and Latin verse which I cannot read without a dimming of the eyes, which I cannot repeat aloud because my voice fails me."

"To escape life as I know it!" Such a desire is not item one of the equipment necessary to a realistic chronicler of the ways of "garret and cellar" poverty among London's lower middle-class. Nor is that confession of *Ryecroft* item two of that equipment, "The world frightens me." Yet notwithstanding such short-comings, and a deficiency of humor, and narrow sympathies, and a restricted experience, Gissing has left us six novels of about the second order of power, and a dozen others that are abreast of the work of much lauded men of our time.

Books of Gissing have inspired or stood as models for a large part of that work. In many quarters, indeed, he is regarded rather as an influence on Bennett, Beresford and Swinnerton than as a novelist of parts whose books we may read with absorption and be left the richer for knowing. In that fashion, and with that result, may be read, certainly, *Thyrza* and *Born in Exile* and *Eve's Ransom*.

Thyrza is not so characteristically Gissing as the two others. It is much in the manner of Dickens. A cheerfulness like that of a Christmas story pervades it so bracingly that, even though its heroine dies as a result of the hero's indecision and snobbishness and caddishness, you rise from its reading, saddened indeed, but far from disheartened or dismayed. It is largely conceived, and crowded with characters. It is full of motives, of conflicts, of contrasts of circles in varying walks of life. Thyrza and her sister Lydia have sunk through poverty almost out of the lower middle-class, and they are maintaining themselves now in a bare sufficiency as milliner's assistants. Yet Thyrza is potentially the lady, in looks and bearing, as well as in character and spirit. *Thyrza* is a variant of the old story of "the flower of the slums," or, in older guise, Cinderella, a petted and tragic Cinderella who has but a peep at the ball and loses her dear delightful prince.

Gissing laid himself out to make Thyrza a character whom men should not forget, and he succeeded, I think, in that endeavor. It cannot be denied, though, that there is strain in the delineation. We see her clearly enough, idealized as she is, of "pale complexion and . . . golden hair." Her eyes were "large and full of light." She had a "gift of passionate imagination which in her early years sunk her in hour-long reverie, and later burned her life away. . . . Her eyes *saw* something, something which stirred her being, something for which she yearned, passionately, yet with knowledge that it was for ever forbidden to her. A face of infinite pathos, which drew tears to the eyes, yet was unutterably sweet to gaze upon." The portrait of Thyrza is as clearcut and complete as Gissing could compass. I have quoted it for this reason, and as an example of at least a dozen of memorable pictures of women in his stories, and also to show that in a story, done in the spirit of Dickens, Gissing is still very much himself.

With the sisters Trent, and Egremont, the younger's lover, there are two groups of some six characters each in *Thyrza* that crowd the foreground of the story. Among the working people are Totty Nancarrow and Mary Bower; Gilbert Grail and Ackroyd; Bunce and Mr. Boddy: and among the upper middle-class groups are Annabel Newthorpe, whom Egremont has admired, and her father; Annabel's cousin Paula and Mr. Tyrell, and the politician Dalmaine; and Mrs. Ormonde. As generally in Gissing, the lower middle-class folk are better done than those of the upper middle-class. These last are often the grandchildren of lower middle-class folk whom business successes have advanced to the upper middle-class.

All these characters I have named are clearly described and some of them really created. All keep in part throughout the novel. Each could be designated by an epithet or a phrase as: Ackroyd the radical; Mrs. Ormonde, the player with the lives of other people; Totty Nancarrow, "like a lad put into petti-coats"; Mr. Boddy, of the violin; Egremont, the idealistic "slummer." Yet although you think of them labelled in this way there is some personality at least in each one. Of them all, however, only the two sisters are notably done. Lydia is touched to life, little stroke by little stroke in the inexplicable way of genius, and Thyrza so fully presented by all the resources of the novelist that we know her thoroughly.

Thyrza has the vice of "dating." The pleas of Ruskin for the bringing of beauty into lives of toil bore fruit in the eighties in many forms of "slumming." That which Egremont follows is of founding a library for workingmen and of giving lectures on literature there. Gissing is not bitterly satirical of this form of "slumming," but he has no faith in it. "It isn't idealists," he makes Mr. Tyrell say of Egremont, "who do the work of the world, but the hard-headed, practical selfish men. A big employer of labor 'll do more good in a day, just because he sees profit 'll come of it, than all the mooning philanthropists in a hundred years." And on this saying Gissing comments, "It is not impossible that Mr. John Tyrell hit the nail on the head."

Born in Exile is simon-pure Gissing. It is made largely out of his own story. It is the prototype of the autobiographical novels that are so persistently with us today. In these autobiographical novels such dramatic power as that of the great novelists is in abeyance; and its sincerity questioned. It is the verdict of authorities accepted in high places that a novelist should write only of what has happened to him. Of course this may be, according to current theory, what has happened to him subconsciously, as well as what he is conscious of having happened to him. Yet one might believe that a novelist should know, by dramatically assuming the position of his neighbor, as George Moore can, what was happening to that neighbor as readily as what was happening to himself subconsciously.

Gissing was troubled by the theory that the one and only way of the novel was the way of Flaubert. He would, I think, be just as gravely troubled by the theories of the psychological school that he is partly responsible for. One of these theories is this that I have referred to, that a man should write only of what has happened to himself. That is true only when the man writing has no dramatic power. If a novelist cannot understand or enter into any other personality and character than his own he had best stick to what he has himself experienced. One might go further and say he had best not write novels at all. Perhaps, though, it is not necessary thus to go further. Perhaps it is axiomatic to say that if a writer has no power of drama, no power of being other than himself, he is by that very fact no novelist at all. Such a belief would drive you to consider not a few novelists of our day as something else than novelists,—Dorothy Richardson, for instance,—perhaps as writers that belong to science and not to any sort of literature.

If our novelist, however, be a Hardy or a Conrad, he can be himself, and his neighbors, and all other human beings he knows well. Without vision, the novelists perish, as surely as the people in mass.

It so happens that Gissing's own story is an arresting one. He has used it in earlier stories than *Born in Exile* but he here uses it with more power than elsewhere. It was this impossible story that underlay his boyish *Workers in the Dawn;* and, in his dearth of experience, he used it again in *The Unclassed,* and, less exactly, in *The Nether World.* Other phases of his life are followed rather closely in *Isabel Clarendon* (1886), *A Life's Morning, New Grub Street* and *In the Year of Jubilee* (1894).

It is in *Born in Exile,* however, as I have said, that the impossible story is transmuted into something like beauty. The chapters about Godwin Peak's boyhood reproduce closely Gissing's boyhood in Yorkshire, where he was born, at Wakefield, in 1857. Peak's giving up of his career at college was the result of a much less serious incident than that which caused Gissing's withdrawal from Owens College as a boy of eighteen. As Gissing had sent Whelpdale to America in *New Grub Street,* the novel just preceding *Born in Exile,* he could not again use that experience of his own for Peak. Instead he hid Peak away in Devonshire, the part of England he loved best. Here Gissing made his hero deny his agnostic youth and study for the ministry of the Church of England that he might so gain caste and be considered by the Warricombes as a possible husband for Sidwell, the daughter of the house. So far as my information goes there is no parallel in Gissing's life for this situation, but there may well have been an episode that suggested it. Sidwell Warricombe is Gissing's most successful portrait of a cultivated girl of the upper middle-class. She is not invented but reproduced from life.

That *Born in Exile* should end unhappily is not inevitable from what we are told of Peak's duplicity. You cannot help feeling that Gissing was aware of his identity with Peak all the time he was writing the book and that his hero was made to suffer as Gissing in a situation similar to Peak's in the Warricombe family would have been made to suffer had the nature of his débâcle at Manchester been made known. Pilfering from one's fellow students to keep one's girl off the streets would not be a pretty tale to tell to the family of a later beloved. The exposure of Peak's assumed orthodoxy need not have been attended with any such calamitous results. Sidwell would have forgiven Peak that readily had he boldly faced her family with the old plea that all's fair in love and war. It was the shadow on Gissing's own life that darkened the way of the lovers in *Born in Exile.* And yet it is true that Peak could not have faced Sidwell's family even after this lesser shame were he largely Gissing. Gissing would not have been Gissing had he so dared.

The irony of the situation in *Born in Exile* is deepened by the legacy left Peak by the will of Marcella Moxey, an old friend of his in London, long in love with him but for whom he could have only friendship. If Sidwell were to marry Peak their independence would be due to the other woman's money. That, apparently, however, was not what continued to separate them, or lack of love on Sidwell's part. Cowardice before her family's opposition, fear of her ability to stand by him, and her own pride, constrained her to take the easiest way out of the difficulty and refuse him. Peak accepted her decision and went abroad. He fell ill and died in Vienna, in exile, as he had lived. It is a coincidence, that Gissing, too, should have died abroad, in the Pyrenees, in 1903.

I have dwelt on *Born in Exile*, not only for its own sake, as a story of more absorbing interest than many of Gissing, but because it so poignantly reveals his inability to forget the results of the Manchester episode and of the impossible chivalry that led him later to marry the heroine of it. There were times when he felt almost a pariah and longed for nothing so much as the scholar's place that had been possible to him but for this fault of his youth. At other times he was proud of his aloofness from the crowd, his loneliness, his individuality that set him apart. In this latter mood he felt himself one of nature's chosen ones, a member of the aristocracy of knowledge and sensibility and power of thought, one of "the few, the very few, that have always kept alive whatever of effectual good we see in the human race."

Eve's Ransom has, from my first reading of it, seemed to me the most original of Gissing's novels. It is the story of a woman who cannot forgive the man who loves her for saving her from a liaison with a married man. After Eve Madeley is saved, after she has accepted from Hilliard everything he has to give, his money, his devotion, all of him that matters, and given him nothing in return, not even real friendship, she marries a rich friend of his, Narramore. Eve has all along cherished a grudge against Hilliard. This affair with the married man she looked back upon as true love, and for it the world had been well lost. She says to Hilliard, "When you took me away, perhaps it was the unkindest thing you could have done." Eve, of course, had never loved Hilliard. Why, then, should she marry him, when she did not love him, and he a poor man? She was not grateful to him. She was afraid of poverty. Now that her real love was over, her fear of poverty was her ruling passion. Why, then, should she not marry Narramore? She did not love him any more than she loved Hilliard, but with the rich man she could avoid poverty forever.

There is a remarkable scene, unemphasized, almost slurred over, at the end of *Eve's Ransom,* in which, as Narramore's wife, Eve thanks Hilliard for saving her. Are we to assume a weathervane has shifted? I think not. We are to suppose that now in the position of an English lady of fortune her girlish dream of a grand passion has shrunk to scant proportions and that she is sincere in saying, "I was all but lost—all but a miserable captive for the rest of my life." It is the close ironic, always dangerous to a story of emotions deeply stirred, but Gissing dares a last page even more unsentimental. It is a week later than the scene in Narramore's garden. Going down into the country Hilliard experiences in the "golden sunlight" of Autumn the last stages of his freeing from the dominance of Eve, a dominance that was almost obsessive. The last words of the book are "And Maurice Hilliard, a free man in his own conceit, sang to himself a song of the joy of life." Not even Hardy goes so far as to show you his hero losing the captivating heroine and crying, "Thank God," for such luck!

In *Demos* Gissing packs into Richard Mutimer all the deep hatred for the proletariat that had consumed him since his early days in London. Years later *Ryecroft* finds him confirmed in his detestation: "I am no friend of the people. As a force, by which the tenor of the time is conditioned, they inspire me with distrust, with fear; as a visible multitude they make me shrink aloof, and often move me to abhorrence. For the greater part of my life, the people signified to me the London crowd, and no phrase of temperate meaning would utter my thoughts of them under that aspect. The people as countryfolk are little known to me; such glimpses as I have had of them do not invite to nearer acquaintance. Every instinct of my being is anti-democratic, and I dread to think of what our England may become when Demos rules irresistibly."

In *The Nether World* (1889) he reveals an even deeper antagonism to the mob. He has here, too, a sense of the menace of revolution, of what may happen "some dreadful, unexpected dawn" when the submerged shall rise, and civilization fall in chaos. Here, in his pictures of the slums, you feel he knows more of the conditions with which he has to deal, that he is surer of his ground than in *Demos*. There are a host of passages in *The Nether World* that cry aloud for quotation, but I have room for one only, a description of Clem Peckover, in whom we have another one of those memorable portraits of women characteristic of Gissing. It is as unsympathetic as that of Thyrza is sympathetic, but as firm and clear as Swinburne's Faustine: "There was no denying that Clem was handsome; at sixteen she had all her charms in apparent maturity, and they were of the coarsely magnificent order. Her forehead was low and of great width; her nose was well-shapen, and had large sensual apertures; her cruel lips may be seen on certain fine antique busts; the neck that supported her heavy head was splendidly rounded. In laughing, she became a model for an artist, an embodiment of fierce life independent of morality."

New Grub Street is a story of "the valley of the shadow of books," of hacks, of authors who give the public what it wants, and of authors who do not. It is a quieting draught for all with literary bees buzzing in their bonnets. Gissing has divided himself into three men, Reardon, and Biffen, and Whelpdale and, for once, in such a division, there is enough to go around. That is because Reardon is the only full-length portrait and the other two brought in just for the sake of giving Gissing an opportunity to air his experiences in America and his theories of writing. It is Biffen who lays down what was Gissing's ideal in his stories of London's lower orders. "What I aim at is an absolute realism in the sphere of the ignobly decent." Gissing saw clearly that there was danger that that way dullness lay. "The result," he continues, "will be something unutterably tedious. Precisely. That is the stamp of the ignobly decent life. If it were anything but tedious it would be untrue." That Gissing, writing very much in the spirit of this declaration, should often, as in *Thyrza*, escape dullness, is remarkable; that he should not always escape dullness is inevitable.

Gissing is under no illusions about his own work. No friend of his could be more candid: "His books are not works of genius, but they are glaringly distinct from the ordinary circulating novel. Well, after one or two attempts, he made half a success; that is to say, the publishers brought out a second edition of the book in a few months. There was his opportunity. But he couldn't use it; he had no friends, because he had no money. A book of half that merit, if written by a man in the position of Warbury when he started, would have established the reputation of a life-time. His influential friends would have referred to it in leaders, in magazine articles, in speeches, in sermons. It would have run through numerous editions, and the author would have had nothing to do but to write another book and demand his price. But the novel I am speaking of was practically forgotten a year after its appearance; it was whelmed beneath the flood of next season's literature."

That, of course, was written in pessimistic mood. There were other times when his work seems better in his eyes, but he usually speaks of it as if it were lacking in "cosmic force."

As most of the novels of Gissing are records of men who fail, the philosophy of life you glean from them can scarcely be a high-hearted one. *Thyrza* is full of his typically disillusioned sayings. Here is one, "After all, he was among the happier of men, for he could look back upon a few days of great joy, and forward without ignoble anxiety." And here another, "Is it not the best of life, that involuntary flash of memory upon instants of the eager past? better than present joy, in which there is ever a core of disappointment; better, far better than hope, which cannot warm without burning." And this a third: "We have to jest a little in the presence of suffering, or how should we live our lives?"

Gissing is, of course, no Meredith, but there is more food for thought in many of his observations upon life than has been allowed by his critics. It is remarkable that one with so narrow an experience should arrive at so many "readings of life."

Nor has the power of Gissing as a critic of literature been generally acknowledged. Some have owned that he has written the best criticism of Dickens that we have, but he has missed full recognition for *Charles Dickens: A Critical Study* (1898) as he has missed full recognition for other phases of his endeavor. It should be remembered, too, that Gissing was one of the first to acknowledge the power of Dostoieffsky, but that at the same time he understood that English fiction should not follow Russian methods, that it must remain insular in its essentials, especially in its point of view. There is no one way of fiction for all the world. "Art is not single; to every great man his province, his mode." Golden words these, but only a fraction of such one would quote if one had the space.

Gissing could appreciate many differing sorts of writing. There was great joy for him in his discovery of a volume of "gentle-hearted" Tibullus "on the stall of the old book-shop in Goodge Street," and an equal joy when he came upon, fresh from the press, a volume of *Barrack-Room Ballads* and found there "the strong man made articulate" by Kipling.

Nor does Gissing make the mistake that so many novelists make when they assume the rôle of critic, of rating the novel as the highest form of literature. He sees clearly that such the novel cannot be unless it is poetry as well. He acknowledges poetry to be the very essence of literature. It is in *A Life's Morning* (1888), just after the great passage on "the sunny spaces of the world's history, in each of which one could linger for ever," that the words are spoken: "To know the masterpieces of literature, pure literature, poetry in its widest sense; that is the wise choice."

There are literally a hundred passages of "poetry in the widest sense" marked in my copies of Gissing, many of them passages which could, I think, stand comparison with all but the greatest in English prose, and a few of them our speech at its best. Some are a little orotund, perhaps, as you would expect of a Latinist, but of perfect clarity and of haunting rhythm. It is seldom such passages are short enough for quotation. He is in no sense an epigrammatist. "It was the hour of the unyoking of men" is one sentence complete in itself; and a second, of another kind, is "Fair, rich land, warm under the westering sun."

It is in his style that Gissing, like Stevenson, is at his best. It is, in fact, in his style alone that his novels reveal a quality of first power. The form of his stories shows slight advance on that of the three volume novel of mid-Victorian days. His gift of narrative is not marked, and though there are scenes of emotion that move you deeply there are few moments of real drama in Gissing. His attributes, save that of characterization, are the still attributes of the essayist rather than the emotional attributes of the novelist. Gissing was the writer born, the novelist made. He was the novelist made by sheer will power, as well made as was possible through the most careful and conscientious artistry working on material never wholly congenial to its gatherer.

It is difficult to place Gissing. There are none of his predecessors with like excellences and limitations. There is no novelist of an earlier time with a distinguished style and a fair power of characterization who was not popular in his own time, but who has grown into some notability in a subsequent time. It is Gissing's fate to be apart, the one of his kind, at least until today. He has never had popularity or even whole-hearted critical appreciation. He is too drab for popularity, and not sensational enough, even in *The Whirlpool* (1897), in which he tried hard for "big effects" in things of the center. It is his drabness, too, I think, that has prevented any coterie worship of him, or a following of enthusiastic critics. Probably he is more read now than he ever was. No book of his that finds its way to the second-hand shops but is snapped up as soon as it is put on the shelves. Yet there is no complete and uniform edition of him, though we have more than once been promised such a desideratum. One sometimes wonders whether his lack of confidence in himself is not communicated as a lack of belief in him to his admirers. It is strange, indeed, that six as good novels as his best do not win him more fame. As it is too many who should know him do not know him, dismissing his novels, in his own distinction, as literary work and not literature. Yet some of them are surely literature, enough of them to make him a novelist only less than great.

CHAPTER XV

GEORGE MOORE, CRITIC

In his bibliography of George Moore, (1852-   ) made in 1921, Henry Danielson gives his author forty-five titles. Several of these represent re-writings of early books, others are hardly more than pamphlets and some are but re-printings or juvenilia or chips from the workshop. If you drop all doublings and inconsequential items, and list as one novel *Evelyn Innes* and its sequel *Sister Teresa,* and the three volumes *Ave, Salve* and *Vale* as *Hail and Farewell,* there remain twenty-one books by which the position in letters of their maker is to be judged. Of these twenty-one the plays, *The Strike at Arlingford* (1893) and *Elizabeth Cooper* (1913), count for little. They are intrinsically of slight value and they have not made history upon the stage. *The Untilled Field* (1903), a book of stories and sketches manufactured especially for the Celtic Renaissance, has but historic interest. It does not come out of an Irish life that Moore knows well as do *A Drama in Muslin* (1886) and so much of *Hail and Farewell* (1911-1914). *The Untilled Field* did nothing to advance the reputation of Moore when it was published and it does not really broaden his field of accomplishment as you consider it today.

Moore is of importance because of his "confessions," because of his criticism, because of some of his novels. By his "confessions" I mean that kind of intimate journalizing he has done in the three volumes of *Hail and Farewall;* and, along with more criticism, in *Confessions of a Young Man* (1888); and, along with a certain amount of fabrication and approximations to the short-story, in *Memoirs of My Dead Life* (1906). There are passages in these books as urbane as a noon in late September.

Leisure is in the air, and peace. Memories of happy days return, not too insistently, and delight, and are forgotten. Other memories that lull as pleasantly float up in consciousness, and have their moment, and pass. And then the mood changes. It is sharp and mocking now, and now a mood of penetrating criticism, of life and of art. This presence of criticism of painting and literature and music in so much that Moore has written is indicative of the real nature of his talent. The man is basically a critic. Even when he is writing of life directly in his "confessions" he is always ready to turn aside and comment on the arts.

The arts and women and a little coaching and going to the races and a playing at Irish nationalism have been about all that Moore has apparently cared about. Religion is theoretically interesting to him. He has written about it a good deal from first to last but you know as you read that religion has not touched him personally. He can feel it dramatically, that is, he can as he has said "kneel at prayer" with Sister Teresa until he can understand her and be at one with her point of view, but that is not at all the same thing as having religion as a part of life. This ability of Moore not only to see things from the points of view of characters so different from himself, but to transform himself for the nonce into these characters is his greatest asset as a novelist. It is his only asset as a novelist other than the style of his maturity that is of the first power. He has not much gift of story-telling, though he does anecdote well, and his characterization is all within a narrow range.

Moore knows certain circles in Paris, artistic and Bohemian, and similar groups in London. He knows, as well as a man of narrow sympathies can know, certain groups in Dublin, or rather he knew them for a little while. That is a trouble with Moore. What he said wittily about Wilde, that he was a lily in a vase, without roots, is true of himself as far as the latter phrase goes. You feel that Moore is without roots, that he has never had a home anywhere despite the Monet and the Sheraton bookcase and the Aubasson carpet that he takes with him on his flittings. And it is difficult for a man without the knowledge that comes through a home to write novels that involve domesticities, as novels of real life must more than now and then. Even when you say Moore knows groups here and there, you wonder whether you shouldn't say he "once knew groups here and there." You doubt whether anything but his devotion to the arts has been permanent with Moore.

By his own confession we know that Moore has often changed masters. That after he realized how shoddy was the prose with which he began he set himself to a serious study of the prose of Pater. That Zola, Flaubert and the Goncourts were influences on his work but only passing influences. That before Pater the true influences were but three. The record of the three is to be found in *Confessions of a Young Man* (1888): "Shelley had revealed to me the unimagined skies where the spirit sings of light and grace; Gautier had shown me how extravagantly beautiful is the visible world and how divine is the rage of the flesh; and with Balzac I had descended circle by circle into the nether world of the soul and watched its afflictions."

There were other influences on Moore in later years, chief among them the influence of Yeats. Moore had never had the style or a part of the content of *Evelyn Innes* (1898) and *The Lake* (1905) if it had not been for his talks with Yeats, his study of Yeats and the new vision of Irish landscape and Irish art and Irish mood to which Yeats introduced him.

Of the three other important novels of Moore than *Evelyn Innes* and *The Lake,* two are done largely on the model of other men's stories or other men's art. *A Mummer's Wife* (1887) is done after Zola. *A Drama in Muslin* (1886) is more wholly Moore's own than any important novel of his. *Esther Waters* (1894), though he found its heroine in the slavey of his lodging house in London and the Barfield home in the south of England, carries in it evidence of a study of *Germinie Lacertaux* (1865) of the Goncourts.

When one thinks of the ten years of youth that Moore spent in France it seems strange that he never wrote about French life in his stories. He spent so much of his time with French people or people who habitually spoke French that in the end English came hesitatingly to his lips, and certain phases of Parisian life, at any rate, must have become familiar to him. He saw little of homes there, but that is as true of his experience of England as of France, and it did not serve as an inhibition to his writing of England. In *Reminiscences of the Impressionist Painters* (1906) Moore writes: "France is the source of all the arts. Let the truth be told. We go there, everyone of us, like rag-pickers with baskets on our backs, to pick up the things that come in our way, and out of inconsidered trifles fortunes have often been made. We learn in France to appreciate not only art—we learn to appreciate life, to look upon life as an incomparable gift." In *Memoirs of My Dead Life* (1906) he seems when writing of Paris almost on the verge of explaining why it is he has written no novel of French life: "I cannot look upon this city without emotion; it has been all my life to me. I came here in my youth, I relinquished myself to Paris . . . and Paris has made me. . . . Although I know the French folk better than all else in the world, they must ever remain my pleasure and not my work in life."

Moore has done eleven novels in all, and one volume of three condensed novels, *Celibates* (1895). Of the novels other than the five that have some distinction, four are early works, *A Modern Lover* (1883), *Spring Days* (1888), *Mike Fletcher* (1889) and *Vain Fortune* (1890), and two of more recent years *The Brook Kerith* (1916) and *Héloïse and Abélard* (1921). Moore has valued *A Modern Lover,* his first novel, enough to re-write it as *Lewis Seymour and Some Women* (1917). It is a poorer book in every way save in proportion and style than the first version. *A Modern Lover* was crudely written, and hurried at the close, but it had a kind of rough effectiveness because of the heat with which it was felt and because of the intimacy of the portraits of Lewis Seymour and Gwennie Lloyd, Lucy Bentham and Lady Helen. It is an ugly story as *A Modern Lover,* a story that is virtually an attack on its hero, a parasitical artist who climbed to reputation by the help of women, and discarded them as soon as they had done what they could for him. As the descriptions of this man's painting resembled to a certain degree those of a popular artist of the time the book had to a slight degree a "success of scandal." As *Lewis Seymour and Some Women* it has had no greater success than as *A Modern Lover,* and it is ugly still, and weak, in addition.

Spring Days (1888) goes *A Modern Lover* one better in ugliness. It must be a great comfort to readers who wish to believe that English girls are of coarse clay. These Brookes sisters are as pretty a trio of vixens as the mind of man could devise. Moore luxuriates in making them catty and cheap and nasty. He is bent on showing you that the England he hates has in it "an artificial, vicious and decadent society." Such a picture is, of course, no more truly representative of the England of yesterday than a dozen of similarly ugly American novels of today it would be easy to name are representative of America as a whole.

Mike Fletcher its author has not rewritten, and, it is reported, is content to have forgotten. It has for hero one even less admirable than Lewis Seymour but one that Moore has not a like gusto in describing. If its author did not wish it to be shocking it is difficult to understand why he included in it so many readings of life of a kind with this gem of them all, "The creation of life is the only evil."

There is good writing in *Vain Fortune* (1892) but as Moore says in his "prefatory note" to the third version of it, the story is "thin and insipid." Even two rewritings have not made it other than that. There are unquestioned graces of cadence and warm glows of atmosphere in *The Brook Kerith* (1916) but the story only quickens to interest for brief moments, being too heavily burdened with treatise-like opinions its author must get off his mind. One of these that he much labors is of the "ultra idealism" of Christ. That Moore should write of Christ at all is an offense to some, but there is such a lack of reality about the book that one can hardly take it seriously enough to be offended or hurt. All of it, too, has been heard so many times over, in polemical writing, if not in the novel, that it is only dogged will that drives you on to the end.

In *Héloïse and Abélard* (1921) Moore has for subject one of the memorable love-stories of the world. From the style he employs to retell it it would seem that he thought some manner other than he had before used was necessary to its age and renown. It is a style at once laconic and heavy, with little beauty in it, but of a timber of its own. He has evidently read up his "period," and he has been amusingly disturbed by a sense of the discomforts of housing of that old day. Now, too, for the first time, he begins to display an interest in natural history, and brings wrens as well as wolves into a snowbound Paris. This is not the first writing in which Moore has attempted to retell a love-story of old time. He quarreled over *Diarmid and Grania* with his collaborator Yeats, and this dramatic retelling of Ossianic legend has never been printed. Those who saw it and heard it performed, however, in Dublin, in 1901, thought it lacked both the nobility and fine scorn of the original. However that may be, nobility is far to seek in *Héloïse and Abélard,* and a great love-story of old time without nobility is nothing at all, not even a travesty.

The five novels that have in them characters which might find place in the great portrait gallery from English fiction begin with *A Mummer's Wife* (1885). That book, like *A Drama in Muslin* (1886), is written without distinction, but there are in it two characters one does not forget. *A Mummer's Wife* marks a great advance in construction as well as in characterization over *A Modern Lover*. Moore had come into power overnight.

Even before Moore had left London for Paris in 1873 he had come into contact with comic opera. One of his family was interested in it as a business so Moore had models for his characters. Dick Lennox is from the life and he is real. Kate Ede is even more of a creation, and she is admirably rendered. She has, perhaps, originated from the girl who inspired Gwennie Lloyd, and Rose Massey in *Vain Fortune,* but she is individualized. The

story of her rise and glory, her decline and fall, is worked out a
little too logically, a little too closely to scale, but she is human
always and she reacts to circumstances naturally.

A Drama in Muslin (1886) has for background the West of
Ireland life to which Moore was born and the Dublin life with
which a landlord of Moore's origin must be familiar at least in
"the season." The story follows the fortunes of five girls from
the convent through their adventurous years. They are distinct,
one from another, though rather conventionally imagined, as
ugly duckling and true swan, and horsey sort of rash impulses,
and cool and rather minxish beauty, and potential nun. As usual
Moore is more interested in his women than his men. If it is not
true that, like D'Annunzio, he can create men only in the image
of himself, the men of his books are more of a kind than the
women, and some of them a good deal like their creator. Moore
uses the device of introducing one Harding, a novelist, very evidently himself, in this as in other stories, so as to keep before you
the suggestion that only this character can be identified with
Moore. The trick is, of course, too patent to be at all deceptive.
A Drama in Muslin is a hard book, a book without shadows, all
black and white. It, too, has been rewritten. As *Muslin* it has
less life than as *A Drama in Muslin*.

Evelyn Innes (1898) is a very determined attempt to make a
thing of beauty out of the cultivation of the nineties. It is a study
of a woman and her career and her loves, of how the career and
the loves work at cross purposes in the end, and how, to regain
her self-respect, she has to seek avoidance of her hopeless struggle by entering a convent. The newspapers send questionnaires
to actresses and singers like Evelyn to ask them how they recon-
cile art and domesticity and struggles like hers fall within the ken
of most of us. There is nothing in the story that is beyond the
experience and observation of the average cultivated person. To
such a person who was young in 1898, who had seen the pictures
Moore had seen, heard the music Moore had heard, and read the
books Moore had read, the story ought to be or ought to have

been at the time of publication, of very great interest. And so it was, but as a cross-section of a known time rather than as the story of a driven fellow human.

The pity is that *Evelyn Innes* promised to be so much more than it turned out to be. Its failure was due partly to its development into a thesis novel, and partly to the overplus of its description of music. The thesis is that conscience will in the end rule both passion and love of art in an English girl, or as Moore himself puts it more briefly, "None can persist in wrong doing." The thesis is not axiomatically true in either form, or as it is revealed in the details of the story. Indeed it is very difficult for the reader to believe that Evelyn would seek escape from the world.

The obvious identity of Frank Innes, Sir Owen Asher, Ulick Dean and Monsignor Mostyn with "celebrities" of the day had something to do with the success of the book, as had its so old theme of duty versus desire. Evelyn herself, who in respect of origin is much more a composite portrait than any of the men, is also—perhaps one should say, therefore—more of an achievement. If there is a great portrait in the book it is Evelyn. *Sister Teresa* (1901), the sequel, impresses as a *tour de force* rather than as a revelation. What is most remarkable about it is that its author should know so much about convents. Particularly remarkable is it that Moore should sympathize with the sister who loves the heavy work of gardening. That is again a proof of his dramatic power. No one who has read Moore can believe he knows by experience that the taste of sweat is salt.

The Lake (1905) might be called by the light-minded largely a gardening novel. Father Gogarty, its hero, is devoted to his flowers and Moore has "gotten up gardening" with great pains. The large effects of landscape, however, are much better done than the details of borders and plots. Moore has caught the very hues and atmosphere of Irish lake and mountain, and he writes of them in a rhythm that is beyond anything that Pater could teach him. It is palpably the writing of Yeats that has shown him the way to these new effects. There is a sense of labor in the characterization, but both Father Gogarty and Rose Leicester, the principals, are completely achieved. Stroke by stroke, Moore adds to the effect of each, until each stands clearly before us. One of them at least has moments of real passion, a rare quality in Moore, who is more often content with the presentation of appetite.

There are many observations upon life in *The Lake,* more, I think, that stick in mind, than in any other of his books. If the truth of these sayings is often questionable their expression is not. Here is one, in pessimistic mood: "Life is, after all, a very squalid thing—something that I would like to kick like an old hat down a road." In *Evelyn Innes* life had been, "a few sonatas, a few operas, a few pictures, a few books, and a love-story."

Man of the world that Moore prides himself in being his experience of life has been very narrow. In *Esther Waters* (1894) his bachelor's lack of knowledge of babies frequently provokes gentle amusement and once downright hilarity. No writer has generalized more freely about women but he has not found out so obvious a fact as that the normal woman has a more lasting interest in children than in men. Even his preoccupation with Esther Waters has not taught him that, though he knows that it is her love of her child that sends her back to William Latch. It is in *Esther Waters* that Moore is at his best, that he shows his deepest understanding of life and true humanity, that he attains a completer unity of effect than is usual to him, and that he achieves his greatest portrait, Esther herself.

Moore's talent for the novel is slight. He has the ability to see life from the point of view and with the personality of people very different from himself; he has style; and he has some power of characterization. If he were not the writer he is, if he had not the personal quality of the familiar essayist, if he had not his malicious wit, if he had not an insight into art that is surpassed by few critics of our day, Moore would not be the figure he is in contemporary literature. He occupies a higher place as a novelist than his stories alone would win for him because of the quality of himself he can put into all his writing. About his place in the future one wonders. Twenty memorable characters, but only one, Esther Waters, surely of the immortals, is not after all a promise of a lasting place in the English novel.

One can better understand the slightness of Moore's whole accomplishment in the novel when one realizes that his life has been almost solely that of a connoisseur. He has been an epicurean, too, in the common sense of the word. It has been his misfortune to have never worked hard at anything or been wholly preoccupied for long with anything but art. This is a misfortune that he shares with many writers of his day. Think of a Scott interested in a hundred things and living the broadest sort of life before he wrote any novels at all. Think of a Dickens with more real living in his boyhood than comes to many novelists in a whole lifetime. Think of a Hardy with a detailed knowledge of a whole countryside. Think of a Conrad with a quiet and unconscious storing up of experience at sea, in London, and alongshore in Malaya. Then think of Moore and—Montmartre, and the little use he made of even that in his writing. Think, too, of the relative sympathies and powers of vision of men of rich and wide experience of life, and of Moore. The man who is a dilettante in life has less chance to be a novelist of broad scope than the man who lives a life of many interests. The dilettante may, indeed, write well, as Moore so surely does, but it is rarely that he will write well about anything but himself. Moore lived intensely enough in the world he created for Esther Waters to achieve greatly in his book of her. That once, only, though, did he succeed in getting outside of himself. He had not the knowledge of life or the sympathy to enable him to do another novel of first power.

CHAPTER XVI

BARRIE AND THE KAILYARD SCHOOL

IN the early nineties Barrie loomed as a novelist to reckon with. Then there were already *A Window in Thrums* (1889) and *The Little Minister* (1891), not great books but good books, books that got around you and led you to believe that great books were to come. Then Stevenson had written, "There are two of us now that the Shirra might have patted on the head." High praise as that was of himself and his fellow Scot, it was justified by what Stevenson had done and by what Barrie had done. Stevenson had, of course, done the more. There were the essays and *A Child's Garden of Verses* (1885) and *The Master of Ballantrae* (1889); and there was just ahead of him *Weir of Hermiston*, left unfinished at his death, but even as a fragment his best work in the novel.

In 1892, when Stevenson wrote those proud words to Barrie of the approval of the two of them by Scott, Stevenson was forty-two, almost of the age at which the Shirra began the series of his Waverley novels; and Barrie was thirty-two, "arrived," and of so sure a place in the affections of readers that they were eager for whatever he would give them. Never was there a fairer outlook for a young man writing novels. And yet Barrie never "came through" as a novelist. He tried to, but he failed. Perhaps it was not in him; perhaps it was because he would not drop the one group of characters he began with; perhaps it was because those early stories had been imagined out of his mother's experience of life, and, with her death in 1896, he was left with only enough memories of her young years to furnish forth *Tommy and Grizel* (1900).

It is a danger to any writer to see life for any length of time through the eyes of another. After that he may not be able to distinguish between what he sees, and what he imagines he sees from having been so long told he sees it. Barrie was taught to see Kirriemuir as it was in his mother's youth and he makes no pretense but it is that Kirriemuir he intends to see, for the purposes of writing at any rate. It is not that distance of time lends enchantment, that he prefers the picturesqueness of yester-day, but that there is no fascination for him in a setting for a story in which he cannot see his mother as a young girl. He tells us of his feeling about the matter in *Margaret Ogilvy* (1896): "The reason my books deal with the past instead of with the life I myself have known is simply this, that I soon grow tired of writing tales unless I can see a little girl, of whom my mother has told me, wandering confidently through the pages. . . . The people I see passing up and down these wynds, sitting night-capped, on their barrow-shafts, hobbling in their blacks to church on Sunday, are less those I saw in my childhood than their fathers and mothers who did these things in the same way when my mother was young."

Another way of looking at Barrie's preference for the past of Kirriemuir as material for his stories is that he is so inveterately the play-actor he cannot live his own life as intensely as he can that of others. From infancy Barrie had listened to his mother's talk of her youth. That talk made what it presented priceless because it was her experience. What better fun for him, what better tribute to a worshipped mother, than to play-act her young days, not only her rôle, but the rôles of all the townsmen of whom she told him. He knew her Kirriemuir as well as his own, and he could play-act it as he could not that which he had himself experienced.

Actuality has an unkind way of asserting itself when a man speaks of his own experiences. It has made many a man give himself away. Make-believe is safer. You avoid personal dis-closures, and assumed emotions do not hurt as do your very own, or, if they do, you can free yourself of them by returning to your own identity. The chief reason a man prefers the play-acting, however, is just that it is more fun. "My puppets," Barrie says, "seem more real to me than myself." It is in *Courage* (1922), his inaugural address as Lord Rector of St. Andrews University, that he so declares himself. He then goes on to tell us about McConnachie "the unruly half of myself—the writing half."

One wonders if there are not more than these two selves in Barrie, as many indeed as there are characters he wishes to enact. Certainly there are three of him. There is the Barrie of the early tales, who sees through his mother's eyes, the Barrie of *Auld Licht Idyls* (1888) and *The Little Minister* (1891); there is the Barrie who writes "dear things about children," the Barrie of *Peter Pan* (1904); and there is the Barrie of the keen penetration of disillusioning realities, the Barrie of *The Admirable Crichton* (1902) and *What Every Woman Knows* (1908), of *The Twelve Pound Look* (1910) and *The Will* (1912), of *Dear Brutus* (1917) and *Mary Rose* (1920). The upshot of *Mary Rose,* to interpret only one of these plays, is that life is but a brief dream in an empty room.

The Barrie that has come through in accordance with the promise of his youth, is the playwright, not the novelist. So, too, has Kipling failed us, as a novelist, after the high promise of *Plain Tales from the Hills* (1887) and *The Light That Failed* (1891). In both instances, of course, the writers have achieved so greatly in other kinds of writing that we can hardly deplore the failure of either to write great novels. Kipling intended novels of Anglo-Indian life of the scope of Thackeray's, he told us, to be written when he had turned forty. They have not come.

Barrie, in *A Window in Thrums,* and *The Little Minister,* promised by his very performance novels of full scope. They have not come. Was it with Barrie, as with Kipling, that other kinds of writing engaged his attention? Or might it be that he avoided the realistic novels that were foretold even in those early excursions into sentiment for reasons analogous to those that caused Hardy to avoid novels after *Jude the Obscure* (1895). Did Barrie feel, as Hardy did, that if he went on he would only give pain?   He would certainly give pain to many of his admirers if they took to heart the symbolism of his plays.   Fortunately, there is so much that is taken at face value there that the hidden and often unhappy truth escapes notice.

It might well be had Barrie turned realist in later novels he had given us stories as stark as certain of his plays, *The Will,* for one.   He can be dour enough, even with make-believe as a buffer, in *The Admirable Crichton.*   There is no tale of his half so heart-searching as that.   Had we a tale from him as realistic as *The Will* it would be as desolating as *The House With the Green Shutters* (1901).   When that terrible story of George Douglas Brown is spoken of as the killer of kailyard sentimentality it should be remembered that Barrie himself was tending toward an equally annihilating power.

The very prevalence of the kailyard kind of writing that his own work had fostered may have turned Barrie against the novel. No matter how immediate and how general the response to domesticities, readers can be given too much of them.   A public moved to tears by one such book may be indifferent to a second just as good, and be almost nauseated by a third.   S. R. Crockett and "Ian Maclaren" were quick to follow Barrie's lead with *The Stickit Minister* (1893) and *Beside the Bonnie Briar Bush* (1894).   The latter book was as successful as *A Window in Thrums* or *The Little Minister.*   Barrie may have been given pause by the flood of sentiment he was responsible for letting loose.   It is true that he went on with writing as sentimental as that with which he won his public.   There is such genuine feeling, however, in *Margaret Ogilvy,* his book of his mother and himself, that one accepts the sentiment of the book as sentiment, not as sentimentality.

There is enough of the roughness and cruelty of childhood in *Sentimental Tommy* to prevent it being mawkish, but *Tommy and Grizel,* for all its melodrama and savage determination to end wrong, turns mawkish more than now and then.   *The Little White Bird* (1902) is hard to bear, though children like those chapters that were reprinted in 1906 as *Peter Pan in Kensington*

Gardens. Not even Dickens in *Dombey and Son* (1848) wallowed more unholily in the pathetic than Barrie in this book. *Peter and Wendy* (1911) is partially saved from sentimentality by its tricksiness and its suggestions of satire and burlesque. Children delight in the ways of its fairies and are only incidentally troubled by what it all means.

The child in the man must never be forgotten when we are searching for the meanings of Barrie's whimsies and puzzles. "Nothing that happens after we are twelve matters much," he tells us in *Margaret Ogilvy,* a saying very close to that of W. H. Hudson in *Far Away and Long Ago* (1918),—"all the interesting part of my life ended when I was fifteen." Even as lately as *Courage* (1922), Barrie has defined his "humble branch" of literature as "playing hide-and-seek with angels." The romancing child to whom make-believe is the half of happiness has its moments of possession of him even in these later years of bitter thought that cannot be hidden. It is this romancing child in him that allies him to all makers of fairy-lore, from the folk to which we used to attribute it to the Joel Chandler Harrises and De La Mares who have latterly remade it.

To makers of boy's books, or of books about boys, to a Mark Twain or a Kipling, to a Shan Bullock or a Forrest Reid, he has lesser affiliations, but affiliations, through *Sentimental Tommy.* The way Barrie has of coming into the foreground of so many groups of contemporary writers makes the rating of him a very difficult matter. He is of unquestioned literary importance, but he is of half a dozen other orders of importance. Like Stevenson, he belongs to writers for the nursery; like Stevenson he belongs to the writers of books about boys; but hardly, like Stevenson, to the writers of books for boys. He has his place, too, among the sons of Sterne, as large a company as were ever the sons of Ben Jonson. Stevenson and Anthony Hope, Locke and Leonard Merrick have, in varying degrees, fewer hours of devotion to "Dear Sensibility" than Barrie, but they have such hours. They all have relaxed in the atmosphere there is about *Tristram Shandy* (1767) and *A Sentimental Journey* (1768), that atmosphere so warm of the sun, so suffused with balm, so exhilarating. Sterne is, indeed, a dangerous influence. He goes to the head, he unsteadies the foothold men have on the earth, and makes them maudlin or uncertain .of their way.

Always, too, you must remember the Scottishness of Barrie. He is the Lowlander in essentials, but there is a touch of the Gael in him, too. The rush of wind in which Mary Rose disappears blew out of the gates of that otherworld to which Ossian was carried when this world was too hard for him to bear. The playboy that is in Barrie, the mastery over him of make-believe, are, I think, of Celtic origin. The sentiment and sentimentality of him are Lowland. There is no branch of the English race has such words of endearment for babies and sweethearts as these Southern Scots. There are tones possible to "bairn" and "bonny," to name but two such words, that make you try to speak them with all the feeling there is latent in them.

It has been difficult for the Englishman to understand the alternate streaks of hardness and softness in the Scottish nature. How is it that the people whose ways and words of endearment are what they are can yet be on occasions so stern with the littlest children and the most cherished lovers. Profession and performance seem, at first glance, to jar one with the other, and their variance to savor of hypocrisy. So Gilbert felt when he wrote *Engaged* (1877). He was doubtless surfeited with the praise of Scottishness that William Black was distributing so widely through a succession of novels that everybody read. Dr. Johnson had been troubled by warring Scottish qualities in his day, and the deplorable quarrel between Henley and Stevenson was intensified by the Englishman's inability to see that the playacting Stevenson was sincere.

In a way Stevenson was the original of Sentimental Tommy, "whose chief likeness," Sidney Colvin tells us, "to R. L. S. was meant to be in the literary temperament and passion for the *mot propre*." Of Barrie himself, however, there is many times more in Sentimental Tommy than of Stevenson. Barrie, too, had in him

> "A deal of Ariel, just a streak of Puck,
> Much Antony, of Hamlet most of all,
> And something of the Shorter-Catechist."

It is those who neglect that "something of the Shorter Cate-chist" in him who misjudge Barrie. The Calvinist is in the foundations of him as surely as the playboy. The Calvinist, when he is a Scot, will have the truth though the heavens fall, and often, it is to be feared, he will take a suspicion of delight in the abomination of desolation that ensues on that disaster.

Such is the Barrie of *The Will*, a very different figure from that described in *The Little White Bird* as "a gentle, whimsical old bachelor," and believed by so many to be the true Barrie. On the whole, though, this Barrie believed to be the true Barrie is the Barrie of the stories and tales and idyls. This is the Barrie of pathos and humor, of make-believe, and sentiment, of charm and whimsy. This Barrie can create character, a Jess and a Leeby, a Hendry and a Tammas Haggart, a Margaret and a Gavin Dishart, a Rob Dow and a Babbie.

It does not seem to me that Babbie is Barrie's most memorable portrait. That, I think, is Jess. There is no doubt at all, how-ever, that Babbie is the favorite of all young men who read Barrie. They all fall in love with her in the most open and unabashed way. Yesterday I used to think that perhaps her impersonation by Maude Adams had something to do with this appeal, but Babbie is just as popular now in a day that knows not Miss Adams. Winsome, tricksy, bubbling with life and spirits, Babbie holds her own with undiminished favor in a genera-tion that is believed to be far more sophisticated than that to which she was first revealed. Young men regard her as Tennyson would have them regard "The Gleam." They would give any-thing to be followers of such a one, whose ways, they think, are not those of a will o' the wisp but those of a guide to lead them to all they hold noble and dear. Rintoul is, of course, a failure. Barrie does not know his character, and so, for all his ability as a play-actor, he has no clearly imagined rôle to fill.

A Window in Thrums has Barrie's most considerable characters in it. Jess is, of course, a picture of his mother in her declining years. Margaret of *The Little Minister* is another aspect of her, and Grizel of *Sentimental Tommy* and *Tommy and Grizel* is modeled after what she was in girlhood and youth. There is something of Margaret Ogilvy in every one of his lovable women, even in Babbie, though there is least of her there. One might find her, too, in several women of the plays, though in them he has drawn from other originals more often than in the stories. Leeby is obviously based on Barrie's sister, and Hendry on his father. Himself he has disloyally transformed into the errant Jamie. Almost all of his principal characters in the stories are based not only on Thrums folk but on members of his own family.

There is no evidence in the stories to show that Barrie has known well many men and women. Perhaps he could know really well only those seen through his mother's eyes. In the plays the range of character is wider, but in most cases the characters are fully developed only when they are like the members of his family circle. In the plays as a whole the characters are not so important as the situations in which they are involved and as the truths of which they are symbols.

There is nowhere an artist a more candid critic of himself than Barrie. In articles on Meredith and Hardy he points out their qualities that make for greatness. These qualities are patently not his in any large measure. It is obvious, too, that he is not secretly treasuring the possession of other qualities that compensate for those he has not. If there is a mock humility in *Courage* (1922) real humility is just as clearly present.

Though Barrie admires Meredith with little less than idolatry that admiration has not led him to make a practice of readings of life such as occur so often in all the many novels from *Richard Feverel* (1859) to *The Amazing Marriage* (1895). Such readings of life as occur in Barrie are very generally asides. Not only does Barrie not speak with authority on the great things of life but he gives the impression somehow of having missed the great things for himself, and of having play-acted only the lesser,

There was precedent in a part of the literature from which Barrie derives for a more searching presentation of life than he has attempted. He has not hesitated to present love scenes whether they are what we usually mean by that term or whether they are scenes of affection between members of a family. He has deliberately avoided in the novels, however, that plumbing of the depths that is so great a forte of the Meredith he so admires. All Lowlanders are fearful of open displays of emotion, and of giving themselves away; so Barrie is but exhibiting a national trait in such reserve. On the other hand, however, he lets himself go in depicting home life, and fairly luxuriates in sentimental domesticities. These domesticities that Barrie loves to picture can be traced back to before the time of Burns. The scenes of home life in *A Window in Thrums* are nearly paralleled by those in *David Elginbrod* (1862) of George Mac-Donald, and in *The Heart of Midlothian* (1818) of Scott, and clearly outlined in *The Cotter's Saturday Night* (1786) of Burns and in *The Farmer's Ingle* (1773) of Ferguson. There are likenesses too, between Barrie and Galt, whose *Annals of the Parish* (1821) presents a minister in Mr. Balwhidder very much like those we meet not only in Barrie but in others of the Kailyard School.

There is more of Barrie in the drama of today than in the novel of today. A. A. Milne (1882-   ) has worked his way into a manner of his own, but he has not forgotten all he learned from his master. And Milne is only the outstanding figure among many playwrights produced in Glasgow and Manchester and London and New York who have gone to school to Barrie. There are a few novelists who, despite *The House with the Green Shutters*, still hold to the tenets of the kailyard school. Of these are Jane and Mary Findlater, who both separately and in collaboration have produced a series of Scots novels of sterling worth.

Two of these are *Crossriggs* (1908) and *Penny Monypenny* (1913). In these books we find not the peasants and artisans so common to the kailyarders but middle-class folk of towns within the influence of Edinburgh. There is a heritage from Miss Mitford and Mrs. Gaskell in the art of the sisters. Alexandra Hope is not unlike certain ladies in *Cranford,* but she is an original creation. She is representative of a type of that large group of spinsters who have not attracted the man of their choice. Alexandra has had to sacrifice a great deal of happiness, too, in the interest of a futile father. The sane optimism of the sisters Findlater is revealed at the close of *Crossriggs.* Alexandra, the man having failed her, is just leaving Scotland for a trip around the world, her father's long cherished dream-come-true. There seems for the nonce nothing in life but the necessity of living. "But," they ponder, "But the roots of the tree of life, in a healthy nature, strike very deep. Again, and yet again, may come a springtime of the soul."

It would be pleasant to take leave of Barrie here in the company of his countrymen. Though he is a slight figure alongside of Burns and Scott they are all three so characteristically Scots, that the slightness of Barrie is not so marked as when you consider him alongside of the great Englishmen. Yet his mastery of pathos forces you to compare Barrie with Dickens. Both have abused their gift of tears, both are what T. E. Brown called "born sobbers," but you will have to search diligently for a third as masterful in this vein unless you cite Brown himself, who has, too, a superabundance of pathos. Humor, Barrie has, but not in anything like the prodigality of Dickens. There is a personality all his own, too, in Barrie, which with his pathos and his humor win him a place in English literature higher than that of men who seem on first consideration of greater parts. It is his plays, though, that make his place sure. Without them Barrie would be only a greater Locke or Leonard Merrick.

CHAPTER XVII

THE LESSER LATE VICTORIANS

LATE Victorian times were crowded with lesser novelists of solid attainment. All but all of these subscribed to ways of writing or to ideals of early Victorian novelists, or of novelists of still older times. Blackmore (1825-1900), whose period of novel writing, 1864-1897, about spanned the era, and Phillpotts (1862-——) who came into his own just before its end, are the solidest of the lot. Blackmore is the most considerable of all the following of Scott, and Phillpotts the most considerable of all the following of Blackmore. Phillpotts represents, too, the Hardy tradition. It may be said that he began with Blackmore and Hardy as masters, and combined with their methods of narrative and characterization and descriptive writing, a determination to say "yea" to life that he found in Nietzsche.

BLACKMORE AND THE HIGHER PROVINCIALISTS

Blackmore, though he wrote to the close of Victorian times, is mid-Victorian in quality. In his stories he often dealt with times long prior to his own era, loving particularly the seventeenth century. That century was to him the chosen time, in which lived and fished his master Izaak Walton, in which lived and gardened that other master of his, John Evelyn, whose *Sylva* (1664) he might have rivalled, had he made the effort, with a chronicle of his own grapes and pears. There is something of the tones of these old devotees of leisure in Blackmore's writing, and a morning-light like that of Scott. All that he has borrowed from his elders, though, he has blent into a warm sunniness of his own. There is a placid after-dinner feeling about Blackmore, a feeling like that contenting men who have dined heavily at a farmhouse, and are lazing around for a little in the sheltered dooryard full of late summer sun. In a little while they will be working all the better for that dinner, but they are inert until it shall be digested.

There is picturesqueness always about Blackmore, a mid-Victorian picturesqueness. It is almost time, indeed, for us all to acknowledge that mid-Victorian things generally are picturesque now, and that late Victorian things are taking on picturesqueness. There are between us and late Victorian times the World War; the readjustments of life through the automobile, the telephone and mechanical devices of all sorts; the drift of population to the cities; the rise of psychology; and the passing of what aristocratic standards in ways of living and thinking had survived industrial democracy.

The little changes that the years inevitably bring total enough in the thirty years of a generation to make yesterday different in the look of things from today. When there is added to these little changes those caused by these greater agencies I have listed, a picture of English life of today is made different enough from that, say, of 1867 to 1897, for that older time, in contrast to this, to stand out as picturesque. It is not so vividly picturesque in externals as the eighteenth century, but it is approximating in picturesqueness the earlier Victorian times.

It is true that there are no books of late Victorian times as picturesque as *Our Village* and *Cranford,* though there are people who are beginning to say that *The Adventures of a Phaëton* (1872) of William Black and *The Little Minister* (1891) of Barrie are bound to occupy a place in the affections of men very like that of the village studies of those early Victorian ladies. The costumes of the seventies and the eighties of last century are quaint to us when we see them on the stage; the china and pottery and glass of that period are approaching Lowestoft and slipware and Sandwich glass in the regard of collectors; and there are signs of a revival of "cottage" architecture. Reprints of the novels of the time as late Victorian classics are imminent, and original editions with illustrations by Du Maurier or Abbey will be valued as are now those older books illustrated by Cruikshank or Leech.

Though the late Victorian novels are approaching picturesqueness with the passing of the years they still suffer the discounting that is the fate of yesterday's fashion. That is, the lesser ones suffer that fate. Meredith, Hardy, Gissing, Stevenson and George Moore hold their values by the genius that is in them. Some of the lesser writers, however, like William Black and Besant and "Ouida" and "Mark Rutherford"—to name four as dissimilar as possible—have all lost a large percentage of their former appeal. Of those who are to our time almost what they were in their first vogue Blackmore is the sturdiest figure. His *Lorna Doone* (1869) is still the half-classic it has been for over fifty years.

When Blackmore died in 1900 Phillpotts wrote it down as his opinion that England had lost one of its three great contemporary novelists, placing Blackmore with calm assurance on the level of Meredith and Hardy. It is difficult to understand so high a rating, but it cannot be brushed away without consideration. Phillpotts unquestionably counts as critic as well as novelist, and his judgment must be weighed. It seems to me that in such an estimate his heart has gotten the better of his head, as will happen to generous natures in moments of emotion. Phillpotts had lost master and friend and fellow lover of country things. He had lost one who was, too, a symbol of what was to him best in all Englishness. When one man has been that to another moderation in speech is hardly possible. It is only, it seems to me, in blood and thews and sinews that Blackmore is of a quality with the two others. There is a substance, a burliness, a whole-hearted fidelity to country ways of thought and speech and action that mark Blackmore as akin to Meredith and Hardy. His range is very much less than theirs, and he can compare in "brain and spirit" to neither. His characterization is of narrow scope, there is little of poet and nothing of seer in him. So hale is Blackmore, however, so wholesome, so deep-lunged and cheerful, so tonic, that many shortcomings can be forgiven him. There are sins of commission, too, to forgive: sentimentality, obvious moralizing, an overplus of fooling, melodrama, a "knack of puffing good people and good things" when verisimilitude demands unbiased presentation of them, a tendency to a regular rhythm in impassioned passages, "purple patches" and a repetition of stock situations and characters from novel to novel.

And yet, find all the fault you will with Blackmore, he is the author of *Lorna Doone*. It had its chance of making an appeal a year and a half after its publication. Queen Victoria's daughter married the Marquis of Lorne in 1871. That was a union popular in Britain, a British princess choosing a British husband, and a man of a rank much less than her own. The similarity of Lorna and Lorne, and the condescension of Princess Louise and Lorna Doone to husbands of humbler station gave the book, as Blackmore said, "golden wings." The qualities that appealed so greatly when the novel thus gained a hearing were just those that endeared Scott to his generation. *Lorna Doone* was romantic; its characters were heroic and simple and easily understood; there was good sport and good feeding and good fighting in it; there was sentiment; there were staunch hearts of the right old sort; John Ridd was Dandy Dinmont and Little John rolled into one, reincarnated and re-formed; virtue triumphed over vice; it was, in short, a book wholly in the English tradition, as sound as Sherwood oak.

Lorna herself, like the ladies of Scott, is less successfully presented than the humbler characters. It is hard, too, to visualize the home life of the Doones in their barracks in the Doone valley. Blackmore has not been able to visualize that life for himself, and so he can hardly be expected, to visualize it for his readers. But the meetings of Lorna and John Ridd at the torrent's head are idylls of a fresh beauty, even if as we read we cannot forget the meeting of Richard Feverel and Lucy by another streamside in a novel ten years older than *Lorna Doone*. The scenes at Plovers Barrows are admirably done. Blackmore realizes that farmstead so clearly that it remains for us, along with the Hall Farm in *Adam Bede* and Talbothays in *Tess,* typical of the best of England's farm homes.

Blackmore was always angered at being written down the writer of one book. He thought there was no such great difference in quality between *Lorna Doone* and other good work of his that it should always be picked out for praise and that other work passed over. The out and out Blackmore enthusiast is of like opinion. One such man will say Blackmore is really at his best in *The Maid of Sker* (1872) and that Parson Chowne or Davy Llewelynn is a greater creation than John Ridd. Another enthusiast will prefer *Cripps the Carrier* (1876) or *Christowell* (1882).

The consensus of opinion, however, through two generations of readers, has declared for *Lorna Doone,* and rightly. It has a large leisureliness, an epic breadth, a wealth of life, a romance in it that are to be found in only the enduring stories. There is not much comment on time and change and the nature of things in Blackmore, here or anywhere. There is always, however, a sense of the presence of a vital personality, of a generous hearted and largely loving man. There is no littleness in him, no faultfinding, no soreheadedness, no satire. There are other characters to remember than Lorna or John. There are Mrs. Ridd and John Fry, Tom Faggus and Jeremy Stickles, Old Huckeback and Ruth, all English to the marrow; and Sir Ensor and Counsellor Doone, of the very flesh of Sir Walter's romantic figures.

There are characters to remember from other of Blackmore's stories. There are heavy courageous men of the order of John Ridd, but of differing fortunes and personalities in the earlier novels, John Huxtable in *Clara Vaughan* (1864) and Bull Garnet in *Cradock Nowell* (1866). And in both of these books, as in *Lorna Doone,* the story begins with the death of a parent.

There is no book of Blackmore that is not sound work, but all are very much of a pattern. He attempts to vary the effect of one and another by making the scene of each story a different part of England. And he does paint in various colors of place.

He is not so successful in varying the motives and passions and situations of his characters. Though at first glance these may seem to be different they turn out to be very much of a piece. *Springhaven* (1887) and *Perlycross* (1894), at the end of his career, are no more distinctive than *Clara Vaughan* and *Cradock Nowell* at the start. What Blackmore had to tell, what he had to show, are best told and shown in *Lorna Doone*.

SABINE BARING-GOULD

Sabine Baring-Gould (1834-1924) is the antiquarian in all his story writing, no matter what form it takes. He is the antiquarian when he would write history, or record folklore, or retell old legends. With a vast store of information gathered from all kinds of sources, oral and documentary, he would never submit himself to the discipline of scholarship, and sift and test and clarify. He is not, in any severe sense of the word, a historian; he is not a scientific folklorist. Nor is he an artist, even of sorts, in his writing he intended as art. He published his first novel *Mehalah* (1880) when he was forty-six and there remained for him forty-four years of writing after that, but he never learned the art of the novelist, though story after story came from his pen. Characterization, too, he failed in, largely because he was content merely to indicate what his people were like, and then to devote himself to the presentation of some queer custom or wonder of the countryside. He could not escape being the antiquarian.

Baring-Gould is as surely the antiquarian untouched by genius as Scott is the antiquarian wholly transformed by genius into the greatest romancer of our tongue. Like Scott, Baring-Gould was a man of prodigious vitality, of interests as diverse as life itself, of a thousand friendships, of a sympathy with all that has ever stirred the hearts of men. He was always so lost in the material he was writing about, however, that he could not bother with its presentation. His stories are without proportion, they have little beauty in them and they peter out into inconsequence. There are curious bits of local lore and custom in them, and, more rarely, vagaries of strange people, or striking situations. They have not been pondered and lived with and shaped with loving care. Worst of all they have not been given any deep significance of any kind. If you would test them put them side by side with stories written by one who is an artist. Put *Dartmoor Idylls* (1896) over against *The Striking Hours* (1901) of Phillpotts and you will see that the sketches of Baring-Gould are only bits of life, that they have not been lifted into the authority of art.

HALL CAINE

No man of potential power ever made less of a great opportunity in art than Sir Hall Caine (1853-   ). There was all the freshness of an unworked field for him in the Isle of Man. T. E. Brown had, indeed, shown the picturesqueness of that island life to the world in *Fo'c's'le Yarns* (1881), but those tales were in verse, and dialect verse at that, and so necessarily of a restricted appeal and little known to the public. Yet instead of following Brown, instead of devoting himself to a patient and loving study of the life of Man and fashioning his stories on what he found there Caine built on "ideas," on old axioms tuned to the hour.

The Bible was to Caine a book of constant study, as much for its situations as for its rhythms. There he found many of his titles and his themes. *A Son of Hagar* (1886) was his second novel, *The Prodigal Son* (1904) his ninth. *The Bondsman* (1890) might be considered a variation of the story of Jacob and Esau, and *The Manxman* (1894) has resemblances to that of David and Uriah. Nor would you have to force matters much to find parallels between others of his stories and stories in the Bible.

It was *The Manxman* that made its day believe that Caine had come to a fulfillment of his promise. The first two parts of that book, as Sir Arthur T. Quiller-Couch pointed out, are well done, the rest of it wordy and self-conscious. What Sir Arthur does not say outright is that the rest of it is extravagant melodrama.   There are dramatic situations, not new surely, but rightly felt and skillfully presented, in that early part of the book, the scene in Sulby Glen, in which Kate Creegan stakes her all to win Philip, the most intense of them. The final scene intended to be "great," the public confession of Philip, is a reproduction of the famous confession of Dimmesdale in *The Scarlet Letter* (1850).

There are elements in the succeeding stories other than these gathered together from Brown and the Bible and Hawthorne. *The Christian* (1897) was not only melodrama of a crude sort but inexact in the reproduction of the life it set out to depict. So untrue were the hospital scenes, indeed, that British medical journals protested against them. Caine had by this time, owing to the great response of the public to his work, come to consider himself an apostle of righteousness. He outdid his former efforts in preaching and theatricality in *The Eternal City* (1901). It is not necessary to consider his artistic decline and fall further than this book. It is all the more deplorable when you consider the literary associations of his youth and young manhood. The friend of Rossetti and T. E. Brown, he must have been well grounded in values and canons of taste. One can only guess at what has caused the change. Perhaps it has been with him as with the Isle of Man. Popularity has been too much for Man. Man has lost, through the influx of week-enders from the Black Country of England, its native tang and savor, its old-time standards. Perhaps Hall Caine, too, has just had to make himself what the public wants.

QUILLER-COUCH

Sir Arthur T. Quiller-Couch (1863-   ) tells us in *Adventures in Criticism* (1896) that "a novelist's rank depends upon what he can see and what he can tell us of the human heart." If that is so, what is the rank of those pleasant and gallant books of his, *Dead Man's Rock* (1887), *Troy Town* (1888) and *The Splendid Spur* (1889)?   Test, too, those other books, *The Ship of Stars* (1899) or *Fort Amity* (1904), by asking yourself how much of the human heart is told in them, and you will have to answer, as you will have to answer of the earlier books, not so very much.   That test does not rank them so high as they should be ranked.

Only *Ia* (1896), of his longer stories, seems to tell us much of the human heart, and even what it tells is not new.   It is, of course, a Cornish story.   It recounts the devotion of a good man Joel Spargo, to a good woman, Ia Rosemundy, who loved and wooed and won a weak preacher man, whom her pride forced her to send away from her.   She was proud of their child, she faced out the village proudly, and when Paul returned to find John a boy of six her pride sent the father away again. In the end she goes to America to give her child a fairer chance than he could have, because of his illegitimacy, in the place of his birth.   Joel is left to face the years alone.   Paul is a creation, a discovery, a man with a personality and temperament unrecorded before.   Joel and Ia are only variants of the constant man and constant woman so familiar in the fiction of all ages.

In the preface to *Brother Copas* (1911) Quiller-Couch tells us that "in a former book of mine, *Sir John Constantine,* I expressed (perhaps extravagantly) my faith in my fellows and in their capacity to treat life as a noble sport."   It was so Ia treated it and so Joel Spargo; it is so all the best of his characters treat it.   That, indeed, is pretty nearly his code for life, and there are few better.   It is the code, too, for his writing. He would wish that also to be "a noble sport."   The pity is he has not the stamina for the game.   He plays in good form, and with an air, but he has not power.

CHARLES LEE

There is more of the spirit of place in the Cornish stories of Charles Lee (1870-   ) than in those of Sir Arthur T. Quiller-

Couch. Sir Arthur, for all his knowledge of boats, is several removes from the cottages in which the fishermen live. Charles Lee writes of them as if he were cottage-born. His books are all intimate, *Our Little Town* (1909), *The Widow Woman* (1910) *Paul Carah, Cornishman* (1912) and *Dorinda's Birthday* (1912). *Our Little Town* is a collection of "Cornish Tales and Fancies" and the others are long stories. *Paul Carah* is the most serious in intention of them, a determined and successful attempt to draw a picture in detail of a puppet Peer Gynt returned to his native Cornwall from wanderings in America. There is humor in the story, as in them all, and the recording of a hundred odd ways of an out-of-the-world folk. There is tragedy in it, too, for there comes to Paul Carah a realization of what he is. He sees himself as others see him, but the playboy in him rallies to his aid and he makes an exit from Porth Julyan more dignified than was his entrance. It is again the woman who suffers. His cousin Jennifer has been taken by his little vanities and easy ways and is left in loneliness when he lightly runs away from the wreck he has made of his homecoming. The story is no more than a good story; the freshness of its material is what chiefly delights us. It is well written, the characterization is clear, the effects intended are made.

Dorinda's Birthday has charm, the prim but far from prudish charm of Dorinda in her white muslin so stiffly starched. It follows the Hardy of *Under the Greenwood Tree* in a far-off way, with bell ringers in place of the Mellstock players. The peasants are faithfully rendered, the descriptions of countryside show a keen sensitiveness to beauty, the prose falls often into a pleasant rhythm. A little more and Charles Lee had been a rival to Miss Keats and Phillpotts.

"ZACK"

In 1896 A. E. Housman published *A Shropshire Lad*. It was a thin volume of verse about the longings of a west-country youth resident in London for those Welsh marches where his earlier life was spent. In 1896 "Zack" began to publish short-stories in *Blackwood's Magazine,* and from 1898 to 1903 she issued in quick succession five books, short-stories and novels, about that southwestern countryside of Devon that she knew. They were *Life is Life* (1898), *On Trial* (1899), *The White Cottage* (1901), *Dunstable Weir* (1901) and *The Roman Road* (1903). *A Shropshire Lad* was acknowledged at once as poetry of power. *Life is Life* was acknowledged at once as fiction of power. Today *A Shropshire Lad* is an integral part of the English poetry that it is expected we should know; it is quoted everywhere; it is steadily increasing its sphere of influence. And until 1922, when the second collection of Housman's verse, *Last Poems,* appeared, there had been no other book of poetry of his to foster interest in him. Yet eight thousand copies of *Last Poems* were ordered before publication, just on the announcement of the book. Today the stories of "Zack" are known only to the few.

Is that the way it is with stories and with poetry? Do stories have in their nature the chance of immediate reception, and quick oblivion; and do lyrical poems have in their nature an inevitable restriction of audience, and the chance of survival among the minority that decade in and decade out cares greatly for literature? It may be that question points the way to a half-truth, but that is not, I think, why it is that *A Shropshire Lad* is a classic today and the stories of "Zack" unknown. Nor is the difference in fate to be charged to a difference in genius.

Gwendoline Keats was acknowledged at once because of the sheer power of the personality that spoke in her stories. Working in old material, the west country life already widely familiar to readers in Blackmore and Baring-Gould, she struck a note that had not been struck before. Her disciplined restraint in the utterance of emotion gave a new quality to her dramatic moments. Her acceptance of the strange ways of providence had in it no protest, no echo of the old, old plea for poetic justice. Her style was her own. There was freshness in her humor, too, though it was of the sort traditional from Elizabethan times. There were characters unmet before, though these were presented in the old way of those middle-of-the-road masters that have carried forward the standards established by Chaucer.

Her weakness lay in the selection of incident and in the architectonics of story-telling. She liked to restrict her writing to moments of intensity, and she failed to connect those moments logically and to arrange them in patterns that would give balance and beauty of form to her stories.

The English novel, as we have all been brought up to know, has not been distinguished for beauty of form. Down to late Victorian times it was characteristically subject to the whim of its writers. It had rambled where it listed, it had sprawled, it had grown inchoate, it had accomplished every sort of form-lessness. Such being its history we can hardly say that the only reason that *Life is Life, On Trial* and *The White Cottage* are neglected is because of their lapses of form. They are neglected, too, I think, for the reason that, despite their many excellences, they are lesser achievements in an old field, the Hardian story of country life; and because, too, they are not quite full scope novels. Stories of a length greater than that of the short-story and less than that of the novel occupy an anomalous position in English literature.

Whatever the reason, it is true that "Zack" is all but forgotten. I doubt if, even from her first recognition, she had ever the public that she deserved. She presents no gloomier reading of life than that of A. E. Housman, but people reading novels will not put up with unhappiness of an unsentimental kind as will people reading poetry. Though "Zack" was published in America as well as in England, and though her books were reviewed at length here, I have never known her to be the topic of conversation when the talk turned to books. Such a failure to hear about "Zack" may be chance, or it may be, as I must believe it to be, an indication that she has not been much read in America. All I have heard of her has been in print, or in letters in response to queries I have made.

If lovers of literature have not read "Zack" they have missed

some good writing. Such is that scene in *On Trial,* gruesome
and haunting, of the death of old Anne. Her last act, on her
death bed, is to get from her lover of old time a letter that he
has found which compromises a young woman. The kindly act
proves in vain, for the letter is not destroyed but goes on
further in its wanderings until it brings about the shaming of
the girl.

There is another scene, in *Life is Life,* in which the adopted
mother of the blind umbrella-mender and that unfortunate
talk about reading in a way that leads to the discovery of truth.
" 'The book has a fine cover of its own,' she said; 'but there,
I reckoned when you laid out your money on such things you
wud have liked to walk in higher life. I ain't come across no
dook, though I've read each page careful.'

" 'Why a duke, mother?'

" 'There ain't nothing scanty about a dook. Set him where
you will, he makes the page look full. I've alles held it a queer
thing that, thinking of dooks as I do, the Almighty has never
seen fit to throw us together; but ther, that's life all over, the
man as admires 'ee most is fate sure to miss 'ee by the turn
of a street.' "

There are admirable scenes of description, too, even in this
early and uncertain story *Life is Life,* of the beauty of the west
country seen in memory all the way across the seas from Australia. There are passages, too, of lyric description in *The
White Cottage,* and the moment of greatest poignancy in all
"Zack." Mark Tavy has been in love with Luce Myrtle since
childhood. They are finally plighted, the girl reluctantly.
"There sommat missing 'twix he and me," she can't help saying.
There comes between them that man masterful with women,
the poacher's son, Ben Lupin. Ben and Luce marry secretly
away from Bere-Upton, and return to "The White Cottage,"
the little house on the cliffs, which Lupin had rented, just before
Mark had made up his mind to take it. There, in the room in
which Mark in dream had seen Luce with their child, he finds
her, on her return to the town. Mark has been away with the

fishing boats and does not know she is married. Without an explanation Lupin takes him to the house. " 'What be 'ee doing here, Luce?' " he queries. "She did not answer. Putting out a trembling hand he touched her, and she raised her head and looked at him. It seemed to Mark standing there that his heart was being drawn from his breast, and peeled piece by piece as a boy peels a willow twig.

" 'I wud ha' been true to 'ee,' she exclaimed at last in a broken voice. 'I wanted to be true to 'ee; but, lad, I jest worn't.' "

Those words of Luce have a poignancy and truth to life not unworthy the art of the great masters.

EDEN PHILLPOTTS

Eden Phillpotts (1862-   ) has given us too much of a good thing. Our delight in his work and his own standing in literature have suffered from the very number of his volumes. Readers who like an author wish to know all of him, to re-read him, to talk him over with others to whom he is also a hobby, to look on him as if he were a rare combination of friend and object of art, to make him a part of their lives. There is too much of Phillpotts for people of average leisure to be able so to know him. His titles total at more than a hundred, and only the hardiest and most voracious reader can assimilate such a number of books of one author. If a novel, or its equivalent in resistance and allurement, be a reasonable week's reading for the man of cultivation, then it would take such a one two years' uninterrupted reading to get to know Phillpotts. There are few of us who have so much time even for our greatest writers, and Phillpotts, true artist that he is, is not of that stature.

In 1913 he made a list of the works that fitted together into "a modest comedy of Dartmoor," planned twenty years before, but that list, although referred to in the "foreword" to the American edition of *Widecombe Fair*, was not printed there. It was not until 1923 that it appeared, opposite the title page of *Children of Men,* a list comprising twenty-three volumes. Meanwhile those who wanted to get the best of Phillpotts had to find out for themselves what that best was. Among so many books that was a long job and attempted by few people. The critics were of little help. They were daunted by the mass of him just as those who read him solely for their own pleasure and without thought of writing about him.

Take my own case as typical of many. Brought up to a reading of Hardy, and finding that Hardy was writing no more novels after *Jude the Obscure* (1895) I was delighted to come upon a review of *Children of the Mist* (1898) that called Phillpotts a worthy follower of Hardy. I read *Children of the Mist* and then went back to *Lying Prophets* (1896) and *Some Everyday Folk* (1893). I found these two books good reading, but I found other stories of Phillpotts which were just "the stuff for which people would pay." Three good books out of twelve titles was discouraging. With none too much money for books I gave up the idea of "buying Phillpotts" until money should be more plentiful. Later, on trying him again in *The River* (1902) I bought a Phillpotts every once in a while, until now I have twenty-odd of his books, chiefly novels, a trio of plays and his volume of verse I like best, *A Dish of Apples* (1921). It is, of course, only the books you own you get to know intimately, so I do not know Phillpotts as I should. I have read perhaps another twenty novels than those I own, most of his plays and all of his verse. As far as my experience goes his better and worse work is poured out indiscriminately side by side, novels that have a place in letters and good journeyman work likely to be popular. You never could buy a Phillpotts as you could a Hardy with the assurance that it would be of its author's best. No one blames the man. He had his living to make, but the practice has been bad for his reputation as an artist. Maybe now that he has scored a great success with the run of his play, *The Farmer's Wife,* in 1924, he can reserve the best of himself for novels that will rank with *Children of the Mist* (1898), *Sons of the Morning* (1900), *The River* (1902), *The Secret Woman* (1905), *The Thief of Virtue* (1910) and *Widecombe Fair* (1913). He has lost none of his power with the years, *Cheat-the-Boys* (1924) having a sharp sweetness and a tragic resignation that makes it a fit companion to its many fine fellows. It is a young-hearted book written by a man past sixty, "sad and unprofitably proud," if we are to take "On Eylesbarrow" literally. It is heartening, indeed, to find him so awake to the wonder of the world, so sensitive to all beauty. In "Experience" he writes:

> "Now I am old, I only care
> How fellow men and women fare,
> Nor challenge eye of passer-by
> Because in truth I mostly know
> The secrets of the heart below."

That is a true word, that he knows "the secrets of the heart." He knows them so well, he knows them so thoroughly in all their infinite variety that he has repeated himself comparatively little, though most of his writing is about a little corner of England. Dartmoor is but a section of Devon, a lonely table-land for the most part, rolling up to great tors and pierced by valleys of streams and rivers. It is not so heavily populated but it may be that Phillpotts knows an appreciable minority of its people. Acquaintances of mine motoring across Dartmoor because Phillpotts had written of it had an experience that illustrated its remoteness and isolation. They ran out of petrol on a by-road and left their car to walk back to an inn they had liked the look of in passing a while before. Tired when they reached shelter they took a chance and left their car for the night where it stopped. Two of them went to fetch it in the morning. When they got within sight of it they saw about it several of the semi-wild ponies of Dartmoor. The ponies were puzzled by it, perhaps they saw themselves reflected in its polished sides. Some of them seemed to be kicking at it. When the men drew up by the car they found its body all dented by the hoofs of the ponies. They had paid their respects to it by their heels. Dartmoor is truly a place of a thousand and one wonders. Phillpotts knows them one and all, and every nook and byway of the countryside.

A friend of mine visits Dartmoor every summer he can get to England. It is the descriptions of it by Phillpotts that take him there. He has read all of Phillpotts, the only man I know who has. There are only a half dozen things in his life more significant to him than these visits and the reading of Phillpotts. The detail of landscape, the careful placing of the characters against their background delight him. Such is not, however, the usual reaction. Many readers and among them some to whom country joys are a large share of life find the descriptions too many and too long. Phillpotts justifies them in the "foreword" to *Widecombe Fair*. "If I deem," he writes, "a forest or river, a wild space, a hill-top, or the changing apparitions of inanimate nature as vital as the adventures of men and women, and as much a part of the material which I handle, then to these things must be apportioned the significance I desire for them. If I choose to make a river a protagonist, or lift a forest, in its unknowable attributes, into a presence more portentous than the human beings who move within it, none has the right to deny me."

That is true: the novelist may, within the laws of its being, do what he will with his novel, but the reader may do what he will with it, too, in that he may skip the descriptions, or drop the novel because of them. But the descriptions are not all that offers resistance in certain of the novels. For all their wealth of incident, their living characterization, their humor and their large lines they are not always easy reading. Such are well worth the effort they entail, but there is undoubted resistance in them. They are long, they are agitating, they provoke brooding. You say: "After all they are very like Hardy, but Hardy was before they were." You do not buy them as you buy Hardy. I may seem to be laboring a minor point, but I am trying to explain why it is that Phillpotts has never come into the reputation a man of his artistry and knowledge and insight should have come into, why for all his popularity he is not by now a classic, as Hardy has been for a generation. It is difficult for the man who is not one of the beginnings in art, and who is far from content to make his best work what the public wants, to win a high place for himself in his own generation. It is the old story of the man who falls between two stools. It is the fate of certain sincere artists who are not of so original and elementary a power as to bend readers to their will.

There is a good deal of talk about his art in Phillpotts, in prefaces here and there, and, at length, and by implication, in the discussions of *The Joy of Youth* (1913). Its most interesting illustration is, of course, in that large part of his writing he calls his "Dartmoor comedy." In the "foreword" to *Widecombe Fair* Phillpotts asks "those few fellow artists and amateurs who have honored me with their interest to the end" to "judge the work [the Dartmoor comedy] as a whole and from no fragment; . . . to consider it is a frieze, carved largely and roughly, whereon victors, vanquished, and spectators of the ceaseless struggles play their parts in the great hypæthral theatre of the Western Moors." He goes on to say: "the workmanship is archaic, yet I venture to claim form and economy of means so austere that the difficulties have often conquered me."

Nietzsche has given him his philosophy. "The purpose of this attempt," he continues, "can be set down in a phrase. I have tried to 'say *yea* to life, even in its most difficult problems, and to display a will to life rejoicing at its own vitality in the sacrifice of its highest types.'" It is in this acceptance of what is that Phillpotts differs from Hardy. Hardy is oftenest protesting at the war between convention and natural instincts, the war of man and nature. He is therefore far more wounding than Phillpotts, who accepts without protest and shows us many of his people accepting without protest whatever happens to them as what must be.

It is a more bracing philosophy than that of Hardy, though

it entails a loss of poignancy in the crises. It helps you to bear what happens to his people as it helped them to bear even the worst. You wish its hardness were extended to other attributes of his writing. There is an overwriting in many of his passages that you feel is sure to flake off with the years as plaster from a stuccoed house. You find this overwriting sometimes in his narrative but it is more common in the descriptions. Phillpotts is, as Robert Frost would say, "versed in country things." Phillpotts knows trees and flowers and birds, the crops from oats to apples; he has a joy in colors and contours; he has a keen sense of the men who have lived in the places he loves, of the generations of men back to prehistoric times. It is a pity that with all this knowledge and rightness of feeling he should let Latinity and ornateness get the mastery of him. Again and again you, reading, are driven to cry out: "If only the writing were as rightly austere as the philosophy of life underlying it!"

Like Hardy again, Phillpotts is best in style in his dialect, best of all when he is chronicling rustic humor. "Nothin' on God's earth—", says Jonnie Beer in *The Poacher's Wife* (1906), "be so uninterestin' readin' as the account of other folks at a revel, if you wasn't there. But with tragical matters the creepiness be very refreshin', and the fact you wasn't there adds to the pleasure. The very heart of comfortable tragedy be to look on other people in the hell of a mess, while you'm all right with your pint, and your pipe drawin' easy." His lyricism, too, is less rhetorical when it finds expression in dialect. In *Widecombe Fair* Daniel Reep, sixty-eight, is dying, just on the eve of spring. He doesn't want to die, his life as love-hunter and poacher has been too sweet.

"And spring coming and all. How cruel well I know how 'tis all happening! The plovers be running about so saucy, down among the rushes in the water meadows, and the trout be moving and the frogs hollering. And the tassels are twinkling, like the lambs' tails, on hazel and aller, and Farmer Coaker be breaking into his great store of roots—the mound he buildeth under the lew hedge. I know it all—to the song of the leastest little cuddy-bum wren; but I shan't see, nor hear, nor smell none of it no more—damn it."

There are times, too, when the King's English of Phillpotts takes on glamour, notably in that so-late novel of his, *Cheat-the-Boys* (1924), where his description of his heroine dead in the water meadow is writing almost Meredithian in its high lyricism. Gilyan is a creation, a portrait for the great gallery I have so often referred to. Chris in *Children of the Mist* is another. Hannah in *The River* still another, and Salome West-away, in *The Secret Woman*, most memorable of them all. Their resemblance to Hardy's women in appearance and ways is obvious. They are a beautiful and a troubling lot. And the men, many of them, are portraits fit for that company of the great gallery, Will Blanchard, Nicholas Oldrieve, Old Redvers and Michael. They, too, are done in the manner of Hardy, and only less memorably. That is what it always comes to in the end. You say of all of Phillpotts, save of his philosophy, how like it is to Hardy. That Phillpotts does not shrink in the inevitable comparison argues him worthy of his discipleship.

That he stands even better the comparison with that other master of his, the author of *Lorna Doone,* reinforces your belief in him as a writer of solid merit. Both of these comparisons with Hardy and Blackmore, on the other hand, make you realize the lack of originality in Phillpotts, as does your thinking of his experiments in other fields of fiction. Diversity of accomplishment, like prodigality of writing, has been characteristic of most of our great English novelists. Yet it is only in the one field of the "Dartmoor comedy" that there is any largeness of attainment in Phillpotts. The fun of *The Human Boy* (1899) like that of *From the Angle of Seventeen* (1913) is not a new humor, and not nearly so good in its kind as the old humor of the Dartmoor series, the humor of Hardy and George Eliot and Shakespeare. Nor are the mysteries and horrors of *The Red Redmaynes* (1923) and *The Voice from the Dark* (1924) new mysteries and horrors. There is more of a way of his own in the gentle satire of his allegorical studies in the classical or mediæval convention such as *The Lavender Dragon* (1923). The vegetarian saurian of this last named book talks in a voice blended of two familiar voices, the voice of the maker of *Erewhon* (1872) and the voice of the maker of *The Crock of Gold* (1912). There is a fresher tang to *The Joy of Youth* (1913), with its talk of the decline of "ruler art" and the passing of the practice of art into the control of the lower middle class, but all this may be traced back to Nietzsche. We are again where we have been so often in this discussion of Phillpotts. What is significant in him is his presentation of Dartmoor life, a Hardy-like presentation of material discovered by Phillpotts himself, but only because Blackmore and Hardy had revealed like material. Phillpotts is a lesser Hardy, tutored to a more cheerful acceptance of life by Blackmore and Nietzsche.

GEORGE MACDONALD

The stories of George Macdonald (1824-1905) have gone the way of most stories with a purpose. They are little read by any part of the generations that have succeeded the generation in which they began to be written, a generation to a large part of which they were a higher sort of sermon. *David Elginbrod* (1863), the first of his novels, was the best of his novels. It was not for its characterization, however, that it was valued in its day, but for its sermonizing and its horrors. Funklestein's practice of the black art was taken seriously. What element of literature there is in *David Elginbrod* is not in these scenes of terror, but in its presentation of Scots character. It handed on the tradition of Galt to Barrie and "Ian MacLaren" and Crockett. Macdonald in other stories made much of second-sight and kindred beliefs of the Highlanders and so carried on, too, the tradition of Scott and Susan Ferrier, and was not without influence on Black, and, later, on "Fiona MacLeod."

Robert Falconer (1868) was the most seriously regarded book of Macdonald; it was a kind of lesser gospel, indeed, in many

of the homes I knew in my youth. It has gone the way of
Alton Locke and most of the confraternity of the "slum" novels.
Sir Gibbie (1879) has had its day, too. Its sentimentality was
once thought to be the highest sort of sentiment. Of all George
Macdonald, prose and verse, there is little vitality nowadays
in anything but his children's stories. There are children quite
a few, still reading *At the Back of the North Wind* (1871) and
The Princess and the Goblin (1871). There are few people
reading anything else of George Macdonald.

WILLIAM BLACK

A half dozen novels of William Black (1841-1898) were more
popular, one after another, than any book of Blackmore save
Lorna Doone. Yet none of them has had much vitality. The
story of his that has lost least of its charm is *The Strange Adventures of a Phaëton* (1872), which was based on a carriage
journey Black made from London to Edinburgh. Changed from
actuality as that story is it has more savor of life in it than any
of the yachting or fishing stories of the Highlands, and his most
believable girl is its heroine—Bell. The lives of *A Daughter of
Heth* (1871), *A Princess of Thule* (1874), *Madcap Violet* (1876),
Macleod of Dare (1878), *That Beautiful Wretch* (1881) and
Yolande (1883) were brief indeed. Most of them had passed
out of vogue by the time of their maker's death in 1898. There
was enough interest in Black, however, at this time, for the
publication of a uniform edition of twenty-eight of his forty
volumes. Black himself had made the rejections and his judgment was followed by his publishers in this reissue.

The uniform edition of Black printed in America is still to
be found in many of our homes. Such a home often boasts no
other complete edition of an English novelist save the inevitable
Dickens. It is almost invariably in city homes that I find
these twenty-eight volumes, bound in a decorous green. From
talk with their owners I gather that a large part of the appeal
of Black was in his descriptions of the landscape in Highlands

and Hebrides. In the heyday of Black, the late seventies and early eighties, two weeks vacation was all that the average American businessman could steal from his desk. Having gone to Niagara Falls or Washington on his wedding journey and having gone to Washington or Niagara Falls on some anniversary of that event, such a businessman would go to other beautiful places on his annual outing; to the seaside, Jersey generally or Newport; to Saratoga or to the Berkshires; to the White Mountains or the Virginia springs; and in such places he would buy and read Black, often in cheap paper editions. Home again, he would reread his Black because there he found so much of the beauty of out-of-doors or so much of a life of leisure that he had but glimpsed on his vacation. Before the coming of the automobile such a businessman, unless he were a commercial traveler, had very little opportunity of seeing far-off beautiful places. Black was the best substitute for the joy of the eyes such a one had had on vacation, so he bought Black in an edition he could treasure and turn to. Black was to him very much as the Currier and Ives prints of Killarney or Yosemite, or as the stereoscopic views he brought home as the record of his outing.

There was a great deal of fun made of the sunsets and other landscape effects of Black, but it is his landscapes that are the best of him. He managed to get into his many Scots novels a good deal of the beauty of Western Scotland, though atmosphere was a something generally beyond his powers. Black thought his descriptions went beyond painting. He had wanted in youth to be a landscape painter and he brought a trained eye to his description of moor and mountain, beach and sea, loch and salmon river. He was eager to get into his pictures more than the painter could. He thought he could add to the landscape painting many accessories that the painter must miss, as bird-song and sound of wind and water, and movements of light and changes of color.

There is little else to charm in his novels than his descriptions. His heroines were thought exquisite by his admirers, but the light and laughter has gone out of the faces of even the most life-like of the sisterhood. Hester, Coquette and Violet are not of the memorable characters of English fiction. The stories in which they are involved are of the slightest, patently concocted, and reflecting little experience of life. There are often quite a few people in the stories, a decent lot most often. He deliberately chose the decent sort to write about. "People are not always committing forgery," he wrote, "or bigamy, or running away with other men's wives, or being falsely accused of murder. I do not know that I ever met anyone who had passed through any one of these experiences, and would rather write about men and women like those whom I have actually known than about imaginary monsters I have never seen."

Instead of such devices as the means of sensations Black used love and death and landscapes, though he grew more chary of death as he grew older. He killed off his heroine in *A Daughter of Heth,* and he killed off his hero in *Macleod of Dare,* and his heroine again in *Wild Eelin,* the novel he published just before his death in 1898. "A novel with a sad ending," he thought, "is remembered longer than one with a happy ending." This was not, perhaps, his only reason for resorting to death for effects. Death is an easy means of sentimental appeal, and he apparently liked tears for their own sake, too. He realized that people felt there was no plumbing of the depths of human nature in his writing. Carlyle had said to him, "Gie us something serious, Willie," and Black did what he could to be serious by killing off his characters. He showed little influence of Carlyle, but it was very evident he went to school to Ruskin. It was the descriptions of Ruskin, not the prophecies, that influenced Black. He applied Ruskin's ways of description to highland and island scenery.

Black did not, however, restrict himself to western Scotland. From the time of his service as war correspondent in 1866 he had delighted in the romantic aspects of German landscape, and in *Kilmeny* (1870) there is almost as much description of the Tyrol and Bavaria as there is of the English midlands where hero and heroine were lady and serving man. Black was fond, too, of Brittany, and he laid the scene of *Three Feathers* (1875) in Cornwall. It was Gaelic Scotland, however, that he loved best, and that his readers most approved as the scene of his stories. He developed a way of presenting this Gaelic Scotland with characteristic bits of scenery and characteristic people, and that way was loved by many late Victorians. They knew just what to expect and they were never unpleasantly surprised. They were prepared, even, for his sad endings, and though they regretted these they at the same time exulted in their pathos.

Formula-like though Black's methods of constructing a story were, that kind of story, with its descriptions and Gaelic-speaking characters and provincial point of view, was a new kind of Scots novel. Since his time we have had William Sharp's way of highland story, in his "Fiona Macleod" phase, in *Pharais* (1894) and *The Mountain Lovers* (1895), and Neil Munro's way of highland story. The Kailyard kind of lowland story came into full luxuriance in his last years, as did the Stevensonian romance. No one of the three ways is very like the way of Black. He differs, too, from MacDonald and Galt and Miss Ferrier, and, still more, from Scott and Smollett. Such as it was the way of Black was his own.

ROBERT BUCHANAN

It was against the grain that Robert Buchanan (1841-1901) wrote novels. What was in him potentially to do was to write poetry, but even that he fell short of doing by that final something that distinguishes facile verse from poetry. Buchanan was visited by inspiration on inspiration with possibilities of realization into authentic poetry, and, on a lower plane, by idea on idea that, had he the power, might have resulted in gnomic verse deeply interesting to his time. His range of subjects was wide. That which most moved his contemporaries was the slum life he presented realistically in *London Poems* (1866). Romance, however, was what he sought in his most highly intentioned novels, both of which had first been projected as stories in verse.

The Shadow of the Sword (1876) is at once "a polemic against War" and a romance of adventure. Its background is Brittany in the days of Bonaparte and its theme that of the refusal of a brave man to consent to conscription because of his belief in the wickedness of war. He will not sacrifice his principles even for his love and he is hunted like a wild animal in the cliffs and caves that were the playground of his youth. Buchanan tried to make it "a simple, strong, natural poem in prose." He wrote it with what for him was great care but he was neither the unresting artist who works and works with his material until it is as near perfection as he can make it, nor the masterful artist who can write out of so clear and sure a vision of what he wishes his work to be that it comes into being with finality of form. There are admirable bits of description in *The Shadow of the Sword,* situations of an exciting sort that had been proved effective from old time, and a picture of Napoleon. The story had a good press, a good sale and as long a life as any story of Buchanan save *God and the Man* (1881).

God and the Man is another propagandist novel, an attack on the hatred of man for man. Its story is that of the hereditary feud between two families in England's fen country, in the time of John Wesley. That worthy, indeed, is credited with being the author of marginalia of its manuscript, supposed to have come down in his family. Richard Orchardson and Christian Christianson, the wronger and the wronged, are left by chance together on a lonely island of the Arctics. Orchardson is spent when the two meet there after the breaking away of the ship; he falls ill, and he is nursed back to a half-life by the man who hated him. Before he dies he is forgiven. Christianson gets back to England in the end and marries his Priscilla, whom Orchardson had tried to win away from him.

As so often with Buchanan the idea underlying the story is fresh and arresting, but, as almost always with him, there is little real life in the tale. That is apt to be the way when

a novelist begins with a thesis rather than with the observation
of life. The bit of life, the characters and their relationships,
with which the story-teller begins, develop into something very
different from what they were in reality, but they give a story
a foundation that figures invented to express a thesis cannot
give.

There are more real characters in *The Heir of Linne* (1887)
than in either of the earlier stories I have considered, and one
of them, Willie Fulton o'Kilmarnock, the drunken and heretical
evangelist, is a character of parts. The story in which he figures
is conventional enough, but he is as nearly a real creation as it
was in Buchanan to do. *Father Anthony* (1899), an outgrowth of Buchanan's residence in the west of Ireland from 1874
to 1877, presents another one of his most memorable characters
and again a man of God. This is Father John, a character
based on the parish priest of Rossport, who did much to hearten
and enliven Buchanan in his stay in Ireland.

The plays that Buchanan wrote were, like most of his novels,
little more than pot-boilers. *Alone in London* (1884) which had
a great success in Philadelphia when Buchanan produced it there
on his visit to America, repeated that success in other places
and for a number of years. Buchanan himself despised it, thinking *Stormbeaten* (1883), the dramatization of *God and the Man,*
his best play of this sort. *Stormbeaten,* too, was a success. It
was his plays that were most popular of his work and that
brought him in the most money. Had he had any head for
business he might have made for himself leisure to do good
work. Spendthrift that he was, his nose was always to the grind-
stone. There is no single lyric, narrative poem, play or story
of his that is not hurried or careless or insufficiently considered.
So, too, is it with his criticism. *The Fleshly School of Poetry*
(1871), his notorious attack on Rossetti, was written precipi-
tately. He lived to repent of it and to recant. In his preface
to the 1882 edition of *God and the Man,* which he had dedicated,
in its first edition, "To An Old Enemy," Buchanan wrote: "That
I should ever have underrated his exquisite work, is simply a

proof of the incompetency of all criticism, however honest, which is conceived adversely, hastily, and from an unsympathetic point of view." It is ironical that it is by this onslaught that Buchanan is oftenest remembered. People say, when his name is mentioned: "Oh Buchanan! That's the man who attacked Rossetti, isn't it?" And it is unjust as well as ironical that a man who was just short of being a good poet, and who was a capable playwright and story-teller should be known only as a kind of parasite of a better man.

NEIL MUNRO

In the earliest years of the century they called him " the highland Stevenson." They knew him then as the author of *The Lost Pibroch* (1896), a collection of short tales, and as the author of five romances, *John Splendid* (1898), *Gilian the Dreamer* (1899), *Doom Castle* (1901) and *Children of Tempest* (1903). He ran serially in *Blackwood's Magazine* and was printed by Henley in *The New Review;* he was praised in the highest terms by the *Athenæum, The Pall Mall Gazette* and *The Spectator;* he was rated with Kipling by Andrew Lang. By 1905 you could buy several of the romances for thirty cents apiece in the January sales.

Neil Munro (1864-   ) deserved a better fate than he has met. A man that could put so much wonder and terror and beauty in the short-story was a man to be grateful for, a man for whom a future in literature seemed to be assured. *John Splendid,* too, was a tale of promise. The man who wrote that should have written better tales than that when he struck his stride. He never struck his stride. He tried hard enough, but it was not in him to get out of himself the best of himself. He tried particularly hard in *Children of Tempest.* That was to have been a romance with the voice of the sea in it, the menace of the sea that is all about Uist of the Hebrides. It was to have been a romance of lovers who escaped an untoward fate by a miracle; it was to have glamour about it and a magical beauty. It was to have had these things in full measure; it has them in scanty measure when it has them at all.

It would seem that the curse that has fallen on so much of the writing of the Highlander since the days of MacPherson had fallen on Munro as it had fallen on "Fiona Macleod." The curse of *Ossian* is the curse of the overwritten, the undervitalized, the curse of an extravagant style and an inability to create character and to body out a story into the proportions of a novel. John Splendid has more of flesh and blood than some of his subsequent heroes, perhaps because he is fashioned somewhat after Alan Breck Stewart. Gilian, the daft dreamer, is a real discovery, but Munro could only paint in a setting for him; he could not devise a story to set him forth properly.

Was the trouble that words got the better of Munro? He was intoxicated with the beauty of the wild countryside of Argyll. He had grown up among the people he wrote about or rather among the descendants of the people he wrote about, for he preferred old times to today as the background of his stories. He was master of a style in *The Lost Pibroch*. How did it come about that the style mastered him and that he came to be content with commonplaces dressed up in proud and flaunting words, he who had once imagined real romantic incident for his short-stories? Was it because he left the highlands for Glasgow, and that romance withered in the reek of Clyde? Or was his trouble that other old curse of the Gael, the dream beyond the power to do?

Other stories followed, *Daft Days* (1907) and *Fancy Farm* (1910) but they were not what the first work augured. Munro had been forced into journalism and he could not escape from the yoke. The newspaper is an exacting master, leaving him who serves it with little energy after the daily grind. Yet other newspaper writers have won their way to freedom and writing worth while. Whatever the reason it is only too true that Munro is not of those so fortunate ones.

CUNNINGHAME-GRAHAM

Robert Bontine Gallnigad Cunninghame-Graham (1852-   )
is hardly a novelist, but one dare not pass by a story-teller of
his parts without mention in an account of the fiction of our
time. No writer in English has come to closer grips with life
in far-off places. Spanish America he knows, as well as the
Spain from which it was peopled; and Morocco, from which
he believes Spain was largely peopled; and his native lowlands
of Scotland. He is strangely free from the prejudices the typical
Englishman loves to carry inviolate even to the ends of the
earth. He is as strangely sensitive to beauty and humanity
in forms his average fellow islander would consider outlandish
or grotesque. English to the core, though, is his love for horses,
his love of wandering, his idolatry of true aristocracy. And
John Bull his very self, in his most inveterate country squire-
dom, is revealed in his dislike of Americans. Is it in the nature of
things that English socialists like Cunninghame-Graham and his
friend Shaw should be so troubled by the spectacle of America?
It is partly, of course, the long affiliation of Cunninghame-Graham
with Spain and Spanish ways, that makes him so resentful of
"States folks." He cannot forgive us the war with Spain.

A bundle of contradictions is Cunninghame-Graham, but in
all his guises he is interesting. Naturally an essayist and writer
of travels, his zest of life and strong kinship with all wild ways
has driven him into many strange human relationships that he
cannot refrain from telling about. He has never troubled himself
to learn the architectonics of writing. And yet so dominant
is the personality of the man that his writing has not only the
words of his talk, but, in ways one cannot particularize, the
tones of that talk, and something of its accompanying gesture
and facial expression. His subjects are often unconventional,
and often, too, his sentence structure. Somehow the lapses do
not matter. There is an intimacy about his writing at its best
that is wholly captivating. You make allowances as you do
for the crustiness and odd ways of an old friend. Always, too,

you feel you are in the company of a man of honor. There is color and delight and romance in Cunninghame-Graham. If you have not read him sample his short-stories by "The Captive" from *Hope* (1910), his travel sketches by "Pajay Cielo" from *Faith* (1909), and his essays by "Falkirk Tryst" from *A Hatchment* (1913). If these take your fancy you will be glad of three hundred more of them, better and worse, that are stored away in his score of volumes.

OLIVE SCHREINER

It is a curious dispensation of providence that the two writers who are most representative of South Africa in English literature should be Olive Schreiner (1855-1921) and Sir Henry Rider Haggard (1856-1925). They were nearly of an age, they both loved veldt and karoo and rand and the constellations that swing over them, and they both "scored phenomenal successes" in the eighteen-eighties with stories of hinterlands unknown before to the stay-at-home world. Yet there were never two writers in greater contrast. Haggard is the teller of gory adventures that befall typical heroes of romance, Olive Schreiner the explorer of the secret places of unusual souls. Sir Henry Curtis, blonde giant on the warpath against cruel Zulus, is the characteristic figure of the one, Lyndall, ox-eyed and proud, champion of woman's freedom, the characteristic figure of the other. *The Story of an African Farm* (1883) won its thousands of readers largely among those who look upon literature as a means to the betterment of life, and *King Solomon's Mines* (1885) its thousands largely among those who look upon literature as a means of relieving the monotony of life. Neither Olive Schreiner nor Rider Haggard is primarily an artist, neither achieved a thing of pure beauty, but each wrote a story that became a classic of a kind.

The fate of Olive Schreiner was not unlike that of most infant prodigies. She never "came through" to real greatness. Much of her *Story of an African Farm* was written before she was twenty-one, while she was governess in a Boer family in the back-country among people not unlike those that Pauline Smith writes about nowadays in *The Little Karoo* (1925). *The Story of an African Farm* was taken to England by its maker when she was twenty-six, in 1881, and published two years later, on the recommendation of George Meredith, who was reader to the publishing house to which she submitted it. It did not succeed very well at first in England, but it sold largely in America from its publication, especially among "come-outers." It was the strongest woman's rights tract that had yet appeared. It might have been expected to lead to still better things by its author but it did not. *Dreams* (1890) is a book of parables something more than propagandist but not much more. *Trooper Peter Halkett of Mashonaland* (1897), with its attack on the Chartered Company of South Africa and Cecil Rhodes, is just a tract raised to the highest power. It stirred up a great deal of discussion but it was not important as art. There is better writing provoked by Rhodes, *The Testament of an Empire Builder* (1902) of John Davidson.

Even before the taking of *The Story of an African Farm* to England Olive Schreiner was planning and working upon another novel. It is referred to as *Saints and Sinners, From Man to Man, The Camel Thorn* and *Perhaps Only*. It never developed into what she hoped it would become and she left it unpublished.

In *The Life of Olive Schreiner* (1924), by her husband, S. C. Cronwright Schreiner, he writes: "The whole novel treats of a little child's care and intensity of love for her baby sister, and then of the same love, more than a mother's love, of the adult woman for the little sister, now grown up and in the grip of a great tragedy." Nor did the long-pondered book, finally published in 1911 as *Woman and Labor,* turn out to be the magnum opus she dreamed of.

There is a telling little study in outline of three generations of a Boer family in *Eighteen-Ninety-Nine,* published along with other "literary remains" in 1923 in *Stories, Dreams and Allegories,* but it is far from a great work. The place of Olive Schreiner in literature depends almost entirely on *The Story of an African Farm.* Its scene is a Boer farm on the red sands of the high and half-desert karoo. There are seven characters of importance. The most clearly realized of them is Tant' Sannie, the Boer woman who holds the farm. With her are, at the story's beginning, two little girls, a step-daughter, and that step-daughter's cousin. Their names are Em and Lyndall. There is a boy on the farm, a dreamer, Waldo, the son of the German overseer of the farm. Upon these folk living quietly with their Kaffir and Hottentot servants irrupts Bonaparte Blenkins, a caricature of a man introduced to make trouble and to afford comic relief. Later comes an Englishman, Gregory Rose, who rents half the farm from Tant' Sannie. The girls grow up, and both Waldo and Gregory fall in love with Lyndall, who, however, does not love either, but a man she meets when she leaves the farm. He, "Lyndall's stranger," is but a shadow of a man, a girl's dream of a handsome and masterful lover, a Mr. Rochester of a younger generation. Lyndall loves him only after a fashion, and she will not be fettered by marriage. She goes away with him, and dies when their child is born. This death is accident, not expiation for her revolt from convention. That is the story that fluttered the dovecotes of the eighteen-eighties. It was written by an intense, an ardent girl, whose personality finds lyric expression in a number of challenging passages and some phrases all but memorable. "When . . . I am strong," her creator makes Lyndall say, "I will hate everything that has power, and help everything that is weak." Lyndall is Olive Schreiner's dream of herself as she wished she might be, a proud beauty who hoped to sway the world to her will as a great actress and free her sisters from the yoke imposed upon them by the tyranny of men. There is no evidence that anything of Jane Eyre went to Lyndall's making but she is nevertheless a sort of emancipated Jane Eyre.

Emerson was one of Olive Schreiner's prophets and Browning another. She came, indeed, from the poets rather than the novelists. Later she found she had much in common with Tolstoi, but she was never wholly in accord with his teaching. There are all sorts of good things in *The Story of an African Farm,* but it lacks coherence. It has no architectonics. It has flashes of insight but there is in it no deep reading of life. It reveals little appreciation of the good things of life, it is deficient in humor, it is strained and, at times, even hysterical. Nor is there much of the beauty of the back-country she so loved. Hills golden in the sunlight and the desert white in the moonlight are but referred to, not painted in in detail. We are allowed to see the room of a farm overseer and the gross pleasantries of a Boer wedding, but surprisingly little of such things. Her chief concern is with states of soul, but even in depicting these she leaves much for us to guess at from hints and intimations. *The Story of an African Farm* is a book of great promise but it is not a great book. That great book never came, although thirty-eight years of life remained to Olive Schreiner after the publication of this path-finding first novel. It was not in her to do the novel she dreamed. Her husband exclaims: "The pity of it, that so beautiful a genius should have been so largely denied, through no fault of its own, the conditions which would have led to its full and glorious fruition." One appreciates the loyalty of the declaration but one cannot believe that her failure was due to any conditions other than the limits of her own nature. She had not the concentration, the knowledge, the experience, the imagination, the power of characterization necessary to full power in her chosen craft. They tell us she wrote much by moonlight, they tell us of the startling luminousness of her eyes, they tell us how she won the admiration of strong men, a Cecil Rhodes, an Oom Paul, a Lloyd George. They tell us all sorts of romantic things about her, of her clairvoyance, of her magnetism; and all of us who have read her know that she could evoke strangeness and wonder. It was a marvellous girl that wrote *The Story of an African Farm*, but that marvellous girl never grew up into an artist of full stature, or into what she would have preferred, a true seer.

MARIE CORELLI

There are certain authors who suggest certain places. Mention "Mrs. Alexander" or Mrs. Walford or "The Duchess" and I see the verandahs of seaside hotels. Mention "Sarah Grand" or Beatrice Harraden or Mrs. Humphry Ward and I see groups of matrons going down dingy and ill-lighted stairs from a hall where they have listened to an earnest and uninspiring lecture by a person of little taste. The latter three writers are associated with the city, and night, and winter.

Mention Marie Corelli (1864-1924) and I see a man no longer young rolling down a bank. The scene is just across the road from a boarding house high in the Berkshire Hills. Three youths, waiting impatiently for supper in a ramshackle summerhouse, ran to his assistance, thinking he had had a stroke. When they reached him they found that it was not from a stroke he was suffering but from *The Sorrows of Satan* (1895). He was clutching the book still, with his thumb in the guilty page, and shaking with spasmodic laughter. Prone on the ground as he was he cried to us: "Look at that and you will know why I fell down the bank." Then he broke out into lamentable expletives. He was short, broad-shouldered and bearded. I remember just what he looked like, his heavy eyebrows, his eyes deep-sunken and gray, and his mobile lips that twitched in an agony of laughter. The youths assisted him to a sitting posture and listened while he tried to read the passage. It was too much for him, so they had to read it themselves. They could see it was pretentious and overblown, but they could not get his joy out of it. I have hunted for that passage in vain, on a re-perusal of *The Sorrows of Satan*. There is only boredom in the reading of it now. I cannot recall that man's name but he remains for me the most redoubtable critic of Marie Corelli I have met, either in the flesh or in print.

MRS. HUMPHRY WARD

Mrs. Humphry Ward (1851-1920) has had plenty of praise, some of it in high places. Henry James thought well of her early work, and Henry James is a critic of insight and power. One might say that friendship had blinded him to her dullness, or one might guess it was another Homeric nod. Fortunately there is

Matthew Arnold to quote against him. Informed in 1881 that his niece had written a story, the *Milly and Olly* of that year, he replied: "No, she has not! If any Arnold could have written a story, I would."

I remember well the furore over *Robert Elsmere* (1888). In those days agnosticism was an issue and we could be greatly excited by discussions of it in a story. Today it is, in such places, as dead and done for as the religious controversy in Charles Kingsley. *The History of David Grieve* (1892) was eagerly awaited, and it was well received. It did not cause such another stir as *Robert Elsmere,* but it was a much talked-of book. So were *Marcella* (1894) and *Sir George Tressady* (1896) and *Helbeck of Bannisdale* (1898) much discussed books, but, book by book, there was less and less heat in the discussion. Mrs. Ward had had her ten years' inning. There was a little flutter over *Lady Rose's Daughter* (1903), but after that her books were calmly received. There were still some of us who continued to read her for the politics in her stories and their pictures of upper class life, and certain others of us who looked into a book of hers now and then because she had stirred us in our youth. *Elizabeth's Campaign* (1918) is the last one I read. It "represents the mood of a supremely critical moment in the war." It is of historical value as a record. Such, it seems to me, is the chief value of all her books, their value as historical records. There is in all of them I have read a clear presentation of a life she knew at first hand, but there is no distinction of style or of story-telling or of characterization. The stories are, on the average, stodgy stuff, with no joy in them and no revelation. You may say that Robert Elsmere is a cross-section of a certain type of his time, but you cannot say he is a fellow of the great characters of English fiction.

BEATRICE HARRADEN

There was a nine days' stir over *Ships that Pass in the Night* (1893). Miss Beatrice Harraden (1864-   ) had her greatest success with this first book. It was the study of a group of people

who were "cases," and it was not without influence in breeding
a whole little school of the sort. It is ill written, morbid and
interesting medically. *Hilda Strafford* (1897) is a story that
shifts its scene to Southern California. There is only one sick
man in it and a great deal more of out-of-doors than there was in
Ships that Pass in the Night. The character of Hilda is firmly
and unsparingly drawn. She is rather a poor sort and wholly out
of place on an orchard in California. The descriptions of landscape are fairly well done, and the landscape is not overpraised.
Miss Harraden admits the spring is beautiful, and the distant
views grand at all times of year, but she truly pictures the brown
monotony and dustiness of a ranch in the dry seasons. There are
nearly a score of books by Miss Harraden, but no other one has
emerged from them as a novel of distinction.

"SARAH GRAND"

"Sarah Grand" is another novelist of one outstanding story.
The Heavenly Twins (1893) shared the honors of its birth year
with *Ships that Pass in the Night.* It was, for all its propaganda,
a better story than Miss Harraden's. Mrs. Frances Elizabeth
Clarke McFall (1865-   ) has been interested in the "Cause of
Woman" from her early years and there are few of her several
stories that are not concerned with some phase of it.

SUMMER READING A GENERATION AGO

In the mid-eighties there was a sufficiency of light reading to
form a background for the gossip of the seaside hotel. Matrons
and spinsters, youngish, middle-aged and old, might be seen in
bevies on the broad porches of "Sea Views" and "Bay Views,"
"Atlantic Houses" and "Ocean Houses," with all sorts of series
in boards or paper, "leisure hours," "seaside libraries" and the
like. There was always a corner in the trunk close packed with
such books lest any hours of those fortnight vacations of Julys
and Augusts should hang heavy on the ladies' hands. The books

they brought to the porches were apt to be of the discreeter authors, the last "Mrs. Alexander" (Anne French Hector 1825-1902), "but not so good as *The Wooing O't*" (1873); or *The Baby's Grandmother* (1885) of Mrs. Lucy Bethia Walford (1845-1915), so comforting to sentimentalists of middle age; or "the best of Mrs. Frances Hodgson Burnett" (1849-1924), *Little Lord Fauntleroy* (1886). Or it might be that the porch books were a Charlotte Yonge (1823-1901), a Mrs. Oliphant (1828-1897) or an "Edna Lyall" (Ada Ellen Bayly 1859-1903), a reissue maybe of *The Heir of Redclyffe* (1853), or *A Beleaguered City* (1880); or a *We Two* (1884).

Intenser stories were reserved by such ladies for the privacy of rooms, or devoured by young girls snugged away under sun umbrellas on the beach—a fresh *Othmar* (1885) of "Ouida" (Louise de la Ramée, 1840-1908); or a *Molly Bawn* (1878) of "The Duchess" (Mrs. Margaret Wolfe Hungerford, 1855-1897), frayed and tattered in its passing down from older girls; or a *Nadine* (1882) almost as worn and old, of Mrs. Campbell Praed (1851-). And when, in the course of years, these romantic girls were married and mothers, they named daughters for these heroines so much loved in youth.

On the porches talk would sometimes go back to thrillers of the past and an older generation of novelists be discussed. *Not Wisely but too Well* (1867) of Rhoda Broughton (1840-1920) would be overhauled; or *Lady Audley's Secret* (1862) of Miss Braddon (1837-1915); or even *East Lynne* (1861) of Mrs. Henry Wood (1814-1887).

The smaller girls on the porch steps and railings and in the pavilions would be employed with "L. T. Meade" (Mrs. Toulmin Smith, 1858-1914), or Mrs. Mary Louisa Molesworth (1839-1921) or Mrs. Juliana Horatia Ewing (1842-1885). There are daughters and granddaughters of those who were these smaller girls reading today old copies of *A World of Girls* (1886) or *The Cuckoo Clock* (1877) or *Jackanapes* (1873) which had seen service in those midsummer days at Beach Haven or Long Branch.

There may be some who think one or another of these women

writers is worthy of a place in a better category than that of "summer reading." "Ouida" has still a following, her books are placed among the "classics" in old book stores, and their sale is not slow. *Under Two Flags* (1867) established her in popularity, and she held that popularity, despite all changes of taste, for nearly thirty years. She had always ignored all criticism of her writing. What she was in *Under Two Flags* she continued to be until she was written out. *Toxin* (1897) was done according to the old recipe. It had that delightful sense of wickedness about it that was summed up in Victorian days in that whispered word "boudoir." Its heroine Veronica Zaranegra, a Venetian beauty, is as intense as Cigarette and as tragically fated. *Toxin* was as compact a melodrama as "Ouida" had ever written, with what she regarded as a powerful theme, the killing of the hero Adrianis by his English friend, Damer the scientist, through a betrayal of professional trust. Yet somehow, it had not, even for staunch admirers, the old glamour. Times had changed and a new order of sensation was demanded.

Several of her novels were dramatized and *Under Two Flags* was a great success, being played by all sorts of companies all over the United States. In its humblest form, played in a tent by wandering actors, it gave to many an American country boy his ideal of girlhood in Cigarette, that lovely and devoted victim of circumstance. "Ouida" had in herself the great gift of caring intensely for life, but she never took the trouble to learn to see things as they are, and she could not distinguish between what was fine and what was false. She was only an entertainer of a generation, not an artist at all.

There are probably others who think Mrs. Margaret Oliphant Wilson Oliphant made a lasting place for herself by *Salem Chapel* (1863). From my point of view, however, it is a document of its time rather than an important contribution to the art of letters. Nor can I see the fineness of *A Beleaguered City* (1880), in which is revealed, perhaps, some Gaelic strain in her Scots blood. Its mysticism allies it to certain books of George Macdonald.

There are better writers among the women novelists of this

period than any of these I have just mentioned. Anne Isabella Thackeray Ritchie (1837-1919) had the disadvantage of being her father's daughter. Too much was expected of her because she was a Thackeray. She was read in some quarters, perhaps, for this reason, but such readers were always listening for some echo of the great voice in the tones of her writing. It was not there, but the tones of a voice somewhat like that of the Mrs. Gaskell she wrote of so charmingly. It is, indeed, in her essays, and in the biographical introductions to her father's novels that I have found her most interesting, and not in *The Story of Elizabeth* (1863) or *Mrs. Dymond* (1885). Her books were always brought home by my father from the circulating library as soon as published, and what he considered the best of them were bought and read by the family. It was a household devoted to Thackeray, but all it could say of his daughter's writing was that it was pleasant. Mrs. Ritchie wrote well, but she did not come upon the kind of experience that her reticent nature could make over into a telling story.

Charles Kingsley's daughter is a more forthright story-teller. Under the pseudonym of "Lucas Malet," Mrs. Mary St. Leger Harrison (1852-   ) won the public with her second novel, *Colonel Enderby's Wife* (1885), and kept that public until she won a larger one with *The History of Sir Richard Calmady* (1901). This last story is a powerful study of a sinister dwarf and his self-sacrificing mother. "Lucas Malet" continued to write on into war times with never failing vigor and did a post-war book, *The Survivors* (1923) that is a valuable record of the times.

Mrs. Flora Annie Steel (1847-   ) one always thinks of with Kipling because of her stories of India. They were published before *Plain Tales from the Hills* (1887). *Wide-Awake Stories: a Collection of Tales Told by Little Children, Between Sunset and Sunrise, in the Punjaub and Kashmir* appeared simultaneously in London and Bombay late in 1884. Scholars were interested in this collection as folklore; children were interested in it as fairy tales; and the public generally were interested in it as a curious revelation of a little known side of Indian life. The book was well received, but it was largely forgotten when the more vivid Indian tales of Kipling began to appear.

On the Face of the Waters (1896) has, however, held its place as a tale of the Indian mutiny. It is a realistic novel set against a most picturesque background, with romantic adventures properly subordinated to the presentation of character. The main characters are four, all well realized. About James Greyman, Kate Erlton and her husband Major Erlton, and Alice Gissing, are grouped a host of minor characters, British and native. Mrs. Steel belongs to the old order of prodigal creators. The story of the fighting that led up to the capture of Delhi is told clearly, and the fortunes of the four leading characters are involved in that struggle with entire naturalness.

What is freshest in the story is the presentation of the Indian characters. Zora, Greyman's native love, is a pathetic little figure, done, it must be, straight from life. And all her native fellows live and move and have their being in what seems reality— Tara, the Rajpoot suttee; Sorna, her brother; Tiddu; Jhungi-Bhungi; Sri Anunda; Princess Farkhoonda Zamani, who foreshadows "Laurence Hope"; Abool-Bukr, the lover of Omar Khayyam; and the Moulvie. I have listed so many that there may be a sense of the richness of the story, and a realization of what knowledge of native life Mrs. Steel possesses.

Her Scots stories are not so striking. They have some affinities with the stories of William Black, and some with those of "Fiona Macleod." Neither *Red Rowans* (1895) or *In the Tideway* (1897) is a fresh revelation of life as was *On the Face of the Waters*. This story, indeed, is her triumph. It is only the element of melodrama basic to her conception of drama and a diction too heightened for continued reading that prevent *On the Face of the Waters* from being a great book, that vitiate what might else have been a fine accomplishment of story-telling.

There were Irishwomen busy with fiction for English readers all through the long Victorian years. Mrs. S. C. Hall was still at the height of her reputation when Rosa Mulholland (Lady Gilbert, 1845-1920) began to publish. *The Wild Birds of Killeevy*

(1883) is a typical novel. She was as prolific of all sorts of stories, Irish and English, for children and their elders, as Mrs. Katherine Tynan Hinkson (1861-   ), who took up a similar task thirty years later with *A Cluster of Nuts* (1894). Both novelists could write well, but both were frankly writing stories for a living. Both cared more for their verse than their prose and both are better poets than novelists, Mrs. Hinkson a poet of a rare simplicity.

Hon. Emily Lawless (1845-1913) did two good novels of Irish life in *Hurrish* (1886) and *Grania* (1892), the one about Clare, the other of the Aran Islands. She knew at first hand the life she wrote of, she had power of characterization, and a style of distinction.

Miss Jane Barlow (1857-1917) is a writer of sketches of Irish life rather than a novelist. *Irish Idylls* (1892), her first book of prose, is her best, but it had many successors of like kind that were almost on a level with it. *Kerrigan's Quality* (1893), *The Founding of Fortunes* (1902), *Flaws* (1911) and *In Mio's Youth* (1917), are novels in intention but hardly in form. They are not so good in their kind as the many volumes of sketches or idylls or short-stories, call them which you will, are in theirs. There is only one character a complete achievement in the novels, Timothy Galvin in *The Founding of Fortunes*. There are a score from the people of Connemara you meet in the idylls, Sheridans, Kilfoyles, the Widow M'Gurk, Mr. Polymathers, Ody Rafferty, Mad Bell, and Con the Quare One among them.

Another Irishwoman who writes with delicacy and charm is "M. E. Francis" (Mrs. Francis Blundell, 1858-   ). She writes more of the Liverpool of her adoption than of the Dublin of her birth. *The Manor Farm* (1902), and *Dark Rosaleen* (1915) are typical, respectively, of her manners.

RIDER HAGGARD

There are two countries graven on the heart of Sir Henry Rider Haggard (1856-1925). They are the South Africa in which he spent the best years of his youth, and the Norfolkshire to which he was born and in which he farmed so successfully for himself and so helpfully to others for so many years of maturity. Save for the decade of his early success writing was not what mattered most to him. For years his functioning as country gentleman and agricultural expert came first, with what energy he had left over going to literary work. One feels, from his writing about the countryside of Norfolkshire, that he would have liked to do justice to it in such books as *A Farmer's Year* (1899) and *Rural England* (1902), but one cannot, as one reads, delude oneself into the belief that he has done justice to it. He belongs, by such books, with the Gervase Markhams and the Arthur Youngs and not with the Gilbert Whites and William Cobbetts.

Rider Haggard went out to Natal as secretary to its governor in 1875, and he passed on to the Transvaal two years later and saw service there for several years. He got to know the Zulus, and wrote his first book on *Cetewayo and His White Neighbors*, which he classifies as "political history," in 1882. Zulus appear again in *King Solomon's Mines* (1885) under the name of Kukuanas, but it was not until *Jess* (1887) that he began to consider carefully the Boers. *Jess* failed to make the impression it might have made were it not for its overshadowing by *She* which appeared just before it in 1887. *She,* though it has not stood the test of the years so well as *King Solomon's Mines,* had an even greater success on publication. It was read the English-speaking world over, and it was translated into many tongues, even into Hindustani. The fabled beauty of its heroine and the terror of its whirling earth-fire that brought immortal youth were a wonder at first, but they were a little too miraculous to last. There is a limit to the tallness of tall stories and Haggard went beyond that limit in *She.* The occult is, too, always a dangerous element in a story. It may be so managed that it will inspire terror, but that terror may give way, on a second reading, to a feeling that the reader was hoaxed by a pretense of terror, that there is no terror at all, but only a trick. So I felt when I went back to *She.*

So I did not feel when I went back to *King Solomon's Mines.*

The chart of the old Portuguese is surely a descendant of that other chart of *The Goldbug* but none the less effective for that. The elephant hunt is still good reading. The picture of the desert with the snow-capped mountains beyond had again the lure for me rereading that it had in boyhood. The whole story seemed to be worthy of a place, humble, indeed, but sure, in the long annals of romance. There was a little of the circus, perhaps, about the Zulu war-dress of Sir Henry Curtis, but the circus has still in itself something of romance. I delighted in that war-dress not only as I delight in a gorgeous item of the circus parade but for its own barbaric splendor. "Round his throat he fastened the leopard skin cloak of a commanding officer, on his brows he bound the plume of black ostrich feathers worn only by generals of high rank, and round his centre a magnificent moocha of white ox-tails. A pair of sandals, a leglet of goat's hair, a heavy battle-axe with a rhinoceros-horn handle, a round iron shield covered with white ox-hide, and the regulation number of tollas, or throwing knives, made up his equipage."

That description recalled to one a succession of warriors in full regalia through the vista of English romance to that viking of "the Ruined Burg," who "hot with wine, in war-harness shone." So, too, the description of the triangled snow-peaks of The Three Witches, leapt into companionship with older and finer descriptions of mountains that stick in my mind. "High, high above us, up into the blue air, soared their twisted snow-wreaths. Beneath the snow the peaks were purple with heath, and so were the wild moors that ran up the slopes toward them. Straight before us the white ribbon of Solomon's Great Road stretched away up-hill to the foot of the centre peak, about five miles from us, and there stopped. It was its terminus."

There is obvious carelessness in detail in that description, but somehow it is memorable. That picture, too, sticks in memory. Bret Harte does it better. "And above all this, etched on the dark firmament, rose the Sierra, remote and passionless, crowned with remoter passionless stars." Yet the description of Haggard

is of a like ancestry. They both go back to that description of
the Alps from the bridge of Schaffhausen by Ruskin and to that
far older description of the Pyrenees in *The Song of Roland,*
where from the field of Roncesvalles the paladins saw the peaks
dimming against the far sky.

The diamond mines themselves are well described, and the adventures in them well recounted, though, like most other romancers, Haggard has to make his heroes unbelievably dull to
allow themselves to be caught in such a trap as Gagool sets for
them. Gagool, that hag centuries old, is the first study of the
character that afterwards appears in Haggard as "She-Who-Must-
Be-Obeyed." Gagool is a shrivelled mummy, no larger than an
ape, and She still in her bloom after centuries, and as shapely as
Venus, but they are in origin one and the same.

There is no more impressiveness in Ayesha, the reincarnation
of She in *Ayesha* (1905) than in the lady of the sepulchres of
Kor. There are again good descriptions of mountains, this time
in some outland beyond Thibet, and some satisfying thrills in the
rock-climbing of Vincey and Holly, but nothing better than the
wonders of *She.*

Swallow (1898) is subtitled *A Tale of The Great Trek.* The
Great Trek was the exodus of Boers from Cape Colony to the
Transvaal in 1836, to escape from British rule. The story set
against this background is conventional enough. It begins with
the description of a Boer homestead in the Transkei, not very
intimately done. The heroine is a Boer girl of mingled French
and Dutch blood, and the hero, her lover, a Scots boy she found
in a kloof after he had been shipwrecked. Suzanne and Ralph
marry but they are parted by the machinations of a tedious villain, Swart Piet, a Boer with Kaffir blood in his veins. Through
the help and final self-sacrifice of a native witch woman, Sihamba,
Suzanne is returned to her husband. The story is supposed to
be told by an old Boer great-grandmother, Vrouw Botmar, Suzanne's mother, but the device does not take Haggard out of his
usual procedure of story-telling. He kills off the faithful horse

which saves the lovers' lives, at the end, against all proper practice in romance, just as he kills off the faithful yak that saves the lives of the two friends in *Ayesha*.

Swallow has been called a truer picture of Boer life than *The Story of An African Farm*. It is not. It is not written out of anything like such a fulness of knowledge as was Olive Schreiner's, but it is presented in a more ship-shape story. *Swallow* is, however, a disappointing book to come after so promising a forerunner as *Jess*.

There is no intimacy of knowledge of the Boers or of their farms in either *Jess* or *Swallow*. Rider Haggard's knowledge of Dutch South Africa is far short of a settler's or even of a sympathetic traveler's. There is more of the countryside in two lines of "Lichtenberg" than in all the many pages of *Swallow*. Kipling has the very tang of it in

> "The smell of the wattle by Lichtenberg,
>   Riding in, in the rain."

Yet *Swallow* is a juster picture of the Boers than Kipling often gives. "A Sahib's War" (1901) is vividly presented, but with a rancor that defeats any propagandist purpose it may have been intended to have. One wonders whether "Piet" was written by Kipling to make amends.

A Farmer's Year (1899) is a better book of its kind than any novel of England that Sir Henry Rider Haggard has written. He tried, no doubt, to make *Joan Haste* (1895) a story of power. It presents two generations of wrong-doing in a family, the sins of the father descending to a daughter who is fated, like her duped mother, to suffer for man's weakness and cowardice. In the end the story becomes a thing of horror, of a madman trying to break into the room into which his wife has locked herself from his fury, and of her murder by him after she has escaped from his house. It is poor stuff altogether, with its only passable parts the description of the sad-colored marsh country he makes its scene. It is somewhat in the manner of Charles Reade, but weaker in characterization and narrative power, and as incredible as Haggard's wildest yarns of Africa and Mexico. And this incredible yarn is laid in so familiar a place as Norfolkshire. Such a choice of locality adds to its incredibility. At the world's end, in Ultima Thule, we are willing to accept the marvellous and are even well-disposed to the incredible, but it is a rare power only that could make us accept so wild a tale with its actors and background people of a sort and a place of a sort we all know so well. Such a power Rider Haggard does not possess. Tell us what you will, we say to him, about outland places, but in England stick to crops and country contentments.

THE ROMANCERS OF THE NINETIES

In 1894 Andrew Lang picked out Kipling, Barrie, Weyman, Stevenson, Conan Doyle, S. R. Crockett and "Anthony Hope" as the chief romancers of the day. He could not help mentioning Barrie after Kipling, even if he had immediately to except him as a good thing of another kind. It was at the annual banquet of the Royal Academy that he delivered his dictum:

"The thrifty plan of giving us sermons, politics, fiction, all in one stodgy sandwich, produces no permanent literature, produces but temporary tracts for the times. Fortunately we have among us many novelists—young ones, luckily,—who are true to the primitive and eternal, the Fijian canons of fiction. We have Oriental romance from the author of *Plain Tales from the Hills.* We have the humor and tenderness—certainly not Fijian, I admit—which produces that masterpiece *A Window in Thrums;* we have the adventurous fancy that gives us *A Gentleman of France, The Master of Ballantrae, Micah Clarke, The Raiders, The Prisoner of Zenda.*"

Lang strangely omits his old friend and collaborater Sir Henry Rider Haggard, but perhaps he regarded him as no longer among the young men. There were other romancers that he might have mentioned though not all of them had as yet written their most captivating stories. Among these omissions are "Henry Seton Merriman" (Hugh Stowell Scott, 1862-1903), Sir Gilbert Parker

(1862-   ), Matthew Phipps Shiel (1865-   ), and Ernest William Hornung (1866-1921).

Kipling is the survivor of this group who most nearly approaches greatness, more nearly perhaps than the Stevenson who is his only rival among them all. Years ago George Moore said he would take Kipling seriously if he came down from his camel, meaning that Kipling could not be truly judged by his Indian stories but that he would have to do stories of England that could be measured against like stories of well-known conditions before he could be accepted or rejected as a writer. Kipling came down from his camel. He did "They" and "The Brushwood Boy," short-stories of first power. He created in Puck of *Puck of Pook's Hill* (1906) a fellow to all Robin Goodfellows and Lob-lie-by-the-fires that sport through the long annals of English fairy-lore. He proved he could write as well about English people at home in England as he could write about English people in conflict with an eastern civilization in India, or about the Indian natives themselves. It remains a fact, though, that he has not written so many stories of power about England as he has about India. From one point of view it is a pity he ever came down from his camel. It is stories such as "Without Benefit of Clergy," "The Man Who Was" and "The Miracle of Purun Bhagat" that reveal Kipling at his best, that is his best in prose. There is no doubt whatever that it is as a poet in verse that he has spoken with the most distinction. "Mandalay," "The Ballad of Fisher's Boarding-House," "The Fires," "The Long Trail," "The Gipsy Trail," "The Feet of the Young Men," "Lichtenberg," "A Song of Travel," "The Mary Gloster," and "The Return" are ten poems of his of a quality better than any of his stories. It is not Kipling the poet that has suffered from his absence from India. It is Kipling the writer of short-stories that has suffered from a long severance from that material that first revealed him to the world. We cannot help wondering would we not have seen the fulfillment of his promise to write long stories of Anglo-Indian life of the scope of Thackeray's had he remained in India. And we cannot help wondering if continued residence there would not have resulted in romances, to which *The Jungle Books* (1894-1895) point the way.

The only long story of India wholly his own that we have had is *Kim* (1901), a picaresque story with romantic incident. It is far from a realistic novel, such as he promised us. The story that comes nearest to such a novel is *The Naulakha* (1892), written in collaboration with Wolcott Balestier. It is crude both in composition and in style, and not of compelling interest. *Captains Courageous* (1897) is a boy's story and not one of the best of its kind.

The Light That Failed (1891) could have been developed into a novel, but, as it stands, there is hardly enough of it for a novel. Dick Heldar and Maisie are definite figures, individuals, people you know on one reading of the story, but you only know certain sides of them. It is with them, as it so often is with the characters of a short-story—you get only a partial view of them. There has not been enough room in the story as it is planned to develop them fully. Kipling has the gift of imparting the personality of his characters to the reader on a first meeting with them. He has also the power to make his characters change as the action develops. Yet he has not, somehow, prepared us for the disloyalty of Maisie. From what we have learned of her in the earlier parts of the story we expect her to stand by Dick when things go wrong.

Altogether, these short novels and approximations to novels of Kipling do not sum up to an important part of his work. The life they present is of nothing like so wide a scope or so varied as that of the short-stories, nor are there in the longer stories any such mystery or wonder as we find in the short-stories. The longer stories, too, are deficient in humor. There is no "Incarnation of Krishna Mulvaney" among them.

The satirist in Kipling is to the fore in these longer stories as in all that he writes but not so insistently as in the short-stories and the verses. It was not as satirist, however, that he first broke upon us back in the eighties, but as the interpreter of the Further East. He was satirist earlier, for *Departmental Ditties* (1886) was his first published book. The spectacle of Kipling during his first decade of publication, 1886-1896, was somewhat like the spectacle of Byron in the decade 1809-1819. Byron, too, was satirist before he was story-teller; and both writers had been stung to their satire by the reception reviewers gave to their boyish first verses. Byron revealed to a wondering world a Nearer East, the East of Greece and Turkish lands, and Kipling to a world equally wondering the Further East of India. From both writers we have a series of memorable portraits. There are enough in the short-stories of Kipling to fill an alcove in the great portrait gallery of English fiction, if sketches are admitted as well as finished paintings. Mulvaney, Ortheris and Learoyd are of this latter class, but they are not wholly original. Mulvaney is a variation of Lever's stage Irishman; Ortheris is a reincarnation of Sam Weller; and Learoyd is a Dandy Dinmont from Yorkshire.

The Light that Failed and *Kim* gave us more portraits to remember than the other longer stories. Dick Heldar, Maisie, the Red-Haired Girl, Lurgan Sahib, the Lama, Kim and the Babu are chief among them. Would there be more fairly well finished portraits of this kind, and more of the highly finished portraits of the kind of the Soldiers Three, had Kipling given us the full scope novels he promised? One wonders. One wonders, too, if Puck will not outlast all the finished few we have.

STANLEY WEYMAN

Stanley Weyman (1859-   ) began with *The House of the Wolf* (1890) and came into general recognition with *A Gentleman of France* (1893), the book Andrew Lang picked out for mention in his Royal Academy address. A son of the Welsh marches he had that interest in France that so many British Celts have felt. In a sense he continued that cultivation of the romance of French history that G. P. R. James had so industriously practiced, but there is more élan and spirit to his stories, a more vivid characterization, and better writing. *Under the Red Robe* (1894) was a book that many of us sat up to finish when it was first published and it was not the only one of Weyman which exacted that tribute from that supposedly ennuied time. Yet it must be confessed that one reason that he could be finished at a sitting was that the best of him even could bear judicious skipping. He is one of those authors that can be "read lightly" without loss of the thread of story.

CONAN DOYLE

Sir Arthur Conan Doyle (1855-   ) is known to all the late Victorian generation and to a good part of the succeeding generation by the *Sherlock Holmes* series. Beginning with *A Study in Scarlet* (1887), and following with *The Sign of Four* (1889), he won almost universal appeal with *Adventures of Sherlock Holmes* (1891). The amateur detective, with his love of good music and George Meredith, with his quotations from Flaubert and his tomes in blackletter, is undubitably a creation of a kind. If you doubt his universal acceptance throughout the English speaking world just refer to old newspaper files or to today's headlines. In the files you will find, on the funny page, the exploits of Sherlocko and Watso in cartoon and print alike, and in the headlines you will find "Detective displays Sherlockian skill."

It is always to be kept in mind that Sir Arthur never took his success too seriously, but that he chaffed his readers and himself in a good deal of the writing about Sherlock Holmes. One wonders why readers were not more of them alienated by that chaffing. Perhaps they were alienated and that is why they have turned today to J. S. Fletcher (1863-   ) and A. E. W. Mason (1865-   ), and in stories such as *The Charing Cross Mystery* (1923) and *The House of the Arrow* (1924) found a solace for the gentle raillery of Sir Arthur.

Doyle did other sorts of stories as well as he did detective stories. His *Micah Clarke* (1888) is an historical novel written in whole-hearted accord with the rules of the game. *The White Company* (1890) takes us from the New Forest to France, and to and fro in France, with good comrades that afford us entertainment all the way. *The Lost World* (1912) most of us have both read and seen on the films. It is an interesting development of the Jules Verne tale. A varied talent is this of Doyle, for in addition to all these sorts of stories he can do effective drama and verse. I never saw Sir Henry Irving act so well as he did in *A Story of Waterloo* (1900), a little play that was used as a curtain-raiser; and I never heard verse more successful at after-dinner recital than "The Guards Came Through" (1900).

S. R. CROCKETT

The kailyard stories of Samuel Rutherford Crockett (1860-1920) have already been referred to. *The Raiders* (1894) and *The Men of the Moss Hags* (1895) are fully as good in their kind, as adventure stories. The Penicuik minister was a good story-teller; and, what is rarer, a loyal upholder of Kirk and Covenant; and what is rarer still, a tolerant man.

ERNEST WILLIAM HORNUNG

Ernest William Hornung (1866-1921) is the creator of "Raffles," the hero of *The Amateur Cracksman* (1899). Before Hornung was that he was the worthy successor of Henry Kingsley (1830-1876) as the Englishman who wrote good stories of Australia. *A Bride from the Bush* (1890) was often spoken of as the best Australian novel since *Geoffrey Hamlyn* (1859). *A Bride from the Bush*, like most of its successors that present Australian life, derives its romance more often from the wonders of the country than from the events it recounts. So does *The Shadow of a Man* (1900), too. This is a typical romance of its day in that most of its complications arise from the wrong-headedness of its characters. Moya Bethune and Rigden are, certainly, of the temperament for misunderstandings, so their foolishness is not so gratuitous as that of the brother and sister who blunder through *Sard Harker*. *No Hero* (1903), with its title from Browning, is a story of English people in Switzerland. It ends with a variation of the kind of trick Frank Stockton used for the denoument of stories and which was used so often in later years by "O. Henry."

"HENRY SETON MERRIMAN"

"Henry Seton Merriman" (Hugh Stowel Scott, 1862-1903) became known by *With Edged Tools* (1894). *The Sowers* (1896) and *Roden's Corner* (1898) were better books, the latter, indeed, falling little short of real fineness. The characterization in *Roden's Corner* is clear and distinctive. You know Professor Holzen and Tony Cornish and Percy Roden, you know Marguerite Wade and Dorothy Roden and Mrs. Vansittart. The story in unhackneyed and interesting. The dialogue is crisp and pointed, but natural always. There are remarks on art and readings of life in *Roden's Corner* that are worth remembering. Of Music it records this dig: "It is the art most commonly allied to vice." Hatred is called "the last, the longest of the passions." There is an arresting moment after the refusal of Mrs. Vansittart to marry Percy Roden:

" 'Why?' he asked, with a bitter laugh, 'What is wrong with me?'

" 'I do not know what there is wrong with you. And I am not interested to inquire. But, so far as I am concerned, there is nothing right.'

"A woman's answer, after all—and one of those reasons which are no reasons, and yet rule the world."

Yes, "Henry Seton Merriman" just escaped being of the novelists that count.

ANTHONY HOPE

Many of us had once a weakness for "Anthony Hope." Most of that many delighted chiefly in *The Prisoner of Zenda* (1894) and *Rupert of Hentzau* (1898), but there were not a few who prided themselves they were judicious in their preference for *Dolly Dialogues* (1894) and for the conversation in *The Indiscretion of the Duchess* (1894). That talk of "Anthony Hope" took us straight back to the talk of Sterne, which as we would expect, "Anthony Hope" admired most of all talk in the English novel. Writing of "My Favorite Novelist" in *Munsey's Magazine,* in 1897, he pays compliment to *Middlemarch* and *Vanity Fair, Esmond* and *The Three Musketeers, Gil Blas* and *Emma,* Byron and Maupassant, Stevenson and Meredith, and then owns *Tristram Shandy* "my favorite perhaps." He goes on to say: "To me, infinitely the greatest charm lies in the talk. In this there is a peculiar flavor, so far as I know, proper to Sterne, and to him only. It has all the discursiveness of actual conversation; the interruptions are as vital as the theme. It is developed through the mouths of characters admirably contrasted. . . .

"Sterne suddenly presents, in a sentence, with marvellous terseness, the point of view most opposed to that which he has been developing; a gulf of difference, intellectual or moral, is shown in a word. . . . This diverse spirit of the interlocutors imparts to the dialogue an extraordinary piquancy, a quality of unexpectedness. The reader never knows what is coming next, and Sterne, quite alive to the value of keeping him in this state of suspense, constantly interrupts the sentence in the middle by a description of the air or the gestures which accompanied the remark. . . .

"There is an absolute sinking of the writer in the character."

What Sir Anthony says of Sterne we may say of Sir Anthony, or rather of that "Anthony Hope" who was before there was a Sir Anthony Hope Hawkins (1863-   ). The talk of *Dolly Dialogues,* particularly, is very much like the talk of Sterne as described above. It is piquant, surprising, exactly in part. It has humor, but it has pathos, also, proving true that old axiom which says that the two are only different aspects of one quality. It is a pathos that, despite its unobtrusiveness, brings us perilously close to tears.

The people of *Dolly Dialogues* and of other of his stories are making life a game, a game that tests all their finesse, their experience, their resource, their long schooling in the control of the emotions. They are ladies and gentlemen who would have been happier had they been simple women and men of no particular social status. Such they would have wished to make themselves did they not know in their hearts that to be simple women and men would not content them. They are those whose habits and codes drive them one way and whose essential humanity drives them another. They are of those upperclass people, who, as Yeats said, do not exhibit their emotions in tones or demeanor, but who look into the fire instead.

It is the tradition to say that the dialogue of Congreve is the wittiest dialogue in English; and that the next wittiest dialogue is that of Sheridan or Meredith or Wilde or Shaw. Granting that Meredith has most wit in the Elizabethan sense, it may be claimed that "Anthony Hope" is wittier, in the modern sense, than any one of the five. His dialogue is brighter and lighter and more worldly-wise, more full of subtle repartee and keen banter and innuendo, more completely realized and more polished, than that of any other English writer, not excepting his master Sterne. This wit is not always apparent in phrase, or in give and take of conversation. Part of it is implicit in the situation, part of it in the characters who are opposed to one another, and a still greater part in the reticences and what is written between the lines. No short quotation can do it justice. You must go to *Dolly Dialogues,* and read, to be convinced that it is so.

It was a short heyday "Anthony Hope" had. Almost all of him which really told was published in the years from 1894 to 1898. Those of us who delighted in the fascinating books of 1894 looked up his earlier stories. Only one of these meant much to me, *Father Stafford* (1891), and that had few of the qualities which made "Anthony Hope" a distinctive author. *Father Stafford* was the old, old story of the priest, this time an Anglican priest, in his struggles between love and vows of celibacy.

A Change of Air (1893) had its fervent admirers, but it never seemed to me to be of his best. Nor was there any later novel as good in its way as *The God in the Car* as a political novel, or as *The Prisoner of Zenda* as a romance of adventure, or as *Dolly Dialogues* as the story told in dialogue. There is a cleanness and lightness and surety of handling in *The Prisoner of Zenda* that makes it stand apart from the press of adventure stories. There is dignity in it and an aristocratic air. Some see in the hero, Rudolf Rassendyll, the ideal type of Englishman, and in Princess Flavia, the ideal queen of romance. There is a great deal in *The Prisoner of Zenda* of the tried material of the adventure story; and its setting of a romantic countryside in German lands had been used before by Stevenson in *Prince Otto* and by Meredith in *Harry Richmond* and by Scott in *Anne of Geierstein*. The famous episode of the yearly exchange of red roses by the separated lovers is perhaps a memory of the yearly meetings of those earlier separated lovers in *The Netherworld* (1889) of Gissing.

It is *Dolly Dialogues* that contain in concentrated form what was most distinctive in "Anthony Hope." Lady Michleham and Mr. Carter are only less memorable in their way than the Widow Wadman and Uncle Toby in theirs. Apt dialogue and firm characterization are to be found in the later novels, but not of the flavor of 1894. Though "Anthony Hope" summoned all his resources to do a fine novel in *Tristram of Blent* (1901), it is not a fine novel, for its very foundation is a trick.

Even now, in the fulness of years and knighted, Sir Anthony Hope Hawkins, is a good journeyman of letters; witness *Lucinda* (1920). There is in none of his later writing, however, the rapture of that of the mid-nineties. Nor is there in it the wit or the verve or the archness that made us think of *Dolly Dia-*

logues as a companion to *Proverbs in Porcelain.* Sir Anthony had his little day, like so many lesser writers. In a few years he gave us what he had to give. His books of the past quarter of a century are the result of a habit of writing rather than of the necessity to write. It was not that he happened to hit the taste of the mid-nineties, and passed with the passing of a current taste, so often a thing of no more than a five years' survival. It was that he had just that one run of semi-genius, and relapsed into talent thereafter. The crowd still delights in *The Prisoner of Zenda* in the movies. Let us hope there are many readers quietly delighting in *Dolly Dialogues* under the lamp.

LOUIS BECKE

It happened that George Louis Becke (1848-1913) published his first book of Pacific tales, *By Reef and Palm* (1894) just a few months before the death of Stevenson. He was an older man than Stevenson, a man who began to write late in life, after an adventurous career as supercargo in trading ships in all quarters of the South Seas, and as a residential trader on several of the islands. So when he came to tell of the life of these islands he had a wealth of memories to draw upon greater than that of any Melville or Charles Warren Stoddard or Stevenson.

It was noted immediately that the episodes of *By Reef and Palm* were artless recitals of actual experiences. It had been noted earlier that *The Wrecker* (1892) and *Island Night's Entertainments* (1893) were, for all their art, thin-sown with facts of Pacific life and lacking in the background that would give atmosphere and color to the stories. Therefore it occurred to many, naturally enough, to wish that there might be a collaboration between the two Louises. Each had what the other lacked, and together, it was argued, they might do great romance. As it was they never met, so far as I can learn, and I do not know that Stevenson ever came upon *By Reef and Palm*. The writing of Stevenson was there for Becke to model himself upon had he so chosen to do, but he could not, apparently, profit by Stevenson's example.

Becke is even weaker in the construction of the novel than in that of the short tale. *The Ebbing of the Tide* (1896) is another such collection as *By Reef and Palm,* neither better nor worse. *His Native Wife* (1896) is in plot very much like several of the sketches of the earlier volumes and the worse for being expanded to the proportions of a novel. Then Becke felt called upon to preach in *His Native Wife,* and to attack the interference of the missionaries with native ways in the Carolines. Tragedy is the result, but the tragedy does not greatly move us. Nor does Becke have more power over our emotions in *Helen Adair* (1903), a tale of the penal days in Australia.

There have been a good many novels about Australasia since the days of Henry Kingsley, and Australasian scenes in a still greater number of novels of English life, but there is yet to emerge from the great island or its neighbors a writer to make such a revelation of Australasian life as Olive Schreiner has made of South African life, or as Kipling has made of Indian life. E. R. Grant Watson may, perhaps, be the man. Already he has done a mainland story of quality in *The Desert Horizon* (1923); and another, for which he seems to owe something to Becke, in *The Other Magic* (1921), a story of the conflict of white man and brown man on an outer island. He is not, though, to the manner born, as was Becke. What Grant Watson has done is to see the South Seas through eyes opened by Conrad, and to write of them in a way that recalls some of the effects of the master.

ARTHUR MACHEN

There are those who hold that demonology is close to the core of romance. There are others who would rather put it that in some romance there are forbidden things, horrors it were best not to study too particularly. Some of us dislike the brooding over such matters by writers of romance as we dislike the preoccupation with abnormality that obsesses some of the realists,

No form of literature, unfortunately, carries with it a prophylactic against such qualities. In a way, however, a taint is more alien to romance than to realism. Romance has always been, traditionally, an escape from the ugly things of life. Tainted romance, then, is less easy to put up with than tainted realism.

So it is that Arthur Machen (1863-   ) is made out a great sinner against the romance he practices; and, it seems to me, rightly. He is not instinctively a story-teller, and he has not taught himself the craft. He has little power of character creation; and his experience of life is, obviously, very narrow. He knows no man well but himself, and he knows no woman at all. He is an essayist, and, often, as such, a bringer of delight. He writes admirably of the landscape and of the Roman past of Gwent; of Carleon-upon-Usk, that white town islanded in its little river; and of the magic of the Graal. He is largely derivative, aping De Quincey and Stevenson, Pater and Wilde. *The Great God Pan* that was a "shocker" in 1894 is dull reading enough today, and *The Hill of Dreams* (1907) moons its tenuous way through long pages that only good writing saves from futility. *The Secret Glory* (1921) has more characterization than most of the earlier stories, and its hero is not continually in need of an alienist. He has moments with which the normal reader can sympathize, but one tires of the harping on the many English institutions that Machen hates, the public school and all its customs in the forefront of them.

The Machen that is well worth while is the Machen of the critical and autobiographical essays, of *Hieroglyphics* (1902), of *Far Off Things* (1922) and *Things Near and Far* (1923). Here the youth " 'degenerate', *decadent"* with "the pathos of the pagan soul," is not so insistently thrust upon us, and there is ripe and illuminating criticism of letters.

SIR WALTER BESANT

Sir Walter Besant (1836-1901) has been compared to Trollope. They are alike only in that both were estimable men, that

both wrote many novels mechanically, and that both left auto-
biographies to be published after death. Trollope had none of
the powers of the novelist in highest degree, but he knew his
England and Ireland, many classes of their people, their institutions, and their countrysides. Besant, with a shrewd enough
estimate of the realities about him to make him a successful
author, knew well only a few corners of England, Portsmouth,
East London and Fleet Street, and even these he knew with
but a shallow familiarity. It was beyond him to have appreciation of depths of any kind. What little wisdom there is in his
writing is worldly wisdom. There is no joy or wonder or sense
of beauty in the man.

Besant knew well the copyright laws and all practical affairs
that bore upon publication. He knew, too, how to make a story
an effective tract. His *All Sorts and Conditions of Men* (1882)
was one of the forces that led to the foundation of the "People's
Palace."

It is held by some that it was James Rice (1843-1882) that
made the collaboration of Besant and Rice successful, and that
Besant's continued prosperity with books after Rice's death was
only the success of the firm carried on by its original impetus.
That is a contention that it is impossible to answer satisfactorily.
It is a fact, of course, that there were three great commercial
successes in the collaboration, *Ready Money Mortiboy* (1872),
The Golden Butterfly (1876) and *The Chaplain of the Fleet*
(1880), and that none of the novels by Besant alone had such a
popularity as these. You will hear oldsters say: "Besant and
Rice were good fun when they wrote together, but Besant alone
was dull." As Besant himself says, he was young when he was
writing with Rice, and ageing when he became "the novelist
with a free hand." For myself I can only say that *All Sorts and
Conditions of Men,* Besant's alone, is the only novel of the whole
series whether by Besant and Rice, or by Besant alone, that
I could get through with easily. And I got through with that
easily because at the time I read it I was interested in "slum
work."

It is the *Autobiography of Sir Walter Besant* (1902) that discloses most nakedly the limitations of the man. After speaking in Chapter X about his collaboration with Rice in a round dozen of books from 1871 to 1882 Besant goes on in Chapter XI to speak of the eighteen he wrote alone in the next eighteen years. He thinks *Dorothy Foster* (1884) the best of these. It is a historical novel of the Rebellion of 1715. He devotes two pages to an account of its conception and development. Four other stories are run over hurriedly, and ten of the remainder tucked away in a paragraph in this summary fashion:

"They are either studies of the East End and of the people, as *All Sorts and Conditions of Men, The Children of Gibeon, The Alabaster Box*—a story of a settlement—and *The Rebel Queen,* or they are stories of today. *All in a Garden Fair* presents an account, somewhat embroidered, of my own literary beginnings. *Herr Paulus* is a story of spiritualistic fraud—I have always rejoiced to think that the story was considered a great blow to Sludge and his friends. *Armorel of Lyonesse* is an exposure of the impudent charlatan who produces artistic and literary works under his own name which are executed by another's hand— a fraud more common, I have been told, ten years ago, than it is now. *The City of Refuge* is a story of life in one of the American communities. *The Master Craftsman* is the history of the politician who makes himself by the aid of an ambitious woman. *Beyond the Dreams of Avarice* is a tale of the evil influence of great wealth. Of course such a theme easily brings to the stage a number of people of all kinds and all conditions. The prospect of wealth corrupts and demoralizes every one— the man of science, the man of pleasure, the colonial, the actor, the American."

If the author of these novels cannot find more to say of their significance than here appears, what can you expect those less familiar with them to find in them. Such critics will be apt to set him down as no more than a cheap writer to a past generation, one who is not reread in their old years by those who read him in youth.

Trilby was for a generation almost a universal character. There can be no dispute about that, however much dispute there may be about the standing of George Du Maurier (1834-1896) as a novelist. She appealed to the men and women who were young in late Victorian times as generally as Lorna Doone appealed to the men and women who were young in mid-Victorian times. No two girls could be more different in character and fate, but each in her way quickened the pulse and touched the heart of a generation.

As we look further back through the vista of the years and see there the imperious figure of Beatrice Esmond we wonder she was not another so to enthrall her day. There was, indeed, no girl of all the many of the greater or lesser early Victorian novelists that was such a charmer. We must turn to the drama to find another that appealed as did Lorna and Trilby. Pauline, of *The Lady of Lyons,* is the nearest approach to them that earlier time can present. There were great numbers of girls named after Pauline, as there were great numbers of girls named after Lorna. The frailty of Trilby prevented a like bestowal of her name on girl babies of the nineties, but the name itself was found everywhere, in all sorts of applications. There were Trilby sausages and Trilby cigars, and Trilby "socials" and Trilby hotels, to say nothing of more vulgar uses.

Trilby is first found, apparently, as a man's name, in a fairy story of Charles Nodier, *Trilby, the Fay of Argyle* (1822). Beyond borrowing its title Du Maurier makes no other use of the fairy tale. What he did use were Murger's *Vie de Bohême* (1848) and Hawthorne's *Blithedale Romance* (1852) and all of Thackeray and his own experiences as art student and artist. Neither *Peter Ibbetson* (1891) nor *Trilby* (1894) nor *The Martian* (1897) reveals the slightest bit of dramatic power in Du Maurier. Stories, episodes, characters, comment—all are personal. It is the pleasantness of the man telling the story, his personality coming out in all sorts of unexpected ways, his gossip about men and books and music and painting, that give the stories a large part of their charm.

A part of the wonder they awakened came from the element of the strange or the supernatural in them all. There is the meeting in dreams of *Peter Ibbetson;* the hypnotism of Trilby by Svengali in *Trilby,* a borrowing of the Priscilla and Westervelt passages of *The Blithedale Romance;* and the sense of the north and the communications from another world of *The Martians.* The same characters appear, under different names, in the three stories, the men with very little variation at all. Trilby is the only dominating character. There are several others we are glad to love or despise, but we forget them all, even the three muske- teers her champions. This trio, by-the-by, is very reminiscent of Clive Newcome and Arthur Pendennis and Fred Bayham.

There are those who try to make out that *Peter Ibbetson* is the real triumph of Du Maurier, but it is not so. The popular verdict for *Trilby* happened to be for the best book of the three he wrote. It is not a very good book, and its author is not a very good writer. Du Maurier just puts down, carelessly and rather amateurishly, the good talk he heard and made on those coasts of Bohemia he frequented. That talk delighted his generation. It is unlikely to delight any other.

WILLIAM DE MORGAN

William Frend De Morgan (1839-1917) is good company. He is good company before he is anything else, and in every sense of the phrase. Artist he is, but it is not as artist that you think of him first. You think of him first as you think of some pleasant old man you meet at the club and talk with long over the coffee. It is difficult to get away from such a one, even when you have come slowly to the conclusion you must get away, pleasant as the talk has been. Old fogies they are both as well as good companions, your friend at the club and De Morgan. You like the leisureliness of them, the absence of guile in them, the gentlemanliness in them, their sincere appreciation of art, but you are with it all a little impatient over their prolixity, their gossip, their very calm. They are a relief from the cheap and hurried and loud that make up so much of life, they bring you relaxation and that freshening of the spirit that only the best company brings, but they are neither of them men of genius and you have spent too much of your time on what is after all only the second rate.

You hate yourself, of course, for such a process of reasoning or instinctive feeling. There is nothing in life better than listening to good talk, and it is a privilege to associate with an old fogy who is a gentleman and an artist. You are hardly forgivable for such an estimate of your acquaintance of the club. You are forgivable for such an estimate of De Morgan. Criticism in itself has no more to do with consideration of feelings than has a surgeon's knife. All that we have a right to ask is that both surgeon and critic are gentlemen.

The upshot of all this discussion is that the stories of De Morgan are too long. If they were written by a man of first power we could discount their length, but as they are not, that length forces itself on our consciousness from time to time as we read. De Morgan is not a great originating force. He is the continuer of the Dickens tradition, and he is under obligations to Thackeray for his kind of comment and to George Eliot for a quality of his analyzing. The spirit of his writing is that of a man freed from mid-Victorian prejudices and conventionalities by love of beauty and lifelong association with painters and other artists. His manner is almost wholly mid-Victorian.

The stories from *Joseph Vance* (1906) to *The Old Mad House* (1917) are as rich a garnering of experience as we have outside of the writing of the great. They are an old man's garnerings from long unharvested fields. There is no other instance in our literature of a man of so rich a nature and so deep an experience beginning to write so late in life. *Joseph Vance* was published when De Morgan was sixty-seven. There was behind him then his career as a designer of pottery and as a potter. There was behind him a long intimacy with Burne-Jones and William Morris and Watts. Life was still sweet to him but memories were now more to him than interests of the day or hopes of the morrow. It was these memories that he now put into a series of novels as other men put them into a biography. Of course, being the man he was, he played with these memories. He selected among them, he replaced old moves made by the better moves that might have been made, and again he put down the past just as he recalled it. He was realist one moment and idealist the next. But always he had an eye on the future, on what would be after death. He yearned to meet old friends again beyond the grave. He had been born to a family interested in psychical research and ghosts were as credible to him as any other sort of wonders.

It is this preoccupation of his with the beyond, as well as his mid-Victorian manner of writing, that makes him so interesting to old people. "Good books all of them," says a friend of mine, "except *An Affair of Dishonor* (1910), each one only a little less interesting than its predecessor. The mainspring was weak before he began to write, and it ran for a less time each time he wound it up."

This same critic thinks that the people of De Morgan are great characters, fellows of those of Dickens and Thackeray. They do not seem so comparable to me. Even those most real, De Morgan is playing with, as if they were dream children, a superior sort of dolls with whom he is juggling, for whom he is building castles in the air, upon whom he is lavishing that affection he would have given, had he had them, to children after the way of the flesh. One is interested in an Alice or a Joe Vance or a Lossie, for De Morgan has breathed into them that kindliness and cheerfulness and toleration and winsomeness that is himself. Those characters that are further from what he was are less clearly individualized. It is the man himself, and no objective power that has come to him from without like a visitation, that makes his books likable. He is essentially the familiar essayist playing with story-writing. There is scarcely any interest under the sun you will not find expatiated upon in these wandering books. I delight in his interest in luster-ware and in street urchins and in anything Italian, and I find myself instinctively looking for familiar essays in little in his stories as well as following the fortunes of his characters. It is their creator, always, and not the characters themselves that most interest me.

SAMUEL BUTLER

In all the writing about Samuel Butler the man the pleasantness of his personality is insisted upon. He had a way with him that won people, it is said, and he was always considerate of others, in little things as well as in important things, whether those others were charwomen in London, or guides in the Italian Alps, or his cosmopolitan friends who, like himself, were interested in ideas. It is not such a pleasant Samuel Butler (1835-1902) that is revealed in his books. That is often the way. There are not a few who are good companions enough in the flesh, but who are unable to invest their written words with any of their kindliness or charm. It is easier to live with these good companions than it is with those who put all the pleasantness there is in them in their writing and reserve their unpleasantness for associates and families. It is not so easy, however, to find good writers among them.

In his writing Butler, it would seem, is both by nature and by malice aforethought out of sympathy with things as they are. Festing Jones believes that Butler's acknowledgment that Beethoven bored him is to his credit. The acknowledgment may be, but the fact that Beethoven bored him is surely not to his credit. With many intellectual interests Butler was a man with a very narrow range of sympathies. The Stevenson he discounted was a far wiser man than he. Butler never discovered, with all his research, that

> "The world is so full of a number of things,
> I'm sure we should all be as happy as kings."

Only in his one book in which there is any gusto save that of fault-finding does Butler rise to real joy in life. It is now "a

quiet gray day" of autumn in the Valley of Mesocco that kindles
him, and now a day, apparently of spring, on Monte Generoso:
"The large yellow auricula . . . I own to being my favorite
mountain wild-flower. It is the only flower which, I think, fairly
beats cowslips. Here too I heard, or thought I heard, the song
of that most beautiful of all bird songsters, the *passero solitario,*
or solitary sparrow—if it is a sparrow, which I should doubt.
Nobody knows what a bird can do in the way of song until he
has heard a *passero solitario.* . . . I shall ever remember it as the
most beautiful warbling that I ever heard come out of the
throat of bird. All other bird singing is loud, vulgar, and unsympathetic in comparison. The bird itself is about as big as a
starling, and is of a dull blue color."

Nobody will quarrel with any man for having a favorite bird
song. Butler may like his rock-thrush better than lark or night-
ingale, but to sweep all other song out of count in a phrase as he
does, does not inspire confidence in his judgment. One must
wonder, does he know other fine songs, as that of the blackcap,
or of song-thrush, or of blackbird. And then to call the yellow
Alpine primrose "auricula"! Is that the scholar's pedantry, or
does it mean that

> "a primrose by a river's brim,
> A yellow primrose was to him
> And it was nothing more?"

I have dwelt on these passages from *Alps and Sanctuaries*
(1881) because they best represent of all his writings his appreciation of the beauty of the world. There is an appreciation
of beauty in some of the passages of the opening chapters of
Erewhon (1872). Those descriptions were memories of the up-
lands of the Upper Rangitata district in New Zealand, where
Butler was a sheep farmer. Butler was later to try to be a
painter, and he should have had even in those early years, the
painter's eye for composition, but there are no bits of landscape
made memorable in words, and no catchings of the lift of the
heart on grassy Alp or by glacial torrent or under spiring snow-

peak such as one remembers from *Song of Roland* or from Ruskin, from Bret Harte or from John Muir. What is best about *Erewhon* is the straightforwardness and simplicity of narrative of these opening chapters. One remembers Bunyan and Defoe and Cobbett as one reads. His prose is not so good as that of any one of the three but it is of the right old English sort. That is about the only loyalty to the past he has adhered to, the loyalty to the direct speech of his ancestry.

The satire in *Erewhon* is not very notable. It is said the clergy of the Church of England have never forgiven him "the musical banks" that attack their oldest forms and sanctuaries. Whatever it was once, this satire is not scathing now, it is only mildly amusing. That is one trouble with satire. It wanes quickly with the years. And another trouble with satire is that it is as apt to be destructive of the man who writes it as of those men or conditions it attacks. If it makes short work of them he is likely to follow them as quickly into oblivion. Like many another parasite, satire, unless it pass to some new victim, must die with the death of that it feeds upon. It is only a satire of unchanging things, such as the attributes of human nature, or a satire that is something more than satire, which has a chance of survival along with the higher literary forms. If the satire have in it something of noble wrath, as sometimes in Donne; if it sound the deeps of human bitterness in a kind of lyric frenzy, as in Swift; or if it discover to us the littleness of life with a sharpness that brings us close to tears, as in Thackeray; if, in short, it is, as I have said, a something more than satire, it may continue to appeal to men as do the lyric and the essay, the story and the play. Otherwise, though we cry, "well hit," and delight in the victim's discomfiture, and thank whatever Gods may be for our own immunity, we quickly forget the satire and pass on to more lasting things.

I am not, of course, considering at all the social use of satire as a means of unseating pretentiousness or of overthrowing wrong. Satire is useful, too, socially, as a stick to beat and rouse stupidity with, or else we could hardly tolerate Shaw. What I am considering is the value of satire as a literary form.

There are some people who can see no good in satire at all, either in speech, or in journalism, or in letters. Blackmore is one of these. In *Lorna Doone,* when he attacks it, he is considering satirical speech of brother to sister, but his generalization is, I take it, intended to apply to all forms of satire. "It strikes me," he writes, "that of all human dealings, satire is the very lowest, and most mean and common. It is the equivalent in words for what bullying is in deeds; and no more bespeaks a clever man than the other does a brave one. These two wretched tricks exalt a fool in his own low esteem, but never in his neighbors, for the deep common sense of our nature tells that no man of a genial heart, or of any spread of mind, can take pride in either. And though a good man may commit the one fault or the other, now and then, by way of outlet, he is sure to have compunctions soon, and to scorn himself more than the sufferer." It is not easy to forget that phrase, "of any spread of mind," even though we believe there is a kind of satire akin to a divine wrath just as surely as a satire that is waspishness.

It is for his attack on the family that Butler is best known. He is known for this attack not only because of his whole-souled abandonment to it in *The Way of All Flesh* (1903), but because of the carrying on of it in play on play of his disciple Shaw. Butler resented with bitterness all degrees of parental control. They all were obnoxious tyrannies to him, but whether because of what he experienced in youth in his own family or whether as his reaction to what he saw about him everywhere in England it is not possible to be sure. It is always to be remembered, however, that Butler was, like George Moore, but a bachelor, and as such deprived of at least half of the experience that comes to most men in the relations of parent and child.

Butler apparently knew little of what had been shown of this relationship by Meredith and Hardy and other novelists of his time whose concern was with the whole of life. He was reading

Darwin and Wallace and their middlemen and not the creative writers. He knows more than does Wells of the English poets but not a great deal more. He is apparently sincere in his contention that he is the only daring soul in the literature of his time. He is not so sure of himself as is Shaw, or perhaps it is only that he is more discreet in the way he puts his claims. He has two mouthpieces for the expression of his opinions in *The Way of All Flesh*. They are Overton, who is supposed to tell the story, and Ernest Pontifex, the hero of that story. It is in Chapter LXXXIV, the last but two of the book, that the meat of the matter is come upon. Up to this time we have seen what a sorry lot were most of the members of four generations of the Pontifex family. Ernest is speaking at the start of the quotation. Overton is the "I" who answers:

" 'There are a lot of things that want saying which no one dares to say, a lot of shams which want attacking, and yet no one attacks them. It seems to me that I can say things which not another man in England except myself will venture to say, and yet which are crying to be said.'

"I said: 'But who will listen? If you say things which nobody else would dare to say, is not this much the same as saying what everyone except yourself knows to be better unsaid just now.'

" 'Perhaps,' said he, 'but I don't know it; I am bursting with these things, and it is my fate to say them.'

"I knew there would be no stopping him, so I gave in and asked what question he felt a special desire to burn his fingers with in the first instance.

" 'Marriage,' he rejoined promptly, 'and the power of disposing of his property after a man is dead. The question of Christianity is virtually settled or if not settled there is no lack of those engaged in settling it. The question of the day now is marriage and the family system.' "

There is no character creation of moment in *The Way of All Flesh*. You learn in detail what sort the various members of the family are and what sort are those with whom they come into contact. Ernest is presented in most detail, quite as "a case" is presented in a medical report. What is recorded of him is believable enough until he falls heir to his aunt's fortune, but you find it hard to realize such a weakling would come to anything even under the stimulating ease of a gilded leisure.

There are those who think the Forsytes of Galsworthy are a disagreeable lot, but the Forsytes are not half so disagreeable as these Pontifexes. Butler has gone out of the way of nature to make them as ugly as he paints them and all their surroundings. A sample of his method is found in his description of the old choir of violincello and clarinet and trombone in the church of Battersby-on-the-Hill. Think of what Hardy makes of the Mellstock choir in *Under the Greenwood Tree*, what he makes of his country-folk. Hardy brings out the humanity and humor of his country folk, Butler the heavy and yokel-like qualities of his. Hardy is concerned with truth and beauty, Butler is concerned with ugliness and the making out of a case. Hardy is an artist, Butler a tract-writer. With his protests Butler may have helped a little toward the amelioration of domestic practices current in his youth. So, too, may Hardy, who has himself protested. Those parts of Hardy are of no artistic value now. If there was any betterment because of what he wrote, those parts of his writing that went to bring it about are no longer bringing about like ends. What lasts of Hardy is the beauty he discovered and revealed. There is no such discovery and revelation of beauty in Butler. *Erewhon,* either as satire, or as dream of a new world, is hardly more today than *The Coming Race* (1871) of Bulwer. *The Way of All Flesh,* praised as it has been, and still is in some quarters, is hardly more than a careful scientific report in the process of being outmoded by fresh scientific research. Its epigrams, say some, will keep it alive. A few of them are really more than epigrams: they are "readings of life." "He who does not consider himself fortunate is unfortunate" is a fair sample. Of sterner stuff than that are sayings that make for immortality. *The Way of All Flesh* still passes in places for a novel, but it is now on the defensive, claiming rank for its historical value. When historical value is the only value argued for what has pretended to be literature you may be sure that book is at the beginning of its end as art.

Walter Pater (1839-1894) was first brought before the readers of novels as the "Mr. Rose" of *The New Republic* (1877) of William Hurrell Mallock. There were few of them who at that time could have known his work well enough to recognize it as the new hedonism the story attacked. But gossip grew busy and by the time Pater published what he called a novel, *Marius the Epicurean* (1885), it was pretty generally known that he was "Mr. Rose" and that he was the apostle of a little cult of worshippers of beauty. What was more important was that after *Marius the Epicurean* there was no gainsaying that he was a master of prose, a writer with a rhythm and a style that were not only distinguished but unlike the rhythm and style of any earlier writer. *Studies in the History of the Renaissance* (1873), *Imaginary Portraits* (1887), *Appreciations* (1889) and *Plato and Platonism* (1893) gave him an authority as a critic and as an analyst of emotions that has known little diminution from the nineties to today.

Gaston de Latour (1896), published two years after his death, was ostensibly a novel, but like *Marius the Epicurean* really a series of essays devoted to the study of an era. *Gaston de Latour* is only a fragment, but, as far as it is finished, just as important as a study of France in the latter part of the sixteenth century as *Marius the Epicurean* is as a study of Rome in the days when an outworn paganism was breaking up under the progress of Christianity. Marcus Aurelius looms large in the one, Ronsard in the other.

It may be said that Pater himself is both Marius and Gaston. Certain it is that there is no characterization of either. There is only a presentation, through a hero created to interest us in the old times of the stories, of views personal to Pater on moral and æsthetic matters. It may be such views as the heroes hold were views held in their times, but they were, too, views held by Pater in late Victorian times. We are told many facts about Marius but we never meet him, and if we see him it is only a glimpse we get. He is present, when he is present, only in some set picture as that in the temple of Æsculapius among the Etrurian hills, and then far off, at the end of a vista, where there is no chance to hear him speak or to feel the influence of his personality.

Pater knew little of life. He was almost a recluse. He was not afraid of life, as Gissing was, but its humdrum and ugly details offended him. Even travel to beautiful places had its burden of boredom, one must willy-nilly brush shoulders with so many average people by the way. One can choose one's books, and, to some degree, those one meets daily, but one cannot choose one's companions on train and steamship, in museum or cathedral, by fabled rivers or Roman ruins. The children of John Bull and Uncle Sam may intrude anywhere, and there are foreigners of even less sense of proportion. So Pater was happier at home than abroad. He gave ordered teas in his rooms at Oxford, and allowed none but beautiful books on his study table. One thinks of Landor's epigram as revealing a restricted life:

> "I strove with none, for none was worth my strife;
> Nature I loved and next to nature art;
> I warmed both hands before the fire of life;
> It sinks, and I am ready to depart."

But the interests of Pater were still fewer. Pater had a love of nature of a kind. There are descriptions in *Marius the Epicurean* that are haunting. He regards out-of-doors, however, first and foremost, as something to make beautiful sentences upon, rather than for itself. "Days brown with the first rains of autumn" is perfect in its rhythm, but is it a good picture of autumn days? Is it not perhaps just a good tone of brown? Just what you would say as you stood before a painting and talked of it?   Art he loved, of course, before everything else. He never "warmed both hands," or either hand, before the fire of life.

It may well be, in the end, despite the unquestionable beauty of his cadenced prose, that he will be kept in mind for his influence rather than for his intrinsic value, that he will be rated high by the historical estimate rather than by the absolute estimate.   You are lulled into a kind of delighted dreaminess as you read his rolling periods.   You relish this phrase and applaud that critical distinction, but it is only the burden of all his writing, his affirmation of the holiness of beauty, that you carry away from the reading.   So it may come to be that he will be best remembered for the writers who have gone to school to him. George Moore is the greatest of his avowed disciples, but Vernon Lee (1856-   ), Arthur Symons (1865-   ), Sir Frederick Wedmore (1844-1921), Lionel Johnson (1867-1902) and George Santayana (1863-   ) are not little people, although of lesser stature than Pater himself, and than the Ruskin and Morris from whom he inherited his tradition.

RICHARD LE GALLIENNE

Richard Le Gallienne (1866-   ) came nearer to the novel in his stories than did most of the *Yellow Book* men.   He had read *Marius the Epicurean* (1885) and *The Picture of Dorian Gray* (1891), and he remembered the rhythms of Pater and Wilde when he undertook stories of his own.   The stories were no more novels than the essays masquerading as novels of his masters. *The Quest of the Golden Girl* (1896) was essays and episodes held together by a thin thread of satirical story.   *The Romance of Zion Chapel* (1898) was a study of "the new idealism" as it affected the famous Noncomformist conscience, with a real characterization, that of Jenny, happened upon by the way.   *Young Lives* (1899) is again a study of the Noncomformists that Le Gallienne seems to know so well.   Its hero is a type of the time, an agnostic dilettante of a pleasure-loving nature, sentimental and unsteady. This story "dates," if ever a book did. The type delineated was just as common at the century's end in America as in England.

Le Gallienne has no native genius for the novel. He has not the dramatic power it demands, and he has not a rich experience of life. He is too self-centered for a novelist, too little interested in the Toms and Dicks and Harries of the world. He is an essayist of charm in the papers of his three series of *Prose Fancies* (1894, 1896, 1900), and in some of them almost a short-story writer. I read "A Seventh Story Heaven" in 1896, when it appeared in the second series of *Prose Fancies,* and I have not read it since, but I have not forgotten it. Le Gallienne's criticism stays by one, too. It is at its best when its subject is poetry. Give him a poet that he admires and few can outdo him in "the art of praise."

"GEORGE EGERTON"

There was a to-do about "George Egerton" in *Yellow Book* Days. There are few who recall her now. Are there more, I wonder, who read now the studied prose of Hubert Cracken-thorpe (1865-1896), or for that matter, the no less studied prose of the other young men who then wrote short-stories in what they were pleased to call the French tradition? They were poets first, most of them, Symons, Dowson, Le Gallienne and Aubrey Beard-sley himself, and if they were not poets fundamentally they were something else before they were short-story writers. Frederick Wedmore, Max Beerbohm, Henry Harland and Arthur Machen all put infinite labor into their writing, but it was moods and at-mospheres they were seeking to catch rather than a character at a crucial moment of life. No one of the Yellow Book group produced a long story of distinction. Few of them, indeed, had any such ambition. The novel was not the vogue with their set. It is to be doubted, however, if any one of them had the energy to drive through to the end a novel of Victorian propor-tions. John Davidson (1857-1909) who was with them rather than of them, was a man of fiery strength, but it seemed to desert him when he tried the story. It is only his prose description of the countryside that even approaches the quality of his poetry.

Crackenthorpe is the most distinctive of the group. Nearly all he wrote has the vice of "dating." Reading *Wreckage* (1893) now we say, "How like the nineties?" *Sentimental Studies* (1895), *Vignettes* (1896) and the posthumous *Last Studies* (1897) are not very different in kind, though in "Anthony Garstin's Courtship" there is a treatment of character and a shaping of narrative that indicate he might, had he lived, tried his hand at the long story. His tragic end and the tribute to him in *Last Studies* by Henry James help to keep him in memory.

Kenneth Grahame (1859-   ) began to write in the nineties, too, but his appeal was for more than a decade. *The Golden Age* (1895) has had a worthy successor in *The Wind in the Willows* (1908). As has so often been the case, a second beautiful book has had power to increase the vitality of a first beautiful book. These books are classics of childhood for what De La Mare calls "the young of all ages."

It was "George Egerton" (Mrs. Golding Bright 1870-   ) that bulked largest of the group to those who took the *Yellow Book* as the gospel of a new faith. It was not that, but another bit of artistic propaganda such as the Pre-Raphaelite *Germ* of the mid century. Still the *Yellow Book* gladly opened its pages to "George Egerton," and helped her to become a celebrity of a cult. Her portrait by E. A. Walton "leads" Volume V, the issue of the quarterly for April, 1895. Aubrey Beardsley had done the title page for her first book, *Keynotes* (1893), a collection of short-stories that were many of them feminist tracts. It was regarded then as a road-breaking book, second only to *The Story of An African Farm* in advancing "the cause of woman."

Where is *Keynotes* now? You do not come upon it often in the old book stores. You do not hear it spoken of. You do not note its influence on short-stories of the hour. And as it is with *Keynotes* so it is with its successors. *Discords* (1894) I did come upon the other day at a book sale, in the American edition, and bought, because of "auld lang syne," and for ten cents. It, like *Keynotes,* has a striking title page, but it, like *Keynotes,* is only a collection of yesterday's tracts. Two other collections of short-stories with musical titles followed, *Symphonies* (1897) and *Fantasias* (1898). The *Wheel of God* (1898), her first novel, has a typical "George Egerton" heroine, of head coldly analytical and "a big hot heart," who twice chooses a wrong man for husband and suffers for both choices. The book is full of plain speaking and revolt. "George Egerton" was still enough of a celebrity in 1901 for *The London Academy* to give her more than a column in its review of *Rosa Amorosa,* but her vogue was passing. She was something of an artist in her way but not enough of an artist to turn to beauty the propaganda of her stories.

THE THREE BENSONS

Each of the three sons of Archbishop Benson tried his hand at fiction, but only one novel of any vitality came of all their effort. Edward Frederic Benson (1867-   ) wrote *Dodo* (1893) when he was twenty-five, but of all the many books of his that have succeeded it no other has won as much consideration. And *Dodo,* after all, was not much more than a book of the hour. A novel by the son of an Archbishop of Canterbury chronicling the audacities of a lively lady was bound to be read. When that lady was quickly identified with a celebrity of the day the book was bound to be read widely. There was, to help its vogue, a certain boyish buoyancy in the book itself. It was little noticed by the powers that were in literature, either in the reviews or in the seats of the mighty, but it was read by the smart set and by that large public to whom the doings of the smart set are a matter of first importance. In America as well as in England *Dodo* was a "best seller." Today its vitality is low enough. It interests, if it interests at all, as a slice of life of its time.

It is a forerunner of *Sonia* (1917), though its writing is much less carefully done than McKenna's. And just as today Sonia re-appears in other stories of McKenna so Dodo reappeared and gave title to other stories of Benson.

Father Robert Hugh Benson (1871-1914) had the family facility with words, but his stories were both thin and tractual. *The Queen's Tragedy* (1906) is saved by its historical content from his usual thinness but you hear in it the voice of the apologist.

Arthur Christopher Benson (1862-1925) was a man of many books, but few of them are novels by intention and perhaps only one a novel in fact. *Watersprings* (1913) is a typical Benson book, with dons and Cambridge and high thinking. In this story you have that faint pleasantness of personality and that urbanity of style that mark the short stories and studies of *The Hill of Trouble* (1903) and the loosely strung journalizing of *The Altar Fire* (1907).

"BENJAMIN SWIFT"

William Romaine Paterson (1871-   ) wrote a first novel of large promise under the pseudonym of "Benjamin Swift." *Nancy Noon* (1896) struck a new note, revealed a young man struggling for expression, seemed the earnest of fine things to come. Those fine things never came. *The Tormentor* (1897) was so much less finished than *Nancy Noon,* so much more lurid and confused, so much less mature, that one was driven to wonder was it earlier work rushed out to take advantage of the good press its predecessor won. *The Destroyer,* more coherent though it undoubtedly was than *The Tormentor,* and more credible than *Nancy Noon,* dispelled the expectation that "Benjamin Swift" would develop quickly into one of the novelists to reckon with. *The Destroyer* was only a book of promise.

Siren City (1899) was better ordered than any of the earlier stories, with its narrative running clearer, its incidents less extravagant, its style more restrained. There was in it that lyric note and those passages of tense drama here and there that had distinguished his writing from the first. *Dartnell* (1899) about extinguished the hope of the hardy admirers of *Nancy Noon* for an ultimate high attainment by its author. Yet the books of "Benjamin Swift" were still reviewed at length, a philosophical essay of his, *The Eternal Question,* being given a whole page in *The London Academy* of May 18, 1901.

All these five years after *Nancy Noon* reviewers who were greatly moved by that story remained faithful to Paterson, and gave good space to book after book that disappointed them. It was by now evident that he was not going to be able to control his real power of drama and his considerable lordship of language, and so to shape his stories that they would take on the sure serenity of high art.

Paterson went on writing novels, averaging one every two years. *Sudden Love* (1922) and *Only These* (1923) have moments of that avidness of life and lyric abandon that marked his first book. He was Meredithian then, he was Meredithian a quarter of a century later. "Love's Old Want," Chapter II of *Nancy Noon,* is the evident child of "Ferdinand and Miranda" and "By Wilming Weir," and not unworthy of its parentage. There is not space for much of it, and meaning and rhythm alike suffer from fragmentary quotation. Yet its marching periods tempt one sorely. "It is the month of Love's high festival. Love thinks that there are only two seasons—Summer and Spring. Autumn is a mere dust-bin, and as for Winter, it is the lumber of the year." If you find that to have something of rhetoric what of this: "Another blackbird had been singing at another window-sill to some better purpose. It was in the country some miles from Dulcet Row; and a young girl had made the blackbird's song an alarm clock, and had risen at its summons. She dressed herself, and went to the dairy, where she drank a cup of cream, and she came out with the cream upon her lips. She stepped stealthily forth into the morning, as stealthy and rosy as the morning itself, and went stealthily up a pathway covered with gray dew, and stealthily over a stile, and then became lost in the woods. A horse in one of the fields neighed and whinnied after her. It was May. Such a dawn as broke over the old farm-house: send a painter rapturous! . . .

"She is merely seventeen, the wonder of the village, whose band of adorers will run to Earth's end to do her hest: Nan herself. Her foot is already on the moor. The sea is rolling Eastward there."

An end must be made. There is more as good. Note how the drinking of the cream and the stealthiness of her going indicate the very quality of the girl. There at the outset of the story is sounded the leit motif of Nan. The pity is that with all the poetry of it, the drama of it, there is a delight in horrors that brings the story to the very brink of absurdity. You think of the Elizabethan tragedy of blood, and of the extravagances of *Wuthering Heights,* and, what is worst of all, you profoundly disbelieve in the truth of what the author tells you is happening. The cardinal weakness is Paterson's lack of knowledge of life. Experience fails him in his crises and he will rely on "invention" that is lamentably close to the melodrama of penny dreadfuls just after an episode that has been close to high tragedy. Paterson has fairly spent himself on his hero, Sparshott the passionate Puritan. Yet, somehow, the character does not "come off." Remade as a comic figure by Besier in *Don* (1910) he is credible, but hardly here in the tragic presentation of *Nancy Noon.*

It is because Paterson bases his stories on theories of things, and then works them out almost as mathematical propositions, that they are lost in a kind of chaos. Hawthorne did, too, you will say. But Hawthorne had more experience of life with which to fill out his theoretical assumptions. He would begin with an idea such as that of the sins of the fathers in *The House of the Seven Gables* (1851), but he knew, from the history of his own family, how disastrously they were expiated by innocent descendants. Paterson has not the experience to justify the assumptions he makes about the passions for the theses of his stories. Without that experience he can only "invent," and in "invention" weakness lies.

Paterson has, too, his countrymen's besetting sin of controversy, what W. H. Davies sees the Scot continuing even in Heaven, where he will "argue his Creator dumb." Early in his authorship Paterson had come to conclusions about "The Function of Art." A paper in *Cosmopolis* for 1897 bears that title and much revealing argument. "The question is, granting that it is the function of art to express, not merely the significance, but the emotional significance of the world, what *is* its significance? . . . Now, the essential character of the world of outward reality is movement, transition, change. That is also the essential character of the inward world of our feelings and desires. But if this is so, and if it is the task of art to reproduce it, then art must in its essence be dramatic, since the basis of drama is movement and change."

And although Paterson does not say that the presentation must be emotional or dramatic, such is the character of his presentation. This insistence on the emotional and dramatic often results in an overplus of these qualities, and, at times in the hysterical and melodramatic. His writing is restless, troubled, disturbed, a revelation of a contentious and cross-grained nature. He delights in things gone wrong. It might be argued, indeed, that it is an article of his creed that things shall go wrong with the characters of his stories. "It was early," he writes in this same "Function of Art," "that mankind saw that all things are on their way to their dooms." This thought is developed until he can say, "For the highest art visits the last destinies of men. The Shadow of the Beyond falls on all great work, this suspicion of the continued drama, compared to which this world's stage is small and these firmaments puppet firmaments." There is in such doctrine something of the spirit of Greek tragedy, and something, too, of the Calvinism of Scotland. There is in it, as in all the essay, an absence of a feeling for beauty and an absence of a sense of proportion which indicate that the shortcomings of his novels are as much the result of a mistaken intention as of a lack of shaping power.

MURRAY GILCHRIST

It is often possible to find a passage in a man's writing that is his credo, that sums up his theory of art and his philosophy of life. It is rarely that you can find a passage that is symbolic of the completed work of the man. There are to be found, however, now and then passages that approach such a symbolism. One of this kind is, I think, that which opens the second chapter of *Willowbrake* (1898), describing an interior in the home of Matthew Pursglove, the hero of the story: "The drawing-room at Thornhill Manor House is a lofty chamber, lighted with two oriels, and hung half-way with Flemish tapestry that depicts scenes from the *Iliad*. Below the coved ceiling runs a frieze in alt-relief, colored with faint shades of red and green and blue—the subject a deer-hunt. The settees and chairs, whose gilding is dimmed so much that it is only visible by candle-light, are covered with silk embroidery; here Phaëton sprawls in Apollo's chariot, there Orpheus plucks fiercely the strings of a winged lyre. Lucilla Pursglove, who wrought these pictures, died two hundred years ago.

"In the window recesses tall lilies, of species rarely seen now, thrust scimitar-like leaves from the yellow amphoræ, which had been found when the barrows on Thornhill Moor were desecrated. On the frail mahogany tables bowls of dried rue and sweetbriar, and tangarine oranges made hedgehog-like with cloves, diffuse a sweet suggestive perfume that rises sleepily to hang in clouds beneath the pargeting of the ceiling."

That passage tells much of the art of Murray Gilchrist (1868-1917). That is good writing. There is richness there, and a sense of rhythm. There is a strong personal coloring to it; it is almost a lyric. There is to note, though, a failure both in the mass effect and in detail. There is no dominating quality stated, nothing to sum up the effect of the whole. We are not told what is the color of tapestry or chair covering, or of the lilies in the amphoræ; though we are told the amphoræ are yellow, and that the frieze is red and green and blue.

As this passage is, so is the whole story of *Willowbrake*. It is incomplete, elliptical, mannered, uncontrolled. The theme is that old rivalry of wrongful and rightful heir, so dear to the groundlings and so provocative of stock scenes. In this story our sympathy is with the aristocrat wrongfully in possession and decidedly against the blustering and plebian claimant, who has an unbelievable change of heart at the last. ˙ It is a Derbyshire story, as are almost all the better novels of Gilchrist, and there are many pleasing descriptions of the countryside and its old farmhouses and manors. Five characters occupy the foreground, Rowland and Richard Wotton, the rivals for the possession of *Willowbrake;* Rowland's daughter Caroline, a little gentlewoman, charmingly old-fashioned; her great aunt Mrs. Pursglove, and that lady's grandson, Matthew. All are clearly realized. Not one, though, is a figure against the sky, as is Anne Witchett, the hoyden inn-servant turned lady of *The Courtesy Dame* (1900).

There is a spirit and pride about *The Courtesy Dame* that give it a place in memory as distinct as that of *Esmond* or *Rhoda Fleming.* Anne, "a fine lady when she pleases, a country wench by nature," is the protagonist in a story that would be incredible were it not as old as the world. A sword has lain between lovers in Norse legend and in Irish, in the *Cormac Saga* and in *Diarmid and Grania.* So we are willing to accept it here, in this tale of the Peaks. Gilchrist does nothing to help us to believe it, but we do believe it. That is always a weakness with him, his little effort to make credible his wonders. Anne, with her "careless mop of bright yellow hair"—and "milk-white skin and wonderful blue eyes of our most perfect type," is not of the temperament of which saints are made, but Gilchrist makes her almost a saint. That, too, we believe, perhaps against our better judgment, but the years have again and again proved to us that wonders do happen. There is a strange beauty about the story's close. Anne, huddled in her window in a cloak of white moleskin, is watching "the snow that curled in trumpet shapes against the glass." She goes to say goodnight to her lover, Lord Bostern, ill in his distant room. He is gone. He has wandered out into the storm. Anne follows and finds him. Together they stagger to the summer house of marble, a place of happy memories.

" 'It is death for you to stay here,' he murmured.

" 'Death whether I go or stay,' she made answer. 'My life is yours; I want nought but to die with you. My Will, how could your Nance breathe when you're key-cold?'

"His teeth began to chatter again; he laughed apologetically. The Courtesy Dame tore away the coverings of her young bosom, and drew him closer still, so that whilst his heart beat his lips should not lack warmth."

The Labyrinth (1902) is wilder romance than *Willowbrake* or *The Courtesy Dame*. Here, too, are portraits of haughty ladies and proud men, and pageants like those on old arras, and lyric landscapes.

This brief word about three books must stand as earnest of the good and bad in the more than thirty that he wrote. Were he always as good as his best Gilchrist would be one of our first novelists. As it is he is a writer with great moments and appalling weaknesses, in selection of material, in style, in the technique of his art. If the day shall ever come when there will be enough people who delight in lyrics in prose to justify an anthology of such passages, Gilchrist will be well represented in that anthology.

LAURENCE HOUSMAN

Laurence Housman (1865-   ) has done many things well. His wood cuts, his poems, his plays, his fairy tales, and his long stories all have the stamp of his individuality. It would be pleasantest to linger over *A Farm in Fairyland* (1894) or *The Blue Moon* (1904), but neither fairy tales nor the hoax, *An English Woman's Love Letters* (1900), immediately concern us. *A Modern Antæus* (1901) and *Sabrina Warham* (1904) do. The one is a Meredithian study of boyhood and youth; and the other a Hardian story of a girl and her lovers. There is in *Sabrina Warham*, too, a plea for youth as winning as Stevenson's *Virginibus Puerisque* (1881). That one has to mention Stevenson and Hardy and Meredith in writing of Lawrence Housman indicates where his weakness lies. He is not original. None of the things he does so well have not been done well by his elders and before he did them.

CHARLES MARRIOTT

Charles Marriott (1869-   ) did a notable first novel in *The Column* (1901). Its manner was reminiscent of Meredith but its material was discovered by the novelist for himself. It was sensitively aware of beauty, of many forms of beauty. Its descriptions of coast scenery rise up before you with the insistence of a place not seen before. Its heroine, Daphne, is a delight, and she has fellows of equal charm in the novels that follow. Ruth of *The Unpetitioned Heavens* (1914) is dearest to her creator, but Hilda Saintsbury of *The Dewpond* (1912) is surely her close rival. Hilda is as provoking as the ladies of Hewlett's trilogy, with which *The Dewpond* has certain correspondences.

Marriott's work has continued to be aware of beauty and of the changing codes of society, to be clearly planned and carefully written, but it has never risen to the position of major work. His stories belong to literature, but they are minor stories. Minor poets have a greater chance of a place in poetry than minor novelists of a place in the literature of the long story. Anthologies keep the minor poets before us, but obviously there can be no anthologies of novels, and the lists of "the thousand best novels" and their like are no substitute for anthologies.

"ELIZABETH"

There are pleasantness and a sunny peace in the early writing of "Elizabeth" (Countess von Arnim). The pleasantness is that of a personality on friendly terms with the world, the flesh and whatever Gods may be. The peace is not the peace of night and rest but the peace of happy labor out-of-doors in a northern by-way redolent of pine forest and sandy heath. *Elizabeth and her German Garden* (1898) is journal in form, but familiar essay in substance, with just enough of incident to bind the casual parts together. *The Solitary Summer* (1899) has all that its predecessor had, humor, lyric bursts over the joy there is in beautiful places and in the sheer goodness of life, shrewd comment on men and manners, quaint incident. Her desire to be amusing has led at times into that very German sentimentality she elsewhere girds at, and there are times when she scores at some cost to dignity. One hates to question "Elizabeth" in anything, but one cannot help seeing flaws in amber.

The Benefactress (1902) is a story, but it has some of that quality of the familiar essay that was so pleasing in the earlier books. It, too, has its store of worldly wisdom, here sometimes expressed with such turns of expression as were later to help make James Stephens famous. "Relations," she writes, "are at all times bad enough. They do less for you and expect more from you than anyone else. They are the last to congratulate if you succeed and the first to abandon if you fail. They are at one and the same time abnormally truthful, and abnormally sensitive. They regard it infinitely more blessed to administer home-truths than to receive them back again." The story is interesting, too, now, in these days after the World War, for its contrasts of English and German ways.

The Adventures of Elizabeth in Rügen (1904) is a familiar journal of a journey around the largest of German islands. There are observations of a weightier sort, in it, too, such as are to be found in the sententious essay. Sentences suggest Emerson and Thoreau. "I wish I could fill my soul with enough of the serenity of such afternoons to keep it sweet forever," and "Every instant of happiness is a priceless possession forever" are two to remember. There are other observations that show how different she is from such weighty souls, and how wise in her unregenerate position. A delectable one of this sort is, "He who has a mission spends most of his time passing the best things by." There are echoes of the "Elizabeth" of these first books in the later ones, but there is never again so contented or so high-spirited an "Elizabeth." Time judges every author by the best that author has done. Let us, too, so judge, and pay no heed to what else came from her pen. The "Elizabeth" of these four books is to be written down as one of the blessed who have added to the joy of life.

Mrs. Ethel Lillian Boole Voynich (1864-   ) published in 1897 a crudely powerful novel, *The Gadfly*. It tried to be tragedy, but it was melodrama, save now and then. Its author made much of an analysis of pain in the hero, Arthur Burton, "The Gadfly." The story is concerned with the struggles of Young Italy for freedom and with the old theme of the conflict of father and son. It is one of the first English novels to show a decided influence of the Russian novels, Mrs. Voynich coming to its writing after much translation from the Russian.

Ellen Thorneycroft Fowler (Mrs. A. L. Felkin) did a "book of the year" in 1898, *Concerning Isabel Carnaby*, and Mary Cholmondeley "a book of the year" in 1899, *Red Pottage*. Neither has proved to be more than "a book of the year," nor has any other novel of either author been more than that.

LEONARD MERRICK

In 1918 writers who were friends of Leonard Merrick (1864-   ) brought about a republication of his novels in a "new uniform and definitive edition." Sir James M. Barrie wrote the introduction to *Conrad in Quest of his Youth* (1903), the first to be reissued, and other novels and a volume of short stories followed quickly, with introductions by such men as Wells, Pinero, Locke, Neil Munro, Howells, Hewlett, Granville Barker, Neil Lyons, and Chesterton. It was a kindly action, and it had the effect it was designed to have. The reissued books sold well and the name of Leonard Merrick was heard wherever there was talk of novels.

But why was such a concerted action necessary? Was it just by accident that stories that proved popular when they so secured a hearing had not previously won that hearing? It is not easy to answer that question. No one answer can wholly account for his comparative neglect and give a convincing reason why it was that he had never won popularity. Nor is it easy in a word to explain why the hoi episkopoi had not accorded him the position these fellow writers of his thought that he deserved.

It is important to remember, in the face of such a tribute as this, that no such acclamation of an author by round robin methods can more than temporarily give authority to him when he has not won authority by the intrinsic value of his work. It is time, and not the writers who are his friends, that will judge the work of Leonard Merrick.

A reason that Leonard Merrick needed such a fillip to his standing with the critics is that he is essentially a writer of "light fiction," if one may use, the adjective as it is used in "light verse." In form his stories are nearly perfect, in their point of view they are marked by an irony a little out of harmony with their lightness of tone. They are neither fish, flesh nor fowl. Certain qualities in them delight all who savor style and appreciate harmony of proportion, and certain other qualities in them alienate just such people. In content most of the stories of Leonard Merrick are lacking in blood and bone and sinew. Their material is often anemic and slight and soft, or it is made to seem so by the presentation.

The stories hark back to Sterne. They are sentimental and satiric both, and they have little deep lyric feeling. They run away from poetry as the writer of society verse runs away from poetry. Their avoidance of poetry and the forthright expression of the deeper emotions is another reason why they are not so highly valued by those whose first concern with literature is as an art.

Conrad in Quest of his Youth is a very charming story of its kind. The idea underlying it, that of a man of middle years unsuccessfully trying to recapture the joys of his youth, is not an unusual one, though it has more commonly animated short-story, familiar essay and verse than the novel. One wonders whether the idea has body enough for a long story, whether it had not better been reserved to such a short-story as "The Call from the Past," in which it is not unsuccessfully used. Maybe that, too, is a reason why Leonard Merrick for so long failed to make a decided impression: that he is essentially a short-story writer. Certain it is that even good writing and pleasantness of personality and wit pall after a time in a short-story too long drawn out. Nothing will take the place of richness of experience and love of life in the equipment of a novelist.

The Man Who Was Good (1906) sounds greater depths than *Conrad in Quest of his Youth*. It is the old, old story of the woman who preferred the worse man to the better. It is a fresh and sincere presentment of that story, with moments of drama of real poignancy. We accept it all as bitterly true to life. And yet to have read *The Man Who Was Good* is not to have had one of the experiences of life that cannot be forgotten. The story fails to impress you as it should because of the lack of weightiness and richness in its writer. Leonard Merrick's is not one of the great natures.

The short-stories of Leonard Merrick are better than his novels for the reason that their sentimentality is less long drawn out. *The Man Who Understood Women and Other Stories* (1908) is the collection of them that has received the greatest praise, the title story having been called one of the great short-stories in English. It is not that. The characters are not realized clearly enough. The man is the man who missed his chance of happiness with the girl, and the girl the girl who was sorry he had not had the courage to take it. We, reading, sympathize, and we are troubled, but we are no more than pleasantly troubled. We are not hurt. We do not care enough to be hurt. And all the while we are aware of an attitude on the part of the writer, rebuking us with an "Ah! if you had the power to take to heart all I mean you would be deeply moved."

When Paris Laughed: Being Pranks and Passions of the Poet Tricotrin (1918) is a series of short-stories made one by a central character common to them all. The various adventures are pretty and gracious, pathetic and tender, humorous and ironic, but they fail to impress you as life. It is play-acting, indeed, that Leonard Merrick is up to in these stories, and in most of their fellows, short and long. Play-acting with characters, and not life, is his concern. In the stories there is always deftness, gayety, pathos, sentimentality, but not reality. And, sometimes, he does not use men and women to play with, but marionettes. Leonard Merrick has not been able, in most of his writing, to outgrow the associations of his old profession of the theater.

W. J. LOCKE

A friend of mine who suffers sleepless nights calls W. J. Locke (1863-   ) blessed among story-tellers. It is not that *Septimus* (1909) puts him to sleep, but that it, read even the fourth and fifth times, has still the power to make him forget his insomnia and all the phantoms that come in its train. Always in the later and mellower books of Locke we can hope to find happy Bohemians who go about doing kindly deeds. *The Beloved Vagabond* (1909) is the typical Locke story. So universally, indeed, has the book been read that a "beloved vagabond" is now an accepted phrase for a certain type of wanderer.

Locke is one of the many writers of the tribe of Sterne. His dialogue is light and easy, and true to part. His sentiment, it may be, passes over into sentimentality, but its expression is managed with such art that the sentimentality does not cloy. The characterization brings people and puppets both before us, but they all add interest to the pleasant tales. He has his lapses, such as *The Red Planet* (1917), a war story, of slight significance, but you can generally be sure, on picking up a book of Locke, to meet whimsically pleasant people and to listen to a clear recital of a good story. There is often very good writing, indeed, writing that falls into clarities of speech you will want to read out loud, and at its best you will hear in it, from far off, drowsy notes of siren song. When he was young, Locke, like many another, wanted to make the world over again, but now he is content in his mazed wistfulness at the strange ways of men.

THE LONDON GROUP

Arthur Morrison (1863-   ) is having a second hearing. His first was in the nineties, for *Tales of Mean Streets* (1894) and *A Child of the Jago* (1896), and it is these same books that readers are going back to today. Both are about the London slums, detailed in method, and with the social background stressed and the characters minimized. There is not much joy in them, but they have the effectiveness of photographic fidelity to the conditions they picture. There were later *Cunning Murrell* (1900), a queer documentary account of witch-finding in Essex, and a return to London slums in *The Hole in the Wall* (1902), a story of a riverside public-house. Such quality as the London stories have comes from a grim grayness of style, a severe objectivity of treatment and a completeness of knowledge of the subject that seems the outcome of cold study.

William Pett Ridge (1860-   ) began to publish in the same year with Morrison, but his first success, *Mord Em'ly* (1898) was later. Of his books that I have read *'Erb* (1903) produces his stoutest contender for 'a place in the great portrait gallery of English fiction. Herbert Barnes is in character about midway between the Richard Mutimer of Gissing who preceded him and the Denry the Audacious of Bennett who succeeded him. He is not so thoroughgoing a demigogue as Mutimer and not so clever as Denry. He is himself, for all this likeness to others,—a character of parts.

The successors of Morrison and Pett Ridge in this field are Edwin William Pugh (1874-   ), Neil Lyons (1880-   ), and Thomas Burke (1887-   ). Pugh has done over thirty books, long stories, short stories, essays and a study of Dickens. *The Eyes of a Child* (1917), says Burke, is the best of them. It is certainly a moving autobiographical story. It speaks of a hard youth as if he who writes were still of the years he chronicles. It is a middle-aged man's successful attempt to recapture his childhood.

There are fresher qualities in Neil Lyons and Thomas Burke. Burke emerged from obscurity with *Limehouse Nights* (1916), pictures of life in London's Chinatown. In San Francisco they would say he shows people "going Chinee." He has done better work than this, very much better work, in *The Wind and the Rain* (1924).

Arthur's (1908) brought Neil Lyons into recognition. *Cottage Pie* (1911) and *Clara* (1912) established him as a writer of sketches of a new tone. *Cottage Pie* is "a country spread," but *Clara* takes us back to London, and Arthur's coffee stall, and the short unsimple annals of the poor.

SOMERSET MAUGHAM

It was *The Moon and Sixpence* (1919) that won an audience for William Somerset Maugham (1874-   ). All that he had before was a following, and he had had that for only four years. *Of Human Bondage* (1915) brought him the following. There had been talk of him then for eighteen years, from the time of the publication of *Liza of Lambeth* (1897). It is not difficult to see why he was so slow to come into his own. There is strength in *Liza of Lambeth,* but it is a brutal and an angry book, with its material and the attitude of its author alike repellent to those who believe in life. And since nearly all who read for amusement and most of those who are interested in the art of letters are believers in life Maugham found few to like his stories.

The title first fixed upon for *Liza of Lambeth, A Lambeth Idyl,* is indicative of the twist in the nature of the man. He has sympathy of a kind for the girl who has her little hour between drudgery and death, but he cannot forego the smart sarcasm of speaking of her so pitiful love story as an idyl. One might excuse that sarcasm on the grounds of youth did like sarcasm not persist even into his latest writing. Apparently he does not distinguish between sarcasm and irony. Certainly he has never attained to irony, and certainly sarcasm is a cheap thing.

The title of his second novel, *The Making of a Saint* (1898), is another indulgence in sarcasm. The story relates the amours and political intrigue of an Italian soldier of fortune of the fifteenth century who seeks refuge from his failure in life in a Franciscan monastery. There were experiences quite in the vein of Boccaccio that went to the making of anything but a saint out of Filippo Brandolini.

In *Mrs. Craddock* (1902) he turns to that corner of Kent in which he was born, the farming country along the great estuary of the Thames. *Mrs. Craddock* is a story of a lady's wooing of a yeoman farmer, her marriage with him, her tiring of him, and her release through his death in the hunting field. Neither heroine nor hero is memorably done; both are presented in great detail, but there is not in Maugham the artist's touch of life. What the man of science can do he does, faithfully writing out his study of them, but there is not a real characterization in the book.

The study of Edward Craddock is proof positive of Maugham's objectivity. The stay-at-home Englishman of virtues at once plebeian and provincial is as far from Maugham himself as a man can be. Maugham is gypsy-hearted, impatient of restraint, restless, with the born wanderer's contempt of settled life. One wonders how he ever underwent the discipline of medical study. It must be that, too, was discovery to him, exploration, a road to new wonders. It is this phase of the man that is revealed in *The Explorer* (1907) and again in *The Moon and Sixpence* (1919). *The Magician* (1908), his attempt at a tale of terror, is negligible. It is but a stirabout of stock horrors.

It is not by such books but by *Of Human Bondage* that Maugham stands or falls. This is the fullest and most detailed presentation of a "case" in English fiction. It is throughout so intimate that it must be largely autobiographical. Maugham has nowhere revealed himself as possessed of an imagination, as Hardy, for instance, reveals himself in *Jude the Obscure*. There is no doubt but that Maugham has striven hard to make his presentation exactly true. Yet at the start there is an error in the observation of human nature that makes us distrust his scientific accuracy and hesitate to believe that he ever practiced medicine. He makes a mother ask what is the sex of the child she has borne only after she has sent for her boy of seven to comfort her in her prostration. If that is a sample of his faithfulness to life he must be a poor observer.

To a reader of Maugham's generation *Of Human Bondage* cannot fail to be very interesting as it recounts so much of the life that was common to all men of the English-speaking countries who grew to manhood in the eighteen nineties. The talk current then about education and literature and music and painting is faithfully reproduced. *Of Human Bondage,* is important, then, from the historical standpoint. But what is its value by the "absolute estimate"? It is a story of great intention, an attempt to give a man just as he is, the attempt that Fielding made in *Tom Jones* (1749). Fielding made his attempt a triumph of art. Maugham would perhaps have been content to make his a triumph of science, but obvious errors here and there, such as the one I have pointed out, precluded that result. *Of Human Bondage* is a careful report on a man child through boyhood and adolescence and youth. It is not a great novel, for its author, for all his power of analysis of character, cannot pass beyond that to the creation of character.

That is the greatest weakness of Maugham as a novelist. But there are other weaknesses. His writing is always a little uncertain, a little like the writing of a man not born to English. He is prone to inversions and unrhythmical as a rule. There is no ease, no urbanity, no mellowness in the man. He is very like a certain type of medical student of the late nineteenth century, a man liberated by science from tradition of many sorts, but not as yet humanized by experience of suffering into that sort of doctor who is above everything else the friend of man. Maugham is a keen student of humanity but hardly an artist at all.

MAY SINCLAIR

As one reads *Arnold Waterlow* (1924) and finds it on the very note of its time it is difficult to realize that Miss May Sinclair began writing in the mid-nineties. *Arnold Waterlow* is not so definitely the presentation of a "case" as *The Romantic* (1920). It is clearly, though, of those studies of personality that have been so frequent since psychology was recognized by many writers as the mistress of the novel. It was in the days when psychology was still the handmaid that Miss Sinclair published what she calls her "first successful novel" *The Divine Fire* (1904). Her art has traveled a long way since that time, it has always kept abreast of the times, it has conformed to the most approved new mode of the forward-gazing writers who believe the novel should be the expression of its period. *The Divine Fire* is romantic, but it is recognizable as Miss Sinclair's by its preoccupation with genius. She has associated much with writers, particularly with those of advanced views, and it is her privilege to write about them if she so chooses. Few will question her knowledge of them, even if she does not know all the "about one thousand celebrated authors" who live in London. They are proverbially difficult to present convincingly in books, and although her presentations are as careful and studied and exhaustive as her scientific faithfulness to detail can make them, some of her artists are not easy of acceptance as men and women.

It has seemed to me, at times, as I have been reading her stories, that she has made the mistake George Eliot made in her later books, of being more concerned to put the latest new thought, and new theory, and new attitude into her stories than to put human beings into them. George Eliot had a knowledge of midlands life, both town and country, in her stories on which her reputation securely rests; and Miss Sinclair has a knowledge of humble Londoners of which she might have made more. It will perhaps turn out in the end that *The Combined Maze* (1913) is her most human story. It is about town middle class people of no particularly striking personality, but it has a stout-hearted girl in it, Winny, whom I remember more intimately than I do any of the strange cases of her post-war stories.

If one should judge of one's novels for their value as records of the time one would have to rate high *The Tree of Heaven* (1917). Written during the early stages of the World War it preserves, without prejudice, the precarious conditions of a sorely tried people. It is not, however, a story of much beauty or knowledge of life or vision. In *Mr. Waddington of Wyck* (1921), she went off, as she says, "on a new tack," and attempted humor. In the estimation of the average reader, apparently she attained it, for the book sold. *The Life and The Death of Harriet Frean* (1922) and *Anne Severn and the Fieldings* (1922) are both technical studies of human beings as "cases," neither of them so futile as *The Romantic*.

What saves these books to literature is their writing. Were it not for that they would belong to science as unequivocally as the writing of Miss Dorothy Richardson. It is a very studied writing, a subtle writing, a writing more aware of the emotions of the moment and of the natural background to that writing than of rhythm or color. It has what she wills it to have, the quality of the feeling of the moment, abruptness now, and now picturesqueness. It is modern, sometimes almost in code, but seldom puzzling and never unintelligible, as this kind of elliptic writing can so readily be. It was not for nothing that Miss Sinclair wrote verse in her youth.

CHAPTER XVIII

THE PAGEANT OF JOSEPH CONRAD

THE phenomenon of Conrad is as nearly a miracle as there is in English Letters. Born Teodor Josef Konrad Korzeniowski in 1857 in Poland, a country without a seacoast, he came to England in 1877, a sailor of three years' experience in Mediterranean and West Indian waters. He came to England because since boyhood he had been determined to be an English sea-captain. And the realization of his hopes was as great a happiness as expectation had promised. From the time of his first understanding of things in childhood, Conrad had been thrilled by the spectacle of England. In Marseilles, when he was seventeen, he first saw the Red Ensign on a British ship, the *James Westoll,* and from that time to his death in 1924 it was to him the symbol of all he loved best.

In 1897, twenty years after he came to England, the name of Joseph Conrad was on the lips of everyone who was on the lookout for what was new and beautiful in our writing. It was in such currency because of *The Nigger of the Narcissus,* which appeared that year in *The New Review.* Though Conrad was the son of a writer, a translator of Shakespeare into Polish, the writing of novels had not been part of the dream that drew him to England. It was not, indeed, until 1889, in a moment of tedium on shore, that he began his first novel, *Almayer's Folly.* For five years he worked at it, off and on, on shore and in hours of leisure at sea in long voyages to India and Malaya. It might never have been finished had not Conrad fallen ill on the Congo in 1892 and been forced to think of leaving the sea.

The story had been inspired by a man Conrad had met up a Bornean river when he was on the little trading steamer Vidar.

This man had so haunted Conrad he had to have his say of him somehow to get him out of mind. The story was finished while Conrad was still at sea, sent to the publishers and accepted, and published in 1895. Few authors, even of some experience in writing, have been able to express themselves wholly in their first serious effort. Yet Conrad, who had written nothing more ambitious than letters before he began *Almayer's Folly*, was able in it to express himself just as he would. The story revealed not only a new world of the East to the Western World but a new temperament that colored the telling of these mysteries of Malaya.

Two years after his first book, with only *An Outcast of the Islands* (1896) between, came *The Nigger of the Narcissus* (1897), as perfectly accomplished a piece of writing as Conrad was to do. With no literary apprenticeship he did two books of a new kind of beauty, and then, in his third book, a masterpiece, and one with no forerunner in older writers. Though his characterization was sure from the very start these first books are most notable for their atmosphere. The menace of the jungle is over the two Bornean novels, and the sea broods threateningly or breaks into violence through many pages of *The Nigger of the Narcissus*.

Tales of Unrest (1898) are studies in the condensed novel, but they are only tentative efforts compared to his five later collections of like sort. *The Idiots* of this early group is after Maupassant; and *The Return* after Henry James, who was to remain the only continued influence of the writers Conrad studied. The tone of this work, the somberly magnificent style that is Conrad himself, were in his first writing; it was methods of story-telling and analysis of character that showed his discipleship to James. Of the Russians whose influence you might look for in a fellow Slav the only one Conrad admired was Turgenieff. That great artist's practice of making every story he told a thing of beauty helped Conrad to a theory of art. That theory he had fully developed within three years of his first publication. In the "Author's Note" to *The Nigger of the Narcissus*, appended to the last installment of that narrative in *The New Review* (November 1897), he tells us the aim of the artist in fiction is to make the reader "see" a "passing phase of life" snatched "from the remorseless rush of time" as it is held "in the light of a sincere mood." Conrad had had from the first the scorn of the true artist for "ideas," which are but passing catchwords, the Shibboleths of an age. His whole intent had been always on life, on character, on story, on atmosphere, on the rendering of all the elements of the novel as a whole.

Lord Jim (1900) gives us his first universal character, the first all men, whatever their experience of life or habits of thought, can sympathize with and understand. Jim is the man who would be a hero. His manhood, however, failed him in the crisis he had been waiting for, boy and man, to prove his heroic qualities. He loses his papers for deserting, with his fellow officers, their steamer full of pilgrims on their way to Mecca when the ship strikes a submerged derelict. Later on Jim goes to Patusan in Malaya and is shot in a petty war, regaining his self-respect in the action that results in his death. *Lord Jim*, perhaps because of the universality of its hero, perhaps because of its cheering instance of a broken life made whole again, gained a greater popularity than had any of his earlier books. Previously it had been largely the writers who had read Conrad, now the legions of readers began to turn to him.

After *Youth* (1902) there was no question that a new writer of the first moment had arrived. This account of a voyage from London to the East, with its tempests and fire in cargo and final disaster, shows the triumph of youth over all difficulties and misfortunes. It is told from the standpoint of the ship's second officer and, of course, records the feelings of Conrad's first trip to Bangkok, and the effect of the East upon him. *Youth* is high-hearted, lyric in its later passages, and thrilled with the lure of Malayan waters. There had been moments of ecstasy in *The Nigger of the Narcissus*. There are moments of an intenser ecstasy in *Youth,* and that deeply true reading of life that, if you have your health, there can ·be no sorrow or trouble that is more than a passing episode when you are one and twenty.

"The Heart of Darkness" of this same year, 1902, is a perfectly done thing of horrors, the story of the way in which living with a subject race in the tropics finds out all the weaknesses in a European and corrupts him utterly in the end.

Typhoon and "Falk" of 1903 are stories of voyages. The one relates the triumph of the faithfulness and courage of a stupid man over wild tempest, and the other the blight and refinement the memory of cannibalism worked on a dour Scandinavian seaman. In Falk's estimation his killing and eating of his shipmate on that weird and terror-haunted drift of a dismasted ship toward antarctic seas was a breaking of an inviolable tradition of the sea, an unpardonable sin, a something not to be lived down but to pursue a man for ever. And yet, the mystery of it was, the thoughts of it all made him less of a hulking brute, more of a man, than he had been before he had sinned.

The constant elements in all these stories of the East are the triumph of the East over the white men; the spell of the lustrous and serene waters of shallow seas under sunlit or starlit skies; the jungle hours so breathless, or so terrible in storm; the brown men so quiet in the background, so faithful and so faithless, so inscrutable always. As you recall Conrad's East you forget sudden blows and thunderstorms, the noise of waves and wind, the cries of angered men, the shots and rushes of the murders and the fighting. A strange hush is over all, a hush broken only by whispering sounds of wind and human speech, a hush, and, often too, a darkness,—the darkness of approaching storm or of night.

The stories that reveal these broken men, that chronicle their vehemence and their resignation, are full of incidents. Thieving and robbery and malignant feuds; murder attempted or done for passion's sake or out of jealousy or greed; shipwreck and piracy and petty wars all have place in them. Yet so indirect, often, are their methods of presentation, so involved the telling of the stories, so much more interested their author in the effect of incident on character and personality and temperament than in incident itself, that the tragedy is often veiled, rendered remote, held in the background, minimized.

As you read Conrad this subjection of incident, this aloofness of presentation of character, this avoidance of poignancy, seems deliberate on his part, the result of a studied detachment like that of Greek tragedy. It results in a curious effect, as if you are listening to words spoken almost out of hearing.

It was *Nostromo* (1904) that revealed Conrad as a novelist of first power. This is a full-scope story, crowded with incidents and characters, of a revolution in Costaguana, a South American republic very like Peru. Nostromo the hero is, like Lord Jim, a universal character, the man who wakes up to find that his years of faithfulness have not been rewarded with the money and power he sees others of no greater deserts possessing. Nostromo would never have been undone morally by his self-esteem had he remained at sea. It was the land, the proverbial enemy of sailors, that found him out. We, reading of him, discover that we are very like Nostromo, in that we are nursing to heart a self-esteem that only needs opportunity to become a canker and destroy us.

Besides its magnificent hero, the captain of stevedores, there are a dozen and more of characters of first importance in *Nostromo,* and of all sorts. There are the old Garibaldino, and Teresa his wife, and Linda and Giselle, his troublingly beautiful daughters. There are Martin Decoud, the Latin American who looks to Paris as the center of his world, and his Antonia and her father Don José Avellanos, aristocrats all. There are Charles Gould, the Ingléz of Sulaco, who allows the silver mine of San Tōmê to alienate him from his wife, and that pathetic lady herself, Doña Emilia. There are Dr. Monygham and Captain Mitchel and Hirsch; and Ramirez and the Morenita and —but one must stop somewhere. There are probably more characters in Meredith's novel of Italian revolution, *Vittoria* (1866), but there are few other stories since those of the prime of Dickens that can boast so many, and almost none in which such numbers are so clearly handled.

After 1903 Conrad did not return to the East for the material of his stories until 1912. In the interim he wrote of the sea, *The Mirror of the Sea* (1906) and "The Brute" (1908); of anarchists in London and Russia and Switzerland, *The Secret Agent* (1907), "The Informer" (1908), and *Under Western Eyes* (1911); of South America, "Gaspar Ruiz" (1908), and "An Anarchist" (1908), besides *Nostromo*. He made a try, too, at an historical novel, *The Duel* (1908) of the Napoleonic wars, the one story of his in which his humor approaches hilarity. Elsewhere it is of a very quiet kind, allied closely to irony.

The reading of Russia in *Under Western Eyes* and the reading of anarchists in *The Secret Agent* bring out a good deal of Conrad's philosophy of life. As a Pole he hates tyranny, particularly the tyranny of Czarist Russia; as a sea captain he cannot but admit a beneficent tyranny is necessary on shipboard. As one whose aversions are disorder, irresponsibility, slackness, and inefficiency, he is strongly on the side of the established social system. He admires the order, the discipline, the tradition, the sense of duty and of responsibility you find in long-established rule, and the centralized power that gets things done. He does not deny there are weakness and corruption in high places but on the whole his inheritance of the code of the gentleman, his experience as a ship's officer and his worship of the Red Ensign as a symbol of life's best, make him a conservative.

The return to the East in *Twixt Land and Sea* (1912) is signalized by three of his most powerful stories. The scene of one, "A Smile of Fortune" is Mauritius, the island off Madagascar, and thus not strictly in the East. Yet the verandah on which you meet Alice Jacobus is above a garden that is heavy with a fragrance like that of Eastern flowers, jasmines you imagine and pittosporums, and the climate and environment have their will of the characters as the East has so often in his many stories of Malaya. The people of the story are not so broken as most of those of the Malayan stories, but they seem held in that tranced immobility and helplessness before difficulties that is so characteristic of all these latter from *Almayer's Folly* to *Victory*. On the whole it is true that it is only the seamen in Conrad who can hold their own in tight places, and they only in tight places of the sea's making. Trouble on land, the people of Conrad find difficult to face, and almost impossible to overcome. Jacobus can do nothing to win his daughter a place in the port's society. Money and civility and family are here of no avail. That poor girl seems to me as surely "a figure against the sky" as Doña Rita of *The Arrow of Gold* (1919). Alice is shunned because of her illegitimate birth, immured almost in her scented garden. She is a splendid woman in body and instinct, but her experiences is that of a frightened child. A lover finds his way to her but her response disillusions him and he leaves her to the ennui she has known for years and to memories of his wooing that will make her days even less tolerable than they were before he came.

Of the two other stories of *Twixt Land and Sea*, "The Secret Sharer" is a Maeterlinckian study of an escaped murderer, a quiet whispering thing; and "Freya of the Seven Isles" is troubled with quarreling and bestial revenge and the loss of sanity.

Chance (1913), strangely, was the story by which Conrad came into general recognition and newsstand sales. It is, among many involved stories of his, the most involved, hard to follow both in incident and in motive. What made it the success it was, was simply its place in Conrad's development. Story by story more readers came under the fascination of his art until there were enough of them won over to an appreciation of him by the earlier and better books to give him a large welcome for the next book that came. It was the luck of *Chance* to be that book. You are at two removes from the story, sometimes, in its telling. Somebody tells Marlow of what happens and Marlow passes it on to the narrator whose words we read. Then Marlow tells the story himself, and Powell talks too. It keeps you busy being sure who is talking. And yet your interest is so keen that you worry it out. And you are exasperated, and repaid for your trouble. You come on things that you cannot forget: the pathos of Flora's childhood, the joy of Captain Anthony's awakening to her love for him; and this passage of description and that reading of life. The man who can say, "That rapid blinking stumble across a fleck of sunshine which our life is" is worth bothering to understand even in his most involved passages.

Victory (1915) and *The Rescue* (1920) are the remaining long stories of the East. *Victory* is so full of action and of scenes of vivid color that it was the first novel of Conrad to be "filmed." It brings Americans closer home than Malaya with two characters that have wandered out of Bret Harte, Plain Mr. Jones and Martin Ricardo. They have the taint of melodrama in them, these two, but Heyst and Alma are as great characters as Conrad has created. "Enchanted Heyst" they called this man so intrepid in action but so afraid of his emotions. Alma, who gave her life for him, and in vain, brought him real living just before life was taken away. His last words, "Woe to the man whose heart has not learned while young to hope, to love—and to put its trust in life," attest Conrad's belief in living just as surely as those other words just quoted from *Chance* attest his sense of the brevity of life. There is more of the sort of comment quoted from *Chance* in Conrad than of the sort quoted from *Victory*, as would be expected of one who writes so often of broken men in backwaters and whose predilection is for tragedy.

The Rescue is the old unhappy story of the lady who loved the serving man. Neither Alice Travers nor Captain Lingard so regarded their affair, but that is the way she would regard it just as soon as she got back to civilization. And to civilization she would have wanted to return within a short time even if he had run off with her as she wished. Barrie's *Admirable Crichton* is of a lesser world surely, but it presents a case very much to the point. Mrs. Travers came as a revelation of unknown and unguessed emotions into the life of Captain Lingard. She came between him and his honor, which was involved in his promised restoration of his Malay friend Hassim to his little state in Celebes. And in the end Captain Lingard sacrificed her to that honor, though she would have left her husband for him at the crook of his finger. She would not have been long happy with Lingard, though, for she was the sort of woman who could not have been content without a high place in the world. It is stressed again and again that she was ill at ease in English civilization, but she was after all of that type of English lady whom T. E. Brown met and railed at on the Pincian in Rome. She was statuesque and distant and proud, and the deck of a little brig with Lascar sailors for audience is too small a stage for such. Remember how Brynhild chafed when she was not at the very center and focus of affairs of her world. Edith Travers is a character of heroic mold, worthy of a place by the side of Lingard, the blond and bearded Elizabethan sea-rover reincarnated in the trader-captain of Malayan seas. Old Jörgenson is a third to these two so memorable creations, a man dragged from a death in life for a brief moment of turbulence at the Rajah Laut's behest.

There is a chance for comment on but one more book of Conrad and that, I think, his greatest, *The Arrow of Gold* (1918). It is beautifully conceived and completely executed. It is of "a wholeness of good tissue" and of a perfected unity. It is the book of Doña Rita. Doña Rita is to be remembered with all the great heroines of legend and history, from Helen of Troy to Deirdre. She is "a woman Homer sung." She leaves her lover after they have known love together but a little while, because she will surely be the ruin of him from the worldly point of view, and because it is problematical that even such love as theirs will last. She deserts him rather than face a time when they two might be "keeping a watch on a love had no match and it wasting away."

The brevity and pettiness and unimportance of human life are as instant to some moods of every thinking man as to other moods of his, its gallantry and blessedness and inestimable worth. You will find realizations of these latter qualities in

Conrad, but he lived so long in his most impressionable years with the immensities of sea and sky always about him, and when he was ashore so frequently among burdened or broken men, that there are more records of littleness and defeat than of largeness and triumph among his stories. Such a result, too, is almost inevitable with one who, like Conrad, has the tragic bias in the very fibre of him, and irony intertwisted with it.

If you could symbolize these stories by one figure it would be that of a man alone on the deck of a sailing ship, at night, raised by the heave of the sea in silhouette against the black and spangled background of the sky. It would be "one of those dewy, starry nights, oppressing our spirit, crushing our pride, by the brilliant evidence of the awful loneliness, of the hopeless, obscure insignificance of our globe lost in the splendid revelation of a glittering, soulless universe."

In certain moods Conrad has a sense that all life is an illusion. He has something of the dreaminess as well as of the resignation of the Slav. Of the sailor, too, perhaps. At other moments he is as matter of fact as any Yankee skipper that ever sailed out of Salem in old days. Do not forget that when he was in command of the *Otago* he was trader as well as master and that he made "the dear old thing earn money as she had never done before." In all his phases Conrad hates turbulence and noise. "After all," he writes in *Notes on Life and Letters*, "every sort of shouting is a transitory thing. It is the grim silence of facts that remains." His creed, it must be emphasized, is one of tradition, duty, order, seemliness, courage, faith, responsibility. There is never a question of his being on the side of the angels. In "Because of the Dollars," he says, "He's thoroughly humane, and I don't imagine there can be much of any other sort of goodness that counts on this earth."

Life is a good thing, he holds, whether it brings more of unhappiness or happiness. "Monsters do change, but the truth of humanity goes on forever, unchangeable and inexhaustible in the variety of its disclosures."

That Conrad is a phenomenon, an unprecedented figure among

English novelists, has to a certain degree minimized his real position. It is so wonderful that a man who could not speak English until he was twenty should become a master of English prose that we are apt to lose in our wonder a sense of how great is that accomplishment. We must reiterate to ourselves his powers; we must summon before us the great pageant of his people; we must remember all the beauty of the world he has gathered into his pages; we must recall his many deep readings of life; we must realize the extraordinary richness of his temperament as it is revealed in his style; we must savor the color and rhythm of life there is in these so many books of his. If we can do all this, then we may come to some true appreciation of him.

The many writers who have come under his influence are a proof that Conrad is one of the "beginnings" in English fiction like Fielding, like Scott, like Hardy. Walpole sees Forster, Lawrence, Beresford, George, Swinnerton, Cannan, Viola Meynell, and Brett Young influenced by Conrad, but Walpole himself, I think, is more so influenced than any of these others save Forster and Swinnerton. One could mention, too, McFee and Tomlinson and Richard Curle; and, in America, Hergesheimer and Eugene O'Neill and—by his own confession—Vachel Lindsay. There are others, too—many of them.

Conrad has struck a new note in our literature; he has introduced into it a quality that was not there before he wrote; he has created at least a score of portraits that must be hung on the line in the great gallery from English fiction; he has told stories that haunt us; he has brought romance back into the novel of our day. And to do these things is to be of the company of the great.

CHAPTER XIX

JOHN GALSWORTHY, GENTLEMAN

IF one chose one's books only for the personality and character and cultivation of their authors John Galsworthy (1867-) would be the most sought after of novelists of today. His books speak his pleasantness, his breeding, his regard for the best in art and thought and statecraft, his kindliness and strength of character, his toleration, his passion for the betterment of all ways of living.

It is idle to pretend that personality and character and sympathies do not influence readers, even readers who take their reading seriously, in their favoring of this author or that. It is all very well to say that the highest realistic art must be objective, and must be valued for its objectivity, but no art has ever been accepted for its objective presentment alone. This man himself, as revealed in his book, will make you accept that book even though its story is repugnant to you, as Galsworthy's sometimes are. That man himself, as revealed in his book, George Moore for instance, will make it repugnant to you, though its story is not in itself repugnant.

The story in a novel is one element of its appeal or a deterrent to its appeal; the quality of the author another element of its appeal or a deterrent to its appeal; but there are, too, those other important elements of the artistry and the insight of the author: the architectonics, the sequence of incident, characterization, surety of dialogue, style, revelation. Galsworthy generally has an interesting and timely story to tell; and the quality of the man himself, save for a streak of improving pedagogue, is all one could ask. If the artistry and seership of him were as his humanity and his knowledge of life! In two novels only, however, the artist and seer in him function nearly as freely as the gentleman, the humanitarian, and the man of experience. These two books were both published when he was about forty: *The Man of Property* in 1906, and *The Country House* in 1907; and, though there is little that is autobiographical in either they are written out of the life he had lived.

Galsworthy was born a suburban Londoner, but his family kept up its associations with the Devonshire from which it sprung, and it is in Devonshire that Galsworthy has now his home. The family prospered in London, and so it came about that he who was to be its most notable member followed that so orthodox round of the English gentleman: Harrow; New College, Oxford; and Lincoln's Inn. Worldwide travel followed his calling to the bar; and in 1897, the cautious first publishing of his early 'prentice work under a pseudonym. "John Sinjohn" was responsible for *From the Four Winds* (1897); *Jocelyn* (1898); *Villa Rubien* (1900) and *A Man of Devon* (1901). The first novel published under his own name was *The Island Pharisees* (1904). It was a wise procedure, this slow approach to his lifework. He did not rush into print with his first experiences, as have so many young men of fortune, but waited until he was thirty to venture his first book.

It was earlier than this Galsworthy had crossed the Indian Ocean on that voyage made memorable by the presence of Joseph Conrad as ship's officer. One cannot but wonder what effect it had on either man. Galsworthy is of the staunchest of Conrad's admirers, but there is slight evidence that Conrad influenced him. Such correspondences of method as there are in the stories of the two men may be directly traced to a common admiration for Turgenieff. If there are origins for Galsworthy in the work of other men they are not obvious. The people he writes about are of the classes that Meredith had written of earlier, and his "lyrical interbreathings" and commentary are in some instances like subdued versions of those of the great Victorian. It is a coincidence, of course, that Galsworthy's novels began to appear shortly after those of Meredith ended with *The Amazing Mar-*

riage (1895).   There is no such direct imitation of Meredith,
however, in Galsworthy as you find in Mrs. Craigie, Hewlett and
Snaith, or even such indirect imitation as you find in E. M.
Forster.   The propaganda of *The Freelands* (1915) allies it
rather surprisingly with so old a book as *Yeast* (1848) of
Charles Kingsley; and certain passages in *Fraternity* (1908)
show the blight that strikes all thinking fathered by Samuel Butler.

   Almost wholly, however, the work of Galsworthy, even in
his beginnings, is his own.   He matured late, as do so many of
the good slow minds characteristic of our race, unhampered by
the too quick facility and imitative cleverness of a "sedulous
ape."   It was a sudden fruition, that of *The Man of Property*
and *The Country House*.   In none of the five volumes from
1897 to 1904 is there more than promise.   And then, in the next
volume, in 1906, one of the two novels that are his masterwork.
In Chancery (1920) was happier than most sequels, but it was
not on a par with *The Man of Property*.   *To Let* (1921) is a
still further thinning of the theme.   The three, with two little
items from the annals of his masterful family, now have place
in *The Forsyte Saga* (1922).   *The White Monkey* (1924) is a
still further, and perfunctory, continuance of it.   *The Forsyte
Saga* impresses by its very breadth of scope, its consideration of
the so many human beings that are numbered among its five
generations.   Yet I cannot but regret that Galsworthy did not
take leave of Irene and Soames in that crashing close of *The
Man of Property*.   What follows is, of course, development of
the theme, rather than variations on the theme, but the old
rapture is not recaptured.

   Soames Forsyte is the man in whose conviction everything he
has acquired, even his wife, is his own to do with as he will.
As such he is a type, but before he is a type he is an individual.
He is the more easily understood just because he is representative of so many of his kind, but less distinct, it must be admitted,
just because he is so universal.   Saying: "How true he is to
life," we identify him with Tom or Dick or Harry, and by
such an identification fail to see him as this one man of Gals-

worthy's creation, Soames Forsyte. Able and tenacious and un-
scrupulous outside his narrow code as he is, Soames is baffled
by his wife and driven to brutality.

Irene, though a universal character, too, is less typical. The
individual woman is not in her lost in the type. Irene is not
easily forgotten, in the pride of her love for Bosinney, or in the
pathos of her return, like that of a wounded animal to its den,
to the house of her husband after her lover's death. Inscrutable, often, in *The Man of Property,* she is made clearer in the
more elaborated presentation of *In Chancery.* She is made still
clearer again, and less lovable, in *To Let.* To Jolyon, Jolyon
the third, to whom she turns after Bosinney is a faded memory,
she is "more than a woman. . . . The spirit of universal beauty,
deep, mysterious, which the old painters, Titian, Giorgione, Botticelli, had known how to capture and transfer to the faces of
their women—this flying beauty seemed to him imprinted on her
brow, her hair, her lips, and in her eyes. 'And this is to be
mine!' he thought. 'It frightens me.' " Perhaps, after all,
Galsworthy has gone to school to Conrad, for this description
is surely of a kind with that of Rita in *The Arrow of Gold*
(1919).

These two, Irene and Soames, are the principals of *The Man
of Property* and *In Chancery,* and much to the fore in *To Let,*
if not quite principals. There are, however, a score other portraits of importance in the trilogy. Galsworthy differs greatly
from the autobiographical novelists that labor so painfully over
the phases of one little life in successive volumes. He can
write of others than himself, understanding men very other than
he is by his breadth of sympathy and by his dramatic power.
Jolyon the second, Jolyon the third, Jolyon the fourth, and
Jon—each is distinct from the other; and Bosinney from the
four; and Monty, brother-in-law to Soames; and Dartie, his
nephew; and James, his father; and so on; and so on; and so
on. Not each is a notable character but each is distinct.

The Man of Property is a hard book. It is hard in subject.
It is hard because it reflects the qualities of Soames Forsyte.

It is hard in treatment, too, as it should be. The charm of a gracious lady, Mrs. Horace Pendyce, who was Margery Totteridge, softens the story of the swift passion of Helen Bellew for George Pendyce, and of its swift passing, that is called *The Country House* (1907). The reflex of that passion upon that institution, the country house, is really more important in the story than the passion itself. Helen Bellew is the wife of a neighboring squire, Jasper Bellew, separated from her husband, and living in London. She is hard, mocking, sensual, incapable of steadfast love, a dangerous woman. George Pendyce is the usual obstinate bulldog of a squire. He is not, however, just sowing his wild oats; the affair has the dignity of a passion to him, even if an unenduring one. Shooting and racing, dancing and drinking, have their place in the story, and, above everything else, the traditions of the squirearchy.

As in *The Man of Property* the Englishman as businessman is satirized, so in *The Country House* the Englishman as squire is satirized. It was to be expected that the man who would indict his countrymen as "Island Pharisees" in his first novel of any parts would continue his attacks in later books. There is no question that both *The Man of Property* and *The Country House* suffer as art from the satire that is in them, and from the propaganda that follows in the wake of the satire. Both satire and propaganda are born of the great love Galsworthy has for England. He is, of course, satirizing himself in all his satire just as surely as he is satirizing his neighbors. And the propaganda he advances is for his own reformation as well as for theirs. His position is very much that of an elder brother who wants to jolt his younger brothers out of ways that reflect upon the family, ways that he owns he himself has not entirely outgrown.

There is mellowness in *The Country House,* a rare quality in any modern novel, and not to be found in any other story, or in any play, of Galsworthy, though there is more than a suggestion of it in that sketch of *A Motley* (1910) that he calls "A Portrait."

Fraternity (1908) is a restless, questioning book. *The Patrician* (1911) a record of disaster, in the affair of Audrey Noel and Miltoun, and a prelude to disaster, in the affair of Lady Babs and Harbinger. *The Dark Flower* (1913) heaps one disaster upon another, and but barely evades a third. *The Freelands* (1915), like *The Country House,* is an account of things going wrong with a county family. It is a raw, combative book, with few interludes of pleasantness or peace. *Beyond* (1917) is a story of high intention, but of less accomplishment, perhaps because it rehashes matter that has been handled before, some of it by Galsworthy, and some of it by Arnold Bennett, in *Sacred and Profane Love* (1905). *Saint's Progress* (1919) is a war novel, compassionate and topical and tedious.

The plays of Galsworthy have not shown such a falling off in power as the novels. *The Skin Game* (1920) is as strong, and as effective on the stage, as any of its predecessors. Galsworthy has expressed a preference for the novel over the play, holding that the severity of form in the latter "starves" a part of the writer; and he has expressed the belief, too, that he is more of a novelist than of a playwright. As I have said in a previous chapter, he is, relatively, more important as playwright than novelist, but not absolutely. The English drama of today is of rather mediocre accomplishment on the whole, the English novel of today of higher accomplishment, and the novels of Galsworthy as novels are better than his plays as plays. His plays loom large only because of the littleness of most contemporary plays.

And yet, despite this expressed preference for the novel on the part of Galsworthy, one who has followed carefully both his novels and his plays cannot help feeling that the plays are now taking what is most vital in him. It is not only that we have no *Man of Property* or *Country House* among the more recent novels, but not one even of the caliber of *The Patrician.* *In Chancery* is not really an exception, for if it have any splendor, it is but a splendor reflected from *The Man of Property.*

The Patrician is comparatively free of that irritating habit

of his of giving a character or place a name that indicates
its quality or function or attitude.   This is a tradition that
Galsworthy, the satirist of tradition, has chosen to perpetuate.
It is to be found in *Everyman* (circa 1475), in Good Deeds;
in *A New Way to Pay Old Debts* (1633), in Overreach; in *Pilgrim's Progress* (1678), in Great Heart; in *Tom Jones* (1749),
in Allworthy; in *Nicholas Nickleby* (1839) in Dotheboys Hall;
and in *The Egoist* (1879) in Sir Willoughby Patterne.   You
might say that with Massinger, Bunyan, Fielding, Dickens,
and Meredith, Galsworthy was in good company in this practice, were it not that it is a practice that the progress of the
years has changed from an accepted custom to an artistic vice.
Galsworthy has a love of it that finds expression in his Forsytes, his Hussell Barter, his Gregory Vigil, his Worsted Skeynes,
his Courtier, his Hillcrests, his Hornblowers.

And, as he is fond of such naming, so, too, he is fond of
that which has been hand and glove with it, allegory.   In that
The Man of Property and *The Country House* and *Fraternity*
are representative of large sections of English life Galsworthy
may be said, in a sense, to employ the symbolic method, but
in none of his important undertakings does he become out and
out allegorical.   In little undertakings he delights in allegory.
For instances, let stand the play, *The Little Dream* (1911);
"A Novelist's Allegory" in *The Inn of Tranquility* (1912); and
the satire *The Little Man* (1915).

Among the many characters of *The Patrician* the only one
whose name stresses his position and qualities is Courtier, that
soldier of fortune, socialistic and red-polled, who talks like
Bernard Shaw.   All these many characters are carefully described, but there is hardly dialogue enough in the novel to
reveal all of them to you with as great a distinctness as you
would like.   Beside Courtier five others stand out, Audrey Noel
and Miltoun, Lady Babs and Harbinger, and that redoubtable
old autocrat, Lady Casterley.   Galsworthy is good at old ladies.
There is another in *The Freelands,* Granny Frances Freeland,

though her constant harping on nostrums brings her close to a caricature.

In almost all of the novels of Galsworthy "love" is presented as irresistible, wholly dominating, obsessing, even destroying—it is passion. And such "love" is, almost of necessity, ephemeral. Very different is the love of Felix and his daughter Nedda in *The Freelands,* "the only kind of love, except a mother's, which has much permanence—love based on mutual admiration." Of the common sort, the devouring passion, is the love of Irene and Bosinney, and of Helen Bellew and George Pendyce. The bond between Lady Babs and Harbinger has not so much of dignity. It is in *The Dark Flower* (1913), however, to which such "love" gives title, that Galsworthy sets out to study it narrowly. He here follows it through its three enslavements of a man, at nineteen, in the mid-twenties and in the late forties. Mark Lennan becomes a sculptor of acknowledged power in the interims between these affairs, but little else than the affairs interest the novelist. It is a study of the man in love, and that almost alone, which he is concerned with in *The Dark Flower.*

Mark changes a good deal in the course of the story, or rather between its three long episodes. In all three episodes, however, the passion comes to him as a visitation rather than as the result of an adventure of his own seeking. In the affair with Mrs. Stormer he is saved by her flight. In the affair with Olive, by her death,—by what was virtually her murder by her husband. In the third affair Mark gets himself out of it unscathed, for the girl's sake, and for his wife's. This last affair was to him, ironically, the most momentous, for though the second cost his lover her life, this parting with Nell Dromore meant that thereafter he would be an old man: "To say good-bye! To her, and Youth, and Passion!—to the only salve for the aching that Spring and Beauty bring—the aching for the wild, the passionate, the new, that never quite dies in a man's heart. Ah! well, sooner or later, all men had to say

good-bye to that. All men—all men!" The obvious reflection
that comes to us as we close *The Dark Flower* is that in such
situations as befell Mark all that a man can do is to remember
that he is a gentleman, and make the best of what is at once
"bale and bliss."

Though Galsworthy is always striving to make life better
it is not difficult to see that it is his settled conviction that
life is a muddle. The muddle, he as obviously believes, can
always be made better or worse. He is not, in his own view, a
pessimist. A pessimist, to him, is a man who has to pretend
that life is better than it is to endure it at all. An optimist,
to him, is one who can see life as it is and keep happy. "To
be kind and keep your end up—there's nothing else in it" was
what Jolyon the father of Jon always said about the way one
should front life, and there is no doubt that this Jolyon speaks
for his creator. Galsworthy has a very keen sense of the passing of youth, of strength, of life,—of Time lying in wait for
all of us and getting even the proudest and most unbending
in the end. He does not hesitate to show us things as things
are, but his liftings of the veils that cover the unpleasant or
the terrifying are, save when he has been driven to indignation,
always quiet and compassionate.

The emotional intensity that marks his plays marked his
novels from the start, crudely revealed though it was in the
'prentice work. I have already written of the great scene at
the close of *The Man of Property*. There is another toward
the close of *The Country House*. Neither scene is new, for
the greatest situations like the greatest plots are alike "stock"
in their essentials. It is the way of presentation that can give
them a fresh significance. The scene at the end of *The Man
of Property* is between husband and wife, the scene in *The
Country House* is between mother and son. Mrs. Pendyce has
been to call on Helen Bellew and has learned that George has
been thrown over. She goes to the studio in Chelsea, which
George had taken to be near Helen. Mrs. Pendyce has a
quivering sense of the love scenes that he must remember have

taken place here, but she keeps everything out of her face and mien but the comfort she would bring her boy. She does succeed in bringing it to him, as much by her silent sympathy as by her caresses. It is not only for its poignancy, that you remember the scene, however. It is bitten in upon you indelibly because as the mother holds her son to her heart, above them "stealthily on the sloping skylight the cat retraced its steps, its four paws, darkly moving spots, its body a faint blur." Is that an inspiration, or only an ironic device?

Galsworthy always makes much of animals. Spaniel John and Roy the Skye, and the horses, from The Ambler to th ? station hacks, have their place in *The Country House*. The are some of them as clearly individualized as the people. A horse is a great comfort to Lady Babs in *The Patrician;* and in *The Dark Flower* the boy Mark establishes a friendship with the goats he and Mrs. Stormer meet on that day of days on the high pastures of northern Italy.

The beauty of out-of-doors delights Galsworthy, but he never makes too much of description, whether it is of the Grand Canyon of the Colorado, or of the countryside in Worcestershire or of the Tyrolean Alps.

Theoretically, Galsworthy holds Art "the great and universal refreshment. For Art is never dogmatic." Practically he often makes art the servant of morality. In this, again, the Englishman that you find in every aspect of Galsworthy reveals himself. Yet moralist though he makes himself, he most applauds of all contemporary writers, W. H. Hudson and Conrad, artists through and through. In fiction Galsworthy pays tribute among men of the recent past, to Turgenieff, Meredith, Tolstoi and Dostoieffsky, but this is, I think, because he believes their art to be formative of that of the novel of his time. In 1911 he wrote in "Vague Thoughts on Art" that the novel was losing the "biographical form achieved under Thackeray" and attaining "a greater vividness which places before the reader's brain, not historical statements, as it were, of motives and of facts, but word-paintings of things and persons, so chosen and arranged that the reader may see, as if at first hand, the spirit of Life at work before him."

It is in this essay, and in its fellows from *The Inn of Tranquillity* that you will find the mature views of Galsworthy on the art of fiction. Read "A Novelist's Allegory," "Wanted— Schooling," and "Vague Thoughts on Art," quoted from just above, and you will know what he is trying to do. In the first he likens the novelist to the old man Cethru, a watchman with a lantern .throwing a meager light in a dark street that is rat-infested, haunted by ruffians, beset by cesspools and li ed by houses in which live an unsympathetic and dull folk. 1 'nally the old watchman is haled into court for revealing thing, by his light that get people into trouble. There, his advo te thus defends him: "And if it be charged on this old m n Cethru that he and his lanthorn by reason of their showin, · not only the good but the evil bring no pleasure into the world, I ask, Sirs, what in the world is so dear as this power to see—whether it be the beautiful or the foul that is disclosed?"

Galsworthy is one moment so enthusiastic about the writing of our time that he would record "this age as the Third Renaissance," but at the next moment he is so temperate that he can write: "Those who do not publish until they can express, and do not express until they have something worth expressing, are so rare that they can be counted on the fingers of three or perhaps four hands." Galsworthy is among that number. And if a person even more temperate in his estimation of the value of novelists today should restrict the number of those who matter to such as could be counted on the fingers of one hand, Galsworthy would still be of them. Hardy and Conrad are great novelists, great in many stories; Galsworthy is almost great in *The Man of Property* and *The Country House;* George Moore in *Esther Waters;* and Arnold Bennett in *Hilda Lessways.* That's the five of them to be counted on the fingers of one hand, with Galsworthy not last of the three lesser men.

CHAPTER XX

MAURICE HEWLETT, "POET OF SORTS?"

THERE have always been ways of escape from the tedium and crass labor of life. There have been the wine-cup, dream, the chosen craft, art, religion, wandering, romance, love, power, and war. Always somewhere in the world one or the other of these ways has awaited the man determined upon escape. None of them ever led, of course, to lasting freedom. The escape effected was momentary, transient, or a swing round the circle that ended where it began. In more recent times, men have tried to invent what seem to them better ways by legislation toward communism or by such an education as will change human nature. To some, who look backward to what has been, as well as around them and ahead, these latterday ways of escape through legislation or education seem as little likely to afford more than temporary escape as the old ways; and to some no escape at all. Can human nature, for instance, possibly be changed?

While the newer hope dominates men, as it does large numbers today, the tried ways of escape will seem to many old-fashioned or childish or futile. To men so dominated there is more promise of permanent freedom from tedium and heavy, stupefying labor through such Utopias as Wells plans than through the older ways. These men will call the plans for Utopia romance and neglect the true romance that has come down the long line of writers from Chrêtien de Troyes to Hewlett. This condition of affairs is contributory to the minimizing of *The Forest Lovers* (1898) and its like by the young intellectuals, who are just now, on the whole, possessed by the humanitarian bias. Such of them as are still possessed by the artistic bias have, at least in part, deserted Hewlett (1861-1923) for less familiar masters of "style" and "romance," and burn incense on the altars of Machen or Cabell, with only a regretful oblation now and then to "Poor Maurie."

The truth is that such have some excuse for their desertion. Not that the new masters are greater than the old, but because the old master has nodded more than now and then. A writer with a real gift for the romantic tale, Hewlett experimented with too many other forms of writing and dissipated his powers. From the start his ambition was to be a poet in verse. The world was unwilling to acknowledge him as a poet in verse—and rightly— but he was unable to forego that ambition and to concentrate on the romantic tale, for the writing of which his inheritance and environment and innate qualifications seemed so surely to prepare him. Like his father before him he was keeper of the Land Revenue Records and Enrollments at Whitehall, and so familiar with details of that mediæval life which his early successes so bravely bodied forth.

To himself, however, Hewlett was first the poet in verse, and not the practicer of that "poetry in the widest sense" Gissing affirms all "true literature" to be. So, no matter how hard Hewlett tried, he was not able to develop for any form of prose writing, save the romantic tale, a predilection decided enough to inspire him to master it, or, if not to master it, to follow one success in that form with another success in it. By chance or by a visitation of power he did just one idyl and just one historical novel supremely well. These are, of course: "How Sandro Botticelli Saw Simonetta in the Spring" and *The Queen's Quair*. By native gift and good craftsmanship he did a body of romantic tales, of the order of "Madonna of the Peach-Tree," very well indeed. Had he put into them such preoccupation and brooding and whole-souled interest as he put into his verses, we should have had, perhaps, one more truly a present-day Chaucer in prose than ever William Morris was a "modern Chaucer" in verse.

Other explanations of the failure of Hewlett to realize the promise of his first decade of writing suggest themselves. He would take the material of his stories more often from books than from life, and this despite his expression of belief that the greater books are made directly from life. In *Lore of Proserpine* (1913) he owns: "All my life I have used other men's art and wisdom as a springboard." It is true, or at least half true, as he goes on to say, that "every poet can say the same." But most writers who count have so used "other men's art and wisdom" only in their formative years.

In a sense Hewlett has reversed the usual procedure, for his first book, *Earthwork out of Tuscany* (1895), is less influenced by "other men's art and wisdom" than much that follows it. *The Forest Lovers* has a glow all its own, but many of its effects are reproduced from Malory. *Pan and the Young Shepherd* (1898) keeps you busy, as you read, writing the names of poets and essayists from Shakespeare to Borrow on its margins, to mark the parallel passages. *The Road in Tuscany* (1904) is full of reminiscences. A group of his novels of nineteenth century life from *The Stooping Lady* (1907) to *Mainwaring* (1920) candidly acknowledges, in style and characterization, his discipleship to Meredith; and *Bendish* (1913), for one, in its introductions of writers and other items, has certain affiliations with *Esmond* (1852). *Lore of Proserpine* may be written tongue in cheek, but it is none the less surely after the "Fiona Macleod" manifestation of William Sharp.

The refashionings of stark tales from *Corpus Poeticum Boreale* (1883), and *Origines Islandicæ* (1905), in the series from *A Lover's Tale* (1915) onward, are very like a confession that their author is not overburdened with stories that cry to be told. It is a great pity that Hewlett did not settle down at an early age in Wiltshire. He loved Wiltshire as deeply in his later life as he did the Italy he knew in his young manhood, and had he subjected himself to the down country's shaping in his formative years there is no knowing what it might have done for him. Or if he had been a man who could strike root again in maturity, as Hudson could, we might have had a story of Wiltshire as native as *A Shepherd's Life* (1910). Hewlett, for all his acceptance by his neighbors, was evidenty a man who could not.

One thinks of Tennyson and his trouble to get themes to write upon, and of his faith in his way of writing about them, when one is confronted with the heterogeneous material of Hewlett. There is the great difference, that, save for certain experiments, Tennyson's style showed only development and no sudden changes as does Hewlett's. Chameleon-like, Hewlett takes color from what he is writing about. If all his books were bound in cloth that varied as their contents the shelf of them would hold a motley crew.

Considered singly, and without reference to their forbears, there are several books of Hewlett, one of this kind, one of that, and one of a third, and so on, that impress you as fine things. Consider all his books together, and you will find that the whole is not equal to the sum of the parts. Taken all together the books of Hewlett do not seem to have a total value that corresponds to the sum of the values they have individually. And that is, not so much that he has repeated himself as that he has achieved so many different kinds of effects that it is intimated to you all cannot be effects of his own imagining. From one point of view this diversity of effects might bespeak breadth, as it surely does versatility, but unfortunately the thought that Hewlett is a chameleon will obtrude itself.

It is more grateful to consider the individual excellences of this story and that. "How Sandro Botticelli saw Simonetta in the Spring" is as fresh and tender as it was on its appearance in *Earthwork out of Tuscany* a generation ago. Story and setting and emotion and words are in complete accord here; it would be another thing entirely told in the large and luxuriant way of some of his later tales. Tragic as it is, it remains an idyl, an idyl that could be rendered perfectly only through the medium of such an April atmosphere as it has.

Turn from this fragile episode to his greatest, if not his most perfect achievement, *The Queen's Quair* (1904). It is a flaunting, challenging book, dealing royally with a great theme, blazoning forth the glory and the shame and the pity of the crowning years of Mary of Scotland. Crucial times for England and Scotland, great issues and great lives are its material. A host of characters pass before us as in the historical romances of Scott. And, here, for once, we may, without danger to Hewlett, compare character for character, Mary and Ruthven and Murray and Morton, with Scott's portrayals of these same royalties and makers of royalties, as we find them in *The Abbott* (1820).

The Queen's Quair begins with Mary in France on the eve of her departure to Scotland and ends with her imprisonment at Loch Leven. All her turns of fortune are chronicled, and at each turn Hewlett presents us with an analysis of her motives and of the temperament that induced the motives. We see Mary in armor, in her mood of dare-devil boy, afield against the Gordons; among her ladies-in-waiting and her pages; bearing herself royally in council; carrying herself with careless calm amid the terrors of the murders of Rizzio and Darnley; beaten and wretched under the mastery of Bothwell. We get to know her as we would a neighbor, thoroughly. And as she is drawn, so are all the other principals drawn, vividly and with personality. All are real creations done after the most careful study of historical documents. They are Hewlett's interpretations in the terms of romance of what history tells us the men and women were.

This characteristic of basic truthfulness, of truthfulness to the kind of fact, if not to actual fact of the story, as well as to the spirit of its time and place, distinguishes Hewlett among romancers. You feel that this is the very life of the time, be it of the Florence of the Renaissance or the Scotland of the Reformation. And the past is revived for us, not only by the study of history, but by the study of the contemporary documents that are the sources of history. This devotion to basic fact leads to what is in fiction a weakness. Hewlett, breaking the old canon that an historical character must not be the central figure of a romance, will make a Botticelli or a Richard I his hero, or, as here, a Mary a heroine, and you, reading, will wonder, "Is this episode in the story an episode from the life of the painter or the Crusader or fated Queen, or is it only the kind of episode that must have happened in that life?" When you so wonder the illusion of the story, as a story, vanishes, and you are left doubting and dissatisfied. If you can regard *The Queen's Quair* and *Richard Yea and Nay* (1900) as studies in the romance of history, and believe them, like Carlyle's, substantially true, all is well; if you do not care whether they are true or not they become merely stories to you, and all is well; and if you regard them as symbols of the times and places they present, all is well. But if you are driven to the histories to find out whether this incident or that is true you feel that your author is not fair with you. Yet, somehow, here in *The Queen's Quair*, you must read on, and in a few pages you forget all perplexity in the gallantry of high deeds.

A far greater offense by the author to his reader is the irony of the close of *Richard Yea and Nay*. The analysis of *The Queen's Quair* is taken as the Normans took the minstrel's recital in hall of a story they knew well, but were interested in because of fresh presentation and fresh interpretation. That the selling of her body by Jehane to the goatish old chief of the Assassins should not in the end save Richard, but should bring about his death—this is rasping irony. And irony is dangerous to romance.

Happily there is no such irony in *The Forest Lovers*. It deals with high, old, impossible things, this romance of the New Forest of the thirteenth century, or, rather, with the wonderful things that only such a place and time could make remotely possible. Here are young life, piping times, romance at the flood.

The great following of readers Hewlett won to himself by *The Forest Lovers* longed for another romance cast in the same mould, but their longing was in vain. *Richard Yea and Nay* was of different composition and form, with too much history in it for such readers, and *The Queen's Quair* of still different composition and form, with entirely too much history in it. And both ended wrong. Certain tales of *New Canterbury Tales* (1901), "The Countess Alys," "Peridore and Paravail," "Saint Gervase of Plessy"; and "The Heart's Key" from *Fond Adven-*

tures (1905), were somewhat in the loved manner, but they were none of them *Forest Lovers* in little. When Hewlett did try to write another such long story in *The Song of Renny* (1911) it was too tragic for those whom *The Forest Lovers* had delighted; and, besides, the old magic of atmosphere was lacking. It did not afford that escape from reality which was perhaps the greatest charm of *The Forest Lovers*.

It is the quality of epic, not of the quality of romance, that is about his retellings of the Scandinavian stories. They turn on character rather than on incident; their people, despite their distance in time and place from the world we know are subjected to many such moral judgments as we subject ourselves to; their themes seldom offer us escape from the problems of our daily lives; in them no voice of "bulbul" drugs us with dreams of paradise.

The picaresque stories, such as *The Fool Errant* (1905) and *Brazenhead the Great* (1911) have their excellences. They have verve, go, swing, vigor, bravery. They are eminently readable, but like so many sorts of make-believe, they but momentarily content us; and they do not remain in memory.

The novels of nineteenth century life are *The Stooping Lady* (1907); the trilogy *Halfway House* (1908), *Open Country* (1909), and *Rest Harrow* (1910); *Mrs. Lancelot* (1912) and its sequel, *Bendish* (1913); *The Little Iliad* (1915); *Love and Lucy* (1916); and *Mainwaring* (1920). These books are not only all more or less Meredithian in style and attitude, but all, or nearly all, are like Meredith's novels in that many of their characters are obviously based on real men and women of their epoch. Senhouse, the gypsying botanist, is of known originals, but, unlike most of the characters made over from life, a composite of three men. There is something of the nature and something of the experience of R. L. S. in Senhouse, though, of course, not so much as in Woodseer in *The Amazing Marriage* (1895) of Meredith. The habits of Senhouse in introducing plants to England from Carpathians or Caucasus are those of a well-known nobleman who was long a concern to the Foreign

Office. The third original is Hewlett himself, whose doctrine of salvation by poverty, Senhouse preaches and practices.

Tom Moore, Samuel Rogers and Leigh Hunt appear under their own names in *Bendish,* just as do Steele and Addison and Swift in *Esmond.* Bendish himself has many likenesses to an even more distinguished poet of their time. Gervase Poore is harder to identify with his prototype in life. Hewlett's criticism reveals him a reader of memoirs, which, one is led to suppose, are the origins of some of these novels.

There are those who hold that the Senhouse trilogy presents the best work of Hewlett. That is not, as I have said, my belief. That best I find in episodes and essays of *Earthwork out of Tuscany,* in certain tales like "Madonna of the Peach-Tree," and in *The Queen's Quair;* and, outside of fiction, in the book of travels, *The Road in Tuscany.* There have been other authors than Hewlett who have fallen in love with a heroine of theirs, but there is no other author I know of who has been so completely bewitched by a heroine of his own creation as Hewlett by Sanchia. This unconventional young lady does not appear in *Halfway House,* at the end of which Mary Middleham, Mr. Germaine's widow, goes away with Senhouse, having escaped the toils of Tristram Duplessis.

In *Open Country* Hewlett goes back into the past of Senhouse, invents a place there for Sanchia, and makes them the best of friends, and, had they been willing to admit it, lovers. When Hewlett wrote *Halfway House,* he had, of course, no thought of Sanchia. As she developed in his mind she became an ideal. Senhouse, of course, was as largely Hewlett himself as either of the other men that went to the making of that prodigy. It was, therefore, impossible that Hewlett could be happy unless his two pets came together finally. So in *Rest Harrow* he parts Mary Germaine and Senhouse, marries her to her old admirer; and then proceeds to separate Sanchia from Neville Ingram, whose mistress she had become. Ingram does not immediately propose marriage to Sanchia on his wife's death, and she leaves his house. In the end, in a scene in which Hewlett's sense of humor fails him, Senhouse and Sanchia come together for good and all.

Hewlett tells us in "The Crystal Vase," one of the essays of *In a Green Shade* (1921): "I have often wished that I could write a novel in which, as mostly in life, thank goodness, nothing happens." He goes on to say that Jane Austen almost did such a novel, and that Dorothy Richardson has done it. Hewlett himself could never write a story in which nothing happens. He must have the surprising, the extravagant, the romantic, sometimes almost the absurd. There is plenty of gossip about as to the originals of *Mainwaring,* but, even though parts of it are from life, knowledge of such actuality fails to lessen your wonder at the amazing situation of the political leader and his wife, who chose to be the servant in her own house rather than the lady of it. And Senhouse is, often, dangerously near the absurd. Hewlett recognizes this, but he so admires the man that he almost persuades himself and his readers that the gypsy philosopher is not the fool of his own theories.

Love and Lucy (1916) is variations on the old theme of the man who fell in love with his wife. Elsewhere Hewlett has expressed his belief that only so can human beings fall in love. Instinct is what brings man and woman together, and in the intimacy of daily life they may, if they are fortunate, fall in love with one another. The hero of *Love and Lucy,* James Adolphus Macartney, is but a latterday variation on Mr. Lancelot of *Mrs. Lancelot.* There is not a great deal of such duplication in Hewlett, however, because he has some dramatic power and does not have to rely on autobiography for the creation of his men.

What Hewlett has not imitated from Meredith is epigram and chorusing. His cleverness does not take the form of good things said by people who never could have said them; and there is little burden of comment on the happenings of his stories. The view of life held by the story-teller cannot help but be there, but he does not stress that view. People are the prey of their impulses, and are more than likely to make fools of themselves. He likes them none the less for that, and particularly approves his women, when, like poor Molly Lovel, of "The Duchess of Nona," they happen to be "handsome fools." He does not go so far as to applaud these "handsome fools" above all other women, but he does applaud women who are lovely and meek. He also applauds women who, like Sanchia, are lovely and long-suffering but not meek. Hewlett is cynical often, and firmly convinced not only that what will be will be, but that generally it does not matter overmuch; that life is taking the good and the bad together.

He grew more sententious after he had turned sixty, and, in his essays especially, indulged in "commentary upon life." "I hope I have neither prejudice nor afterthought; I know that I have, as we say now, neither axe to grind nor log to roll. Politics! None. I want people to be happy; and whether Mr. George make them so, or the Trade Unions, whether Christ or Sir Conan Doyle, it's all one to me. I have my pet nostrums, of course. I believe in Poverty, Love, and England, and am convinced that only through the first will the other two thrive. I want men to be gentlemen and women to be modest. I want men to have work and women to have children."

So much for his attitude toward life. Now for his attitude toward art: "If I am to deal with life it must be in my own way, for there's no escape from one's character. I may be a good poet or a bad one—that's not for me to say; but I am a poet of sorts. Now a poet does not observe like a novelist. He does not indeed necessarily observe at all until he feels the need of observation. Then he observes, and intensely. He does not analyse, he does not amass his facts; he concentrates. He wrings out quintessences; and when he has distilled his drops of pure spirit he brews his potion. Something of the kind happens to me now, whether verse or prose be the Muse of my devotion. A stray thought, a chance vision moves me; presently the flame is hissing hot. Everything then at any time observed and stored in the memory which has relation to the fact is fused and in a swimming flux. Anon, as the Children of Israel said to Moses, 'There came forth this calf.'"

To some this will mean only that Hewlett did not prepare so carefully for his stories or for his verses as he should. Such will say the confession explains the lack of plan, of fundamental brainwork underlying his writing. It is to be remembered, however, that this is only one saying of his, a saying about one kind of work. Very different was his mood, very different his methods of composition, in *The Queen's Quair*, of which he wrote that he had read all the state papers relating to Mary, and of which the architectonics could not obviously have been arrived at spontaneously during composition. Then he believed that book to be an "illumination of history from within," and that "The illumination of history from within is, in fact, the business which I make bold to believe at this hour my business—and to that I intend to devote what life remains to me." That was written in 1904. The intention was not fulfilled. Hewlett was a man of moods.

One thing, however, he always clung to, the necessity of form. In *Earthwork out of Tuscany* he said: "Form is your safeguard. Lay hold on form; you are as near to Essence as may be here below." One thing, too, he has always practiced and that is a decorative style. There is little doubt that it is the man himself, of the very texture of him, not plastered on the outside of his stories. And yet it is often elaborated too far; we long for the relief simplicity would bring. We feel that Hewlett, like the Rossettis, must have made lists of "stunning words," gathering them from his reading of poetry and the old romances. At his best he uses them very well, with a right feeling for rhythm as well as for color; at his worst he uses them lusciously, allowing them to burden the rhythm of his prose.

It is as a teller of tales that Hewlett is most to be valued, of such short tales as are to be found in *Little Novels of Italy, New Canterbury Tales, Fond Adventures* and *The Spanish Jade*, all work of the decade 1898-1908, when their author was in his late thirties and his forties. These tales are by no means all of an equality of accomplishment, but there is not one of them that is not gallantly told and not one of so little inherent interest that having been begun it can be put aside unfinished by the reader with keen human sympathies. There are one or two of them that are decorations chiefly, groups of figures like those on tapestries, and none of them without decorative features, but all are concerned with characters of flesh and blood.

"All romantic invention," Hewlett believes, "proceeds from people or from atmosphere," and that belief is founded on his own practice. Character and atmosphere underlie all his stories and give them a substance often wanting in romance. It is his girls that are most memorably delineated, as was to be expected of so thoroughgoing a Meredithian. "Literature being a man's art," he says, "is at its best and also at its worst, in its dealing with women." That is as it may be, but there is no doubt that Hewlett is at his best in painting their portraits. His gallery of these recalls his master's, and invites comparison with that crowded assemblage. That you can think of the two groups together without the total effacement of Hewlett's is a high compliment to him. There is a higher compliment, though, that honesty compels one to pay, and that is that the painting of the pupil is worthy of the master.

It is a pleasure just to list them, for the "sweet symphonies" of their names: Simonetta, Isoult, Vanna, Ippolita, Selvaggia, Alys, Paravail, Jehane, Mary, Aurelia, Virginia, Hermia, Manuela, Sanchia, Stangerd, Stanvor, Helena! That's not the half of them, but it must do. It is a keener pleasure to let the names conjure up image after image as one cons them over—if you can. I have named those that quickly rose in consciousness as I went over the list of the stories. More images throng round me as I think of the heroines of Meredith, but from no other writer than Meredith do I recall more than from Hewlett.

If Hewlett had command of all the powers of the novelist or romancer in as large measure as he has this of portraiture of girls he would be a great writer indeed. Unfortunately he has not. There is in almost every one of his stories a flaw in the telling, in the credibility of some incident. Even "Madonna of the Peach-Tree" does not go scatheless, treasure after its kind that it is in atmosphere and temper and writing. "How Sandro

Botticelli saw Simonetta in the Spring" is a perfect idyl. *The Queen's Quair*, too, completely realizes its intention. It is an historical novel of such knowledge and understanding and insight, of such structure and progression of incident and characterization and style, of such artistic execution, of such power over the emotions, that it gives pause to you, having finished it, as only a great book can, as perhaps one other handling only of its heroic theme has been able to do, the *Bothwell* (1874) of Swinburne. And, after all, a group of romantic tales not to be paralleled in any other writer of his time; a perfect idyl; and a historical novel that is a true "illumination of history from within," are not so slight an equipment for the voyage down the years.

CHAPTER XXI

H. G. WELLS, JOURNALIST

WELLS owns proudly that his writing is not concerned with life as it is. It is in his preface to Swinnerton's *Nocturne* (1917) that he makes confession: "Personally I have no use at all for life as it is, except as raw material. It bores me to look at things unless there is also the idea of doing something with them. I should find a holiday, doing nothing amidst beautiful scenery, not a holiday, but a torture. In the books I have written, it is always about life being altered I write, or about people developing schemes for altering life. And I have never once 'presented life.' My apparently most objective books are criticisms and incitements to change."

If you could take Wells (1866-   ) at his word it would not be necessary to say much about him in a book that is concerned with literature. That large part of his writing which is tracts could be left to the sociologists and that which is entertainment could be filed away for those tired hours and sleepless nights all of us must face now and then. But despite the words just quoted there is another part of Wells. "All Gaul is divided into three parts." There is the part represented by *Thirty Strange Stories* (1898), which made him known to America. There is the part represented by *Anticipations of the Reaction of Mechanical and Scientific Progress upon Human Life and Thought* (1901), with its prophecy of airplanes, its advocacy of a world-state and its belief in the perfectibility of man. There is the part represented by *Love and Mr. Lewisham* (1900), *Kipps* (1905) and *The History of Mr. Polly* (1910). These stories, the first and second largely "presented," despite the denial of Wells; and the third with a decided Lockean element

404

in it, are made out of the only life that Wells knows about by having lived it without self-consciousness, the life of a section of the lower middle-class in London, suburban London, and the outer suburbs of London in Kent.

The fantastic stories and the pictures of future states are all "gotten up" out of the study and reading of Wells. The stories of the so-called "big issues" of the day, from *Tono-Bungay* (1909) to *The Secret Places of the Heart* (1922) are "gotten up," out of a limited experience, by reportorial methods. Wells is not a storehouse of experiences and observations of case on case of such situations as that of *Marriage* (1912). He knows one such case in his circle of acquaintances; he studies that case very carefully; he gathers together all the "stuff" he can about it; and he "writes it up" with all that energy and verve that make him the "star-reporter" of our day.

In some of his other stories on "big issues" Wells has apparently followed that other device of the reporter in subjecting himself to the experiences he wishes to write about. In this place and that, in reading *Ann Veronica* (1909), for instance, you feel that here is a record gained not casually in the natural way of life, but "gone out after" and "gotten" as a reporter "gets" an assignment. Anyone who has been through the journalistic mill will recognize the signs of the method. A result is, of course, information "secured" in a hurry, not knowledge gained as lasting knowledge must be gained, slowly as the progress of the year.

Even a slight analysis of the plots of his stories indicates how narrow has been the experience of Wells. If you list the number of them that have some pretensions to literature as fifteen, you will find that more than half of them present one or another phase of the same story. The coming of a woman between a man and his life-work is almost the whole story in *Love and Mr. Lewisham, The New Machiavelli* (1911), *Marriage, The Passionate Friends* (1913) and *The Secret Places of the Heart*. I do not say it is almost the whole book, but almost "the whole story." In each one of the books other than the first-named, there are large shovelings in of passing issues of the hour, of "ideas," of propaganda, sometimes to the extent of half the number of words of the book. In five others of the fifteen the coming of a woman between a man and his ambition is part of the problem of the story: *Tono-Bungay, Ann Veronica, The History of Mr. Polly, The Research Magnificent* (1915) and *Joan and Peter* (1918). Other situations are dominant in *Kipps, The Wife of Sir Isaac Harmon* (1914), *Bealby* (1915), *Mr. Britling Sees It Through* (1916) and *The Undying Fire* (1920).

Of the three books of Wells that count most as literature *Love and Mr. Lewisham, Kipps* and *The History of Mr. Polly,* this cardinal observation of life by Wells is almost the whole theme of one, has no appreciable place in another and is responsible for a part of the action in the third. It may be that advocates of Wells will say that in his preoccupation with this theme he is reflecting life as he has observed it. Their observation may confirm his and it may even be true as a general proposition that fifty percent of men have to chose between a woman and their hoped for way of life. Is that, though, a reason why a novelist should write again and again on one theme? Selectiveness is at the very basis of art. Wells has, of course, shifted the scene from one story to another, and changed somewhat the characters, but he has not been able to vary his situations or his people very much.

The truth would seem to be that Wells had had since boyhood little time for living or for the observation of life. He is a man who is always working, always acquiring information. He has never once since youth, apparently, loafed and invited his soul. Wells himself approached a realization of the necessity of leisure when he wrote "nothing done in a hurry, nothing done under strain, is really well-done." Yet in that other sentence, quoted at the start of this essay, "I should find a holiday, doing nothing amidst beautiful scenery, not a holiday, but a torture," he reveals his essential nervousness, a nervousness that approaches the fidgety. That association of the "raw material" life, with which a novelist begins, to what one sees on a holiday is a little inept. If you interpret the passage to imply a similitude between "beautiful scenery" and "life" you will be driven to graver wonder. Wells has not been able to see much that is beautiful in the life that has passed before him in England. It has always had ugliness in it for him, and wrong-doing that must be quarreled with. To Wells this attitude of his seems a virtuous one, and not just one he happens to find fun in holding. He does not deny for a moment that he allows moral purpose to interfere with the art of the novel. He glories in allowing it so to interfere. He does not at all mind being dubbed a journalist because his chief concern is with the issues of the hour and not with essential things. "I would rather be called a journalist than an artist," he writes Henry James, apologizing rather defiantly for the satire of James in *Boon* (1915).

Wells, doubtless, would welcome one saying that there is no mellowness in him. Mellowness, he might say, was but precedent to decay, or at least to age. And he, Wells, is yet unripened, and triumphantly young. The unrest of Wells has, however, never seemed to me to be the unrest of youth. It has always seemed to me to be rather the unrest of the "outsider." That largely. And, partly, the unrest of the reformer. In America it is difficult for us to understand how a man born as Wells was in England feels toward the system and the ruling caste of which he was so manifestly outside, both governmentally and socially. Here we are all, in the older English sense, hopelessly middle-class, but since we do not recognize that fact it is of no importance in our lives.

Wells has told us, with the candor so characteristic of the man, of his humble parentage and of the condition of his people. The son of a shopkeeper and professional cricketer, and one who himself served as a draper's assistant, his clear head and tireless application won him a way into London University. He did brilliant work in science there but he never went on to Oxford or Cambridge. The fact that his mother had been in service, and that his father's father had been gardener to a noble family made the "outsideness" of Wells the more marked.

That Browning had a forbear a butler, that Lamb's father was

a servant, did not set either against the social order to which
he was born. Wells reacted differently. His appreciation of the
fact that he was "outside" did not impel him to try to get
"inside." It impelled him to make over the social system so that
the rule might be by an aristocracy of intellect rather than, as
it was in England until recently, by an aristocracy of birth. Of
course, there were other reasons, his pedagogic temperament, his
efficiency-expert's bias, but there are references in his books, particularly in *Tono-Bungay,* that show his sense of being an outsider was a main reason.

Wells felt the old system was weakening the manhood of the
country, from aristocracy to peasantry, that industrialism with its
"wage-slaves" had cost the commonalty dear. He still feels in
the foundations of him the zeal and the confidence of the reformer. He has the reformer's "divine discontent," but he
possesses, too, another attribute that is unfortunately often to be
found in the reformer, that of being a "Meddlesome Matty."
"It bores me," he says, "to look at things unless there is also the
idea of doing something with them." He likes to set things
straight for the sake of setting them straight as well as for the
betterment of life. He does not realize that the man who wants
to better things is not necessarily superior morally to the man who
does not. The man who wants to better things may be actuated
merely by the pleasure he has in that kind of a chore. It may
be advantageous to society to have such a bettering man about,
but that does not make him more moral than his neighbor who
does not have pleasure in that kind of chore. As Yeats sees it:

> "The Light of Lights
> Looks always on the motive, not the deed,
> The Shadow of Shadows on the deed alone."

Wells grows less sure, however, as he grows older, that he is
always right, and he becomes less sure of the perfectibility of the
human race. As he has had always the courage of his convictions we can follow his change of belief from book to book. No
writer of our time has so largely conducted his education in

public. The convinced Fabian of the nineties is less sure than the partially disillusioned advocate of the Collective Will of the twenties. In *The Passionate Friends* Wells was still of his early belief that education through schools and through pamphleteering was a cure-all. He is less certain, though still hopeful of that, in *The Undying Fire*.

Once, in *The New Machiavelli*, Wells seems to have had a momentary sympathy with the party of tradition, even if he never would allow any authority to tradition. "Life is rebellion, or nothing" is his slogan. Inevitably tradition revenges itself on Wells for his scorn of it. He cannot escape the pitfalls of those who neglect tradition. Had any considerable proportion of his knowledge of life or of his standards been handed down to him through his family he would not trust so wholly in education by pedagogues. That schooling is a panacea is so old a cry in America that we take it for what it is worth. Helpful as it is when it disseminates new-won knowledge of immediate use to society, and helpful as it is when it hands down the history of what has been, to prepare men for the living of what is and what shall be, we know such education has very definite limitations. We know that the home and its traditions are more influential than the school even among a forward-looking people such as we are. We know that the school cannot compensate for that which the home without traditions fails to give. We know that unless we can perpetuate by all the agencies, home, church and school, the best of what has been, the future is indeed uncertain. Wells is so struck by the evil of today that he cannot realize there are many valuable things of today in danger of being lost to the world.

It would serve no purpose to discuss further the value as tracts of the writing of Wells. It is, perhaps, worth while in passing to point out that his tracts are not always of much value as tracts even, that for all his sincerity and well-informedness he is but guessing his way on like so many others with "the rapture of the forward view." I have dwelt on this averseness to tradition of Wells for another reason. That is to emphasize the old truism that tradition has a good deal to do with literature.

It is a truth too little insisted upon, that a writer who has made his story or poem, his essay or play, ten per cent original, is very original indeed. If ten per cent of any writing is its author's very own, in the sense that it has never been before, that author has struck a new note in literature. Nine-tenths of all writing must be a re-saying, at the best on the note of a new personality, at the worst on the note of a new age, of what has been said before. It is folly, then, for an author to think that he can reject what has been handed down to him. Wells has not, Wells could not, for all his declarations. His material, so far as life itself goes, is just what all men have had to write about. He differs in his treatment of it from writers to whom writing is an art: from the realists, by refusing to "present" it as it is, to be loyal to life in depicting it; from the romantics, by refusing to color it with that strangeness and wonder that are in all legend and in all haunting places.

The so-called romances of science of Wells, those suggested by Jules Verne, his stories of eras, golden or gray, yet to be, are not romances at all; they are fantasias. They are written with differing intentions: a few are just tall stories; others are pleas for Utopias; and one at least, *The World Set Free* (1914), was an accurate forecasting of certain phases of the World War that so shortly followed its publication. Wells is, then, to a degree, a true prophet, in the sense that what he predicted has come to pass. To some people he has been what Emerson calls "a prophet of the soul," one who brightens the world with his sayings. He is taken very seriously by some such followers, one going to the length of declaring that Wells has brought "the age of materialism definitely to an end." It is through what he calls his "series of books upon social-religious and political questions" that it is believed such a consummation has been reached. These books fall wholly outside the field of discussion of this study of the novel, but similar topics force their way into his stories, and compel at least a word of comment.

Other men who belong to literature by a part of their writing have had a like failing. No novelist with a purpose, however, before Wells, save George Eliot alone, has been regarded as a prophet. Her later work, *Felix Holt* (1866) and *Daniel Deronda* (1876) especially, were regarded by many as almost inspired. Among novelists not given to novels with a purpose George Meredith is almost the only one ranked with the prophets. Most of the English writers of the past hundred years who have been so ranked have been essayists. Matthew Arnold was a minor prophet, as was Macaulay. Macaulay, a better writer than Wells, is one who, in his fidelity and easy effectiveness and bludgeoning power, is in a way a forerunner of him. Ruskin, like Arnold, is still an influence, if no longer quite a prophet. Carlyle and Emerson, still have honor even in their own countries, yet neither is the prophet he was to his own generation. They live as George Eliot does, not as prophets but as writers, often memorable for readings of life but just as often for the moments of living they have caught in imperishable words.

Rosamund Marriott-Watson attempted a book of *Great Thoughts from H. G. Wells* (1912). It was a selection intended in all kindliness but in effect it is unkind. It is not "great thoughts" it reveals but hit or miss observations, very few of which are even well put.

There can be very few "readings of life" in Wells, because "readings of life" are possible only to men who ponder about life, who give themselves leisure to track things out, who are curious about life. Wells is not of these. What he is after is not to see life as it is, to understand it, but to change it. He assumes it is bad and tries to make it better. No one doubts his sincerity or his high aim. Nor his well-informedness. There is not, I suppose, anywhere in the world, "a better informed man" than Wells. Our American phrase exactly fits the man. He is in no sense a scholar; there is no field of learning or research in which he is an expert. Yet there is no other man who comes to mind that could do so monumental a tract as *The Outline of History* (1920), nor any other man for that matter who could so ingenuously own his hope of moulding all human thought anew with a book. One wonders whether Wells is not after all the simple soul his Kipps is. His belief in the efficacy of print is childlike. "Anything wrong with anything?" he asks himself. "If there is, I'll write a book about it. That will make it better." In his own simplicity of heart he believes the world simple, too. And maybe he is right.

To return to literary matters. It is difficult to stick to them, they have so little part in Wells. Does he tell a story well? Yes, fairly well. Has he humor? Yes, a little. Has he style? No. Has he power of character portrayal? Some, but not much.

There is Aunt Susan in *Tono-Bungay*, the one portrait of distinction in all his interminable writing. There are Mr. Lewisham and Mrs. Lewisham and the homely girl in the laboratory. There is Chaffery too. These four from *Love and Mr. Lewisham* are well drawn, though they have not the life of Aunt Susan. There are Kipps and Ann Pornick and Helen Walsingham and Chitterlow from *Kipps*, three of them done in Wells's way, and Chitterlow pure Dickens. There are Mr. Polly and Uncle Pentstemon and Uncle Jim and the fat landlady in *The History of Mr. Polly;* and there might have been the Red-Headed Girl. These are the characters that matter in Wells.

There is hardly need to mention the heroes and heroines of the books on "the big issues." Those books already read like day before yesterday's newspaper, and when their issues were new ideas the leading characters were but mouthpieces. *Tono-Bungay* and *Ann Veronica* are the best of them. What Wells regards as the emotional close of the first is, however, so stuffily and humorlessly sentimental that it turns banal and you try to forget it in ribald laughter. And *Ann Veronica* that made so pretty a flutter in its day is now but yesterday's revolt of the daughters. Day before yesterday's was *The Woman Who Did* (1895). The novels of that revolt go all the way back to *Jane Eyre* (1847), which was that, but a good deal more.

One hero, though you call him Capes, or Remington, or Trafford, talks his way through the series of these topical stories. He is Mr. Lewisham blossomed out, and less of a man for the blossoming. There are reappearing heroines, too, though there is more variety to them than to the heroes. Margaret in *The New Machiavelli* is but Helen Walsingham of *Kipps* in another guise. Marjorie in *Marriage* is but Ann Veronica having her way as wife as she had previously had her way as daughter.

"Gotten up stuff" burdens Wells painfully in these novels of the "big issues." *Marriage* has the heaviest load. It is at the close of the story you find the most of it. After Marjorie has driven her husband to commercialize his science so that they may live as she would Trafford tires of it all and tells her he is going off to Labrador for the winter to think things out. Marjorie goes, too. There are detailed pictures of an arctic winter, well enough done but with no suggestion that Wells has himself endured such hardships or has looked on such desolate beauty. The spendthrift is reformed by playing squaw to her husband, by saving his life. The end presupposes that the reconciliation will stand the strain of London seasons to come.

The Passionate Friends is a tract against jealousy—that among other things. That Wells should believe it worth while to attack that fundamental passion reveals the simplicity of soul in the man to which I have referred before. It reveals, too, his courage. There is nothing he will not attack, and no defeat leaves him daunted. In *The Undying Fire* (1920), however, there creeps in a note of weariness: "I talk. . . . I talk. . . . and then a desolating sense of reality blows like a destroying gust through my mind, and my little lamp of hope goes out." It is Job Huss talking but the words are the words of Wells.

There is little evidence in the writing of Wells that he has been influenced by Tolstoi, but his general attitude toward the relation of novels to art and life is not far from Tolstoi's. Samuel Butler has been an influence on him, in little things as well as great. The escape by balloon in *Erewhon* (1872), for instance, is repeated in the escape by airplane in *Tono-Bungay* (1909). Wells was a close and loyal friend to Gissing when Gissing needed friends but that friendship brought about no discipleship. Wells had been more of an artist, perhaps, had he heeded his elder's example. Meredith, rather strangely, Wells has admired, particularly *One of Our Conquerors* (1891), but unless the earlier concern with big business inspired the choice of that theme for *Tono-Bungay,* there is no sign of imitation following the admiration.   Dickens is an obvious influence, especially in the books of lower middle class life.   Huxley, under whom Wells sat in London University, was a greater influence over him than any novelist; and the Fabian Society and the reading it led Wells to was an even stronger influence than Huxley.   There is no evidence anywhere in Wells that he is familiar with English poetry or essay or drama, or that he has read widely in the great novelists of the past.

Wells is a man made out of his own time if ever there was one.   And as he is of that time that time has responded to him and acclaimed him.   His admirers, too, have been not only the general public but portions of the intelligentsia, and many of his fellow writers of a younger set.   These last have been led into this admiration, largely, I think, by the optimism of the man over the possibilities of tomorrow.   What they regard as his practice of Tolstoian precept is, undoubtedly, also an element in their appreciation of him.   Tolstoi said that a great writer "should stand on the level of the highest life-conception of his time." There they believe Wells has stood, and therefore he is their prophet.   Such a fealty is a pleasant phase of human nature but it has been fraught with disastrous consequences to the writing of those offering it.   He has steered many an unfortunate away from art and into the writing of tracts.

Mr. Britling Sees It Through has had the greatest popularity among the books of Wells and as great an immediate popularity as any English book has known.   It is a popularity that has passed with the World War, of the reaction to which it was a record.   Such, indeed, has already been the fate of most of his novels.   Only *Love and Mr. Lewisham* and *Kipps* and *The History of Mr. Polly* bear rereading with any degree of patience. These are what Wells has to rate him.   And these give him now the standing of a lesser Gissing in whom there is a streak of Locke.

CHAPTER XXII

OF ARNOLD BENNETT, HARD WORK AND BEAUTY

AN infinite capacity for hard work has made Arnold Bennett (1867-   ) the artificer of seventy books. It has made him a skilled craftsman in the construction of long stories, short-stories and causeries; and a craftsman only less skilled in the construction of plays, travels, criticism and manuals of self-improvement. It has made him the author of *The Old Wives Tale* (1908) and of the trilogy, *Clayhanger* (1910), *Hilda Lessways* (1911) and *These Twain* (1916). It has made him, that is, in at least four books, as much of a genius as an infinite capacity for hard work can make any man; and, through the sixty-odd together, the most successful tradesman of letters of our day.

Bennett is of the frankest of men and of the most arrogant. The frankness appears in all his writing, that which he would have creative and that which is critical. The arrogance appears chiefly in his critical writing; it would be out of place in the stories that are intended as art, and Bennett is resolute in suppressing himself when his art demands that suppression. It is in this suppression of himself that he so differs from Wells, the rival in productivity with whom he is so generally bracketed. Bennett is concerned to be an artist, as Wells is not, and Bennett is an artist in some of his books,—in so far as his native powers will permit. Bennett, of course, is not one of the originators; he is derivative, with a theory of selection of material derived from George Gissing, and a theory of attitude derived from George Moore and the French masters of George Moore, and a style derived from George Moore himself.

The frankness of the man is at its sublimest in *The Truth About An Author* (1903): "An author once remarked to me: 'I know enough. I don't read books, I write 'em.' It was a haughty and arrogant saying, but there is a sense in which it was true. Often I have felt like that: 'I know enough, I feel enough. If my future is as long as my past, I shall still not be able to put down the tenth part of what I have already acquired.' The consciousness of this, of what an extraordinary and wonderful museum of perceptions and emotions my brain was, sustained me many a time against the chagrins, the delays, and the defeats of the artistic career. Often have I said inwardly: 'World, when I talk with you, love you, and hate you, I condescend.' "

There is arrogance for you, but underneath a note of self satire. That note has sounded earlier in the book: " 'After all, it's nothing!' I said, with that intense and unoriginal humanity which distinguishes all of us. And in a blinding flash I saw that an author was in essence the same thing as a grocer or a duke." So, too, he avows in *A Great Man* (1904), of at least one kind of author, the concoctor of fantastic stories with fascinating plots. Such an author, of course, Bennett had proved himself, when this was written, by *The Grand Babylon Hotel* (1902). That he was a good deal more than that sort of author he had also proved by *Anna of the Five Towns* (1902) and *Leonora* (1903). *A Great Man* might, of course, be interpreted to mean he was utterly sure of himself. No one not so sure, it is arguable, would have dared the satire of a popular novelist, possible of identification with himself. And yet *A Great Man* is, I believe, a confession of humility, advertently or inadvertently, whatever else it may also be, a paying off of scores against others, let us say. The too great protestations, recurrent in his critical writing, about the infallibility of his judgments of literature, as those of a "creative artist," are confirmatory of his lack of confidence in his own achievement. The very fact that he has never been able, after much experimentation, to find a way of writing of his own, either in form of story or in style, is of course an acknowledgment that such humility would be justifiable.

In *Books and Persons* (1917) Bennett scornfully hustles *The London Times* out of court because of its remarks on Trollope's methods of composition. *The Times,* it appears, said the confession of Trollope in his *Autobiography* (1883), that he obliged himself to write two hundred and fifty words every quarter of an hour was "a fatal admission." Bennett counters: "How can the confession affect his reputation? His reputation rests on the value of his novels, and not in the least on the manner in which he chose to write them. And his reputation is secure."

To all of which we agree, as well as, for the purposes of argument, to the next sentence: "Moreover, there is no reason why great literature should not be produced to time, with a watch on the desk." No "reason," we'll say, but ask what "great literature" has been so produced? If there were cases of "great literature" so produced Bennett would cite them as Exhibit A and Exhibit B and Exhibit C. Trollope has not produced "great literature," nor has Bennett himself, whose methods he has owned many times are as business-like as Trollope's. Bennett is, of course, instinctively if unconsciously, defending himself in defending Trollope.

The frankness of Bennett about his ways of composition should be hailed everywhere as a mordant of the sentimentality with which too many invest literature. No one should think the less of either Trollope or Bennett for their confessions. Yet there is no doubt that the confessions explain certain limitations of their writing. Both are deficient in exaltation, which is a thing of moments and cannot be forced to be present whenever a man sits down to write. It may, of course, visit the writer on revision, or it may not. And this habit of Bennett of doing so much per day or per week, and the determination of the length of the story before its writing is begun, may account, too, for the too great length of most of his books. *Clayhanger,* of the books intended as art, almost alone could not be improved by compression.

It may be that this addiction to too great space for the telling of his stories, this willingness to let "invented stuff" stand side by side with writing that is the result of experience, that is real creation, is a habit acquired in his years as a journalist. Journalism, in all its forms from the higher hackwork to reporting, has given English literature, in old time as today, a good many of its great men. Defoe comes out of journalism, and Dickens, and Kipling, to name but three prominent examples. Journalism is a good school for writers, but like other schools, it leaves those who pass through it with some habits that are better sloughed off. A man of greater originality than Bennett, a man less eager to apply this short-cut or that tour de force of journalism to literature, a man less inured to the habit of turning off his column a day, might have written less and better "stuff."

That Bennett might have done better "stuff" than he has if he had done less is debatable. With his experience and with his powers you may say it is a wonder that he does not amount to less than he does, as well that he does not amount to more than he does. When you think of his practice of composition, his regularity of output, his habit of printing every thought that has ever come to him, his preoccupation with the mercantile aspects of writing, you wonder that his work on the whole is not much poorer than it is. It is not, on the average, as thin as work done after so little forethought might be expected to be. And when you think of the knowledge of life that Bennett reveals in his best stories, his gift of characterization, his power over words, you wonder why these best stories should nearly all fall so far short of greatness as they do.

It is, perhaps, that Bennett has in many instances not given his stories time to grow in his mind. Concentrating himself on themes that seem good to him, he has developed them quickly and well, with sure craftsmanship, but without that completeness of life that comes after such preoccupation as Conrad confesses to in the writing of *Nostromo*. The material of the stories of Bennett seldom has richness; the stories do not seem to be written out of an abundance of experience; they impress you with no sense of reserve strength; he seems to have told you, when he is through, all he knows about his people and about life; he has apparently exhausted himself in each book. Repetitions occur in little things as in great. Adeline, the first fancy of the hero of his first novel, *A Man from the North* (1898), is very like Marguerite, the first beloved of the hero of *The Roll Call* (1919). The heroes of the two books, the one a law clerk and the other an architect, Richard Larch and George Edwin Cannon, are very like too, perhaps because both have in them so much of Arnold Bennett.

Observations on life are not very frequent in Bennett. He does not often intrude himself as chorus and comment on the doings of his characters. He would have his stories objective. And yet when he does comment, comment in one book is apt to be very like comment in another. He has observed, for instance, that old truth as to the effect of the arrival of men in a house full of women. As he puts it in *Leonora* (1903): "The social atmosphere was rendered bracing by this invasion of the masculine; every personality awoke and became vigilantly itself." Eight years later he wrote in *Hilda Lessways* (1911): "The entrance of George Cannon into the parlor produced a tumult greatly stimulating the vitality and the self-consciousness of all three women." A score of such parallels between the two books might be recorded, and similar parallels to these in a third and fourth book. If you double-columned Bennett in details you would find that he uses over again the simile of young girls escaping almost imperceptibly from the room where their parents are, as fox-terriers escape from the presence of their masters. He is very fond, too, of applying the "wild deer" and "fawn" metaphors to young girls, indulging in them insistently. As one considers these duplications, more particularly the many duplications of character, one wonders if Bennett has not had time to "put down the tenth part" of what he had "already acquired" in 1903.

The first book of Bennett does not overflow with experience and observation of life. It is a young man's book, a modest, unpretending account of the experiences of a youth from the pottery towns of Staffordshire during his first years in London. It is natural and interesting, but not very interesting and not alarmingly natural, as some of its successors were to be. The characterization is rather faint, and the writing lucid and unaffected. The story is simply and clearly told. The hero has a very tepid affair with a very nice girl, the niece of an old man employed in the law office in which Richard Larch is stenographer and clerk. They try to love each other, but he fails. When she sees he cannot love her she goes to relatives in San Francisco. Lonely, the young man marries an uneducated and unrefined girl who is a cashier in a restaurant. He gives up his "literary aspirations." *A Man from the North* is truly and neatly done, very much in the manner of Gissing.

The Grand Babylon Hotel (1902), its successor after an interval of four years, is a book made to sell. It is well made for that purpose. It still sells. It has had many successors, some out and out melodrama, like *The Gates of Wrath* (1903); others what Bennett calls "fantasias" like *Teresa of Watling Street* (1904); or "stories of adventure," like *The Card* (1911); and some "idyllic diversions," like *Helen with the High Hand* (1910). The books of this group, whether their scene is the Five Towns of Staffordshire where Bennett was born; the London of his journalistic days; or the Essex coast along which he has yachted: are of varying degrees of excellence in their kinds. They fall together only because all are potboilers. Some of them are very conscientiously written potboilers; many have moments of more than potboiling excellence. Two, at least, are altogether delectable, *The Card* and *Helen with the High Hand*.

One could make out a case for *The Card* as the most original of Bennett's books. It is light, very light, but with a new kind of lightness. It is full of surprises that are really surprises. It has an air all its own. It is hard and bright and glittering, to *The Old Wives Tale* what the mediæval fabliau was to its contemporary romance of epical sweep. *Helen with the High Hand* is light, too, and bright and trifling, but it is not so original. It is, like so many of the superficially cheerful but really cynical novels of today, of the school of Sterne. Bennett apparently excepts the author of *The Sentimental Journey* from the scorn he lavishes on most other English novelists, barring George Moore, since the days of Richardson.

These two, Richardson and Sterne, are approved because the one is so honored in France and the other so devoted to France. The label "made in France" goes just as far with Bennett as it does with George Moore. A chapter in *Things that Have Interested Me* (1921) explains "The Desire for France" that is a ruling passion of Bennett. That desire visited him when he was a clerk in his father's law office in the Five Towns; it dominated him in his London years; and it drew him across the Channel to live just as soon as his writing became such that he could do it where he would. Bennett had nine years of France, most of them in Paris, and yet France gives him the material of very little of his writing. And, curiously, the France he has drawn on most largely in his stories is the France of the Franco-Prussian War, in the third part of *The Old Wives Tale*. There are passages from the France of later years in *Sacred and Profane Love*, and in the misnamed *Paris Nights* (1913), which is something more than clever journalism, but not much more.

Your United States (1912) is of a similar order, but not so good a book. It goes up like a rocket with an account of New York so highly colored it outdoes even the description of that city by Wells in *The Passionate Friends* (1913). It comes down, the deadest of sticks, with Chicago and the rest of the "States." Bennett had a moment of insight when he guessed the "provincials" he saw sightseeing in Washington to be more typical of America than the mixed crowds of the great cities, but such moments of insight were seldom his in America. His prejudices prepared him to like us; he did like us; but his book about us has very little to do with anything but externalities, and on the whole it is not even fair reporting.

The London novel of his early years that is not fantastic I have already spoken of, *A Man from the North,* and I have spoken, too, of the satire, *A Great Man.* There are four other London stories, not fantastic, of recent years, *The Pretty Lady* (1918), *The Roll-Call* (1919) *Lilian* (1922), and *Riceyman Steps* (1923). Of these *The Roll-Call* has an interest that is not its intrinsically because its hero is George Edwin Cannon, the son of Hilda Lessways.

The Pretty Lady is a compound of boudoir and war-work and interior decoration, a sentimentalized scented thing, with parts of it quite in the manner of the *London Nights* (1895) of Arthur Symons. At the start the book is satirical of the privileged and unproductive gentleman of means, but it ends as an appreciation of him. Are we to understand that Hoape is made into another man by the war; or is Bennett, radical and laureate of the lower middle-class, discovered as the Englishman who, despite class prejudice, must love a lord?

Lilian harks back to *The Odd Women* (1893) of Gissing. It is the problem of the daughter left penniless by the death of a doting father and without a training that enables her to earn a living.

It is not in these London stories that the Bennett that counts is to be found. Nor is that Bennett to be found in the plays, pleasant as the most of them are, and picturesque as were the tableaux of *Milestones* (1912), the one of them which had a lease of life after its first production. Nor is he to be found in the criticism; nor in the books on the trade of letters, valuable as they are practically to those beginning to write, and as dispellers of moonshine about writing from those who read. Nor even in the chatty familiarity of *Things that Have Interested Me: Series I and Series II* (1921-1922). Nor, of course, in those books of self-improvement, like *How to Live on Twenty-Four Hours a Day* (1911), that make Bennett the Sir Arthur Helps of our day. *Friends in Council* (1847-59), by the bye, is listed in *Literary Taste: How to Form It: With Detailed Instructions for Collecting a Complete Library of English Literature* (1911), so there is little doubt of the parentage of such books of Bennett.

The Bennett that counts is the Bennett of the novels of the Five Towns. Here in this pottery district of Staffordshire Bennett was born; here he grew to manhood; and here he has found the material for all of his writing that the hardened reader can take seriously as art. One cannot help feeling about Bennett as one feels about Kipling. Had either lived longer in the place of his birth we would have had more writing of worth from him. There is a savor about Bennett's stories, short and long, of the Five Towns, that his books about other places have not. Only among the potsherds has his writing strong roots.

These hard rough people, who feel it just they should reap as they have sown, are his own people. Prejudiced, provincial, dourly Protestant, they have the right stuff in them. They have backbone, determination, fight, the will to get on. They are not lovable, perhaps, but they are dependable. They hate pretense, and an air of superiority, and injustice. Radicals in politics, with a tendency to communism as a political creed, they are strongly individualistic man by man. They are taciturn, a bit soreheaded, and subject to wild orgies at fairs and other times of license. We know such people well in America, with the changes they have suffered wherever they have gone since they came to New England three hundred years ago, and their very selves unchanged in factory towns, such as those on the Delaware, for instance, from Frankford to Trenton. Viking blood and a bleak climate, Dissent and industrialism, have made these Midlanders a very different people from the farm and village folk of the South of England.

Bone of their bone is Bennett, despite his desertion of them for the languors and art of Paris. His inherited Puritanism he has sloughed off, for worse and for better, but in most other respects he is still a man of the Five Towns. Like the Five

Towners Bennett is malicious; a little truculent; dry always, with flashes of wit now and then; and the very devil for work. In "The Death of Simon Fuge" he has revealed cultivation among them, and the designs on Wedgewood and other ware from Staffordshire are symbols of the taste existent there from older times. And yet Bennett tells us that he had seldom heard beauty discussed up to the time he was twenty-four. Perhaps it is his own experience he is recording as that of Twemlow in *Leonora,* who on his return to "Bursley" after years abroad is "astonished to find that beautiful which once he had deemed sordid and commonplace."

As John Davidson, in "A Ballad in Blank Verse on the Making of a Poet," realized the picturesqueness of industrialism in Glasgow, so Bennett realizes it in his Five Towns and records it in his Five Towns stories. The flares of the furnaces at night are a joy to him; and even the squalid ugliness revealed by daylight was "squalid ugliness on a scale so vast and overpowering it became sublime."

The two trilogies of Five Towns life are of different orders. *Anna of The Five Towns* (1902), *Leonora* (1903), and *Sacred and Profane Love,* (1905), now renamed *The Book of Carlotta,* are studies respectively of a young woman of the lower middle-class; of a woman of forty of the new rich; and of a woman of artistic temperament, from her youth to maturity. The other trilogy is two tellings of the love story of Edwin Clayhanger and Hilda Lessways, with reaches back into the separate lives of either, in *Clayhanger* (1910) and *Hilda Lessways* (1911); and of their life when, older, they have become husband and wife, in *These Twain* (1916). *Whom God Hath Joined* (1906) and *The Old Wives Tale* (1908) rest the total of these novels of the Five Towns at eight.

Tales of the Five Towns (1905), *The Grim Smile of the Five Towns* (1907), and *The Matador of the Five Towns* (1912) reduce to little more than a volume when you find that constituent short-stories are reprinted from one collection to another. With eight novels and this sheaf of short-stories the fiction that is a serious presentation of the life of the Five Towns totals at nine volumes, not a large proportion of his output of stories.

Anna, Leonora and Carlotta, the heroines of the first trilogy, are not typical products of the Five Towns, though Anna is less removed from the typical than the two others. Leonora is the charming woman of forty as she is anywhere, and Carlotta the artist in revolt against what she considers a dwarfing environment. *Sacred and Profane Love,* after an arresting onset, fades away into stuff gotten up in the way of journalism, in the London and Paris scenes. This petering out is of the same kind I referred to in considering *Your United States,* a corollary, it would seem, of his theory of so many pages a day.

In its quiet way *Anna of the Five Towns* is the best of the three but like all the early work of Bennett it is without depth. *Leonora* is very successful in the delineation of the heroine and her three girls. The men, as is usual in Bennett, are less firmly drawn, perhaps because men do not interest him nearly so much as do women. Only the young men fashioned in his own image and the old boys who are "cards" or "characters," and George Cannon, make much of an appeal to him. Arthur Twemlow, who brings back her youth to Leonora, is sentimentalized; and a great opportunity is missed in John Stanway. This manufacturer, baffled as *pater familias* by the younger generation, and driven to dishonesty and final disaster by the failure of his speculations, is so universal a character that had Bennett given him to us as completely as he has given us queer old Uncle Meshach he would have been sure of a place in the great portrait gallery of English fiction. Bennett fails to make him such a character, solely, I think, because he does not care much for him.

There are always present in the writing of Bennett signs of his study of George Moore, but there is no book in which there are so many such signs as *Leonora.* The fall of the sentences is often Moore's; words are used again and again as Moore uses them; and characters are presented and their motives analyzed in the very way of Moore. In *The Old Wives Tale* concern with the whole life-stories of Constance and Sophia frees Bennett, in large degree, from the influence of Moore. Moore has no more than a passing interest in old women, so he does not provide Bennett with models for the sisters after their days of youth. Bennett is interested in them, as he is in all that is human.

The Old Wives Tale impresses, like the novels of Richardson, by its very bulk. It is a study, as Bennett phrases it, of "What Life Is," and "What Life Is," as Bennett sees it, is a squalid thing, at least when one considers the life of the usual sort of person. One wonders if it is his belief that the mere numerical preponderance of the drab and monotonous and painful days blots out the days which are memorable for happiness or revelations or wonder, if life is the great grind rather than the great adventure. It would seem he did so believe and that what of sublimity he found in life was like that of the Five Towns, "squalid ugliness on a scale so vast and overpowering that it became sublime."

One doubts if Bennett, when he began *Clayhanger,* had any notion of it as the first volume of a trilogy. It seems that that use of it must have been an afterthought, from the standpoint of art an unfortunate afterthought. As it stands *Clayhanger* is incomplete,—perhaps deliberately so that he might have the fun of re-writing the situation from the woman's point of view. There is an unpleasant suggestion of a trick about the two versions, or at least of a device like that of the serial that ends a chapter with a situation that compels you to buy the next number of its magazine to see how things turn out. Were *Clayhanger* and *Hilda Lessways* and *These Twain* condensed into one novel we would have a better book than any one of the three. As they are *Hilda Lessways* is the only one of them a completely achieved work of art. It has not the depth of *Clayhanger,* it is not written out of such a fulness of knowledge as that first study of the situation; we have that curious feeling we so often have while reading Bennett, that there is no perspective in the novel, and no richness of experience in the mind and emotions out of which it was conceived. Only in *Clayhanger* is Bennett revealed as greater than his art; in all the other stories you wonder rather that the man you find back of the book could have done so well. To Bennett "the most precious of all faculties" is "the power to feel intensely," and yet human as he is the emotions revealed in his books are but a part of the many emotions man is heir to. Sex is, of course, the source of most of the emotions he is concerned with, and the desire for gain provocative of most of the rest. He considers, too, those that arise from the restlessness of youth, the thirst for adventure, the itch for notoriety, the lust of power. There is little concern with the emotions arising from nature or religion, and, despite his interest in painting and music and literature hardly more with the joys of art. It may be the lack of interest in the arts in the Five Towns explains the little account of them, outside of *Sacred and Profane Love*, the Hilda Lessways trilogy, and some moments of *The Old Wives Tale*, but in religion certainly there has been a deep interest throughout all the years he is dealing with. "Hanbridge, Bursley, Knype, Longshaw and Turnhill" are still strongholds of Evangelical Christianity.

In *The Truth About An Author* (1903) Bennett tells us that his first novel was to be "the usual miraculously transformed by Art into the Sublime." To that "sublime" of course he never attained in *A Man from the North*, nor in any other book he has written, but it has certainly been the endeavor he has made in all these novels of the Five Towns. The usual has been transformed into something fine in the Hilda Lessways trilogy, at any rate. Hilda is his most completely presented character and his most memorable. This passionate dark slip of a girl of *Clayhanger* and *Hilda Lessways*, who "generally acted first and reflected afterwards" is an indubitable creation, and the woman she became in *These Twain* what we should expect such a girl to become. Constance, too, from *The Old Wives Tale*, is completely realized, Sophia not so completely. Those three, with George Cannon, from *Hilda Lessways*, seem to me the characters that have most body, most reality, of all in these books of the Five Towns, though Mr. Povey, of *The Old Wives Tale,* and Annunciata Fearn's father from *Whom God Hath Joined,* and Edwin Clayhanger are memorably rendered, too.

With their intentness on objectivity there is little place for a philosophy of life in the novels of Bennett. For that we need not be sorry in a day when so many novels are little else. And yet it is not difficult to see where Bennett stands. As we would expect of a man who turns his back on the past in matters of art, he is against tradition in social and economic matters. It is Bennett who says with Edwin Clayhanger that in a strike the workmen are always right. In *The Feast of St. Friend* (1911) Bennett has a chance to be more explicit and he is more explicit. He finds that "it is a curious fact that the one faith which really does flourish and wax in these days should be a faith in social justice." And he finds not only all rightness on this side, but all the angels too: "In England, nearly all the most interesting people are social reformers: and the only circles of society in which you are not bored, in which there is real conversation, are the circles of social reform. These people alone have an abounding and convincing faith. Their faith has, for example, convinced many of the best literary artists of the day, with the result that a large proportion of the best modern imaginative literature has been inspired by the dream of social justice. Take away that idea from the works of H. G. Wells, John Galsworthy and George Bernard Shaw, and there would be exactly nothing left."

That saying is not, I think, set down in malice, though it might be so interpreted. Fortunately, it is only half true. If it were wholly true Wells and Galsworthy and Shaw would have no place at all in literature. It serves, however, to point out sharply that Bennett, though his sympathies are with the propagandists, is too much of an artist to have fallen a victim to their inartistic methods. The compromises of Bennett have been wisely made. He has put his preachments into *The Feast of St. Friend* and into his "pocket philosophies"; he has put his potboiling into these and into his fantastic tales; he has put the best that is in him into his novels of the Five Towns. That best does not win him a place among the great artists of the English novel, but, in *Hilda Lessways* at any rate, wins him a place just short of theirs.

CHAPTER XXIII

THE NEO-GEORGIANS

"But many young fail also, because they endeavor to tell stories when they have none to tell." Trollope, *Autobiography*.

"For surely no one who cordially and truly either hates or despises the world will publish a volume every three months to say so." Peacock, *Nightmare Abbey*.

"Whoever reads *The Human Comedy* thoughtfully will learn from it that the niche we should reserve for the abnormal is a very small one and that the man of talent should refrain from introducing it into his stories." George Moore, *Conversations in Ebury Street*.

"It is running a very great risk to dispense with nobility of soul either in literature or life." William McFee, in a review of *The Judge,* by Rebecca West.

For the past thirty years and more no great English novelist, save Conrad, has swum into the ken of our generation. Even those of us who hold to "the rapture of the forward view" and would welcome such another could we find him are forced to admit there is but Conrad. Moore, Phillpotts, Barrie, Bennett, Hewlett, Wells, Galsworthy, Maugham—each in his way has done work that arrests our attention for more than the moment, but no one of them is of the Titans. Nor has any one of their generation, save Conrad, done work in the novel that is as good in its kind as is the work of W. H. Hudson in the essay, or of C. M. Doughty in the travel-book, or of Synge in the drama, or of Masefield in verse. There is more real distinction, too, in the writings of lesser poets,—Sturge Moore for one, W. H. Davies for another, and Ralph Hodgson for a third,—more individuality, a fresher vision of the beauty of the world, than in any novelist that has gained a hearing since 1900.

D. H. LAWRENCE

There was hope that a new novelist of power was to be when *Sons and Lovers* appeared in 1913. D. H. Lawrence (1885-   ), however, has never realized the promise of that book. A writer of his experience and insight, of his lyric delight in beauty, of his individuality and gift of characterization, has no need to wander into the byways and purlieus of life to achieve originality. All he had to do was to be himself in his handling of the normal phases of life that are the time-honored and sanctioned material of the English novel. An author so original in his personality did not have to avoid what had been written about. He could have made over into a new beauty experiences that were common to him and to all who live natural lives. But he was afraid his "stuff" would not be "new stuff" if it had been used by other novelists before him; so he wandered into the most devious places to find fresh material.

When he did find what he thought was new it was not really life hitherto undiscovered, but life that the traditions of English civilization had decided it was best not to write about. Lawrence unfortunately not only writes about such life but delights in its exploitation. *The Rainbow* (1915) and *Women in Love* (1921), which might have been things of beauty, are things of ugliness— fine art struck by blight. And as the material of his art is blighted, so, too, is the shaping power of the artist. There is no such figure in any of the later stories as the mother, Mrs. Morel, in *Sons and Lovers*. That the original of this character was a part of his life before she was remade in his imagination is proved by her reappearance as Mrs. Holroyd in the play, *The Widowing of Mrs. Holroyd* (1914). Lawrence is less himself, too, in these later stories, parts of *The Lost Girl* (1920) reading like a rewriting of parts of Forster's *Where Angels Fear to Tread* (1905).

JAMES STEPHENS

If James Stephens (1884-   ) were an out and out novelist instead of a poet at play with philosophy in tall stories I had begun this chapter with him. In *Mary Mary* (1912), *The Crock of Gold* (1913) and *The Demi-Gods* (1914), he has given us a reading of life, that, despite obligations to George Meredith, is a newer revelation of the wonder of things than that of any story-teller of his generation. Dunsany alone vies with him in freshness of effects, but most of his wonders are of another world than ours. The world of Stephens is lighted by the sun we know and the old familiar moon, but it is somehow transfigured at intervals into a thing of strangeness and wild delight. Here in Stephens is a humor we have not had before; a smiling delight in little things; a full-lunged heartiness that drives away doubt in a great gale of laughter. Here is a sympathy with all that is human; a welcome to all weathers, to the weathers of the spirit that we call moods, and to the weathers of out-of-doors that bring rain in the face or sun to warm us. Here is a pageant of people low and high, Mary Makebelieve and Mrs. Makebelieve in their lofty tenement in the Dublin slum, and the big policeman and the thin youth; philosophers and their wives out of faery, Pan himself and the great god Angus Og, men of the Royal Irish constabulary and a Caitilin that is as surely a symbol as Kathleen-ni-Houlihan; a tinker girl Mary MacCann and her father Patsy and their donkey, and the guardian angels of all three that come down to earth and go gypsying with them. There are characters that live, too, in his retelling of the epical stories of Ireland, in *Deirdre* (1923) and *In the Land of Youth* (1924). Deirdre and Naisi and Conachur are made at once human and kingly in their fated lives; but Etain and Nera and their fellows retain, as they should, their places among the shee.

Here, too, are lesser things, a gift of epigram that owes nothing to Wilde; satire of Irish weaknesses; a romancing that beats all the many varieties of romancing in recent Irish writers—

witness the story of Brien O'Brien and the threepenny-bit; and words like the flowing water, which are never allowed to run away with the sense.

E. M. FORSTER

Three other writers press forward for consideration for the place of primacy among the younger generation of novelists. They are E. M. Forster (1879-   ), Sheila Kaye-Smith (1887-   ) and James Joyce (1882-   ). All three are loudly championed by this or that group of their generation. The originality of the attack of E. M. Forster has been appreciated from the appearance of his first book, *Where Angels Fear to Tread,* in 1905, but it was only when *The Longest Journey* (1907) and *Howard's End* (1911) had been added to his list that it was realized what strength there was in him. There is so much of his time in his work that it has likenesses to other contemporaneous writing, such as *Maurice Gest* (1908), of her who writes under the pseudonym of "Henry Handel Richardson." *Howard's End* is not, of course, a "musical" novel, and *Maurice Gest* is as wholly concerned with music as is *Evelyn Innes.* It is in their steady deliberation over the lives of everyday people of the middle classes in cities, people who are what is generally called "cultivated," that the two writers are alike. There is something of the influence of Gissing in both, of the Gissing of later years who had added other sorts of people to the "ignobly decent" that were the study of his earlier years. Forster has the knack of making his people stand before you in the flesh at your first meeting with them. He has the gift of bestowing personality with a touch. His people are real to you, often painfully real, from the start. Little by little you learn all that human beings can know of one another, all the tricks and manners of them, their standards, what to expect of them; and so they no more often surprise you by what they do than do kin and friends. There is no book of his in which the characters do not make lamentable mistakes, mistakes that affect the whole course of

their lives. These mistakes may be accidents, of which life is
so full, or they may be inevitable to such people as the characters
are and no more accidental than sunrise. It is this intimacy
of knowledge of his people that you enter into that makes you
aware of the strength of the man. At times you are almost ap-
palled by your intimacy of knowledge. You yourself are very
like these people of Forster's, and, but for the grace of God,
you might be as weak and as wanton as they.

SHEILA KAYE-SMITH

Sheila Kaye-Smith is more fully the follower of Hardy than
Forster is the follower of Gissing. Her strength is more evident
than the quiet strength of Forster. She has not, of course, the
Hardy quality, though she comes close to it at times; his resentful irony over "what man has made of man" is inimitable; but
she has much of the Hardy technique, and subjects very like
his. What a student may learn of a master she has learned
from Hardy. Before her Eden Phillpotts and "John Trevena"
had subjected themselves to a like drill, but she is an apter pupil
than either of them. She does not know her Sussex as Phillpotts knows his Dartmoor; she is always just a little the outsider;
for all her labor her writing has never the smack of the soil.
All, though, that the sympathetic outsider may learn of a community she has learned of hers. And in her succession of novels
from *The Tramping Methodist* (1908) on through *Sussex Gorse*
(1916) and *Little England* (1918) to *Tamarisk Town* (1919) and
Joanna Godden (1922) she never fails of large effects. *The End
of the House of Alard* (1923) almost alone of her books is lacking
in dramatic intensity.

Sussex Gorse has for hero a more implacable and more successful Michael Henchard. He is a man who sacrifices his family
and himself, this Reuben Backfield, to the betterment and en-
largement of his farm. You will not soon forget him, derivative
from Hardy though you call him. He, too, is of the seed of
Lear, a figure against the sky as you look back through the long

vista of the English novel to *Troilus and Cressida*. Monypenny of *Tamarisk Town* is a creation more wholly her own. He is so wholly her own that the book which presents him conforms to the formula she threatens to harden down into, a man with the choice between happiness and a dream that it is almost imperative for him to follow. This man generally wobbles, and is wrecked. There is nothing heroic about Monypenny, and there is something almost heroic about Reuben Backfield. Heroic unquestionably is poor Joanna Godden, a woman who won the fight with the farm that Bathsheba Everdene was unable to win, but who was mastered by a lover more tinsel even than Sergeant Troy. Yet Joanna triumphed in the end; for her child's sake she would not submit to wedlock with its unworthy father. Joanna, too, is a figure against the sky.

There is little originality in Sheila Kaye-Smith, but there is power, and she can write. There is in her, perhaps, a tendency to overelaboration, but she is guiltless of "purple patches" that daub the fine story-telling and finer characterization of Phillpotts. Nor does she ever lapse into the sensationalism that mars "John Trevena" in *Furze the Cruel* (1907), *Heather* (1908) and *Granite* (1914).

JAMES JOYCE

James Joyce began with George Moore as master. Perhaps one should say, "as guide" rather than "as master," for perhaps, Joyce had no master in English. The French naturalists had done before him almost all that he has done in *Dubliners* (1916). What else there is in that book that is not himself has been found under the pilotage of George Moore. There is even more to delight Moore in *The Portrait of the Artist as a Young Man* (1916) than in *Dubliners*. Like Moore Joyce is deeply concerned with art, and religion, and sex. Like Moore he enjoys controversy, and, again like Moore, he has the juvenile's desire to shock. This shocking is of a sort more mature than that of Moore and less forgivable. It is supported by a knowledge of many phases of life; a knowledge of the ways of Irish clerics;

a knowledge of psychology that has a basis in medical study; a knowledge of the vagaries of the artistic temperament.

We have all had experience of the youth who sets out deliberately to cut up ugly. Joyce, artistically, is in the state of that youth. To him people are such out and out hypocrites that life is intolerably disgusting. Let us pull the mask off things. Let us see the people of Dublin just as they are. Let us have the truth about art and artists. Let us, in *Ulysses* (1922), give honestly and completely, the whole life in detail of a group of people for a day; let us do it in a lingo that will really render it; let us put it all down in the kind of code in which we register thought and sensation in our minds, not in the formal English of literature. The Joyce of parts of *Ulysses* is in style as far from the Joyce of *Dubliners* as a man may be from his past. There is a sniffing at putrescence in *Dubliners*: putrescence is pursued with a delighted yapping in *Ulysses*. All this is very interesting to the alienists; it appeals to them as only an unusual case can.

There is little of delight in these books. There is little of life as most of us know it. There are "slices of life" neatly mounted on slides as if for the microscope in *Dubliners;* there is a family row in *The Portrait of the Artist as a Young Man* that is good writing and good drama; there are comments on life in *Ulysses* that challenge and compel consideration. Yet all in all *Ulysses,* yet all in all Joyce, is a pitiable waste of potential genius. Wordsworth defined poetry as emotion remembered in tranquillity, and in so defining it gave expression once and for all to a basic truth of art. No matter how turbulent the material of art, the final rendering of that material must attain serenity, the calm of what has come to be. There is no serenity anywhere in *Ulysses*.

THE NINE CONTEMPORARY GROUPS

There has been mention of masters in speaking of some of the novelists of the younger generation. There might have been, with reason, more mention of masters. Lawrence, for instance, in certain of his writing, uses methods of Hardy, but he is so definitely *sui generis* that an influence that helped to mould him was not insisted on. Hardy and Moore and Henry James, all of whom owed something to French fiction, are pervasive influences throughout a large part of the English fiction of today, though it may be said that Hardy alone is followed by anything like a school. Sterne is still an influence but not so potent as he was with the writers who began to publish before 1900.

If you delight in marshalling your writers into groups you can list at least nine such among recent novelists. There are the Trollopians, elders among the younger generation, W. B. Maxwell and Archibald Marshall chief among them. There are the Meredithians, "Benjamin Swift," "John Oliver Hobbes," Galsworthy and Charles Marriott among the elder writers, and J. C. Snaith, C. E. Montague, E. M. Forster, Cannan, Walpole, McKenna and Francis Brett Young among the younger. Few of these are so consistent disciples of their master as the Hardians are of Hardy. Meredith is a freeing rather than a controlling influence. These men are Meredithians only in the sense that they have gone to Meredith for guidance and have written for a time in his manner. And it is equally true that some of them in this group, as in other groups, have gone to more than one master, as Bennett for instance has gone to Gissing and George Moore.

The Hardians are Phillpotts, "Zack," and Charles Lee among the late Victorians, and Bullock, "John Trevena" and Sheila Kaye-Smith in more recent years. There is a strong influence of Hardy, too, in two novels of E. Œ. Somerville and "Martin Ross," *Naboth's Vineyard* (1889) and *The Real Charlotte* (1894), but you could not call Hardians writers who found a way of their own in *Some Experiences of an Irish R. M.* (1889) and became known the world over for a new humor. Nor could you write down H. A. Vachell (1861-   ) a Hardian, for all the Hardian manner of *The Soul of Susan Yellham* (1918). His early work inspired by California savors of Bret Harte, and the years brought other modes until he fell under the influence of Hardy.

There are those who use the novel as a tract after the manner of Samuel Butler, H. G. Wells of the older contemporary novelists, W. L. George and Cannan among the younger. Galsworthy and Beresford, too, have been influenced, though only momentarily, by Butler.

There is the modern school of terror, owing something to the Stevenson of *Dr. Jekyll and Mr. Hyde* (1886), but harking back consciously to Maturin and Beckford. Arthur Machen is of this group by such of his writing as *The Great God Pan* (1894) and Robert S. Hichens (1864-   ) of it by *Flames* (1897). So, too, is Algernon Blackwood (1869-   ) of it by *The Lost Valley* (1910) and *The Bright Messenger* (1922). "The Wendigo," one of the tales of *The Lost Valley,* is the most blood-curdling tale since Poe. Robert Simpson (1884-   ) is of it by his *Bite of Benin* (1917), and Michael Sadlier (1888-   ) by *Privilege* (1921). Brett Young (1884-   ) is of it by *Undergrowth* (1913) and *Cold Harbour* (1925); Forrest Reid of it by *Pender Among the Residents* (1923); and V. Sackville West, of it by *The Dragon in Shallow Waters* (1922). Masefield, too, has experimented in this manner, rather disastrously, in *Sard Harker* (1924).

There is the school of Gissing, in which Bennett began, though he is more frank in his expression of obligations to George Moore, the later and dominant influence in his making. W. L. George, too, has studied Gissing, as he has studied Wells and Butler, and Zola, and Turgenieff, and Dostoieffsky. Yet no matter how far afield George ranges for methods and material the stamp of Gissing's way of presenting London life is upon his writing always. Walpole shows the influence of Gissing, too, as do "Oliver Onions" and J. D. Beresford and Allan Monkhouse. No English writer not of first power has, during the past twenty years, had so wide and deep an influence as Gissing.

There is the influence of George Moore. It has not, as I have said, brought into being a group of writers dedicated to the ideals and methods of Moore. Yet all English fiction written by those who began to write after the publication of *Esther Waters*

(1894) has been different because of *Esther Waters*. *Evelyn Innes* (1898), too, has been an influence. It is in the thoroughness of detail, the carefulness with which every word is used, the laborious workmanship, the naturalistic fidelity of contemporaneous English fiction, that we note the influence of Moore. It has come across the seas to us in America, where in *John Cave* (1909) and *Barbara Gwynn* (1911) of W. B. Trites we have his methods carried out with the most exact faithfulness. Bennett and Stephen McKenna, Norman Douglas and Michael Arlen, four very different writers, are partly what they are because of George Moore.

There is the influence of Conrad. It is to be found, says Hugh Walpole in his *Joseph Conrad* (1916), in "all the more interesting younger English novelists." That is true, particularly true of Walpole himself. His later writing shows his discipleship. Conrad is to be found in McFee and David Bone and Tomlinson, who are, like their master, writers of the sea. Conrad is to be found in Richard Curle. Virginia Woolf has felt his spell. America has followers, too, that reveal his methods, Hergesheimer in the novel, O'Neill in the play, and Vachel Lindsay in verse.

There is the influence of *The House with the Green Shutters* (1901). It is not often that a first book of an author is so well received on publication and remains for so long a model for other writers to copy as this study of Scottish life by George Douglas Brown (1864-1902). It portrays the rise and fall of James Gourlay with a fidelity that was new to English fiction. Gourlay is the big man of a little Scottish town in the eighteen-fifties. He is in a way fashioned after Michael Henchard, but there are other influences than Hardy in the book. Galt is remembered, and a certain lurid quality seems to indicate obligation to Balzac. Maybe the young author had read Dostoieffsky, too. There is the Russian's willingness to accept things as they are in *The House with the Green Shutters*, but there is not the Russian's tolerance of everything human.

There are resemblances between this story and *Furze the Cruel* (1907), the best book of "John Trevena," that seem to prove a direct influence of the elder book upon the younger. *The Valley of the Squinting Windows* (1919), for all "Brinsley MacNamara" professed the desire to be an Irish Dostoieffsky, shows him building up a story on the very lines of *The House with the Green Shutters*. That Brown did not live to write another book was unfortunate for English fiction. He revealed more power and freshness in his one book than any of his immediate contemporaries, the men who began with the new century.

There are, of course, other groupings possible of these writers I have mentioned. One could have divided them into the foreign and native schools of English fiction, with sub-groups of French naturalists, Russian realists, Tchekoffian impressionists, etc., etc. It has seemed more appropriate, however, in a book which aims primarily to consider the English novel in its relation to other forms of English literature, to group the writers under the English masters they have followed.

It has been pointed out that a distinguishing characteristic of the great novelists from Fielding to Conrad is their wealth of creative power. All the English novelists who are really of first power have written not only many novels but long novels, novels that teem with people, with experiences, with life. Mrs. Gaskell is remembered for *Cranford* (1853); Mrs. Craik for *John Halifax, Gentleman* (1856); Blackmore for *Lorna Doone* (1869); Mallock for *The New Republic* (1877); Shorthouse for *John Inglesant* (1881); "Maxwell Gray" for *The Silence of Dean Maitland* (1886); and George Douglas Brown for *The House with the Green Shutters* (1901)—each one for a single book.

Several of these writers have done other good work than the one book mentioned, but not one of them has written another book that is memorable in the sense that the one mentioned is memorable. And after all not one of these books is really a great book. They are all books that were famous in their day, that are important according to "the historical estimate," that have a place in social history, but that are already discounted as art. Richness of experience and richness of imagination would seem to be a *sine qua non* of the great novelists. A style, a romantic fancy, even a new note struck, cannot atone for thinness of quality in the novel. It is the absence of richness that makes us doubt the lastingness as novelists of writers of such unquestionable worth as Stevenson and E. M. Forster.

Conversely, imagination that can spend itself prodigally, richness of material, energy, verve, vitality, make us greet their possessors with hope of their greatness. So it was that we welcomed Compton Mackenzie (1883-   ) and Gilbert Cannan (1884-   ). Young men with so whole-hearted an attack, and dowered with so large and so varied an experience, should carry far, we thought. Yet neither has come through. It is not that either has written too much that they have not taken a sure place in literature, but that neither has found his way to that final something which lifts talent into genius.

GILBERT CANNAN

There is not about the writing of either Mackenzie or Cannan, interesting as that writing is as a reflection of the world about us, that largeness, that inevitability, that memorableness of characterization, that distinguish the great novelists. Cannan has tried many ways of writing, aping now Meredith, now Synge, now Butler, now Rolland and now the Russians, but whether his form be play or novel it falls short of the expectations it arouses. *Peter Homunculus* (1909) was a brilliant start for a young novelist. As so often with beginners his hero was himself. Unlike the more dramatic novelists he has not been able to get away from himself in his more mature writing. Though he puts many men into his books whose originals are other than himself his heroes remain largely Gilbert Cannan. *Old Mole* (1914), with its chief character so different at the start from his creator, should have freed Cannan, by its success, from this habit, but once well under way in the story, he cannot refrain from using his hero as his own mouthpiece.

Cannan is an angry young man in these earlier stories, a young man at quarrel with the way things are in the world, and, often, a young man with a hatred of life. This hatred of life has deepened with the years, despite momentary relapses; and there is therefore denied to him, as there always is to such a one the ability to render life faithfully. One wonders whether back of the Manchester in which he was born there is not a Scottish past of his family. He is often the typical Scot of the soreheaded type, and Scottish blood, as in *The Stucco House* (1918), sometimes accounts for the ways of his characters.

Cannan can be very weak in his writing. He would be well disposed indeed who could find anything good to say of *Mummery* (1918). And yet it has its admirers, for it is about the theater, and our age is theater-mad. Cannan himself is dominated by theatricality. There is a tendency in him to force the note, to louden the effects, to sneer nasally at all that fails to please him. There is always a sense of hurry about his writing, and when he does stumble on beauty he is too much in haste to see it clearly. He is very sure about things, too sure for one who would pose as a seer. It is only out of long travail of living and of thinking about living that wisdom comes.

If there were only characters that we could not forget in Cannan, we would not so much mind the chaos of his stories, but there are not such characters, even in such Dickensian oddities as Old Mole and Matilda. They are certainly not to be found in the gray Gissing-like portraits of *The Stucco House*. With all his vehemence and assurance Cannan has never wrought out a way of story-telling of his own, or done work of first power in the way of any other writer.

COMPTON MACKENZIE

Compton Mackenzie is as unconventional as Cannan, but far more engaging. And though he began, in *The Passionate Elopement* (1911) and *Carnival* (1912) and *Youth's Encounter* (1913), in the young man's habit of writing about himself, he has gradually grown more and more objective in his writing. He never writes about anything beyond his experience; so there is, in a sense, a rather restricted field for him to select from;—the sheltered life of childhood, which he remembers very vividly; the awakening of youth; Oxford; the stage; Bohemia; and the church. One's memories of his early books are of pretty writing. *Sinister Street* (1914) takes its place in mind as a typical exhibit of the autobiographical novel, but once we meet Sylvia Scarlett we are come upon a real characterization. Mackenzie has written too much about her, but she remains an achievement, a creation, a personality, a portrait with a definite place among the remembered women of English fiction.

Sinister Street (1914) towards its close; *The Early History of Sylvia Scarlett* (1918); and *Sylvia and Michael* (1919) are dominated by her; and again in *The Vanity Girl* (1920) her vital personality shares our interest with that of Mackenzie's most complete characterization, Dorothy Lonsdale. Dorothy is your cold beauty, whose every action is determined by her fixed purpose to get on in the world, to be of the first in England. This ambition she attains in the end by a personal sacrifice that would be appalling in one less avid of place. Her every act is consistent, her progress is as inevitable as that of the seasons. One does not doubt the mad impulses of Sylvia, her generosities, her runnings away from the impossible situations she gets herself into, but her character, for all its reality, falls without the experience of most of us. Michael is very carefully detailed, but despite the obvious autobiography that goes to his making we never know him fully.

Nor do we so know his replica in other situations, Mark Lidderdale in *The Altar Steps* (1922); *The Parson's Progress* (1923) and *The Heavenly Ladder* (1924). This trilogy follows the development of an Anglican priest through various stages of Anglo-Catholicism until he submits to the Catholic Church.

It would seem that the reappearance of the same characters from book to book controverts the claim made for real fecundity of imagination in Mackenzie. Yet it really does not controvert that claim. Mackenzie knows so much about his characters and the many people whose lives touch theirs that you never have the feeling that there is worked over material in their reappearances. Take *Sylvia Scarlett*, for instance. Its heroine suffers such vicissitudes of fortune, knocks about among so many differing sorts of people, that one wonders how in the world Mackenzie had the experiences he must have had to imagine what he makes happen to her. His infinite detail convinces you of the reality of it all, but there is in him such a flair for the romantic that the somberness one expects of realism can never settle down over his writing. You cannot call the man who wrote the lyric passages of *Plasher's Mead* (1915) a realist.

Until Mackenzie took up his trilogy on Mark Lidderdale, his novels were of a sort to appeal to many kinds of readers. But a priest's troubles with ecclesiasticism and discipline and ritual could appeal widely only if they were powerfully presented. That they are not. The mere massing of material about the cardinal situations of life had its share in the impressiveness of the early work of Mackenzie. When he attempts a story of less universal appeal his lack of power becomes evident.

J. D. BERESFORD

The mien of J. D. Beresford (1873-   ) is very different from that of Mackenzie. That of Mackenzie is of a man after dinner, at ease with the world. That of Beresford is the mien of a man after breakfast, after a lodging-house breakfast in London, who sits down to hard writing with no greater stimulus than that of weak tea. It is downright good writing, most of it, of Beresford, laborious writing faithful to life, writing worthy of all respect, but a bit dull. Led astray by Wells, Beresford can sink into such work according to recipe as *Revolution* (1921), but at his best, in the first of his work that he preserved, he falls just short of a hard fineness. *The History of Jacob Stahl* (1911) is interesting as all sincere human documents are interesting, but it is no more than interesting. There is nothing quickening, of the color of delight, of the lift of life at full tide about it.

A Candidate for Truth (1912), Vol. II. of the Jacob Stahl

trilogy, is just a little thinner and a little grayer than Vol. I; and Vol. III, *The Invisible Event* (1915), dims almost to blankness. *Those Lynnekers* (1916) takes us up the social scale from the level of the trilogy, and there are more contrasts in the story, but it reads as if it had been task work. It is driven through doggedly to the end. It is true in the main, very true of the scenes between Dickie in revolt and the rest of the family, but it is dull, often deadly dull. There is little humor in Beresford, and lyric passages are rarer than humor. There is one real portrait in his many books, Betty Gale, a gracious portrait that does not thin away to nothingness as do almost all his intended personages.

His artistic creed is old and orthodox. "The essential thing," he holds, "is the accurate presentation of the commonplace." That is the creed George Eliot preached so often, and practiced so successfully. She was nourished, however, on a local lore rich in humor and open eyed. Beresford has no such treasure to draw from; he must trust to his lean experience alone.

The story, as story, as a puzzle the intricacies of which we are eager to solve, does not usually amount to much in Beresford, but in *The Prisoners of Hartling* (1922) the revolt of certain members of a family against the tyranny of its old head keeps us reading until the book is finished. Should Beresford continue to break away from the autobiographical novel there may be a new development possible in him, but he has advanced little during the past ten years. The Jacob Stahl trilogy is sterling work for all its reiteration of facts and too much discussion of the art of fiction, but its three parts constitute a severe test of the novelist. The adage may be true, that there is a good book in every man's life, but it does not follow that there are three good books in every man's life.

There are intimations of fine things in Beresford, but they are seldom realized. What he says of Wilfred Hornby in *Housemates* (1917) is damagingly true of himself. "Indeed, I am not a true artist. I have the power of conception but not of creation. In my drawing and in my writing, I present but the pale, weak model of my desire." In *An Imperfect Mother* (1920) is the proof of this admission. The story was intended to be a study of "a slight departure from the normal" in Stephen Kirkwood, "due to a severe, nervous shock in his early childhood." Beresford conceives *An Imperfect Mother* as a "case" presented in terms of art. It deviates, fortunately, into something other than a "case," even if it falls short of fineness. It is a story of sorts. A vivid scene at the start, a parting that is real drama, then pages on pages that are inconsequential, and then another moment of drama, less impressive than the one at the start, and then a summary, in the good old way, of what happened after the fall of the curtain—that's all. And that all is not enough, and J. D. Beresford knows it.

HUGH S. WALPOLE

Hugh S. Walpole (1884-   ) is better known in America than either Cannan, or Mackenzie, or Beresford, but he is no more of a power. It is difficult to find one personality, one Walpole, running through all his many books. The author of *Maradick at Forty* (1910) is one man, the author of *Mr. Perrin and Mr. Traill* (1911), another, the author of *Fortitude* (1913), a third, and the author of *The Golden Scarecrow* (1915), a fourth. There are, of course, qualities constant to Walpole in all his phases. He is never without a plot; he is pleasant; he is always the gentleman, which all novelists, unfortunately, are not; and so it is that even when he presents life as you know it cannot be, there is the interest in his writing that good company always affords.

Why should one novelist not lie about life like a gentleman now and then, with the motive of making things easier and safer and more pleasant and more beautiful, when so many novelists lie about life like cads, for the sake of making things harder and more dangerous and more disagreeable and uglier? And whatever his vein Walpole always writes fairly well, though he seldom awakens wonder and never rises to revelation. He is very wistful about childhood, devoting *The Golden Scarecrow* (1915) and *Jeremy* (1919) to its all important littlenesses, and dallying long over the childhood of the heroes of other books, as over that of Peter Westcott in *Fortitude*.

A too great preoccupation with childhood and youth, indeed, is not only one of the weaknesses of Walpole, but of a large part of all the fiction of his generation. It is very easy to maunder and sentimentalize over young years. A reason for this preoccupation is that life irons out the average man in his first years of bread-winning, and the differentiating characteristics that distinguish early youth disappear. It is easier to find children with individuality than youths with individuality. Another reason for this preoccupation is that his school life, being relatively far in the past to the young novelist, gains the enchantment of distance. Forrest Reid (1876-   ) is an even greater sinner in the exploitation of childhood than Walpole. Both his first and second novels, *The Spring Song* (1917) and *Pirates of the Spring* (1920) are concerned almost exclusively with boyhood and adolescence.

On the page opposite the title page of the fifth edition of the English imprint of *Maradick at Forty*, a book first published in 1910, the books of Walpole are listed as "novels," "romances," "books about children" and "belles-lettres." One wonders if this is the author's division of his work. It is easy to see why *The Wooden Horse* (1909), *Mr. Perrin and Mr. Traill* (1911), *The Dark Forest* (1916), *The Green Mirror* (1918) and *The Secret City* (1919) are listed as "novels." It is not so easy to understand why *Fortitude* (1913) and *The Duchess of Wrexe* (1914) are listed as "romances" along with *The Prelude to Adventure* (1912) and *Maradick at Forty* (1910). Of these four stories only *Maradick at Forty* is certainly a "romance," though all the other stories have in them elements of romance.

Fortitude is a story written to a theme rather than a story written to make something beautiful out of a dream of life or out of an experience of life. It drifts away from life as almost all theme stories always have done. Peter Westcott is made to find out early in life that courage is all that matters, the courage to endure as well as the courage to do; and because he must have all kinds of unhappiness to prove that courage is all that matters, to prove true the theme of the story, things happen to him in the story that would not inevitably happen to such a one in life. The scenes in Cornwall in the early chapters of the book are hardly more than crude melodrama. The school scenes are the usual two and two makes four sort of filling incidental to school chapters in the contemporaneous novel. The scenes in the book-shop in London, and the scenes of Peter's married life are manufactured to order, not observed from life. Of all the London scenes only those of the boarding house have the ring of truth.

The Green Mirror (1918) is the best novel of Walpole. It tells how Katherine Trenchard revolted against her mother and won freedom for herself and her alien lover. Her mother had determined to bend Katherine and Philip to the traditions of the house of Trenchard, but the younger generation was too strong for her. From one point of view *The Green Mirror*, too, might be looked upon as a theme novel, or thesis novel, but as the story it tells is one well-known in literary circles in London, it is probable that in this case Walpole fitted the theme to the story, rather than the story to the theme as is usually the pro-cedure in the novel with a thesis. We believe that Mrs. Trench-ard was defeated, as we do not believe, in *Maradick at Forty*, that Mrs. Maradick was even partially reformed. Mrs. Trench-ard, too, is a character to remember, Mrs. Maradick a character to be amused over a while and then forget. Mrs. Maradick is but the typical wife who has come to regard her husband as a necessary article of household gear. That, and that only, James Maradick is to Mrs. Maradick, until jealousy and the genius of a wonderful place, Treliss in Cornwall, cause a re-adjustment of her attitude. Cornwall, indeed, is the place of places to Walpole, treasured for a childhood there and many revisitings, revisitings in the flesh and revisitings in dream.

"OLIVER ONIONS"

"Oliver Onions" (George Oliver) is the author of *In Accordance with the Evidence* (1912), *The Debit Account* (1913) and *The Story of Louie* (1913). There are other titles in his list, quite a few of them, but they hardly count. It is the trilogy only that you remember without effort. Most of what he has written crumbles away in memory; but once you have met Evie and Archie, those cheapest of lovers; and James Herbert Jeffries, with his ape's face and his will to have Evie that stops at nothing; and Louie, so fine, so mad, so brave in disaster: you have characters of another clay altogether, people that will go with you further on the way down the years than the usual chance acquaintance of detective stories.

For detective stories are what, fundamentally, the novels of the trilogy are. They are more than that, they are faithful representations of smart Alecks and cheap Janes from the lower middle class of London. Here for once is no autobiography, but stories told objectively, and humanly, too. Elsewhere "Oliver Onions" is apt to turn to fantasia, or to satire, or to themes of the hour, or to tricks. Here in the trilogy he is the story-teller with a thrilling yarn about real people. Are the three stories of such appeal because we are all at heart devotees to the detective story and do we rise to acclaim them because in them "Oliver Onions" has made the detective story intellectually respectable? Whatever the reasons the appeal of the stories cannot be denied.

It is disconcerting to find a man who can do work at once so human and artistic as this trilogy manufacturing such a tale as *The Tower of Oblivion* (1921). This is an attempt to make a good yarn out of the tragedy of growing young. Derwent Rose, a novelist, incredibly well-preserved at forty-five, finds himself becoming by fits and starts rapidly younger. His friend, the popular novelist, Sir George Coverham, tries to shepherd him through his second experience of certain adventures usual to the years from sixteen to forty-five as these years unroll reversely on his flight back to youth. Within the year Derwent Rose is a youth of sixteen, and a suicide, though perhaps he had reverted to a point from which he might have begun to grow old again. One wonders if George Oliver was not some night at a cinema when there were flashbacks or when the film chanced to be reversed. He would do in the novel what was done by the film. He manages the many difficulties of his plot with a good deal of dexterity, but no effort could make such a subject worth while. I would not have mentioned *The Tower of Oblivion* at all were it not symptomatic of one of the great weaknesses of contemporaneous English fiction, the search after new effects. Such an experiment is interesting, too, for its relation to that part of the Faust story in which his youth is returned to Faust as the greatest gift possible. To Derwent Rose the return to youth was a hellish thing because it involved him again in the mire he thought he had waded through once and for all.

FRANK SWINNERTON

Our intellectual snobbishness is a little troubled, perhaps, if we happen to like "Oliver Onions." Even intellectuals, however, can afford to admire Frank Swinnerton (1884-   ). Of all disciples of Gissing he is most faithful to the London vulgar. It is often the London vulgar in revolt that he presents, the London vulgar of the younger generation. Swinnerton sympathizes with that revolt, though he is seldom a propagandist and therefore a more accurate presenter of the life he has chosen to write of than many of his fellow novelists who pattern their writing after that of Wells. Gissing, of course, presented youth in revolt, but he was seldom in sympathy with that revolt, or with revolt of any kind.

Nocturne (1917), a longish story built up on the model of the short story, is the most praised book of Swinnerton; and *The Three Lovers* (1922) the most popular. Quick dispatch of the story, fidelity to his characters, and good writing mark *Nocturne,* yet it is not among the tales one returns to again and again as one does to *Barry Lyndon* or "A Smile of Fortune," for the joy one has in brave or beautiful art. *Nocturne* is a cold study, too detached in its telling to win one warmly. The personality back of the story, the personality of its narrator, which the artistic canons of our generation hold not to matter if the story is told well objectively, matters greatly in *Nocturne*. We would have our authors stick to their proper job and not interfere with their characters once they create them. That is the theory we hold to, but as a matter of fact we must know our writers to be on the side of the angels or we cannot be happy in their company. That we are not sure of Swinnerton in this respect is always a drawback to our joy in reading him, as it is, more pronouncedly, in reading Somerset Maugham. The intense curiosity about life of Swinnerton, and his concentration in the study of it lead him to discoveries of what life is that we are glad to have him share with us. There are rejoicings here and there, however, over human weakness, that are hard to endure. They reveal, in *Nocturne*, a personality that alienates, that creates a kind of repulsion for which no pleasantness of words can atone.

There is always more or less of a strain in reading Swinnerton. He never relaxes. There is little humor in him, little of that pleasantness that comes of leisured living and leisured writing. Could he, in his youth, have been turned out to grass for a season or so, we would have had a writer of more profit and delight.

It is ironical a better book of Swinnerton than *The Three Lovers* (1922) should not have been his best seller. Even *Coquette* (1921) is a better book, and ten years before *Coquette, The Casement* (1911), had a freshness that has now worn off of his writing. *The Three Lovers* is just the usual thing. It is the old story of a girl's perils before she finds safety with the right man. It is that old story up-to-date. It has all the semblance of reality about it, it is neatly written, it carries easily enough a good deal of sharp analysis of character, but its significance begins to lessen as soon as you have finished it. That is not the way of stories that are real discoveries in life. Such conjure themselves up in memory again and again, as do the poems you most care for, to the deepening of their appeal on each such recall.

J. C. SNAITH

J. C. Snaith began with his best book, *Broke of Covenden* (1904). That may have been the one story that there was in him to write. It showed its author was a gentleman who knew his Meredith, and a group of people from "county" down through "the lower orders" of a country community. The squire who gives title to the book is a character of a type very familiar in the English novel, but he has individuality. He is solid, too, very solid, as solid as Squire Western himself, and plagued with a whole bevy of Sophias. Broke is, I think, himself an influence, perhaps not directly, but collaterally at any rate, upon the head of the house of Clinton that Archibald Marshall studies from so many angles.

There is not so firm earth under the feet of the characters in his succeeding novels. *William Jordan, Junior* (1907), is another "beloved vagabond"; Araminta, "the Goose," of *Araminta* (1909), a real "phantom of delight"; Henry Harper of *The Sailor* (1916), a bringer of romance in the good old fashion to a world tired of tracts and "slices of life," and Harriet Sanderson in *The Time Spirit* (1918) the patientest of patient Grizels. I have used the familiar phrases to describe these principals of Snaith because those principals themselves are all, in part at least, recapturings of familiar characters from the English literature of yesterday, and because there is, more often than not, the use of other men's words in their description and in the recital of their doings. Snaith is far from a great writer, but his ways are ways of pleasantness and peace is with you at each story's end.

W. L. GEORGE

W. L. George is the noisiest of the English novelists of his generation. He uses not only the novel to shout out what he thinks about men and things, but journalism and the lecture platform. He is a good journalist, too; he writes with shrewd judgment about his fellow novelists; and he knows how to say the startling thing from the rostrum. That is the trouble with George, this love of the startling thing; and his habit of choosing "stuff" that he has to go out of his usual routine of life to obtain. In reading him you do not feel that he has, despite his varied experience of the professions and of business, a great fund of experience to draw upon. You feel that George, after the fashion of the Wells who was once his master, studies up the career of the leading newspaper potentate of his day when he wishes to write *Caliban* (1920), just as very early in his career he "worked up" a seamy side of life for *A Bed of Roses* (1911). In *The Confessions of Ursula Trent* (1921), on the other hand, he is full of his subject. A certain sort of men's talk that we all have known is drawn upon largely for the "stuff" of this novel, and it is supplemented by what seem first-hand versions of a certain sort of women's talk we are not all so familiar with. Yet is it natural that Ursula should have thought out as minutely as she is quoted as having, these difficult and intimate questions? And certain doubt arises in our minds as to whether she was really "county," as George maintains.

It had been better were there "county" in George. It has traditions that tend to keep parliamentary the written word. Brutal frankness is a delight to him, as is, too, a defiance of the conspiracy of silence there was once in print about certain matters. Now that there is more of such matters, relatively, in print than in life, one grows tired of them, especially when they are thrust upon us in so strident a style.

George is always in a hurry, too, to get things said. Maybe he feels that, did he not say, as soon as he thinks of it, this or that, he might change his mind and not be able to say it with conviction. On the whole, though, he is sincere; and, moreover, able to see himself as others see him. When he writes of novelists in "Litany of the Novelist," he is, of course, speaking in his own defense. "We are queer people," he writes, "nasty people, but we are not nastier nor queerer than our fellows. We are merely more shameless, and exhibit what they hide. We have got outside, and we hate being outside; we should so much like to enlist under the modern standard, the silk hat, and yet we are arrogant." This queerness and nastiness in the case of George is not balanced by many compensating powers on the other side of the account. Had he beauty or wisdom or insight we might not so much mind the queerness and nastiness and arrogance, or were Victoria or Bulmer or Ursula a really great portrait.

STEPHEN MCKENNA

It is the misfortune of Stephen McKenna (1888-   ) to be dominated by his Sonia. She is far from the woman of Dostoieffsky who rises before us at mention of the name. She is an English lady of today who has the gift of bringing trouble upon herself and upon the many that love her. She is to her creator not only a loved puppet, but the woman of today, a symbol of what the war and the forces that led up to the war have done to England's best. So captivating is she to McKenna that his sense of humor is atrophied altogether as he chronicles her vicissitudes.

Sonia (1917) has not so many such lapses as *Sonia Married* (1919), but the little circle of oldsters, her admirers, whose concern about her indiscretion and waywardness and disloyalty is recorded in so minute detail in the latter book, are difficult to take seriously. They are, indeed, provocative of downright and unholy laughter. Sonia is still one of the group whose fortunes we follow in *Tomorrow and Tomorrow* (1924), the eighth volume of his mirroring of one time and set in England.

There is no doubt that McKenna is to the manner born, and there is no doubt that he can find in the ruling caste he knows so well warrant for all he sets down about it. Whether what he sets down is typical of that class, or only what may be found in that class, is another matter. Art of a kind has always found the exceptional more arresting than the usual, and McKenna has many predecessors in his methods of selection. *Midas and Son* (1919) is a very serious attempt at a cross-section of the ruling class that met the War, but I cannot help wondering

whether it will not eventually take its place as history rather
than as art. There is knowledge of life in it, and an ironic sympathy with all its differing puppets, but there is, for all the effort
to portray a master of men, not a creation of character in the
book. Knowledge of life and good writing are not all that go
to the making of a good novel.

One must question, indeed, whether McKenna is interested in
his stories primarily as stories or as exhibits of the age. If one
has read his *While I Remember* (1919), a book of his reminiscences of the generation that was of military age at the outbreak
of the World War, one has read what is most significant in his
stories. The novels are really elaborations of the themes of *While
I Remember* and variations upon them. The novels give con-
crete and detailed illustrations to the reading of the times he puts
into such passages as this:

"In so far as it is true to say that the English ever lost their
heads, they lost them between the March offensive and the
December general election of 1918. For more than four years
there had been the relaxation of bonds which is natural when
life is no longer secure: sexual relationships became increasingly
promiscuous, marriages were contracted, abandoned and dissolved
with reckless disregard of private morals or public responsibility;
and the craving for such excitement as would bring forgetfulness
led to the excessive indulgence of every physical appetite. . . .

"In a short phrase, the restraints of modern civilization were
burst on the resurgence of primitive man. Honorable, kindly,
fastidious, gentle and reserved spirits dragged back across the
ages, lied and cheated, fought and bullied in an orgy of intrigue
and self-seeking, of intoxication and madness. Only in this way
and at this price could those who had fared delicately and lived
softly endure hardships which for generations or centuries had
been removed from the average experience of civilization; the
bravery of the savage emerged, hand in hand with the savage's
ferocity, his licence, his superstition and his credulity."

If I am interested in such social history as this I had rather
have it frankly as history than tricked out in a story invented

for the purpose of revealing it. It is a too sweeping statement to say that there is hardly more in the trilogy *The Sensationalists* (1920-1921) than you find in the chapter of *While I Remember* from which the above passage is taken, but it is true that the heart of the reading of life of *Lady Lilith* (1920), *The Education of Eric Lane* (1921), and *The Secret Victory* (1921) is here in the social history.

FRANCIS BRETT YOUNG

Francis Brett Young (1884-   ) is another novelist who writes well, who has a keen sense of the irony of life, who has studied seriously the architectonics of the novel. Like McKenna he has written many interesting books, but he has written only one memorable book and that not a novel. *Marching on Tanga* (1917) is at once a travel sketch and a narrative of a military expedition. There is terror in it, but there is humanity and sheer beauty too. Unlike McKenna, Brett Young writes of many conditions of men. He has worked in the manners of several of his elders, done 'prentice work with several masters. *The Tragic Bride* (1920) was said to mark his emancipation from all influences and an emergence into a manner of his own. And yet for all the evident truth of *The Tragic Bride* as a record of life, it is a book whose story might have been imagined by any one of a half dozen writers of today. It is life as we all know it, it is absorbing reading, it has moments of beauty, but not enough beauty or gusto or revelation to send you to it a second time. There is little to link it to the man who wrote *The Red Knight* (1902), which takes us to an imaginary kingdom in the Mediterranean. *The Crescent Moon* (1919), *Pilgrim's Rest* (1922) and *Woodsmoke* (1923) are about Africa, where Young served against the Germans. *Marching on Tanga* is his record of that campaign.

There is a great deal of Conrad in *The Crescent Moon,* the best of the three, but there are reminiscences of other authors of our day as well. The very title is that of a volume of child's verse by Tagore, and that tumbled west country of England that Housman and Masefield both so love is background to Eva Burwarton as the narrator envisages her on the railway platform at Nairobi. The very words of Housman are woven into the writing, which in this passage does not suffer by contrast in their presence. We meet against Ludlow and Usk, Wenlock Edge and Clee. Brett Young is a poet, too, as every writer must be if he is to be of first power, no matter what form of literature he follows. There are memories here of Conrad, Godovius the planter being not a little like Schomberg and Zangiacomo rolled into one, and M'Crae, though of so different an origin and story, somewhat in the situation of Heyst. The girl from Far Forest in the Welsh marches is her creator's own, but a type of the women of her countryside first and an individual only after he has disposed of her in his mind in that rôle. Many of the scenes recall "The Heart of Darkness." That is inevitable with the background of the two stories the African hinterland. Every admirer of the fine quality of his work wishes Brett Young would write more in the vein of *The Young Physician* (1920), of the English life he was born to, and that he find in the end a place as much his own to write about as Shropshire is Housman's.

Young is too much of an artist to be wanting to show his versatility by writing about here, there and everywhere. His way to mastery is not in thus escaping from himself. That is indeed a dangerous practice in an art in which so much depends on the personality of the artist. There must be more than one of his readers that is looking forward to a novel by him on the life of that "high Shropshire upland of late hay" his picture of which so kindles one at the start of *The Crescent Moon*. That way, and not through imitating Machen, greatness lies.

"BRINSLEY MACNAMARA"

"Brinsley MacNamara" (A. E. Weldon) in his *In Clay and Bronze* (1920) tells us of a young novelist, Martin Deignan, who would be an Irish Dostoieffsky. As the novel is obviously autobiographical we are perhaps warranted in assuming that such, for a while at least, was the ambition of "Brinsley MacNamara." There are no studies of abnormality in any book of the Irishman but he has approached his task of depicting the Midlands to which he was born with all the frankness and completeness of detail of the Russian. And to "Brinsley MacNamara," too, nothing is common or mean or too low for human interest and compassion. In so far as he has the power, and art will permit, he tells us all about his characters.

Two other books than *In Clay and Bronze* have followed *The Valley of the Squinting Windows* (1918), *The Clanking of Chains* (1919) and *The Mirrors of the Dusk* (1923). Neither is particularly important as art. There is no great characterization in either. Nor is *In Clay and Bronze* comparable to *The Valley of the Squinting Windows*. As is not unusual with writers who are less than great, his first book is his best. It tells the story of John Brennan, the son who was to expiate his mother's sin by becoming a priest, but who became instead a drunken loafer like his father. It spares us no detail of the sordidness and meanness and weakness it has to relate. It is a book of great power. There are figures against the sky in it, Nan Brennan, and John, her son, and Padna Padna surely. If it has any beauty in it at all it is that pointed out by its author as "the beauty of tragic reality." The book has been publicly burned in the townland it depicts and it has become a bone of contention wherever Irishmen meet. It will soon cease to be that, and be that better thing that it has always been, a sombre work of art, "gray and quiet," and dominated by an irony that drives the sentimentalists almost mad.

THE NOVEL IN IRELAND.

Things are picking up with the novel in Ireland. The peasant drama of the Abbey school, followed by Irish independence, has made possible a realism in the novel that the Irish public would not accept while it felt that the putting of the best face on all

Irish matters was necessary for the cause of independence. "Gerald O'Donovan," indeed, had begun his careful and candid revelations of clericalism in *Father Ralph* as far back as 1913, and *Conquest* (1921), at any rate, of its successors, has kept up to the level of this first book. The writing of "Gerald O'Donovan" is uniformly good, his knowledge unquestionable; he has an infinite capacity for hard work; but his characterization is not sure, and his comment on men and things hardly more than mediocre.

There are possibilities in Liam O'Flaherty. *Thy Neighbor's Wife* (1923) tells us a good deal about life on Aranmore. It is an intimate and picturesque story, but it runs away most unwarrantably from its predestined tragedy.

Eimer O'Duffy has tried hard to give an unprejudiced account of the drift of events in Ireland that led to the uprising of 1916 in *The Wasted Island* (1920). It is, however, but another contribution to social history.

Daniel Corkery (1878-   ) in *The Threshold of Quiet* (1917) records the conflict between the work-a-day and spiritual lives of a group of young people in the suburbs of Cork. It is not nearly so good in its kind as his plays, *The Yellow Bittern* and *The Clan Falvey*.

Seumas O'Kelly (1881-1918) lived just long enough to do the best that it was in him to do. His masterpiece, *The Weaver's Grave*, published in 1920, two years after his death, was almost his last work. It is not a novel; it is not a short story; it is a something, in proportions, between the two. It is a capturing of primitive things, grotesque, wild, malign, with undertones of sorrow that rise and fall and rise again until they all but break into keening. The novels *The Lady of Deerpark* (1917) and *Wet Clay* (1923) are of little importance. What counts in him is a play or two, a little sheaf of sketches and short stories and *The Weaver's Grave*.

Back in 1902 William Buckley was much praised for *Croppie's Lie Down*. It is a grim and gallant book, but it has had no successors in kind. The stories of *Cambia Carty and Other Stories* (1907) do not amount to much.

Canon Hannay (1865-   ) began with high intentions. *The Seething Pot* (1904) and *The Northern Iron* (1907) are serious attempts to portray Irish life, the one a political novel of the end of the nineteenth century and the other an historical novel of the end of the eighteenth century These two are the best of the five books, all realistic, that he wrote before he discovered the Rev. J. J. Meldon. They were not appreciated as he had hoped they would be. He shrugged his shoulders and had another try. The result was *Spanish Gold* (1908). The Rev. J. J. Meldon made this tale of hidden treasure a best seller. "George A. Birmingham," as the Rev. Mr. Hannay called himself on the title pages of his books, had struck a new lead, and this he has worked industriously ever since, permitting himself only one or two attempts at the vein with which he began. Since the public would not have him on his chosen terms, and would have him as a farceur, he accepted its decision. He is more, of course, than a farceur. There is satire of Irish institutions even in the lightest of his many stories of adventure; there is a little bitterness over his defeated dreams; but he is too game to question or complain. There is a long list of these diverting tales, if no other one of them is so diverting as *Spanish Gold*. *General John Regan* (1912), *Inisheeny* (1920) and their like are good fooling all of them, but without that relation to life that makes *Some Experiences of an Irish R. M.* (1899) and its successors of Miss Somerville and Miss Martin so much better writing.

Shan Bullock (1865-   ) is another Irish story-teller who has not panned out as he promised. *The Squireen* (1903) creates for us in Martin Hynes a figure we do not forget, and *Dan the Dollar* (1905) tells us what his fellows who have stayed at home think of the returned American. There is graciousness in *Hetty* (1911).

St. John G. Ervine (1883-   ), like so many of his countrymen, has done but one good novel. It is *Mrs. Martin's Man*

(1915). *Alice and a Family* (1915) has a charm that is akin to Barrie's. *Changing Winds* (1917) and *The Foolish Lovers* (1921) are but books of the hour. Ervine knows the people of County Down; he likes to paint the dour side of them; he can give life to their portrayal. Like *The Magnanimous Lover* (1907), *Mrs. Martin's Man* has the ring of reality. Like the play, it is close packed with knowledge of Ulster ways, and Ulster attitudes toward things, and Ulster reactions. Belfast casts its shadow across the story, and Belfast's creed oppresses it, that creed whose first article is a strong affirmation of the glory of work.

WALTER DE LA MARE

Walter de la Mare (1873-   ) made his place with a poem, "The Listeners," but he is to many now as much story-teller as poet. The stories that are praised today, and praised without stint, are *The Return* (1910), and *The Memoirs of a Midget* (1922). There is in these that same something withheld, that same something mysterious, that same something inexplicable that distinguishes so large a group among his poems. Even his sympathy with all little things, however, cannot remove a suggestion of unpleasantness from the dwarf as heroine. One has the same sense of distress in reading *The Memoirs of a Midget* as one has in seeing midgets exploited in the circus and upon the stage. *The Return*, on its reissue twelve years after its first publication, had a remarkable press, especially in places of the severest literary judgment. That its eeriness is native to the story, and not foisted upon it, as all phases of the supernatural are so apt to be in the romances of today, is true enough, but the story does not come home to us with the insistence of fact.

NORMAN DOUGLAS

There is a strange bias, too, in Norman Douglas, another writer with an enthusiastic following. As one who has delighted in books of travel from the time in boyhood I delved into *Pinkerton's Voyages,* I was interested in Douglas from the moment I came upon his writing in *The English Review.* Yet for all the charm of *Siren Land* (1911) and *Old Calabria* (1915) there is something sinister in them, as in his other books, and always a pottering over petty details,—very differing impediments, the one repellent, the other boring. *South Wind* (1917) is more of a novel than his earlier books, but it is hardly a true novel. Douglas seems sometimes to forget whether he is writing a travel book or a story; he fails to fuse his fact with his fiction into one whole. What should be the objective parts of his story seem almost an intrusion upon his memories of his own experiences of people and places. It is these memories that he must set down first, that are his chief interest in his writing. Along with these memories he gives us a bit of story now and then, rather casually, just for form's sake perhaps. He has not taken the trouble to blend these memories with his imaginings of the doings and emotions of his characters.

They Went (1920) is a baffling book. It assumes the guise of an historical novel, but it would seem to be mostly satire, satire of what you will. Its heroine is so sublime an example of "my lady loves her will" that you feel Douglas cannot be serious in his portrait of her. What it's all about is a question. Perhaps it does not matter, for there are in it recapturings of lost yesterdays that are a joy to everyone brought up on the classics, and bits of grim humor unlike anything in the writing of his elders.

The writing about life at sea in the stories of William McFee (1881-   ) is so bracing one is not too critical about their qualities as novels. One is apt to bracket him with David W. Bone (1874-   ), the author of *The Brassbounder* (1910), as one who knows the sea and ships and can tell a good story, and let it go at that. Conrad will, however, sooner or later come to mind and force the reader to regard McFee and Bone more critically. Then there is H. W. Tomlinson (1873-   ), who does not try to turn his experiences of travel into stories, but leaves them just travels, or puts his broodings over them into essays. *Casuals of the Sea* (1916) made McFee known to most of us. The experiences it recorded were those of McFee, but he was indebted for the opening of his eyes to Conrad. Since *Casuals of the Sea* McFee has published *Captain Macedoine's Daughter* (1920), *Command* (1922) and *Race* (1924), the last a story almost wholly of the land. There is a wealth of material in the two sea stories, *Captain Macedoine's Daughter* and *Command*. Indeed, there is too much material in the latter for McFee to get into his story without distortion of it. There is romance in both stories, as there is always in Conrad, and such a bustle and richness of life as one finds in the talk of men of crowded hours. All sorts of women and men throng the pages of *Command*, some a little melodramatic and some that are to be swallowed only because the book is after all a traveler's tale.

John Masefield (1876-   ) is no novelist. He can write a boy's story like *Martin Hyde,* which bids fair to run such a course as *Treasure Island* ran; and he can do something of a finer kind in *The Lost Endeavor* (1910). His sea-tale, *Captain Margaret* (1908), is much less successful in its kind, and the two stories that are realistic novels in intention, *Multitude and Solitude* (1909) and *The Street of Today* (1911) are interesting only because Masefield wrote them. *Sard Harker* (1924) has one great piece of writing in it, a description of a Central American swamp, but the rest of it is scarcely more than a loosely strung succession of strange things seen. Masefield must content himself with a first place among the poets and dramatists of his time. In no form of prose fiction has he equaled *Nan,* or *The Everlasting Mercy,* or "Sea Fever," or "Here in the Self is all that men can know."

VIRGINIA WOOLF

The new freedom is supposed to have brought as much experience into the lives of women as there has always been proverbially in the lives of men. If it has, their writing, frank as it is, does not reveal such freedom. After all a good deal of this freedom of women is of the sort that George Sand knew and wrote about day before yesterday, and a good deal of it, too, of that other sort that Miss May Sinclair began to write about yesterday. It may almost be said, indeed, that Miss Sinclair has founded a school. Mrs. Virginia Woolf and Miss Dorothy M. Richardson owe a good deal to her.

Virginia Woolf writes about phases of life that she has discovered for herself, just as Katherine Mansfield did in the short-story. Such discoveries as Mrs. Woolf's have perhaps been made before, but these rediscoveries are set down with such freshness of emotion that she makes them her own. She is not content to "belong to the old proud pageant of man." She represents the antithesis of the sentiment announced by Flecker in his "Ballad of Camden Town":

> "Why should we think,
> We who are young and strong?"

Mrs. Woolf wants to know what is the meaning of the pageant of life, what is behind the show of things, what are the eternal verities. She materially widens our knowledge of the emotions in *The Voyage Out* (1915), her first book, but eager as she is she has not been able to push her analysis further in her subsequent books. The leisurely life of a long voyage is so tensely felt, the rather dull round of experiences when South America is finally reached chronicled with such wholesouled absorption, the inexorableness of death brought home so keenly, that the many who admired the story looked forward to a truly fine accomplishment when Mrs. Woolf should have ripened and found a great theme.

Night and Day (1920) was disappointing. Anger at being of the family of a great writer is the most deeply felt emotion in the story. It is not an uncommon but not a particularly dignified reaction. We have all met the people who wished to be appreciated for themselves and not because they came of a distinguished ancestry. Such a resentment at emphasis on family is not appealing and it certainly is not enough to furnish the emotion that should underlie a story. Mrs. Woolf, the daughter of Leslie

Stephen, and the granddaughter of Thackeray, has evidently found such distinction hard to endure.

Jacob's Room (1923) does not do much more than mark time in the progress of Mrs. Woolf. There is penetrating analysis in it; there are many short passages of lyric feeling, some of them better done than all but the best of imagist poems; but there is not enough story, or characters of enough body, to hold our attention to the end. It is to be assumed, I suppose, that these books of Mrs. Woolf, like those of Miss Dorothy M. Richardson, are to depend for their appeal, in the last resort, on the revelation of the personality of the author. To stake all, or nearly all, on personality and personality alone, is a dangerous choice. No writing can be really great that has not a great personality revealed in it. Ibsen, despite the objectiveness of his plays, is revealed in them, sombre, aloof, all-knowing, haunted by the incredible romance of life. Only in the greatest writers, however, will personality compensate for the lack of objective interest. Ibsen, for one, makes the objective interest of his plays so great, with their fated people involved in such strange yet common toils, that many are hardly aware of the Titanic personality that broods over them. The novelist is, of course, the showman of life, and the showman must have something to show.

DOROTHY M. RICHARDSON

I cannot pretend to more than curiosity about the writing of Miss Richardson. That curiosity, however, would have been satisfied with one reading of one story. It was a sense of duty that drove me further. The only satisfaction I had, indeed, in any one of them was in seeing "how the wheels go round." Friends tell me that they are valuable psychologically as a sincere record of the static progress of one woman through certain years of youth. That may be, and it may be, too, that they are a new development of the art of fiction. They seem to me to be more wholly written for their author's own self than any books I have read.

The titles of all four I have read interested me—*Pointed Roofs*

(1916), *Backwater* (1916), *Honeycomb* (1917) and *Revolving Lights* (1923). I had a mild interest, too, at the start, of the kind one has in a diary, but once I was through them I could remember little of them but their method. Diaries can be fascinating, but this writing in the fashion of notes for a diary leaves one reader, at least, cold and undesirous of following the course of the "stream of consciousness flowing on." Her elliptical way of writing is defended as "thinking aloud." Perhaps it is, and undoubtedly it appeals to some of her generation. Passages in *Ulysses* could hardly be had she not developed the method they follow. At times Miss Richardson seems on the point of giving us little poems in prose of the sort of which Mrs. Woolf has done so many, but just as she is about to speak out something interferes and we have the something significant that we expected left unsaid, or said without that significance that will make it memorable.

STELLA BENSON

From *I Pose* (1915), her first story, it has been evident that Miss Stella Benson was for turning the second rate that she saw in life into something better than second rate. She delights in beauty and she can at times find words worthy of the beauty that delights her. *The Poor Man* (1923) boldly tries to make a kind of grotesque beauty out of the doings of twopenny people. The landscape of California helps her to a more obvious kind of beauty. Her indifferently interesting people motor to the Yosemite, and moments among the foothills of the Sierra Nevada, and moments by the Big Trees, and moments in the villages of box-like houses all but deserted in the decay of mining take their place with the best description we have of California in Bret Harte and King and Muir.

There are characters in *The Poor Man*. The "poor sickly thing" that gives title to the story stands before us clearly and acts and speaks and fails to act just as such a one would. Emily Frere, whom he loved and who herself loved another in vain, save for her moment, is another creation. So are Tim McTab, the journalist, and Lucy his wife, creations. These English characters are presented against a background of Bohemian Americans we have all heard of as existing in San Francisco, but that only English writers seem able to find. There are scenes of real drama in the story, the last one of all the most poignant. In this scene Emily turns against her wretched adorer and strikes him in her agony. That scene has a damnable way of coming back to mind. They are a cheap lot, the whole of them, and why should you care? Tragedy is the overthrow of something great, is it not? This is the overthrow of something little. And yet, as Brett Young says:

> "Ah, God, how deep it stings
> This unendurable pity of small things."

And yet, how long will you care what happened to Emily Frere and her "poor man"? Does Stella Benson want you to care? It may be she does not. It may be that the generation of young people who had to "meet the war" were so hardened by their experiences that they blessedly lost something of the power to feel and so do not make us feel, when they write, as we think we ought to feel about unhappiness. Or is it that our now caring and now not caring come from the very personality of Stella Benson? Do the tricksy air and elphin aloofness from the significance of things that give quality to certain parts of *The Poor Man* carry over to the parts that might be movingly human and act as a prophylactic against sorrow?

"REBECCA WEST"

"Rebecca West" (1892-   ) is intolerant of most things that have been. She has a sharp tongue, courage and an ax to grind. Man as opposed to woman has always had too much made of him in this man's world. She is going to document him truly. Wherefore *The Judge* (1923). *The Return of the Soldier* (1918) is but tentative. *The Judge* is her first real attack. Its thesis is:

"Every mother is a judge who sentences the children for the sins of the father." That thesis, like most theses, has its percentage of truth, but it is advanced with too great sweepingness to win sympathy. There is too much analysis of neuroticism in the story, too little humor, too much bias, to win it acceptance as a "slice of life." Things may be as bad in certain places in this world as they are said to be in this story, but they are not taken so seriously by those who suffer them as "Rebecca West" would have us take them. The effect of her intense seriousness is therefore almost a distortion of life.

"Clemence Dane," like "Rebecca West," is a pseudonym. "Rebecca West" is Miss Cecily Fairfield, out of Edinburgh, and "Clemence Dane" is Miss Winifred Ashton, of Southern England. Miss Ashton began as a schoolteacher; and, wisely, she began writing about what she knew most about, a girl's school. *Regiment of Women* (1917) is a book about girls in a school, a protest against their absorption into a wholly feminine society during their formative years. As in so many books with a thesis the characters are but pawns in a game. They are as they are to prove the thesis. This is, too, much the status of the characters in all her stories and plays. The underlying ideas are more interesting to her than the people who develop them.

Legend (1919) is a story of a pow-wow among a woman writer's friends shortly after her death to decide just what was the secret of her character. She must be handed down to posterity as what she really was. Joyce may have taken account of the method of *Legend* in the plan of *Ulysses*, though the germ of *Ulysses* is in *A Portrait of the Artist as a Young Man* (1916). *Legend* is wholly a record of one conversation, nearly two hundred pages devoted to the happenings of two hours. *Wandering Stars* (1924), too, is well written, and full of good things, but like *First the Blade* (1918) it lacks characterization. "Clemence Dane" has yet to prove herself a novelist. The plays, all three of them, are better art, *A Bill of Divorcement* (1921), *Will Shakespeare* (1921), and *The Way Things Happen* (1923).

"E. M. DELAFIELD"

One thinks of what George Eliot wrote of Jane Austen when one reads the novels of "E. M. Delafield" (1890-   ). These are "novels written by a woman, an Englishwoman, a gentle-woman," and not mere projections of states of hysteria, mistaken for revelation of soul, by a young person freed from all national moorings. The novels of "E. M. Delafield" present people who are something more than types of the hour. Canon Moorhead is as much a reality as any cleric out of Barchester, and Sir Julian Rossiter, universal as the gentleman is, is the kind of gentleman one cannot find in any other race than the English. The daughter of Mrs. Henry de la Pasture, and the stepdaughter of Sir Hugh Clifford, "E. M. Delafield" knew a home in which the art of life and the art of letters were alike matters of first importance. Her mother is a novelist who believes a novel should be a story and her stepfather a writer of sketches that are transcripts from life and romance in one. *Zella Sees Herself* (1917) was written during the World War. It is one of the thousand and one studies of adolescence that are characteristic of the time. It is saved by its humor.

Tension (1919) marks a decided advance toward maturity of power. Pauline Marchrose, its heroine, is a likeness caught, photographically perhaps, but clearly. She is not harmonized with the rest of the picture, but stands out independently from it. Lady Edna Rossiter is only less clearly done. There are four men, each distinct, and half a dozen subsidiary characters just sketched in. "E. M. Delafield" knows something about some-body else than herself, a kind of knowledge not too common among our novelists of today.

The Optimist (1921) is another fulfillment of a modest inten-tion. It is not a tumultuous story. "E. M. Delafield" follows Maeterlinck in his belief in the power of static drama. She puts her belief into the mouth of Sir Julian in *Tension:* "On the whole the big calamities, such as battle, murder, and sudden death, are no longer essential to constitute crisis. The same reactions in humanity's present stage of development are produced without any visible action or events. Our consciousness has shifted to a more complex level." Perhaps, but a story that is so composed makes greater demands on its writer than are made on that writer when he is dealing with "the big calamities." There must be, as I have had to say so many times, a real power in the story-teller to offset the lack of drama in the story. "E. M. Delafield" accomplishes what she sets out to do, but the quietness and subduedness of her writing spreads a certain grayness over all her work. 'I hat grayness would surely result in monotony were it not for her humor, and sometimes it results in monotony despite her humor.

"Clemence Dane" resorts to violence in her stories and plays to escape from a too uniform quietness. We would not have "E. M. Delafield" seek a like way out. We only wish that she had the intensity, the insight, the revelation,—the genius in short—that would make her work, perfect in its kind as it is now, of a kind of larger importance.

Other women who have made places for themselves in the literature of the past fifteen years are Rose Macaulay, Eleanor Mordaunt, Ethel Sidgwick, Amber Reeves, and Viola Meynell. Miss Macaulay has won a popular success with *Potterism* (1922). This was after she had published her full half-score of novels, at intervals of approximately a year and a half. They are a varying lot, with satire as their most valuable characteristic. In *Orphan Island* (1924) the satire is perhaps most concentrated, but at its severest tolerant, almost kindly. Except at its intensest, satire is, however, in the long run, of poor service to a novelist. It seldom wears well, and when it is satire of manners, often passes with the foibles that provoke it. It may be dead as a door-nail in five years, or even less. Often, too, it is but a device to hide the absence of constructive writing, and always it is the hardest of literary modes to make beautiful. Miss Macaulay has other excellences than satire, but she has no freshly discovered beauty of life to reveal. She has no distinctive vein of her own at her best; she is more than a merely clever person, but not a great deal more. At her worst, as in *Mystery at Geneva* (1923) she can prose most pedestrianly.

Mrs. Mordaunt, although most of her writing has been done since 1909, belongs by practice and sympathies to the previous generation. She knows what she writes about whether her characters be of the servant class or professional people or "county." She chooses people to write about to whom things inevitably happen because of their avidness for life. This habit leads her into melodrama. She realizes melodrama as weakness, but she risks it rather than be dull. *The Family* (1916) is the book in which she is all at once all she can be. All she knows by observation and experience and insight is presented here and poignantly. There is plenty of criticism of early twentieth century England as comment on the story, which chronicles the vulgarization of a family that had started out with traditions of gentility. *The Pendulum* (1918) and *The Processionals* (1918), too, are stories of families of Irish and English folk as they were tried by the great war, and found not wanting.

Miss Sidgwick is a careful, almost a precious writer, of that family of Bensons with ink in their blood. She is all that is refined and cultivated, she is almost exquisite. It is her appreciation of the comic spirit as Meredith has interpreted it that prevents her from becoming the æsthete. That appreciation is particularly keen in *Jamesie* (1918), an interesting experiment in the story told by letters. She loves to write about lives in which art dominates, and it is in such writing, in *Promise* (1912) and in *Succession* (1913), that she carries her art, in certain directions, beyond the points attained in those directions by her master, Henry James. If Mrs. Wharton is Henry James clarified, Miss Sidgwick is Henry James refined.

Amber Reeves restricted herself to three novels during the six years of her first period of novel writing, 1911-1916. That is in itself a promise of leisured writing, a kind of writing sadly to seek among the novelists of the time. There is nothing hurried or forced in any of the stories, all three of which are about just the sort of people we all know. *The Reward of Virtue* (1911) is a story of the troubles a woman has in reconciling herself to the botheration a husband is until she gets used to him and has a child to take her mind off him and his irritating ways. *A Lady and Her Husband* (1914) is of sterner stuff, with a commonplace domineering male done to the life, one Heyham. *Helen in Love* (1916) is the most original of the three. In it Miss Reeves is as frank as her heroine could be to herself as to just what such a girl demands of love and life. It is a chronicle of philandering, a good deal of it cheap. In the end we have a strange return to a first love, and the surprise of a happy ending. There is a deliberative quality about all three books, and ease, and a sense of surety that augur still better stories when the years and imagination have given her a real richness of life. They have not given it to her in *Give and Take* (1923). That is just a good official document about a Government Department in war-time.

Miss Meynell would not be her mother's daughter if she could not write. The pity is that she has not a great deal to write about. Happily she sticks to her own experience, and her own observation, writing out with simplicity and completeness all the little that has come her way to know. There is the charm of naïeveté about her stories; a child's enthusiasm in her discoveries; a winning way with her. The stories from *Lot Barrow* (1913) on are all of a piece. *Columbine* (1915) shows no more knowledge of life than *Lot Barrow*, and *Second Marriage* (1918) no more knowledge than *Columbine*. She might well call herself, as her mother Alice Meynell did before her: "a poet of one mood in all my lays."

Gilbert Frankau (1884-   ) is his mother's son. Like "Frank Danby" he writes of the Bohemian side of Philistia, and with an avidness of interest and a rush of words that gives you a sense of being talked to breathlessly. His first book was a long novel in verse, *One of Us* (1912), dedicated to Byron and written in high spirits. There was further verse during his war-service and his first novel in prose, *The Woman of the Horizon* (1917). It combines travel book and the pursuit of that ideal woman that has inspired so many stories in verse as well as in prose. There have followed *The Seeds of Enchantment* (1921), *The Love Story of Aliette Brunton* (1922), and *Gerald Cranston's Lady* (1924). These books are packed full of all sorts of issues and signs of the times. There is much world-wandering in them, and imperial questions of all sorts are discussed. There are considerations of the condition of England in the days just before the World War, and during the War, and after the War. There is social satire and feminist propaganda and joy in the beautiful places of the world, but save in Gerald Cranston, the man of Big Business, not many notable creations of character.

THEODORE FRANCIS POWYS

Theodore Francis Powys (1878-   ) has his own vision of the world. As you read him you think of the Hardy whose Wessex Powys has chosen to write about; you think of Caradoc Evans, who earlier than Powys saw peasants as clods and little more; you think of Lascelles Abercrombie, whose *Adder* (1914) is a forerunner of *Black Bryony* (1923) in its concern with the splendor of sin. With an evident knowledge of all English literature, with an instant awareness of that Hebraism and Hellenism so vitally a part of that literature, with measurable obligations to Hardy and Evans and Abercrombie, Powys is still original. What he writes down in his stories he has found out for himself in the byways of Wessex. There is in his writing a surprise that the peasants are as he sees them; they are a discovery of his come upon suddenly in his maturity. No man who had known a people in boyhood and had a knowledge of them as an inheritance could find so few sides of their natures as does Powys, or so few characters among them. One hazards the guess that it is but recently Powys has settled down in his corner and studied its people carefully. He has caught their dialect and their slow ways of speech and thought. Like Maeterlinck he insists on the constant repetition of words and phrases in their talk.

In almost all the stories of Powys, in *Mark Only* (1924), in *The Left Leg* (1923), in *Hester Dominy* (1923), in *Black Bryony* (1923), for four, there are likenesses in character and situation. Again and again he chooses to center the interest in a clergyman of weak character; a successful farmer; an innkeeper; a storekeeper; a carpenter; farm laborers; a roadmender; or the inevitable village idiot. They are a loose lot, women and men alike, unworthy the pastoral setting in which they drag out their lives. And the setting itself, the landscape of it at least, fails often in its beauty, or turns sinister, or resolves itself, at seasons, into mud. Powys has moments when all he can find in the country is mud and dullness.

It is the townsman's view of the country one meets in Powys. What he finds there is there undoubtedly, but so much else is there that he does not find! I pretend to no more than a traveler's knowledge of Wessex, but I know so well so many country places, long-settled, in America, where one can find, side by side with what Powys finds in Wessex, other things of the best of life, that I am sure his picture of sensuality and cloddishness and petty villainy and superstition reflects but a part of what is about him in the village that reappears in his stories as Dodderdown or Madder or Norbury. I think of what an indictment of back country towns in New England even one who knows them well might write in "mudtime," when the frost is going out, and people have been cooped up all the long winter; and I know that, human nature being human nature the world over, Powys must have given us only a partial view of his village. Think, too, what others have found in this same southern England that Powys writes of; what Hardy has found, and Phillpotts, and Jefferies, and W. H. Hudson, and you have the needed corrections to his biased vision.

Powys is not very skillful in plot. He has to rely there on a greater malevolence in humanity, and on a more total depravity in inanimate things than are usual in our world. Such a villain as Charles Tulk in *Mark Only*, or Mr. Mew in *the Left Leg*, is scarcely credible. A portion of this crudity of character and incident and construction may be due merely to his inexperience in the architectonics of the story, as it was with Emily Brontë, but there is unquestioned crudity in the very fiber of Powys.

Trying hard to be as implacable as life itself Powys cannot help but betray himself as the sentimentalist. He is wounded by what he has found a decaying countryside to be. Probably he once thought the country had many aspects of Arcady and he cannot content himself now that he has found it has but few. Even his humor cannot save him from crying out his disappointment. Nor can his keen appreciation of the poetry of landscape and stables and "low life" bring him enough joy to atone for the cruelty and ugliness he sees everywhere. Irony, like sentiment, he would avoid if he could, but, like sentiment, irony creeps in to prevent the objectivity of presentation he desires. Before he turned to the novel Powys wrote *Soliloquies of a Hermit* (1918), and something of the quality of the essayist survives in the storyteller. Powys is a man of strong personality, and it is this personality, hurt by what it finds life to be, and, at times a little dazed by life, that is what is most distinguished in his writing. Tolerant he still manages to be, but unlike many tolerant men, he cannot manage to widen his vision of life. That vision remains as narrow as it is original. Within his restricted range, Powys is an artist of real power, a creator of living people, a poet of a sort.

Of the younger men three have forged rapidly ahead in the past few years, A. E. Coppard, Douglas Goldring and Stephen Hudson. Coppard and Goldring are both poets as well as storytellers. In his best novel, *Margot's Progress* (1920), Goldring has done an admirable character study of a Canadian adventuress who found her triumph in wedding an English gentleman brought her no more than the satisfaction that she had got what she had longed for. This lower middle-class girl had trampled her way up through the social levels over a score of men of dishonorable intentions toward her, but she had never known love. Without love she found life of little worth. She could not be content with

her honors as an English lady. She sloughed off her gentleman
and won the man she loved. In *Nobody Knows* (1923) Goldring is amusingly satirical of the youngest generation.

Stephen Hudson is another presenter of biography in detail.
He likes ugliness and he succeeds in depicting it. He confines
himself to a few characters but he crowds his stories with the
minutest analysis of every emotion and thought and happening
that the few characters experience. *Richard Kurt* (1919), *Elinor
Colhouse* (1921) and *Prince Hempseed* (1923) make up the
trilogy by which he has won a hearing. They are obviously after
Proust.

If the tales of A. E. Coppard were as good as their titles, they
would be very good indeed. *Clorinda Walks in Heaven* (1922),
Adam and Eve and Pinch Me (1923) and *The Black Dog* (1923),
all three whet one's appetite for their reading. *Hips and Haws*
(1922), too, is delectable as the name of a volume of verse. No
one of the tales is strictly a novel, though *The Black Dog* might
well have been one. As it is, it is a condensed novel. It is as
fantastic in its way as any little novel of Italy of Hewlett, with
irony in the end snuffing out its slender flame of romance.
Orianda is as charming as her name, but he who would be her
husband is not content to be her lover and else she will not have
him. There is but the one way out for him, the ignominious way
of flight. There are moments of beauty in the tales of Coppard,
but more moments of prettiness. His danger is he may go the
way of Richard Le Gallienne. His romance may be no more than
the romance of youth. Middle age may smother the artist in
him.

MARSHALL AND MAXWELL

Archibald Marshall (1866-   ) and W. B. Maxwell are competent story-tellers, men that have learned their trade. They are
both something more than that. Maxwell, the son of "Miss
Braddon," was born to the art as surely as Trollope, and he has
made a creditable place for himself in the safe and sane form
of story. He has no distinction, save that of good breeding, in

his novels; but he writes lucidly of what he knows. He tells you about certain people in a good deal of detail, but he fails to make them very interesting. A typical book of his is *The Day's Journey* (1923). It is the account of the finding of nobility in what passes for cheapness. Heber and Bird, pals from youth, are past forty when their crucial experiences begin. Both are unfortunate in their marriages, and both, perhaps, deserve to be, for they have little motherwit, and experience has taught them nothing. They are scarcely better than a pair of fools, but they are very human in their folly. They go to the World War old men, and not well, and in the end they have each other to quarrel with and chum with. That so much is all one should demand of life is apparently the creed of Maxwell.

Archibald Marshall was a god-send to all English speaking people during the World War. He brought what pleasantness and leisure of ancient pathways he could to the generations shaken by the threatened overthrow of their world. The older generation suffered, in addition, from the breaking of old ties that synchronized with the War and that came of it, and by the passing of old customs with all their ease of use and wont. That generation turned with a glad sigh to Marshall and found heart-ease in his stories. There, at any rate, were still home-enchanted things.

Marshall is often compared to Trollope, and with a certain justice. He is like Trollope in his content with the usual. And he is like Trollope, too, in that he does not make the usual distinguished or noble or romantic. Nor does he make the usual instant to us, as if it came to us through gossip. He merely makes the usual mildly interesting. This is as true of the Clinton series as a whole as it is of a short-story like "The Bookkeeper." There is interest more than mild, of course, in such a yarn as *The House of Merrilees* (1905), but for a detective story it leaves the reader "more than usual calm."

There are a number of popular novelists, our contemporaries, for whom I have not found place in this book. Some of these I have read and judged of too slight significance for mention, but there are some that should, perhaps, be listed. "Richard Dehan" (Clotilde Graves, 1863-   ) and Robert Keable (1887-   ) have their thousands of readers, as did "F. G. Trafford" (Mrs. C. E. C. Riddell, 1832-1906) and G. A. Lawrence (1827-1876) in mid-Victorian times. It has been the function of such writers to be entertaining to a generation, as it has been the function of literally hundreds of lesser fry. Perhaps a few among these many have hoped to be something more than entertainers. One, perhaps, has intended prophecy, and another has dreamed of a story truly art. Most of them, however, are of that sort, numerous in all conditions of business, who are content to give the public what it wants, who have no inkling of the artist's delight in making a new beauty for himself and his fellows.

Some critics say that if there are not any imposing figures among the younger novelists there are significant changes in the forms of the novel they write. Yet can any practices of little significant writers be deeply significant? To one who has watched novelists of yesterday who were portents to many readers wither away to nothingness, Miss Dorothy M. Richardson and James Joyce seem little more than symptoms of the time, and Aldous Huxley and Ronald Firbank and Michael Arlen only passing irritations.

You read a great deal about the breakdown of form in the novel, but that breakdown in form is so seldom in evidence in a novel of power that the old art of the long-story seems likely to go on developing through its traditional forms. Galsworthy thinks that *The Spanish Farm* (1924) of R. H. Mottram is a new kind of literature closely allied to the novel, and, apparently, indicative of a new way of development. That may be. Speculation is a pleasant pastime, but it does not establish facts. Nor does speculation establish values. It is this slight relation of speculation to criticism that has kept speculation as to the future of the novel in the background in this book. Nor has it seemed germane to the purpose of the book to discuss much the trend and tendencies of the novel. What of beauty its writers have achieved in the art of letters has been its concern.

There are, no doubt, writers of real parts whom I have missed. I only recently read Mrs. Mary Webb (1883-   ) whose writing is keenly felt and freshly phrased. *The Golden Arrow* (1916) is a good deal of a book. I almost missed *The Orissers* (1923) by L. H. Myers (1882-   ). I had heard it was a mastering, a desolating book, but I found it to be something less than that. It is sincerely written, carefully worked out, very typical of our time. Its people move in a Conradlike trance. None of them can prevent disasters that threaten, though they are forewarned. They have not power enough, or wisdom enough, or adroitness enough, to ward off what is clearly seen to menace them. Or it may be it is not their weakness that renders them helpless but that they are held immobile by some force of destiny and that what is willed by fate to happen would happen whether there was effort to avoid it or lack of effort on the part of feeble humans.

There are writers I may have failed to include because of reasons of classification. I have hesitated about Max Beerbohm (1872-   ), one of those who add to the joy of life. *Zuleika Dobson* (1911) and *A Christmas Garland* (1912) have given me as much pleasure as I have ever had from the lesser forms of satire. Yet I have not written of Beerbohm because it seems to me he is essentially the satirist and not the story-teller.

The general level of excellence in the writers who have come to be known in the past fifteen years is high, indeed, but there seem to be none of the great among them. Lawrence, Stephens, Forster and Brett Young are the best of them. All four I should say write with more distinction than Peacock, Kingsley, Reade and Trollope, but will they, we must wonder, last as long? Where now are reputations of twenty years ago equal to those of our four of today, the reputations of Charles Marriott, Charles Lee, "Benjamin Swift" and Anthony Hope? And how do our four compare with men of that generation who are still in vogue, Bennett, Phillpotts, Galsworthy and Wells? And are any of these names so far mentioned in this paragraph names of novelists of the highest rank? And if not, what is the status of the English novel today? Such questions make us thankful that we have had two great novelists with us during most of the first quarter of the century, Hardy and Conrad, and thankful, too, for George Moore.

INDEX